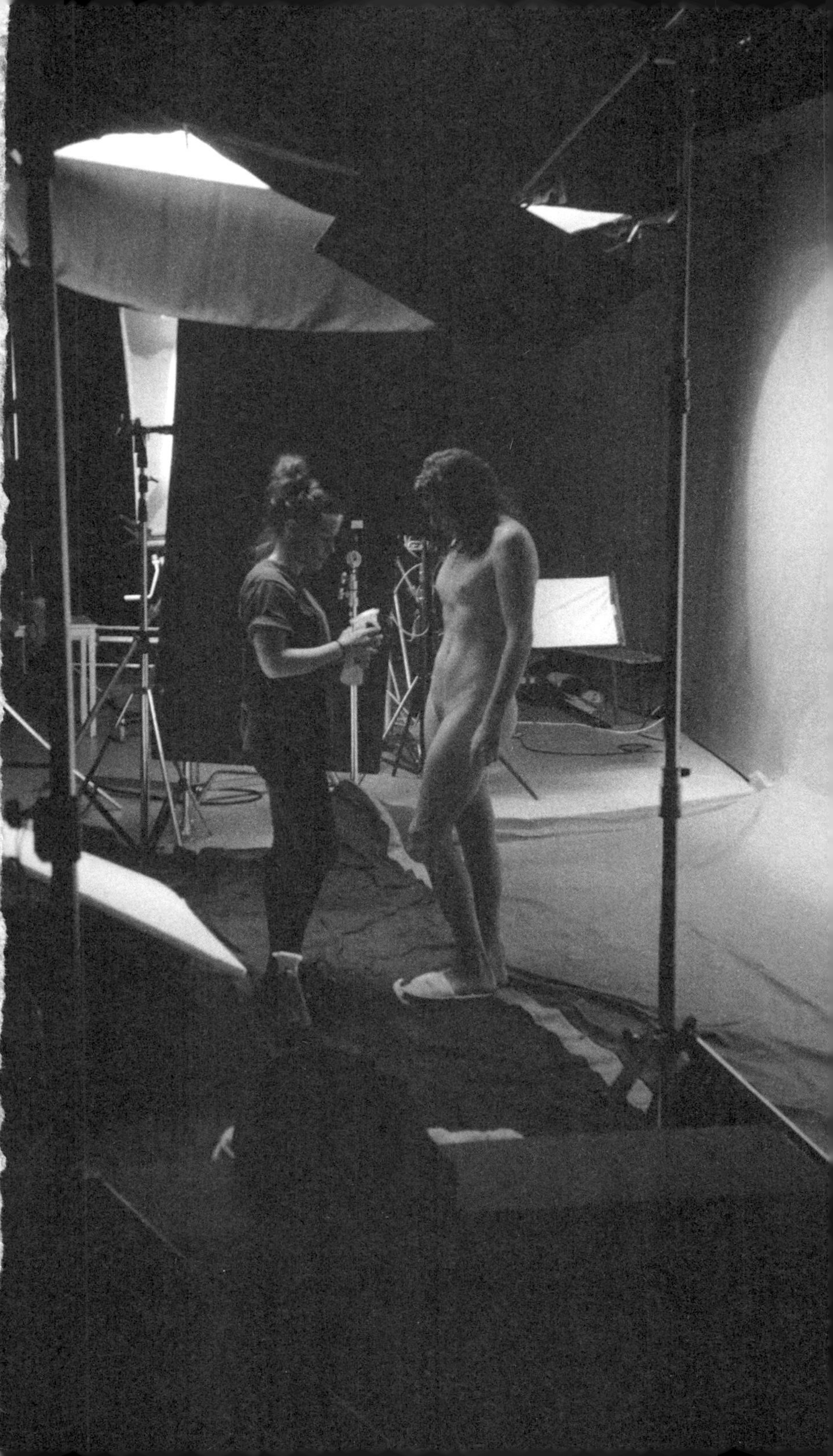

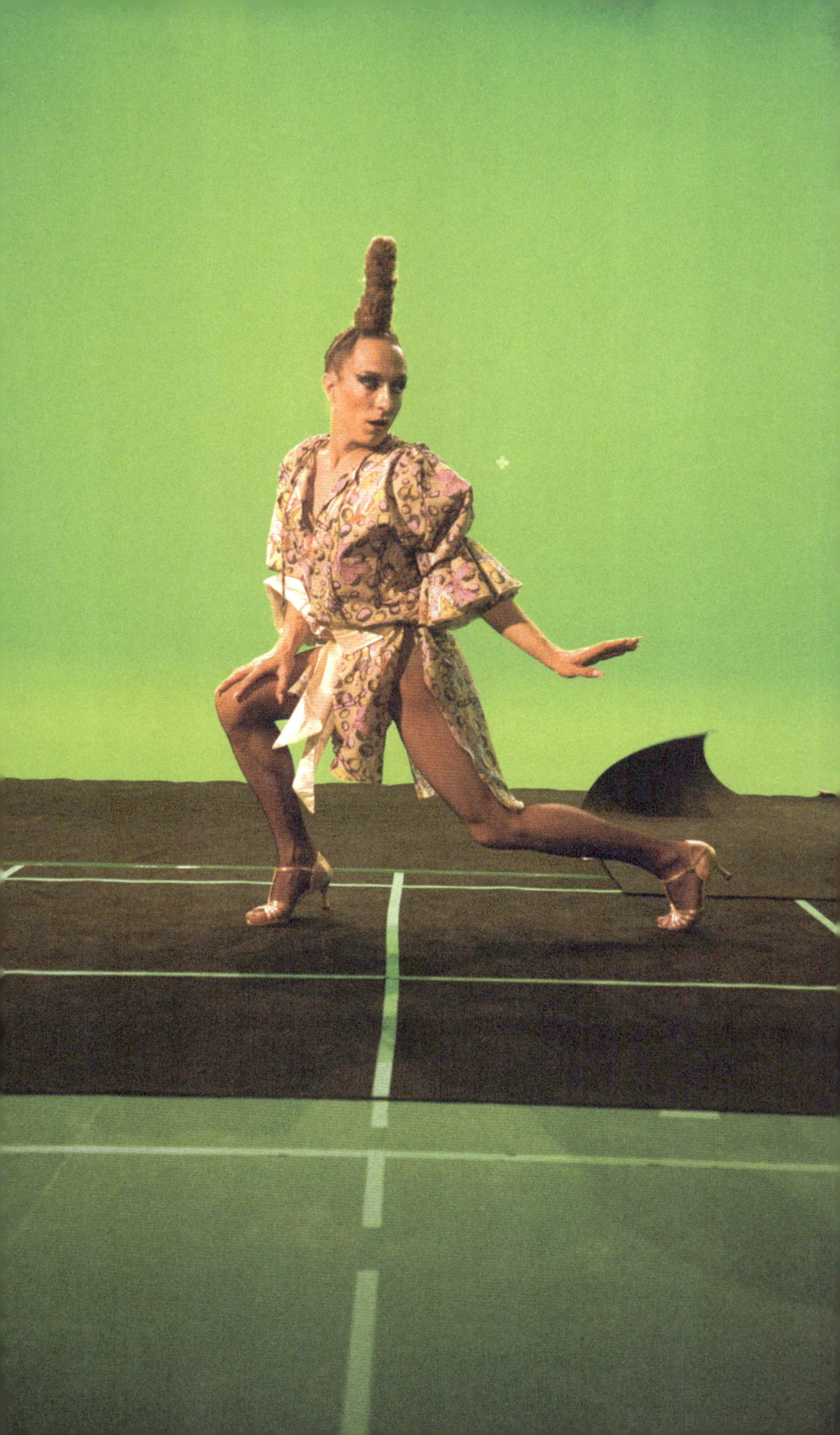

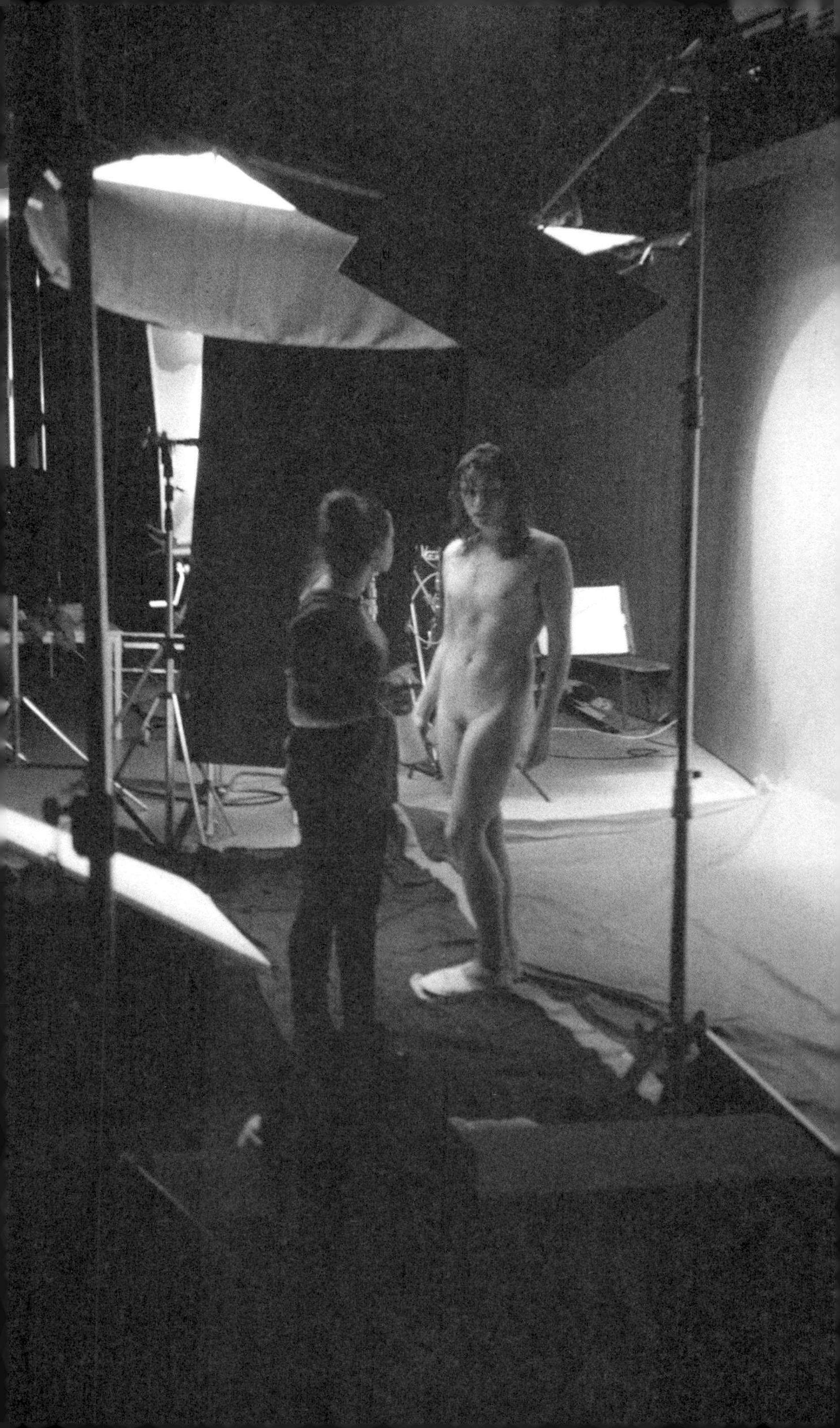

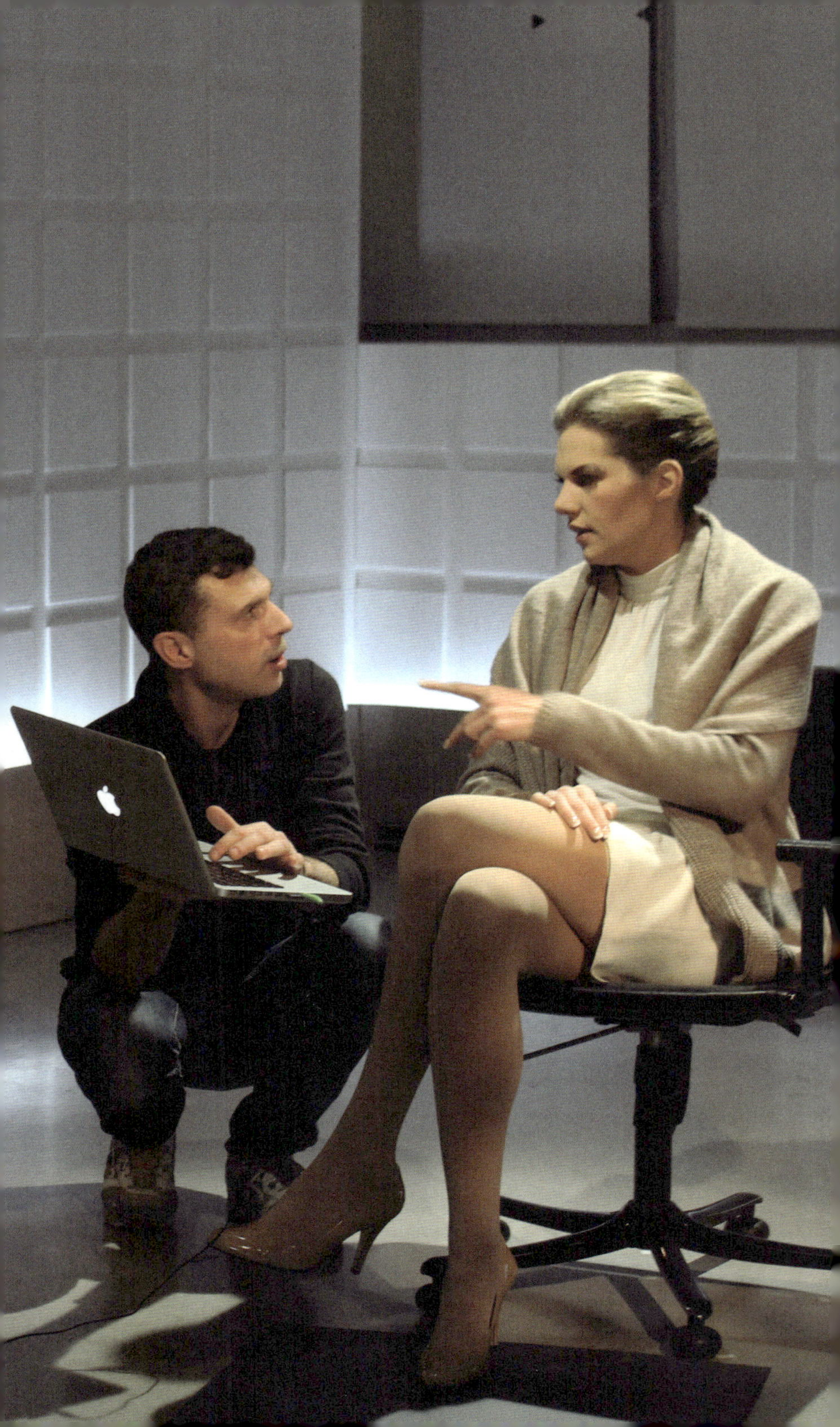

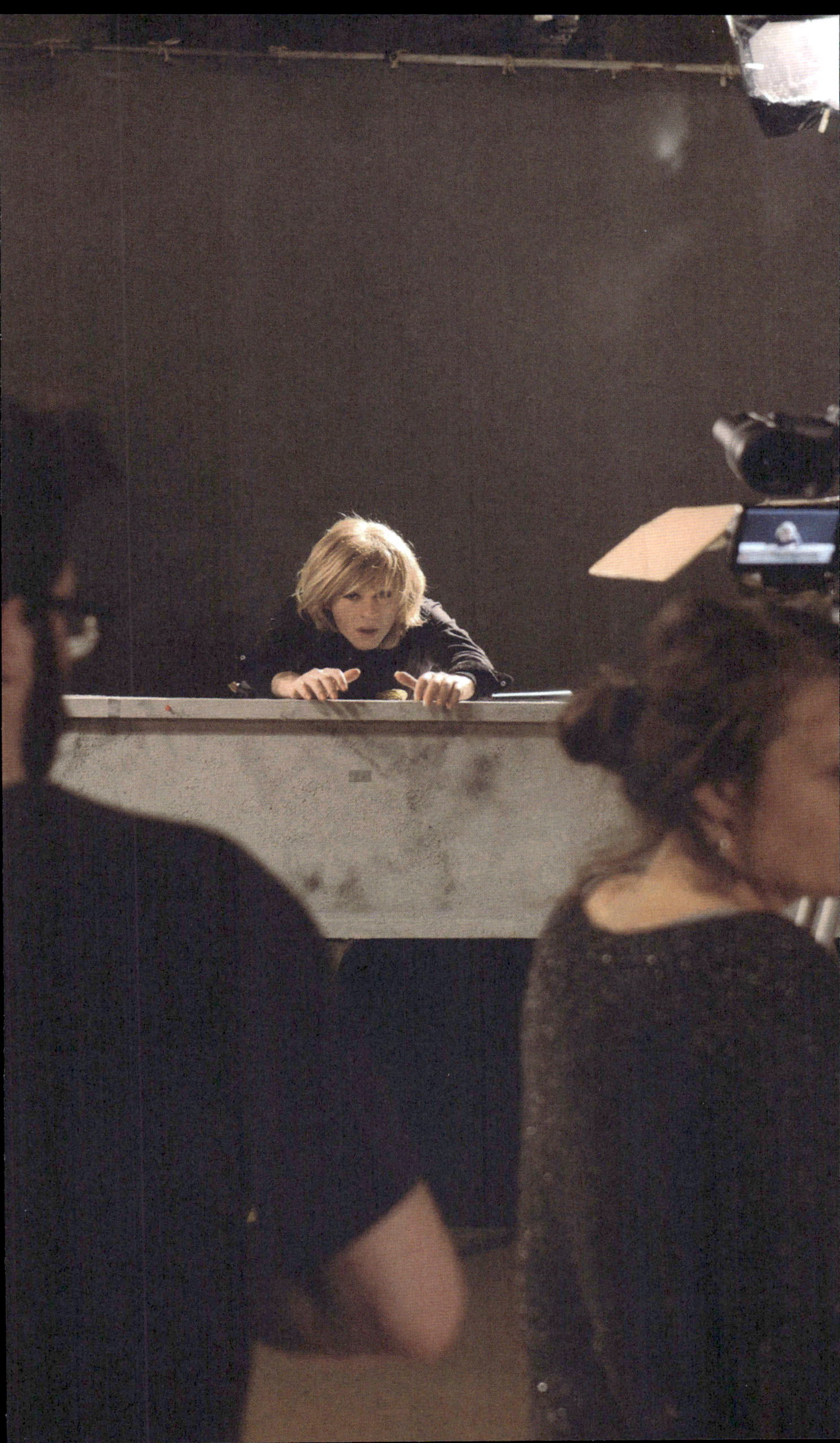

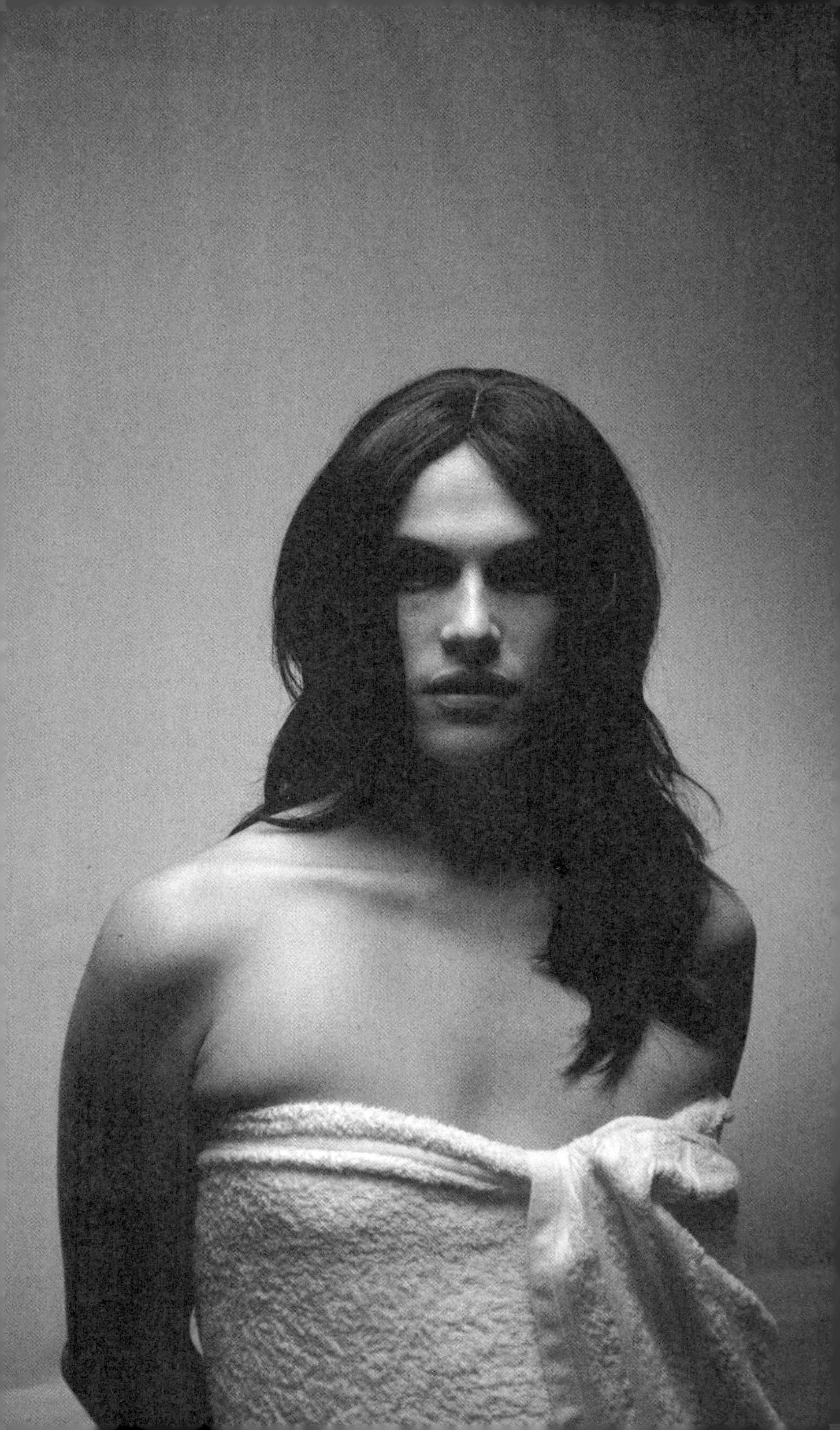

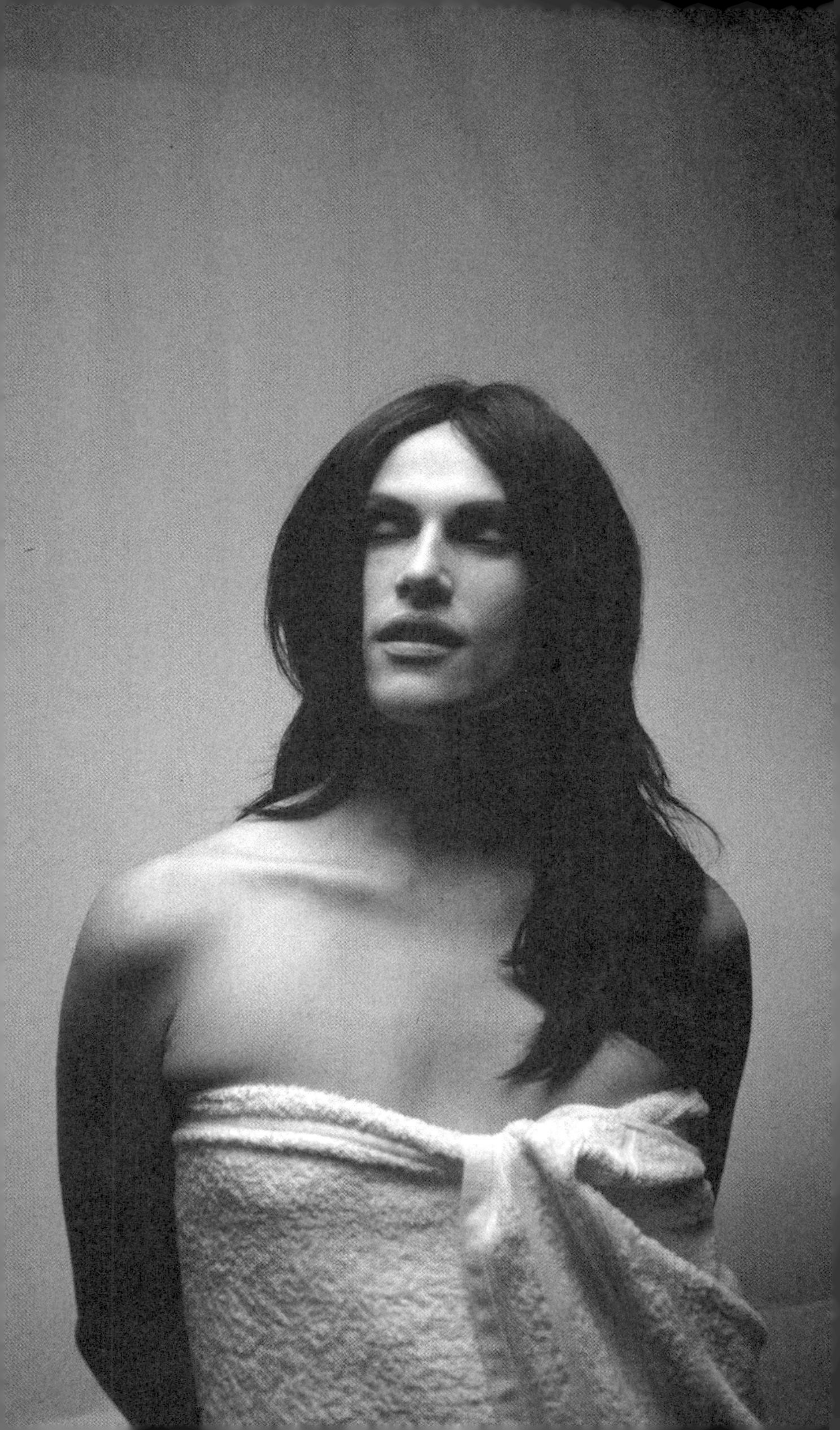

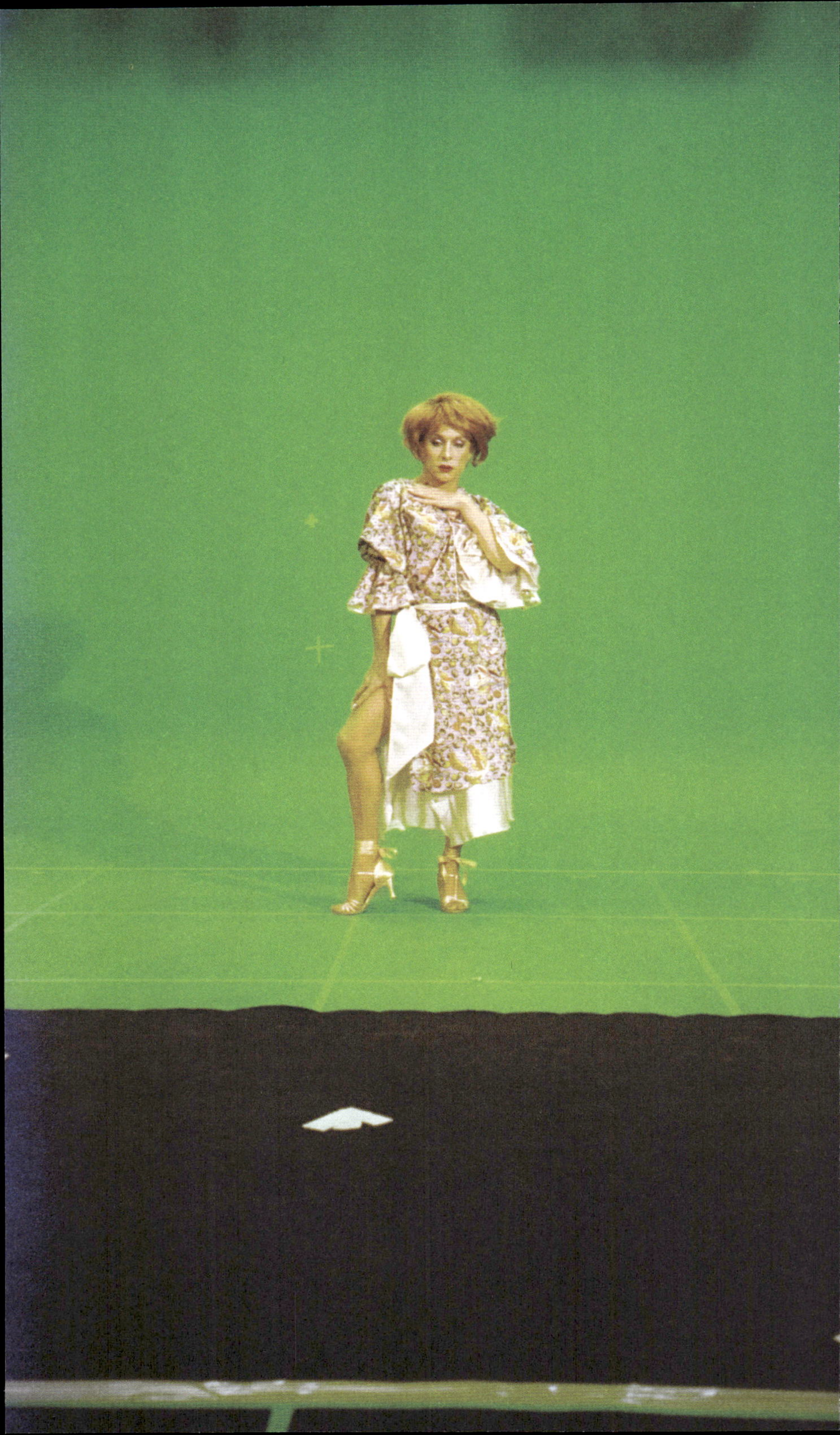

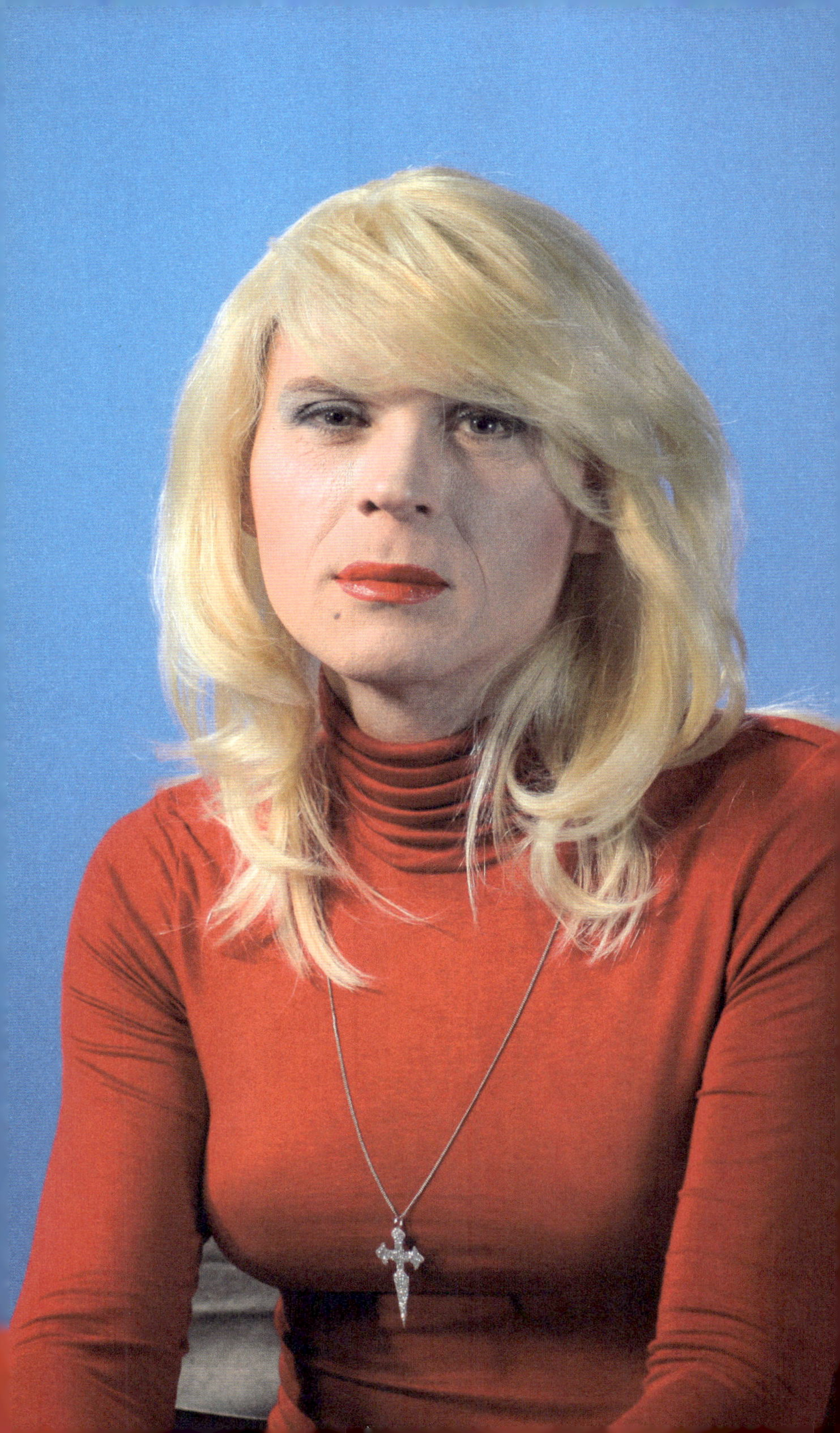

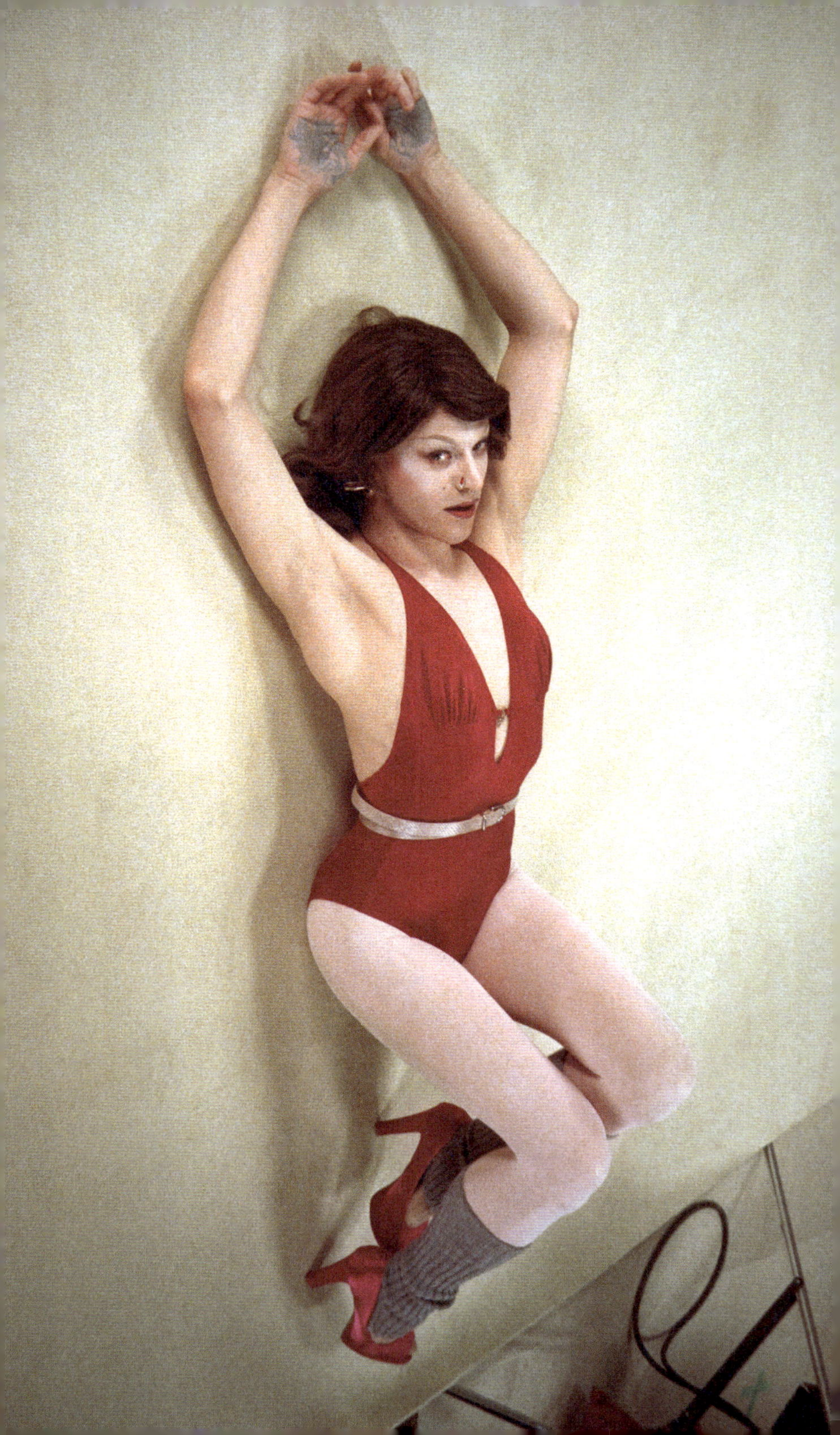

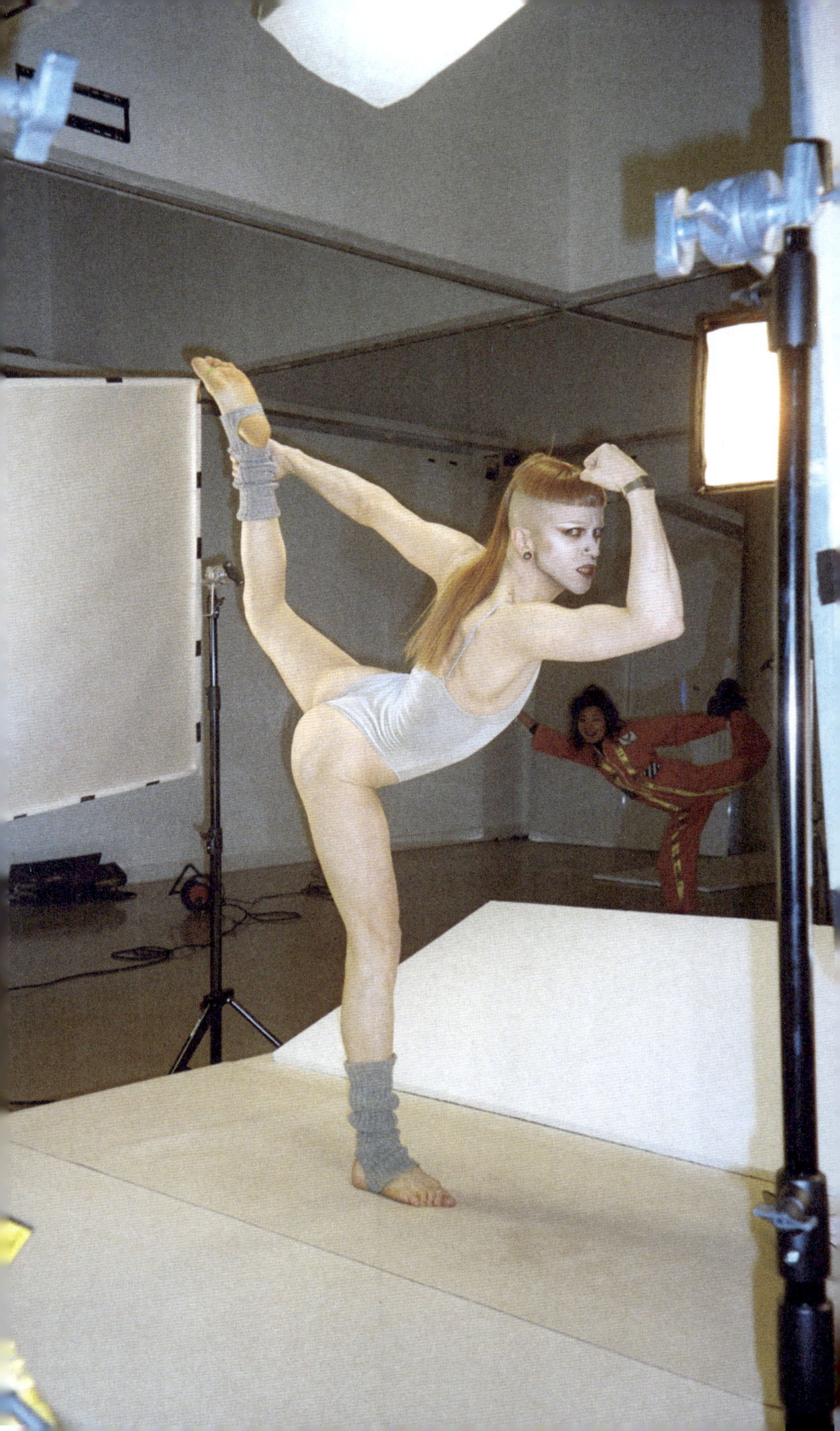

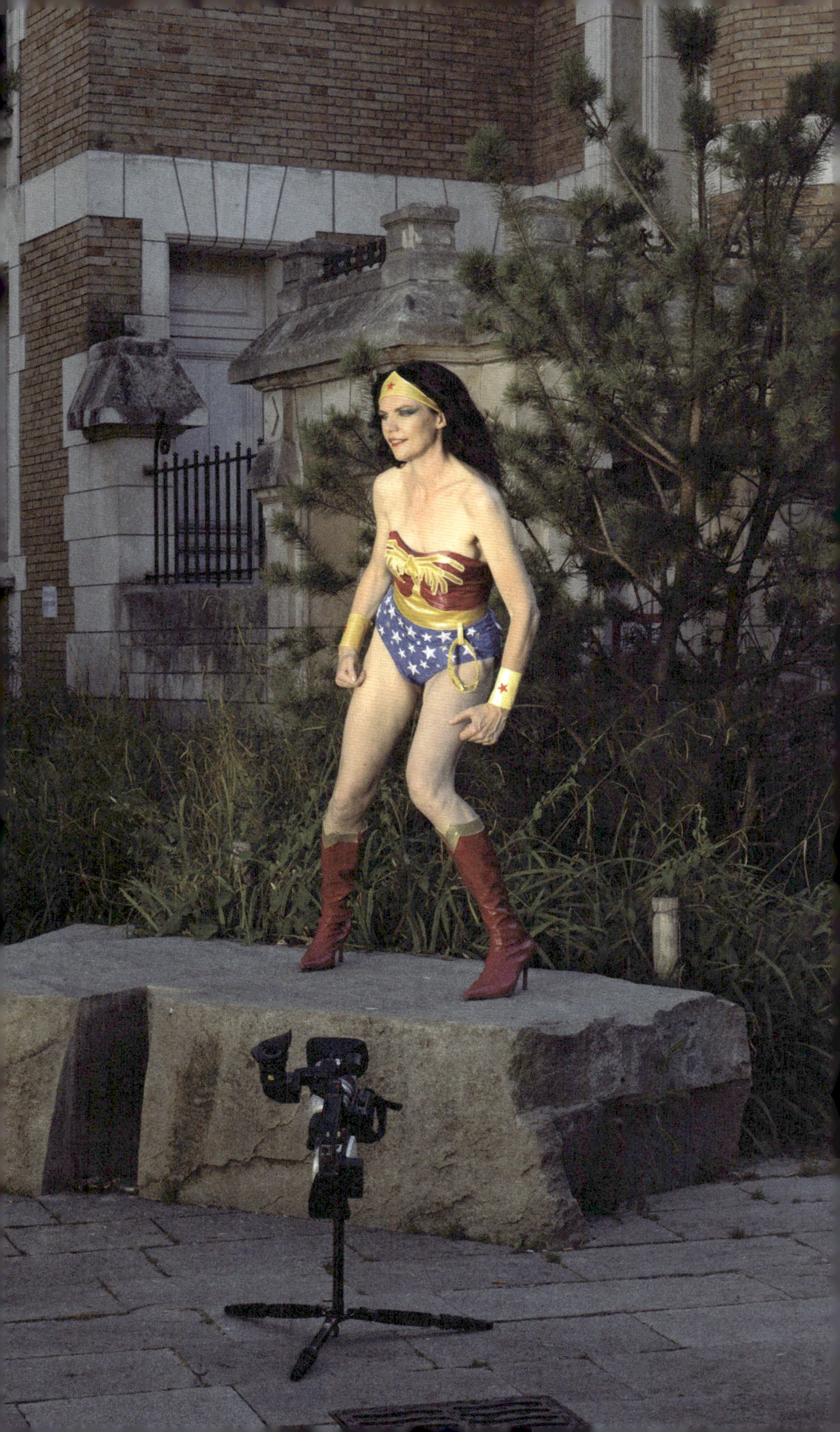

BRICE DELLSPERGER

TWELVE BODY DOUBLES

Mousse Publishing

TABLE OF CONTENTS

BODY DOUBLE XXIX

2'58"
AFTER MIKE NICHOLS' POSTCARDS FROM THE EDGE (1990)
2013

CAST
BRICE DELLSPERGER &
NATACHA LESUEUR

IMAGES
JORDANE CHOUZENOUX

EDITING, SOUND DESIGN
& SPECIAL EFFECTS
BRICE DELLSPERGER

SET MANAGER
GILLES MARTINEZ

TECHNICAL TEAM
JENNIFER DUJARDIN, MICHAEL
LANOUILH, JULIE FOTI, WILLIAM BONNET,
JEAN-FLORENT WESTRELIN, ROMAIN ECK

PRODUCTION
BRICE DELLSPERGER; TRANSPALETTE -
EMMETROP, BOURGES

COLLECTIONS
FRAC CORSICA, FRANCE;
NMNM - NOUVEAU MUSÉE NATIONAL
DE MONACO

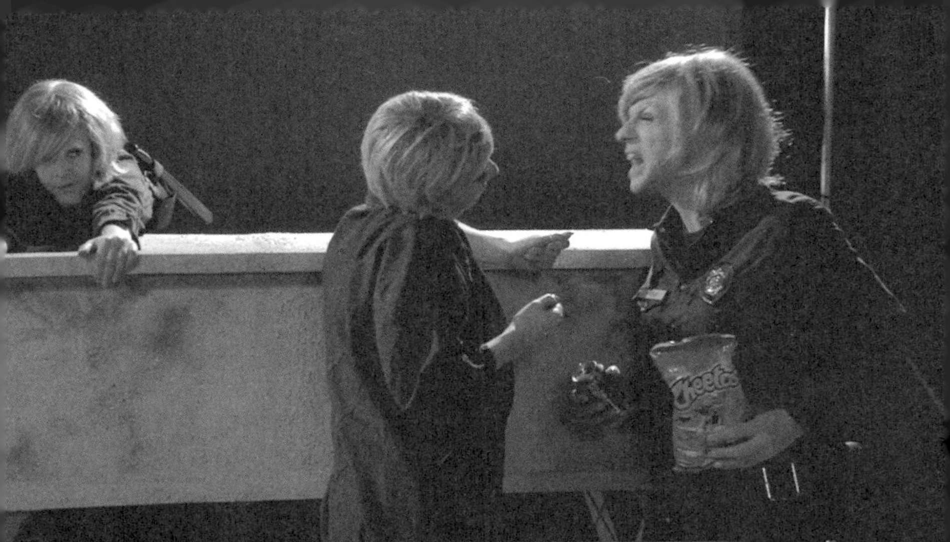

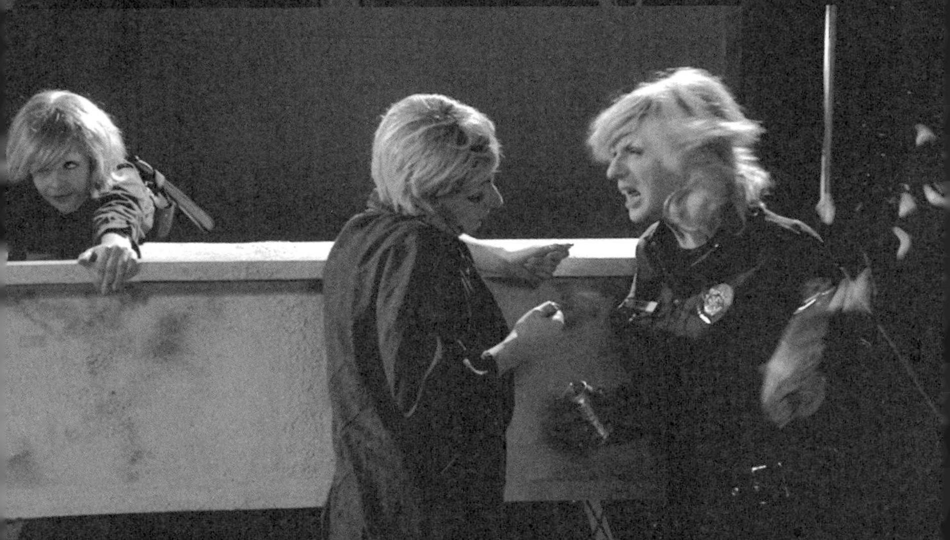

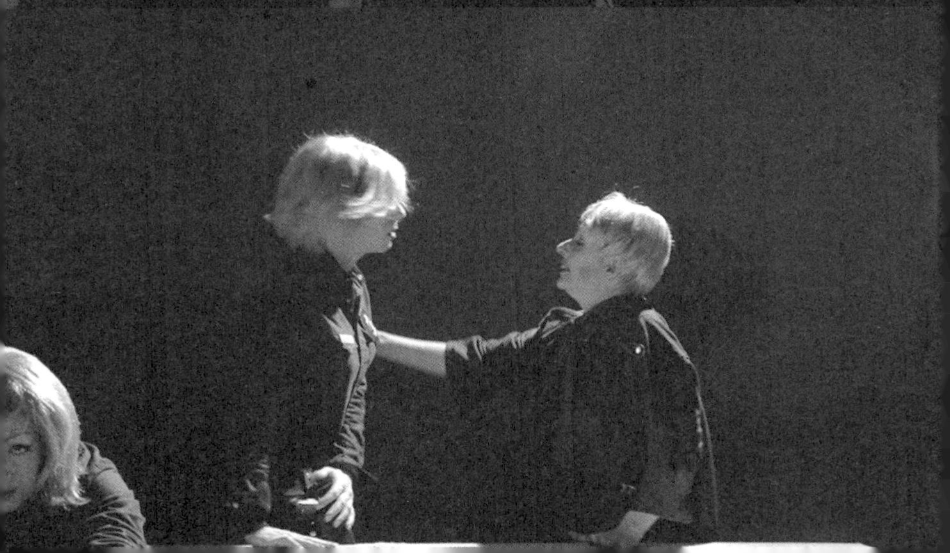

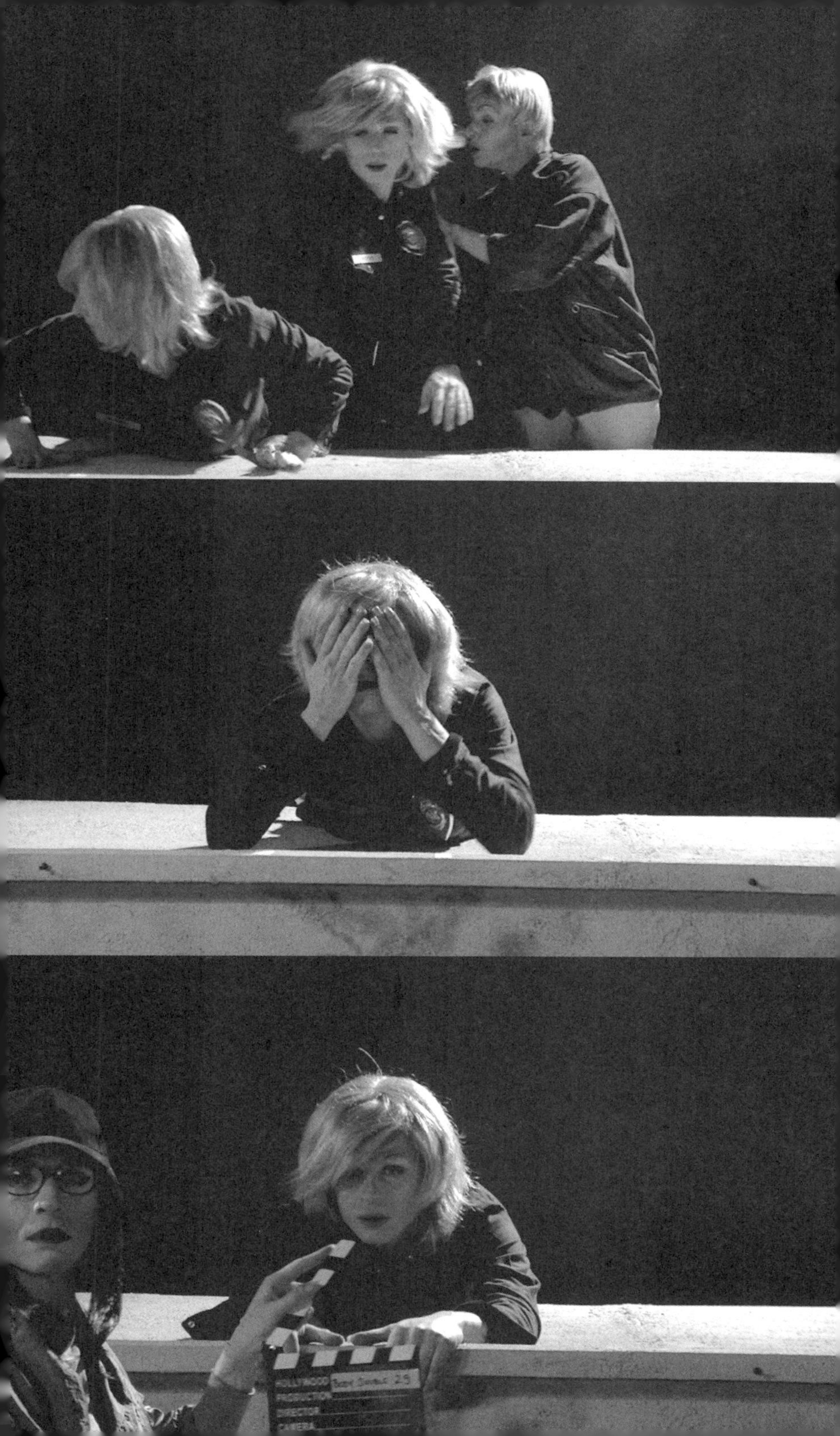

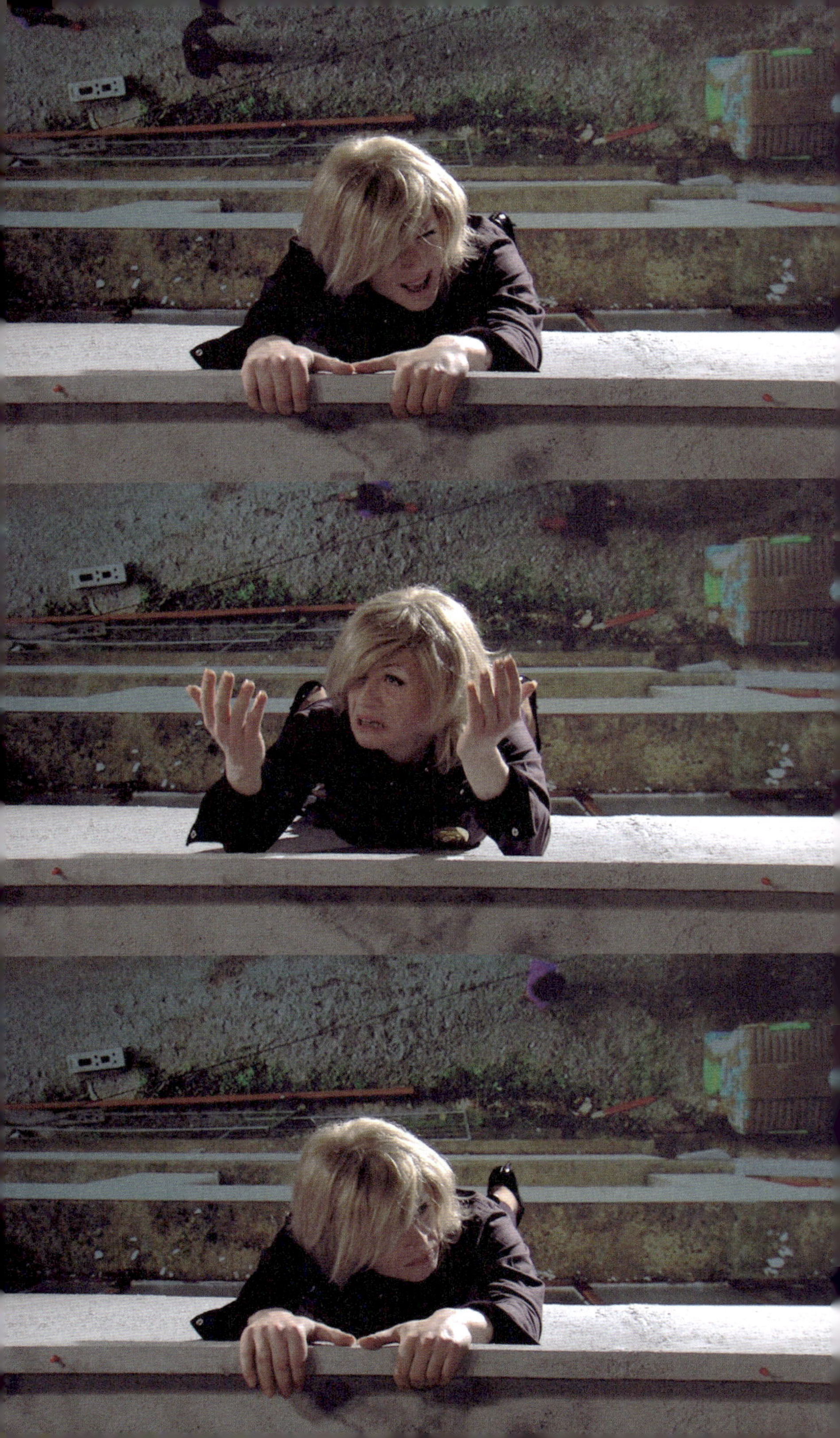

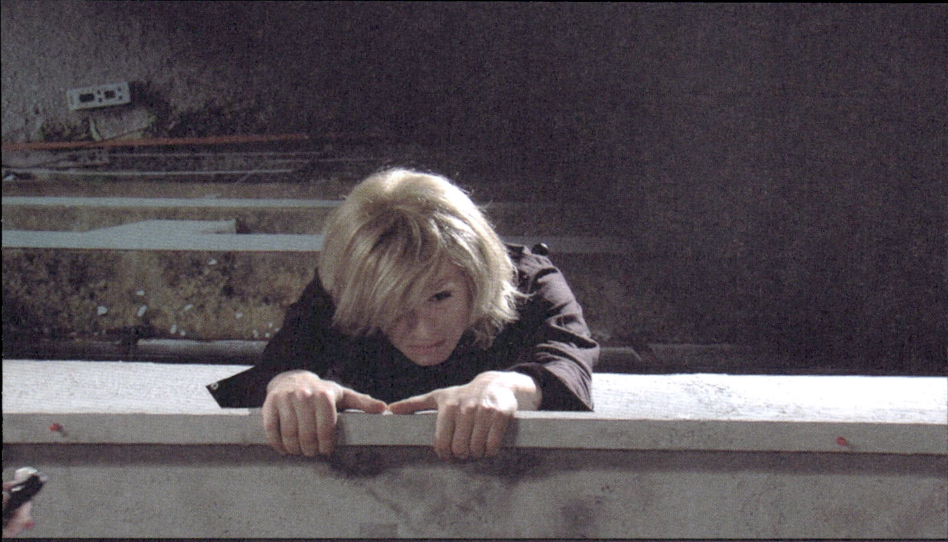

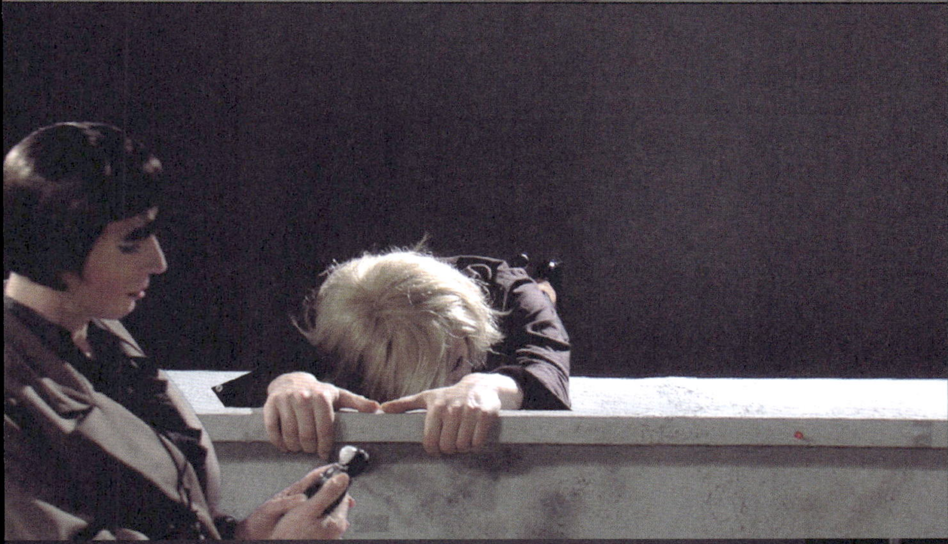

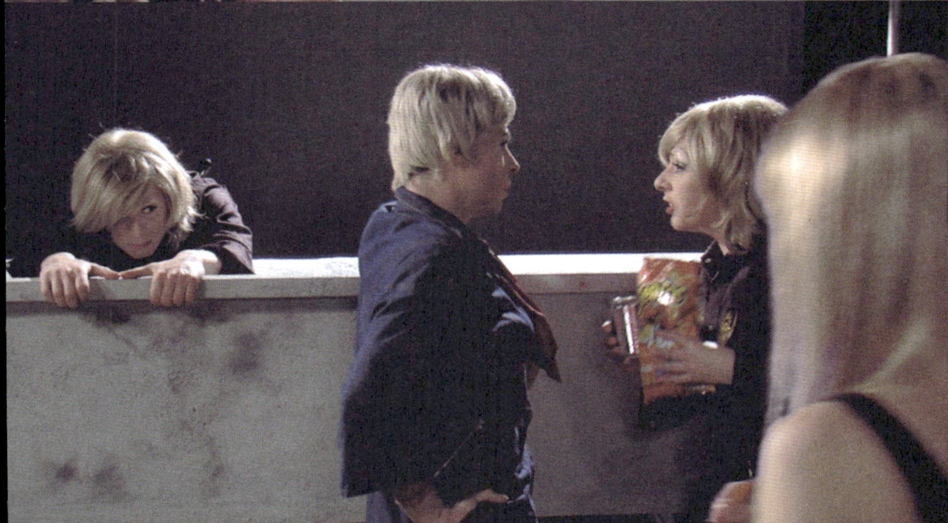

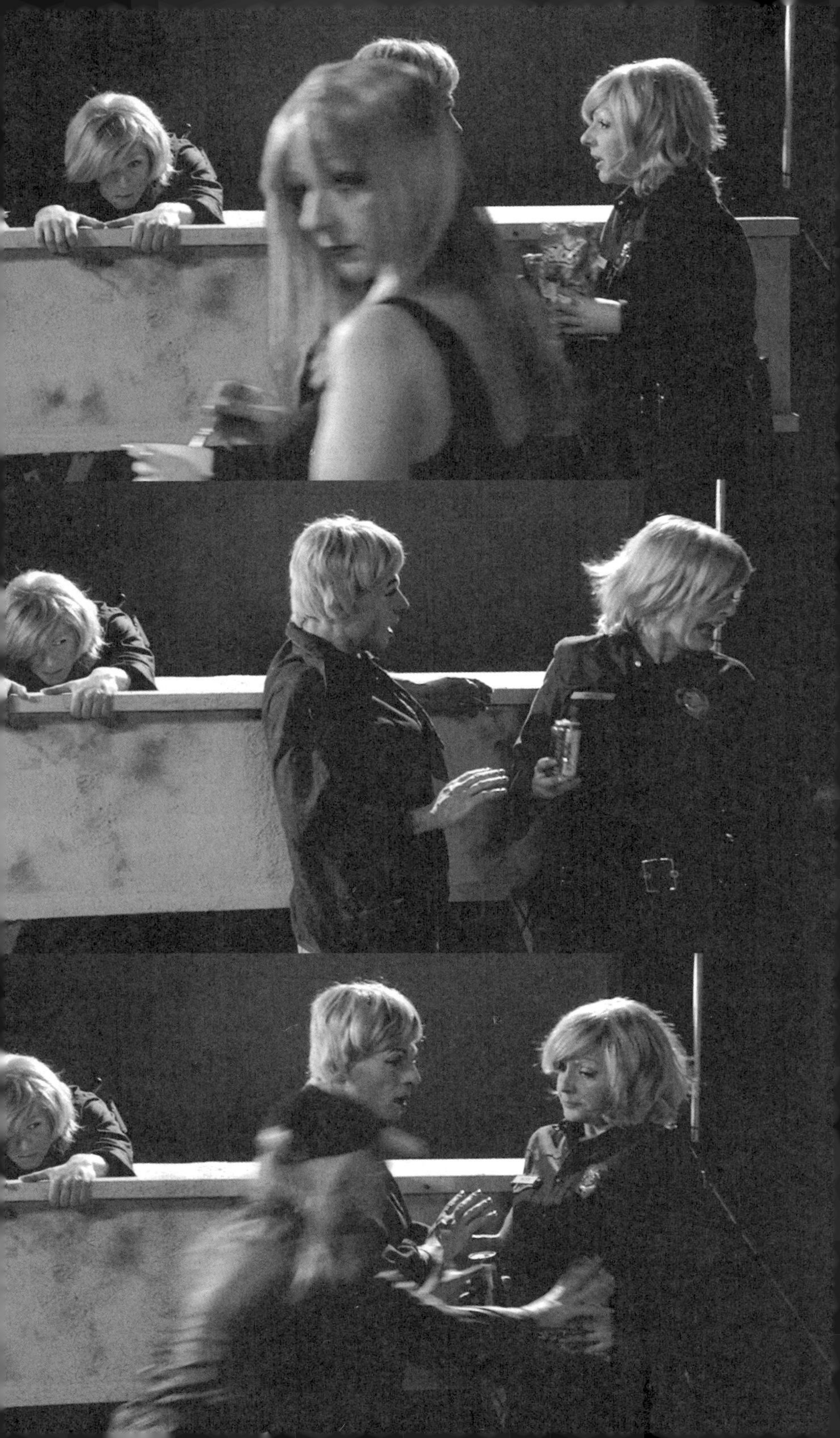

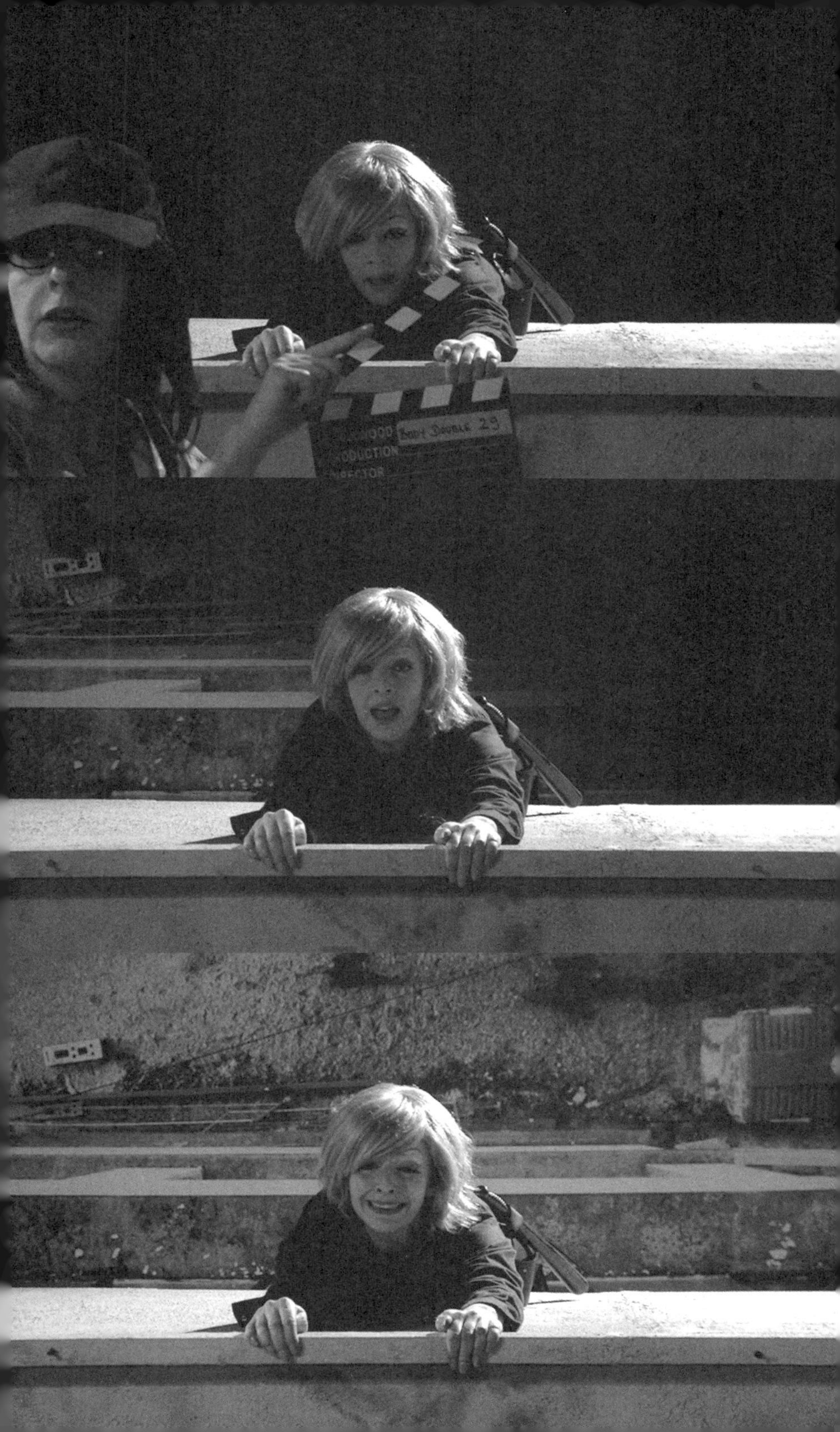

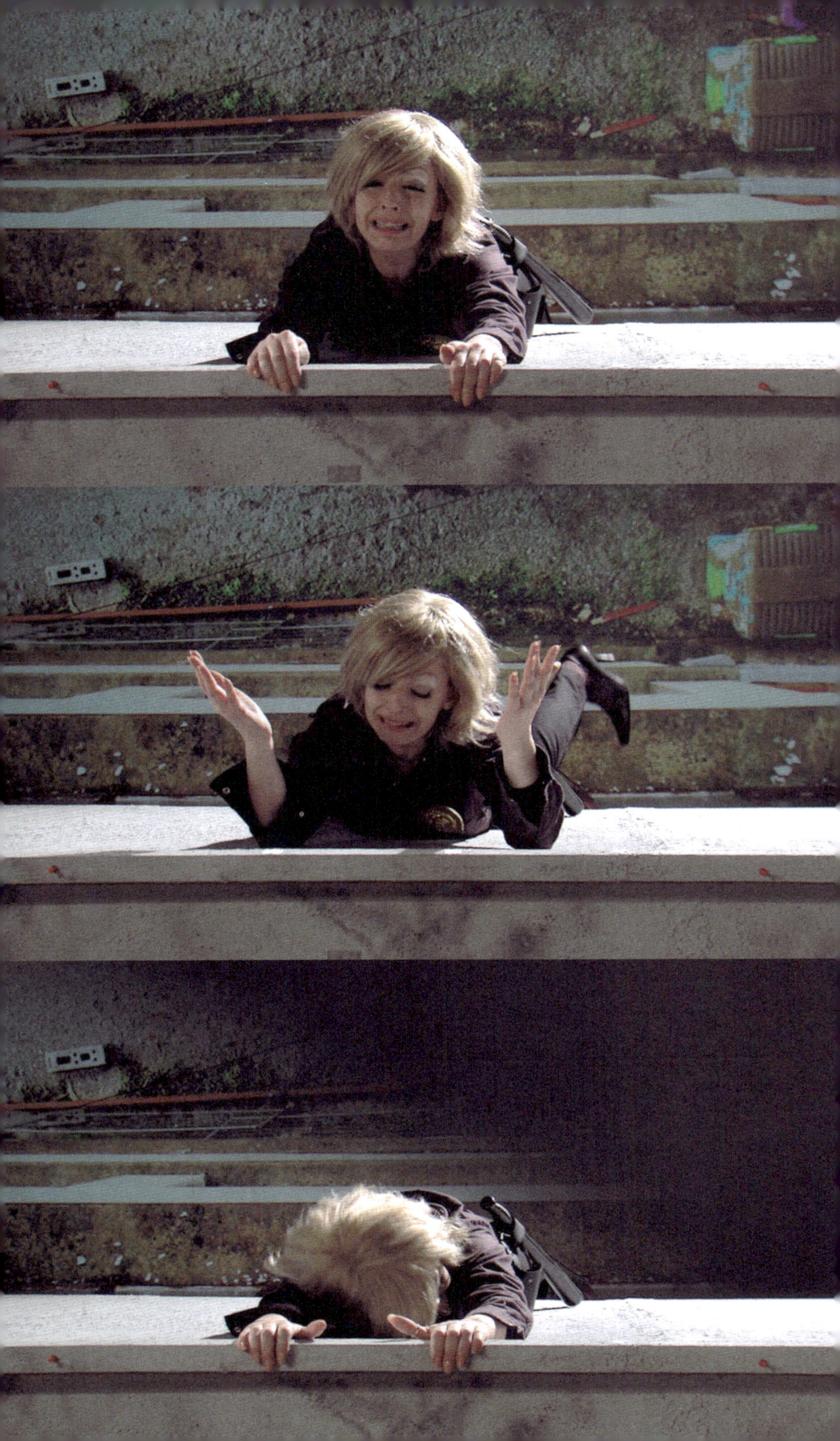

BODY DOUBLE XXX

2'49''
AFTER BRIAN DE PALMA'S DRESSED TO KILL (1980)
2013

CAST
BRICE DELLSPERGER

IMAGES
NICOLAS PERGE

EDITING & SPECIAL EFFECTS
BRICE DELLSPERGER

PRODUCTION
BRICE DELLSPERGER

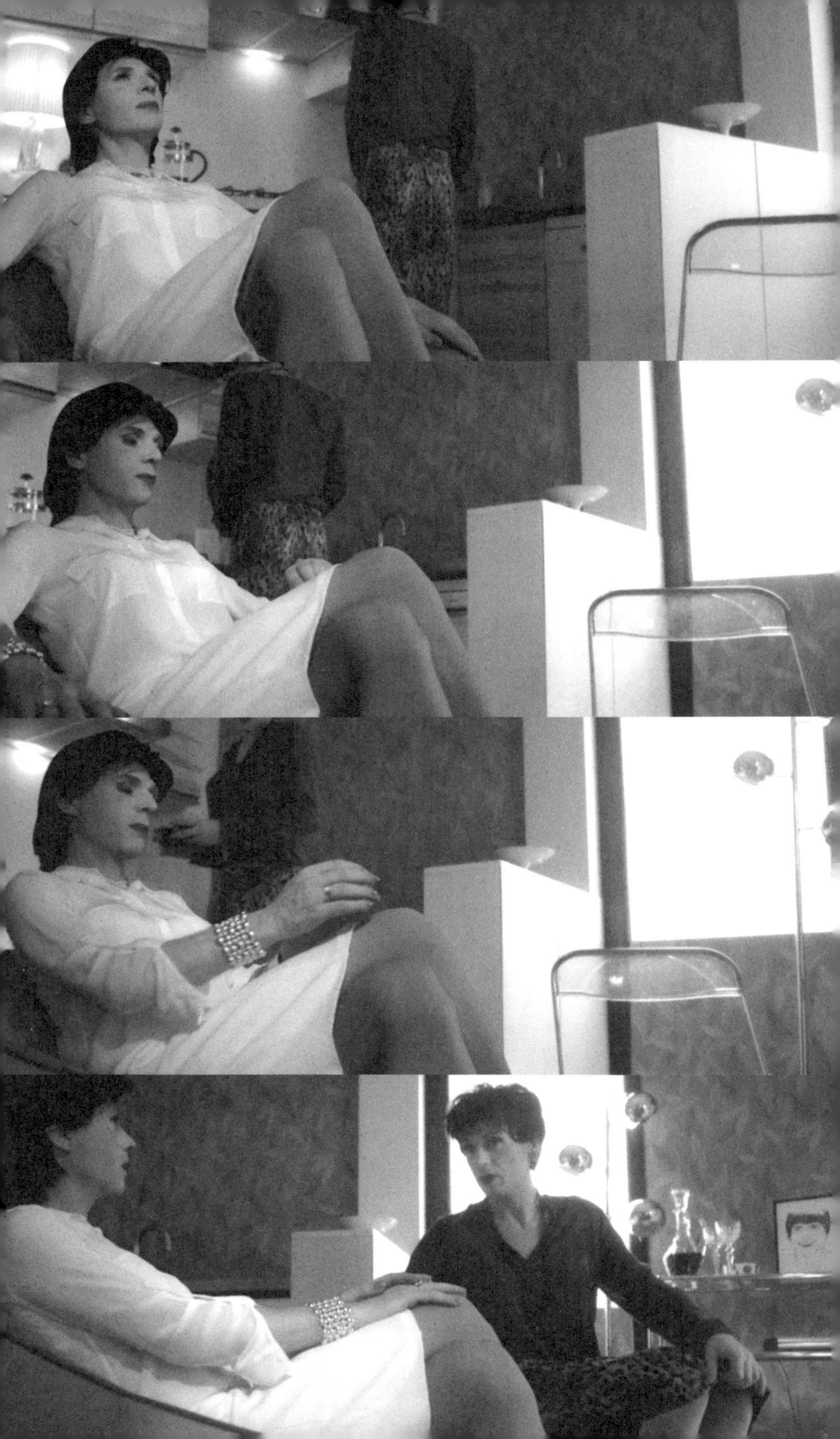

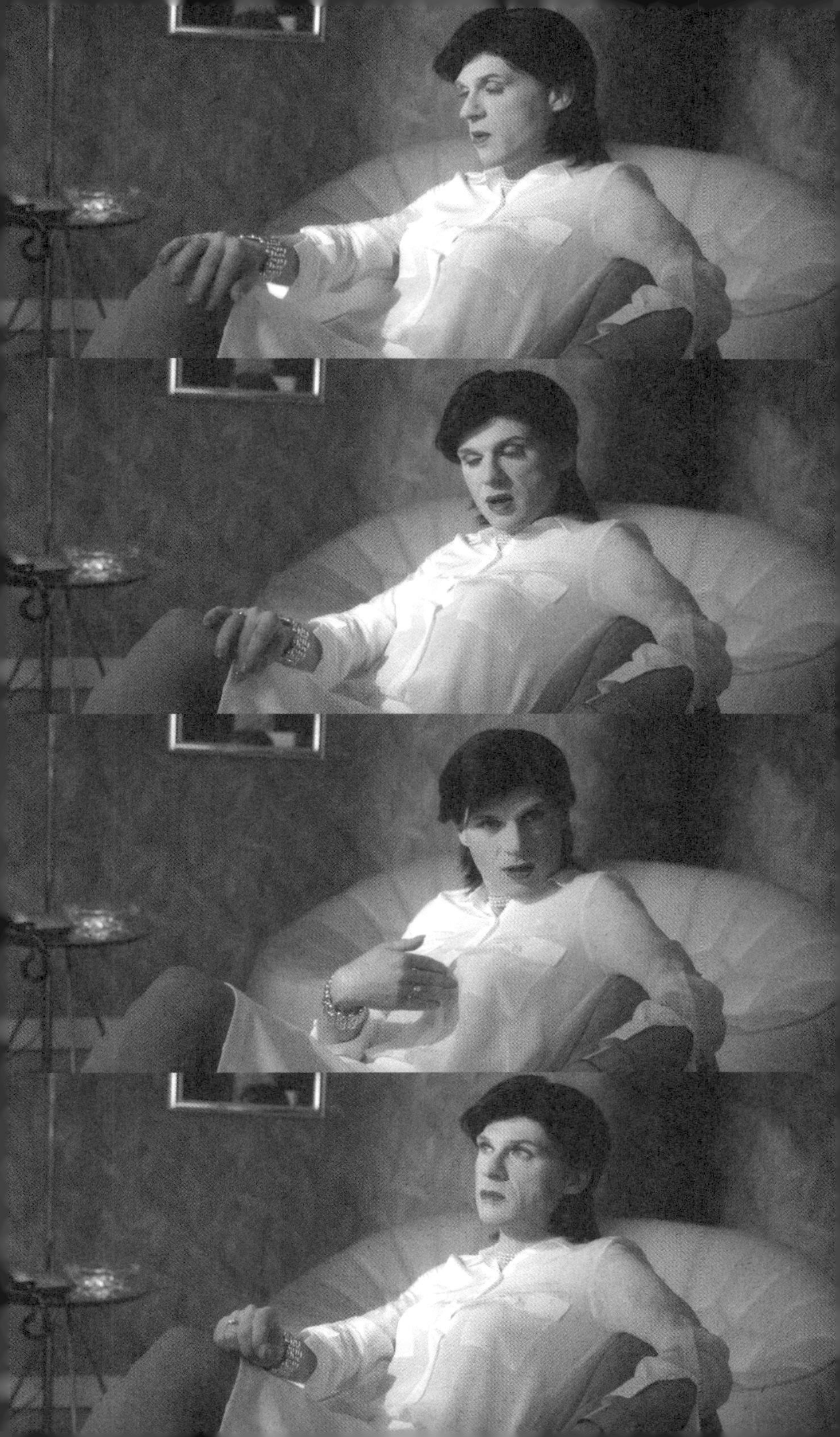

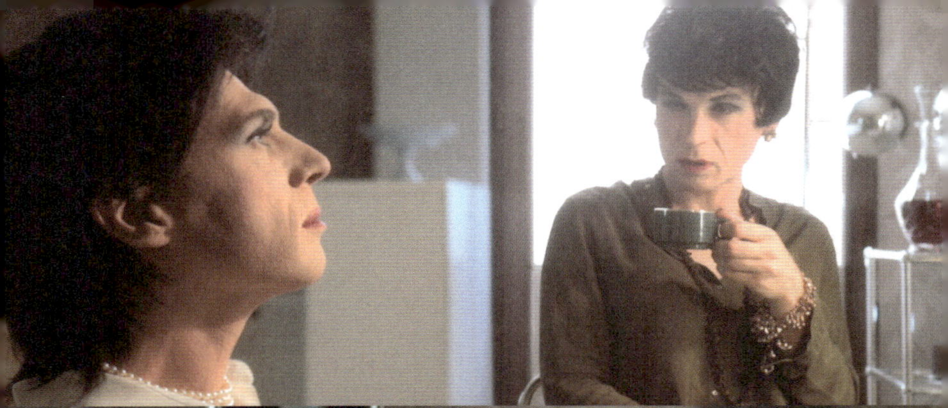
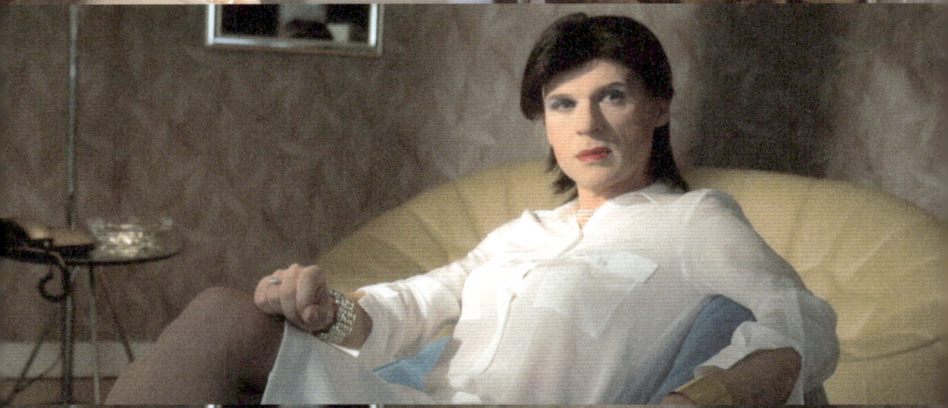
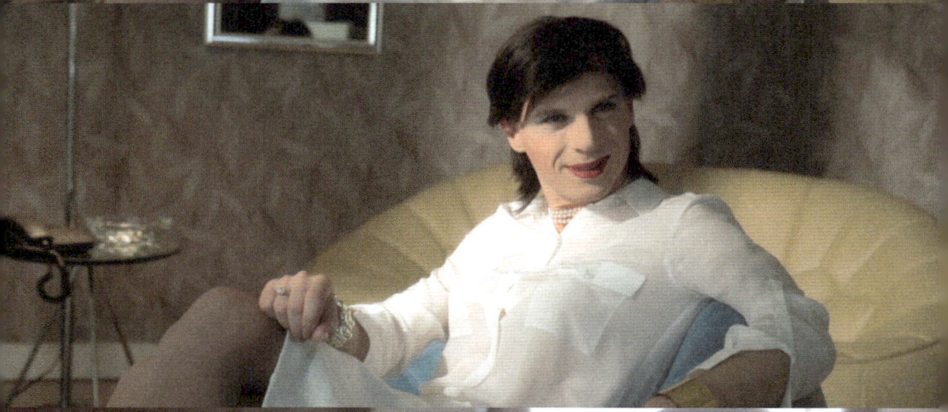
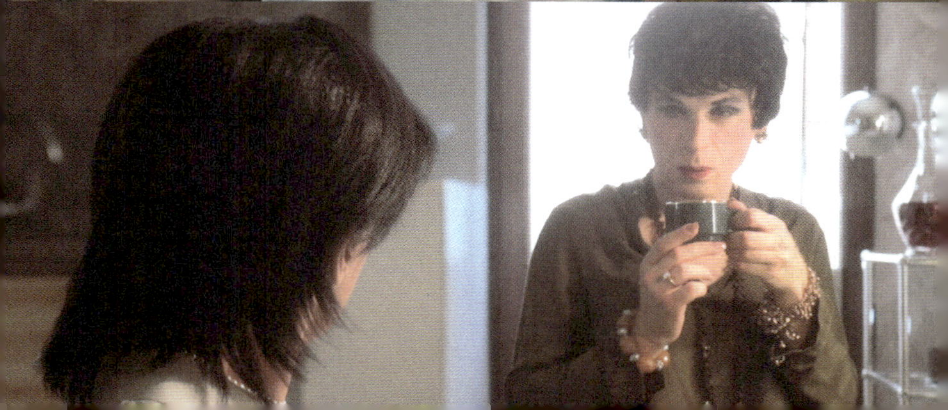

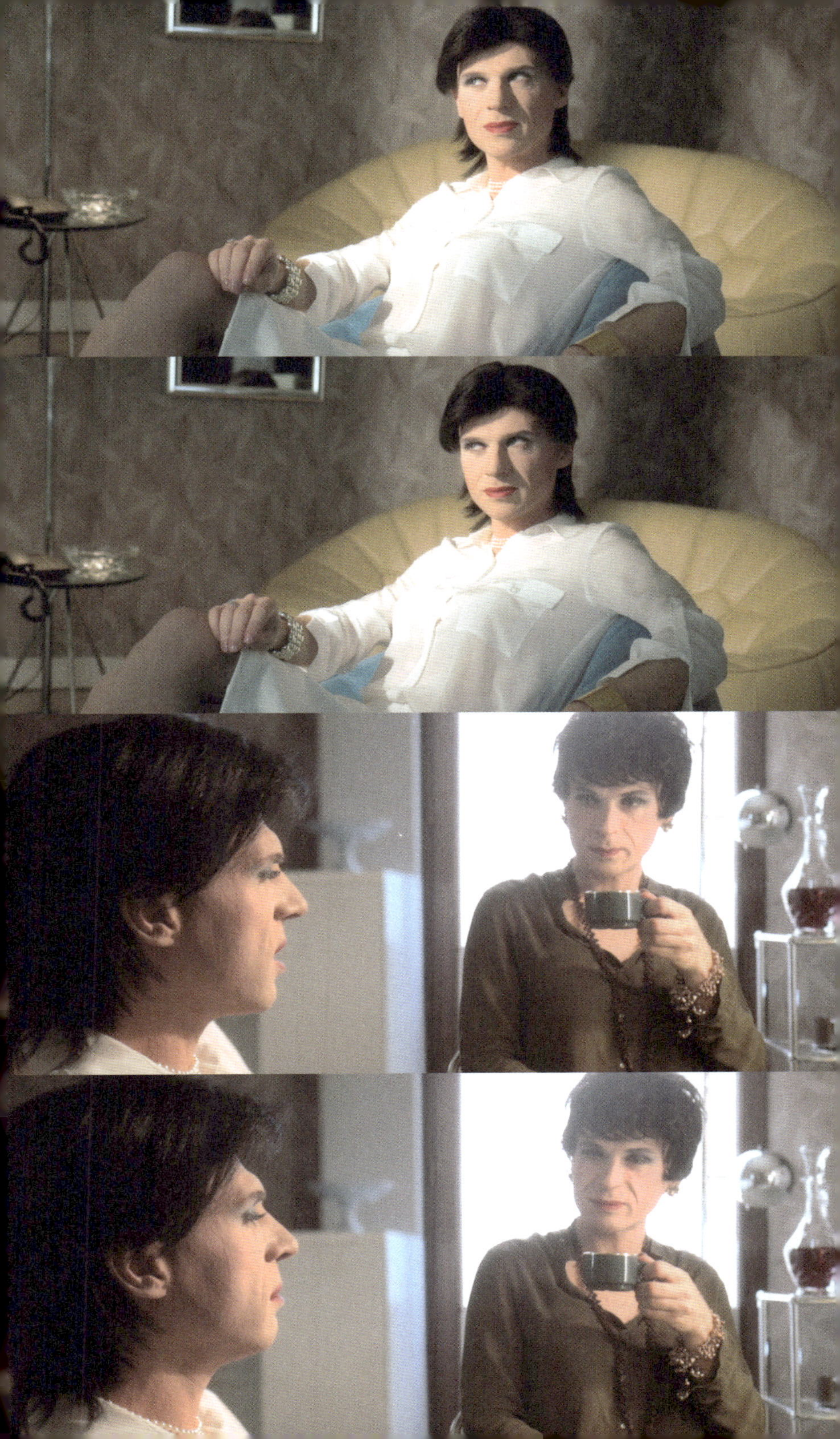

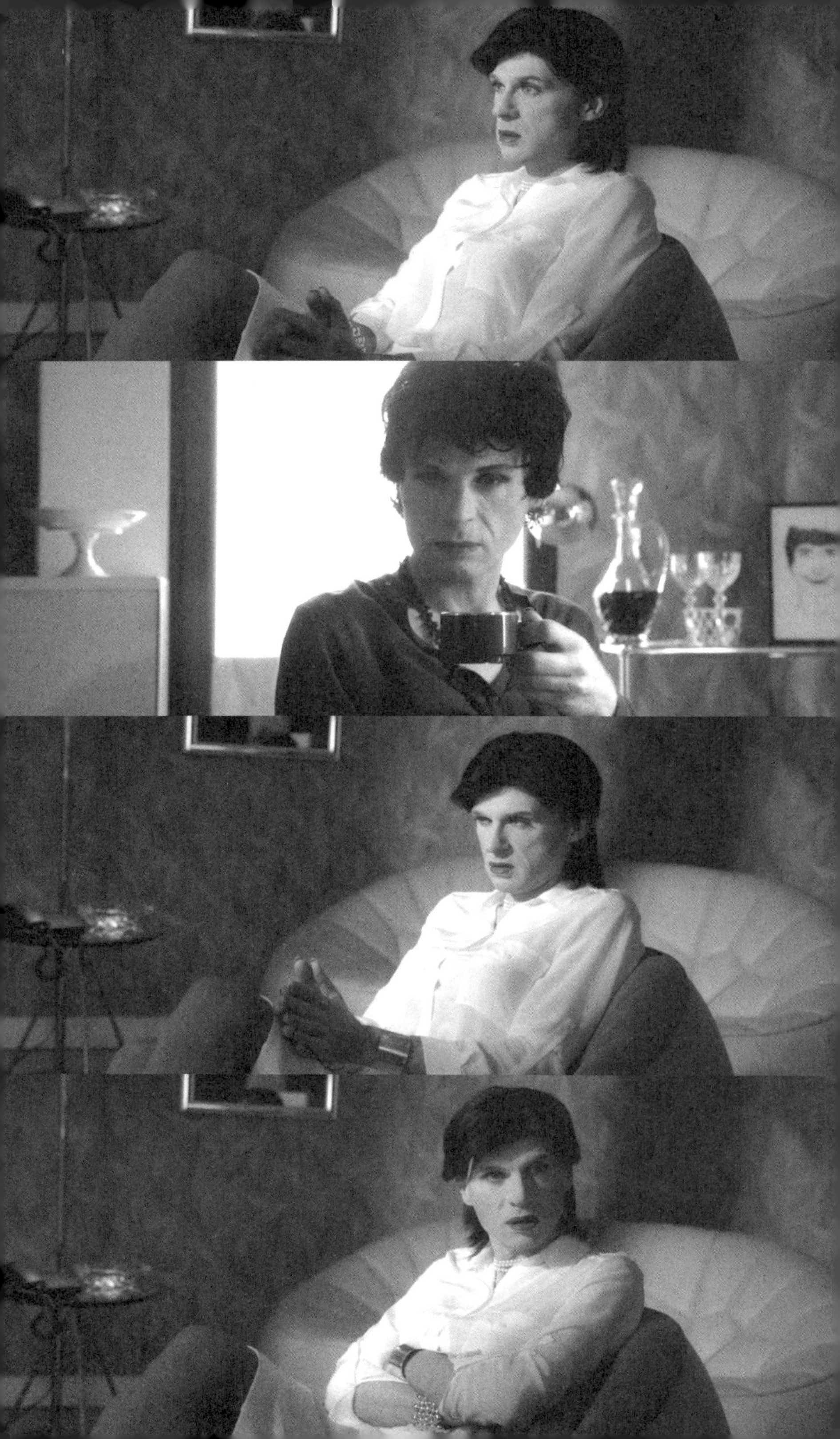

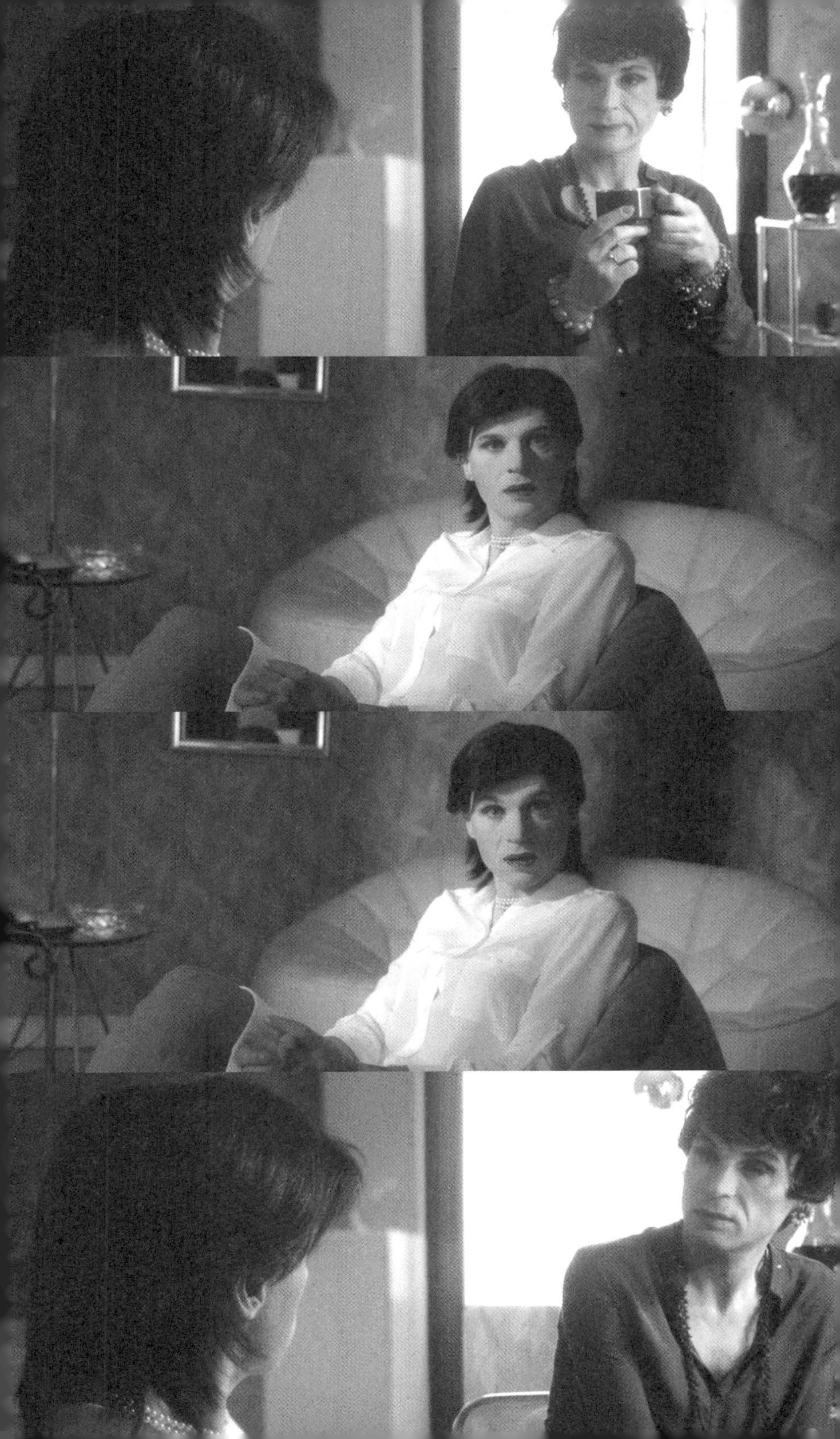

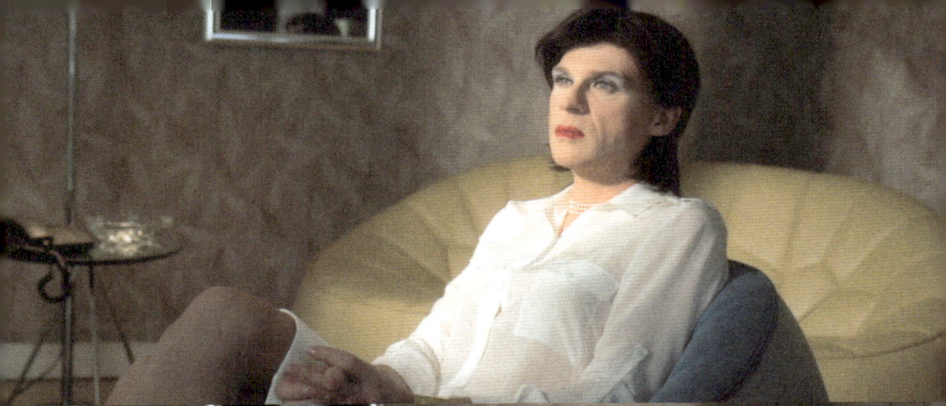

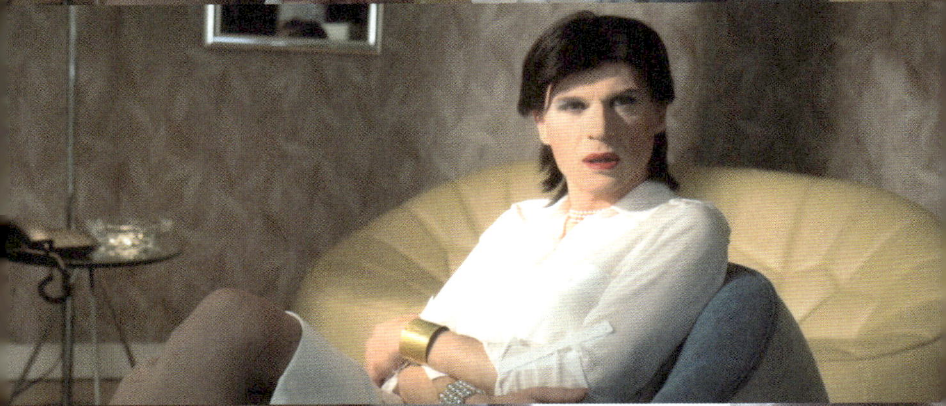

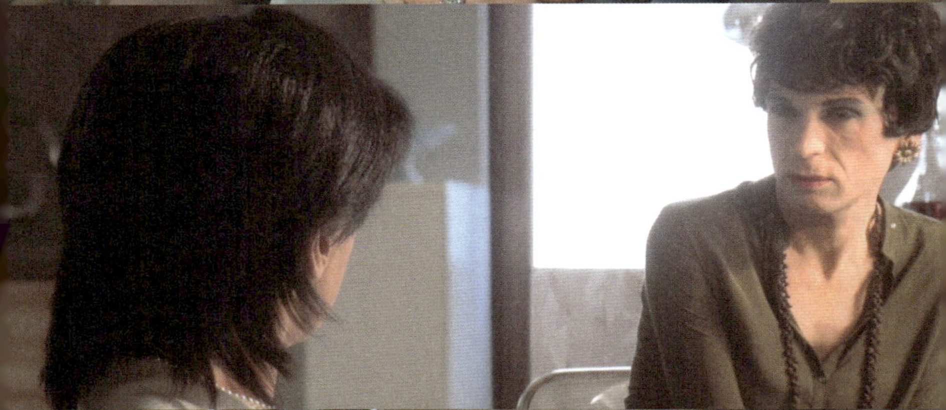

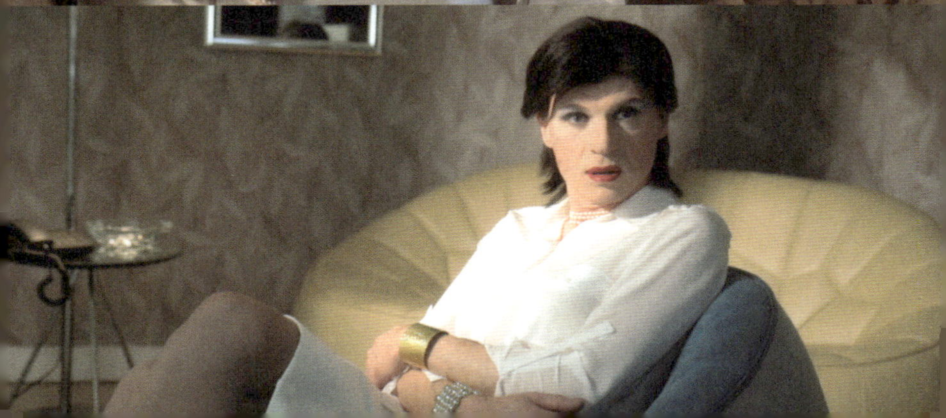

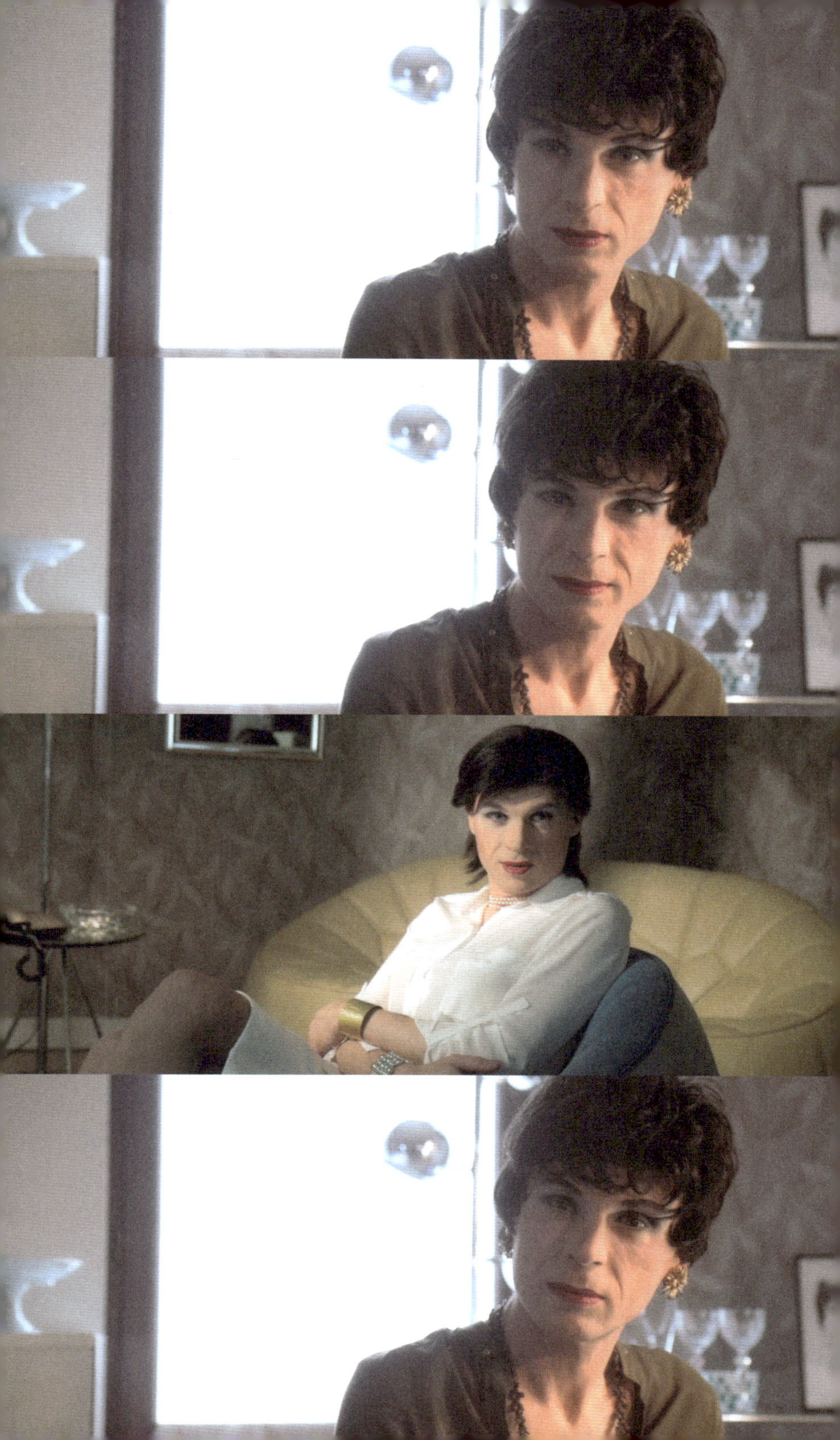

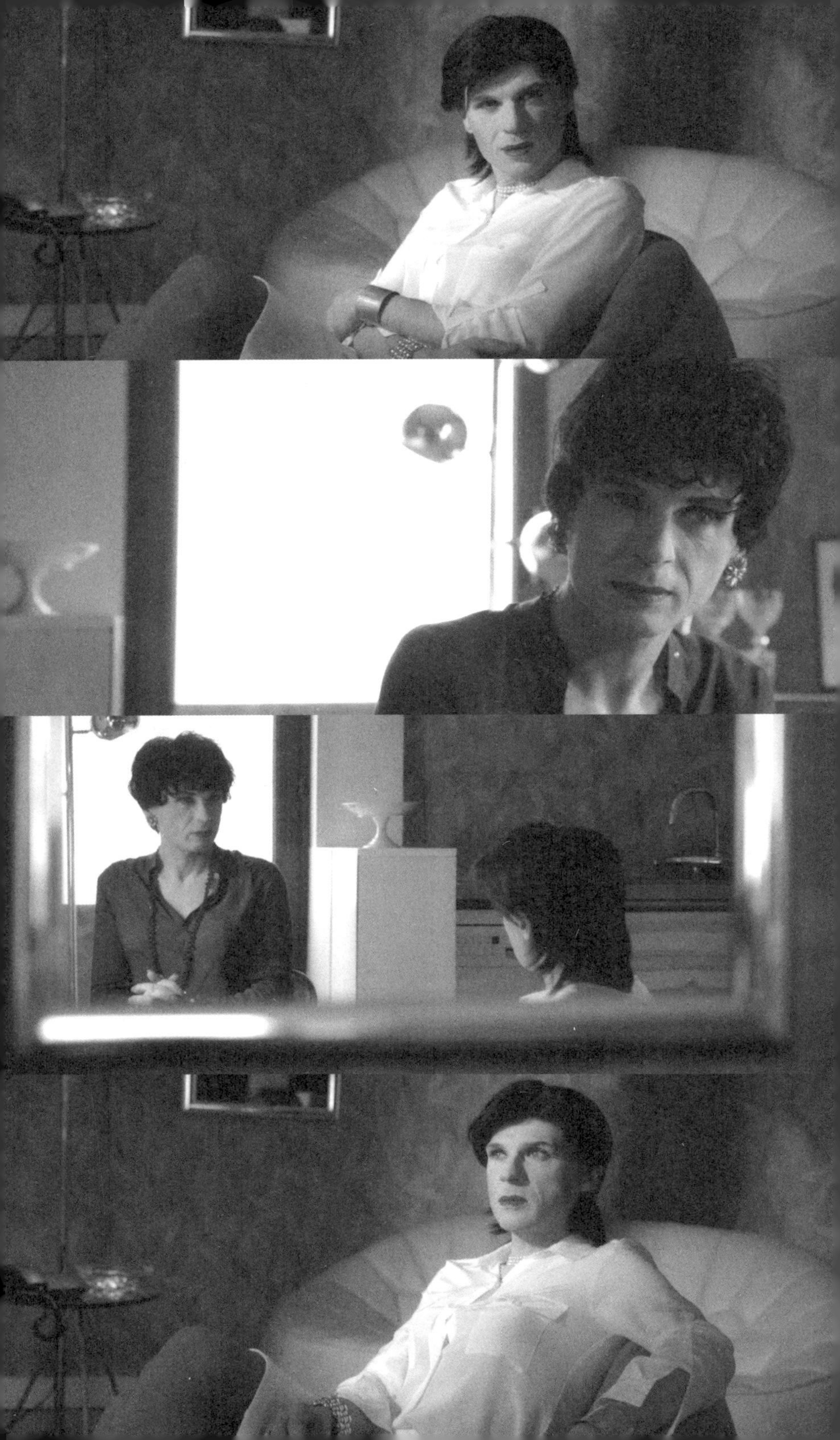

BODY DOUBLE XXXI

4'31"
AFTER PAUL VERHOEVEN'S BASIC INSTINCT (1992)
2014

CAST
EVA SVENNUNG

IMAGES
JORDANE CHOUZENOUX

EDITING, SOUND DESIGN
& SPECIAL EFFECTS
BRICE DELLSPERGER

TECHNICAL TEAM
DANA COLIN, SOPHIE DESBORDES,
NAÏA LASSUS, PAUL MIGNARD,
BAPTIST PENETTICOBRA

PRODUCTION
BRICE DELLSPERGER; AIR DE PARIS

COLLECTION
FRAC POITOU-CHARENTES, FRANCE

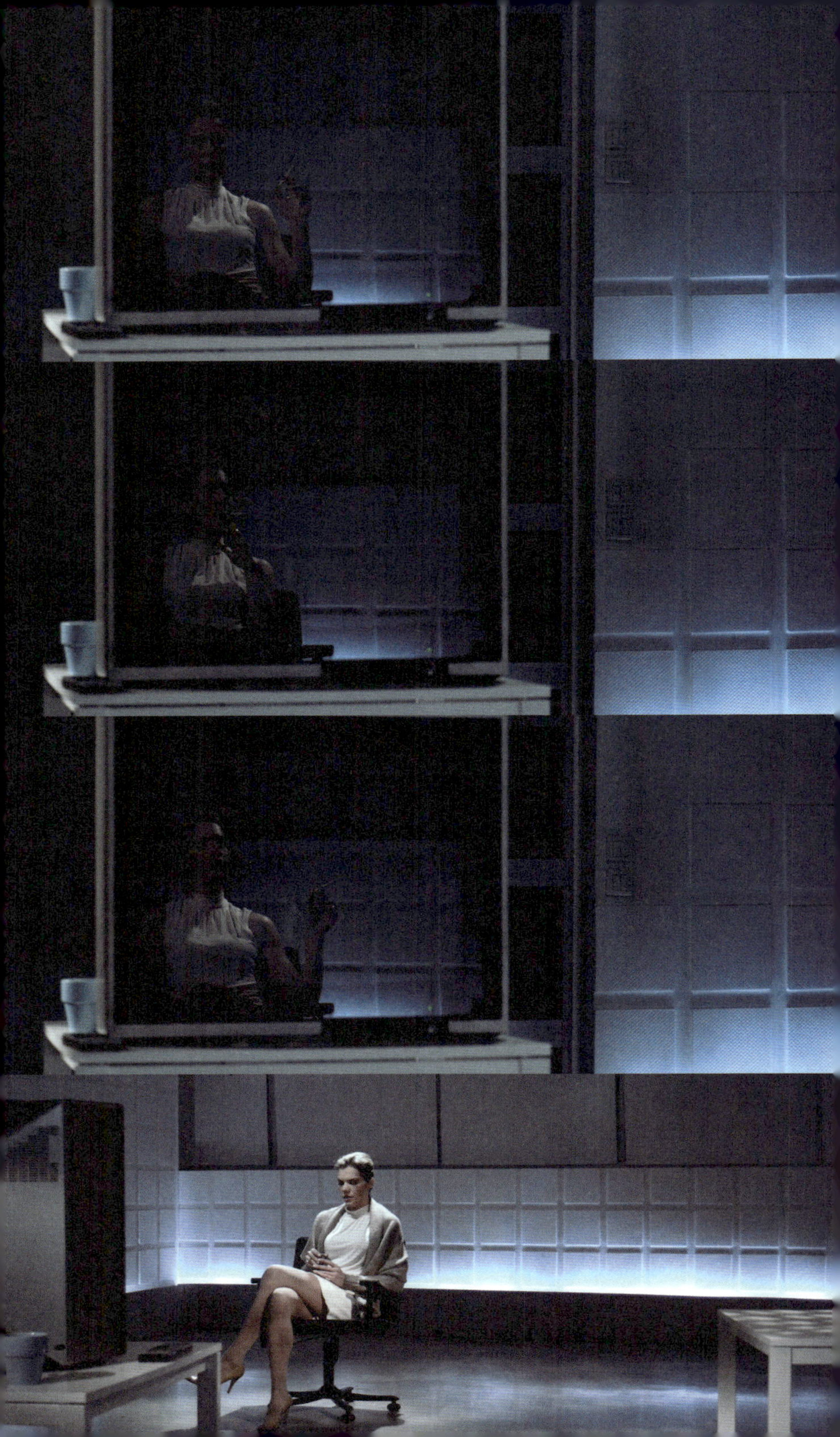

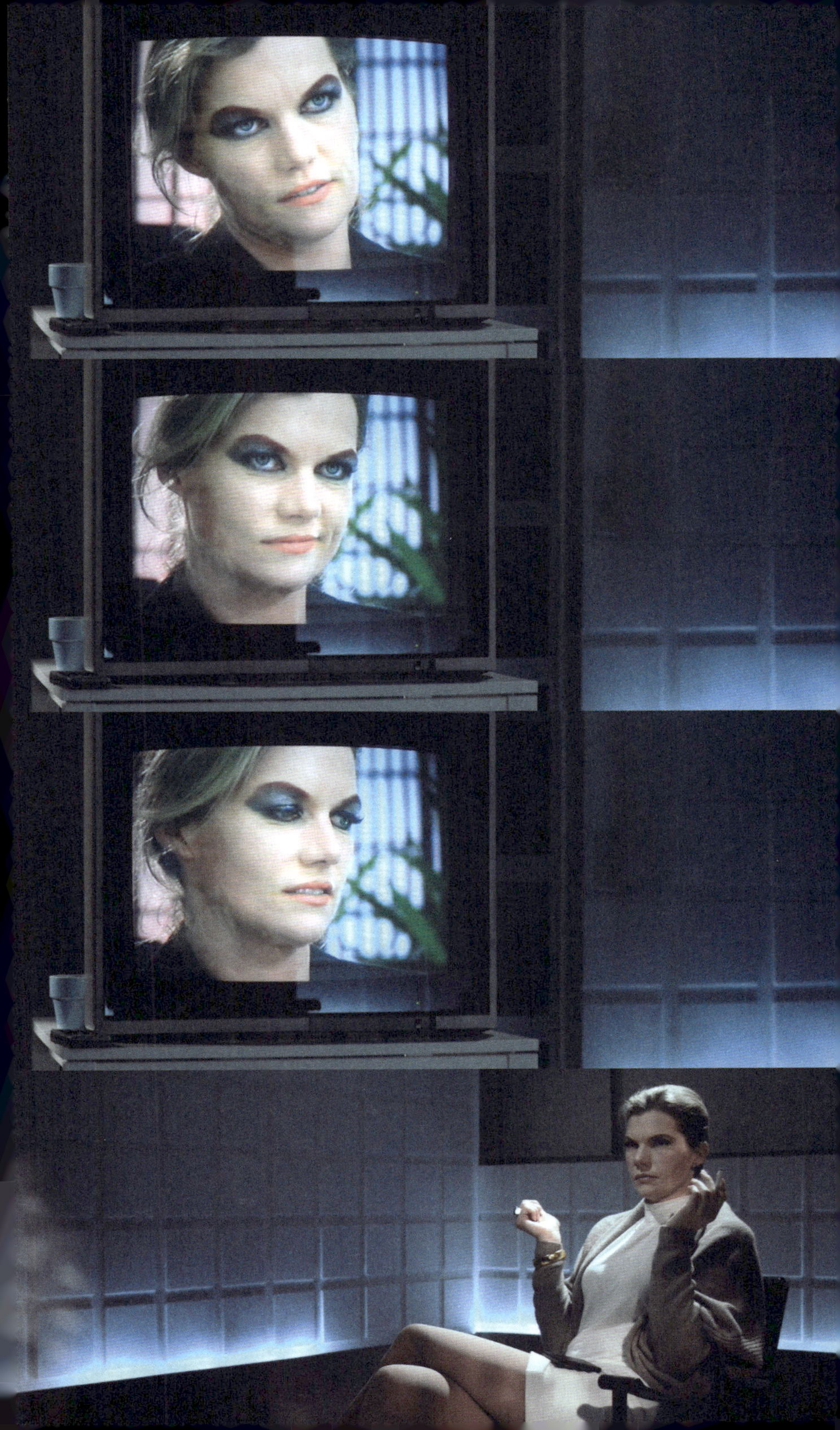

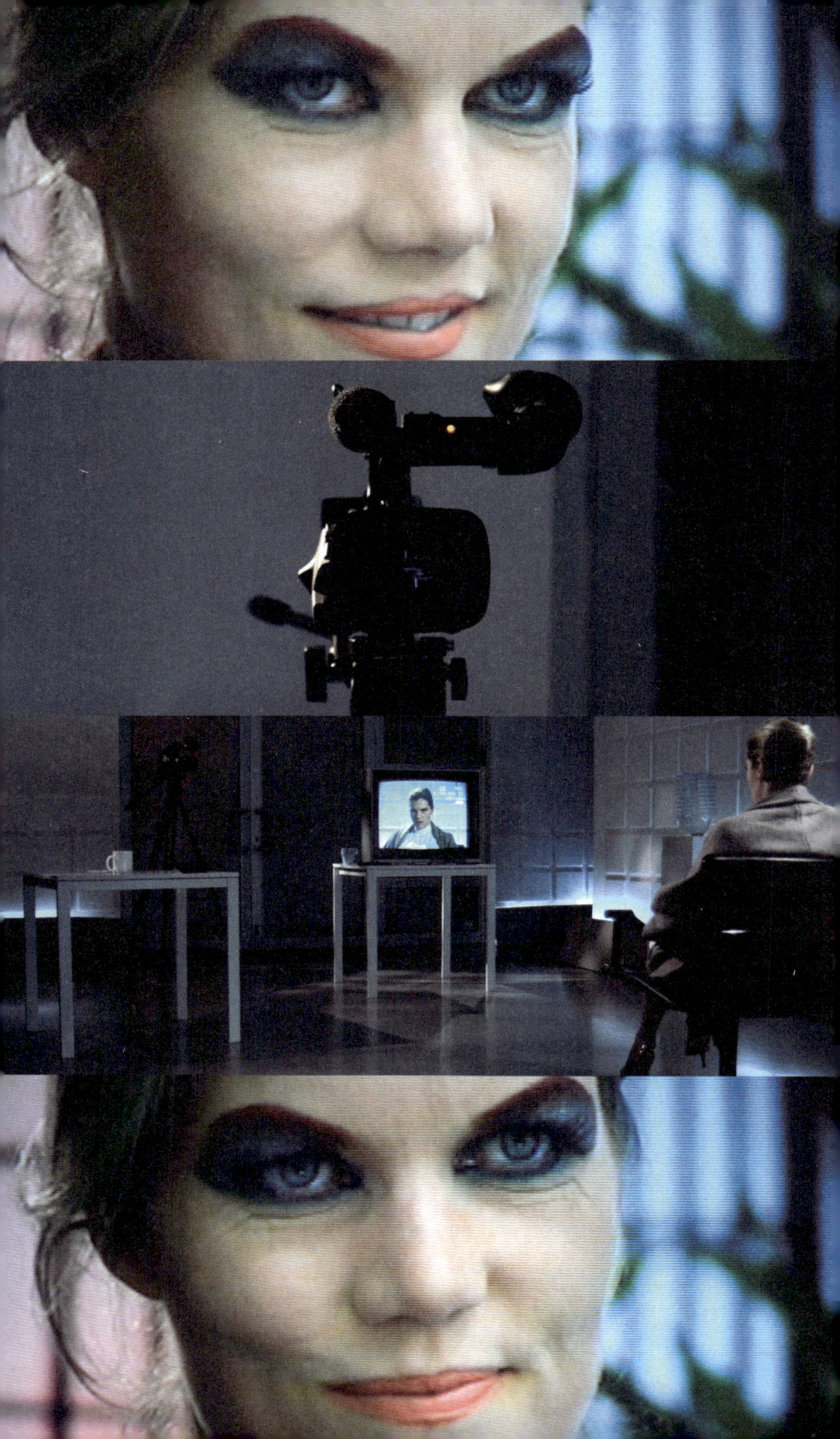

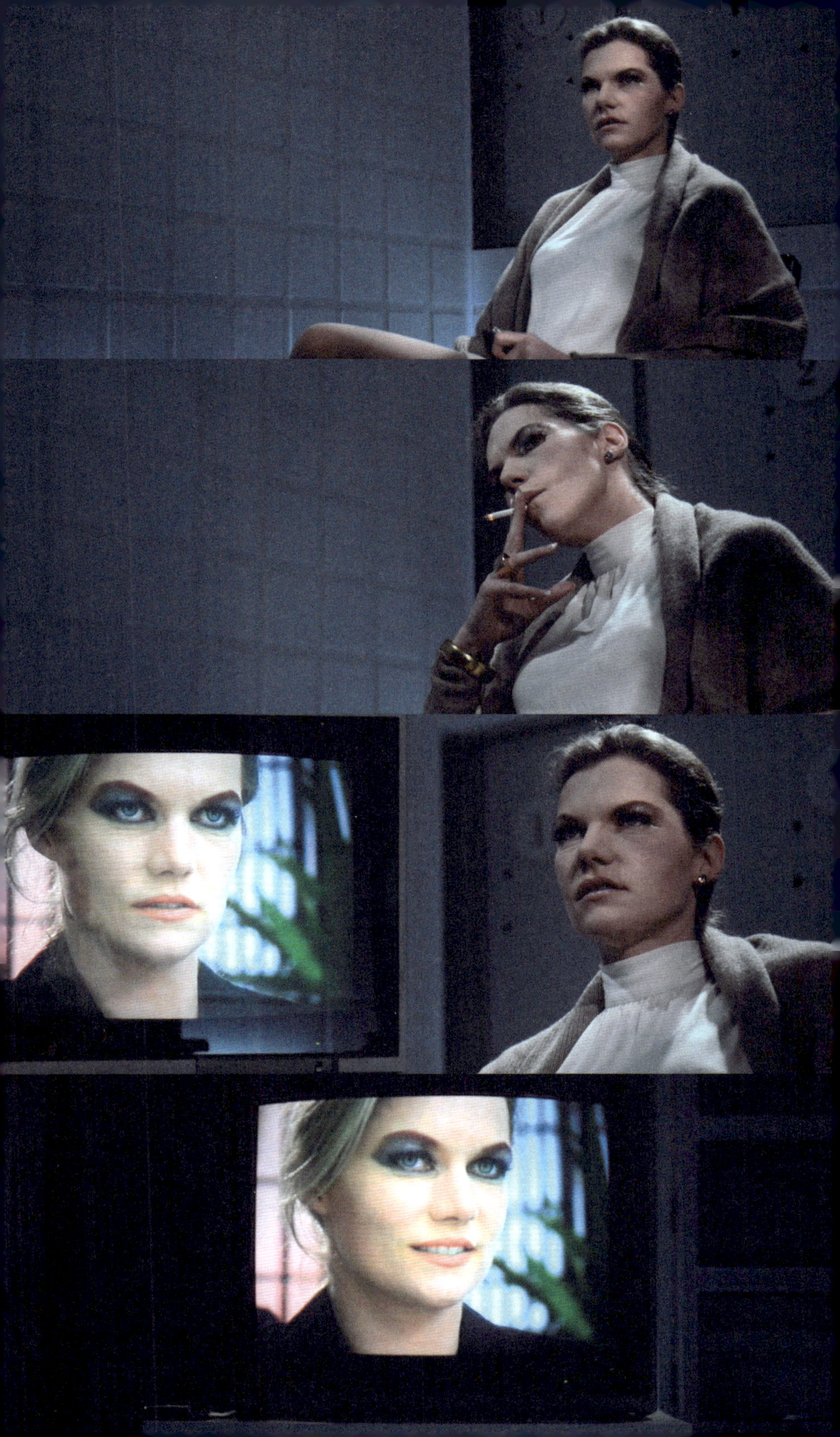

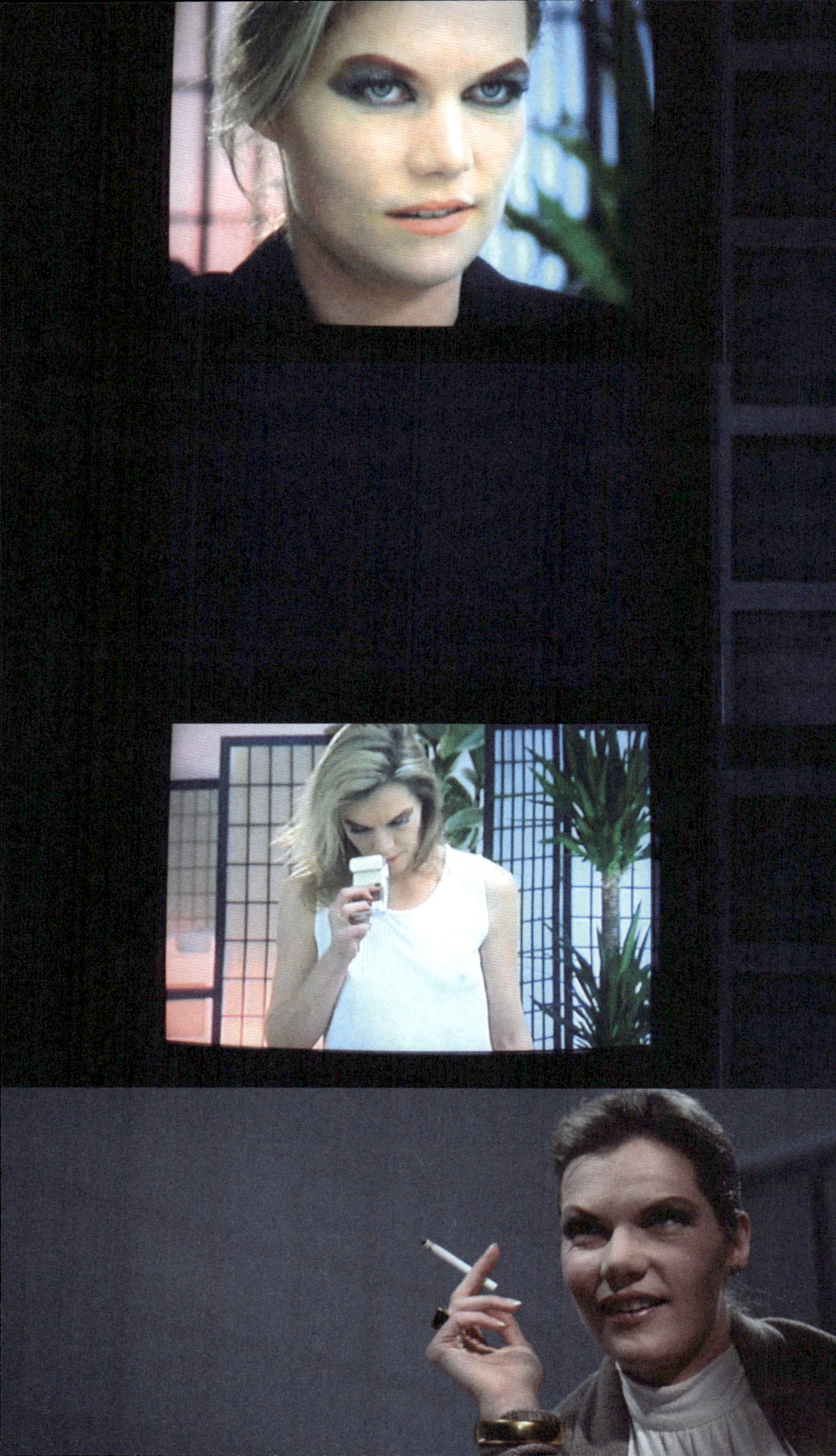

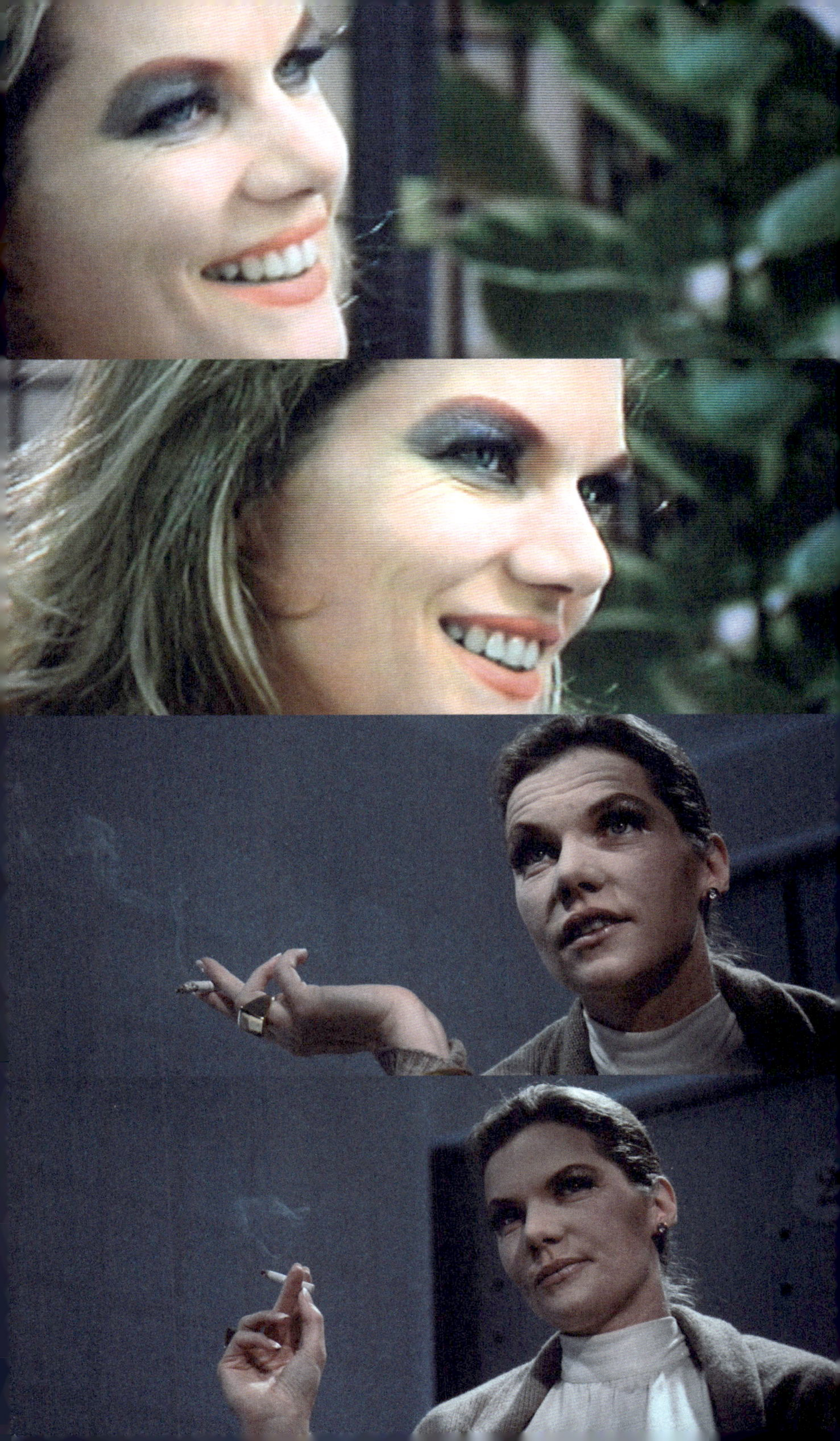

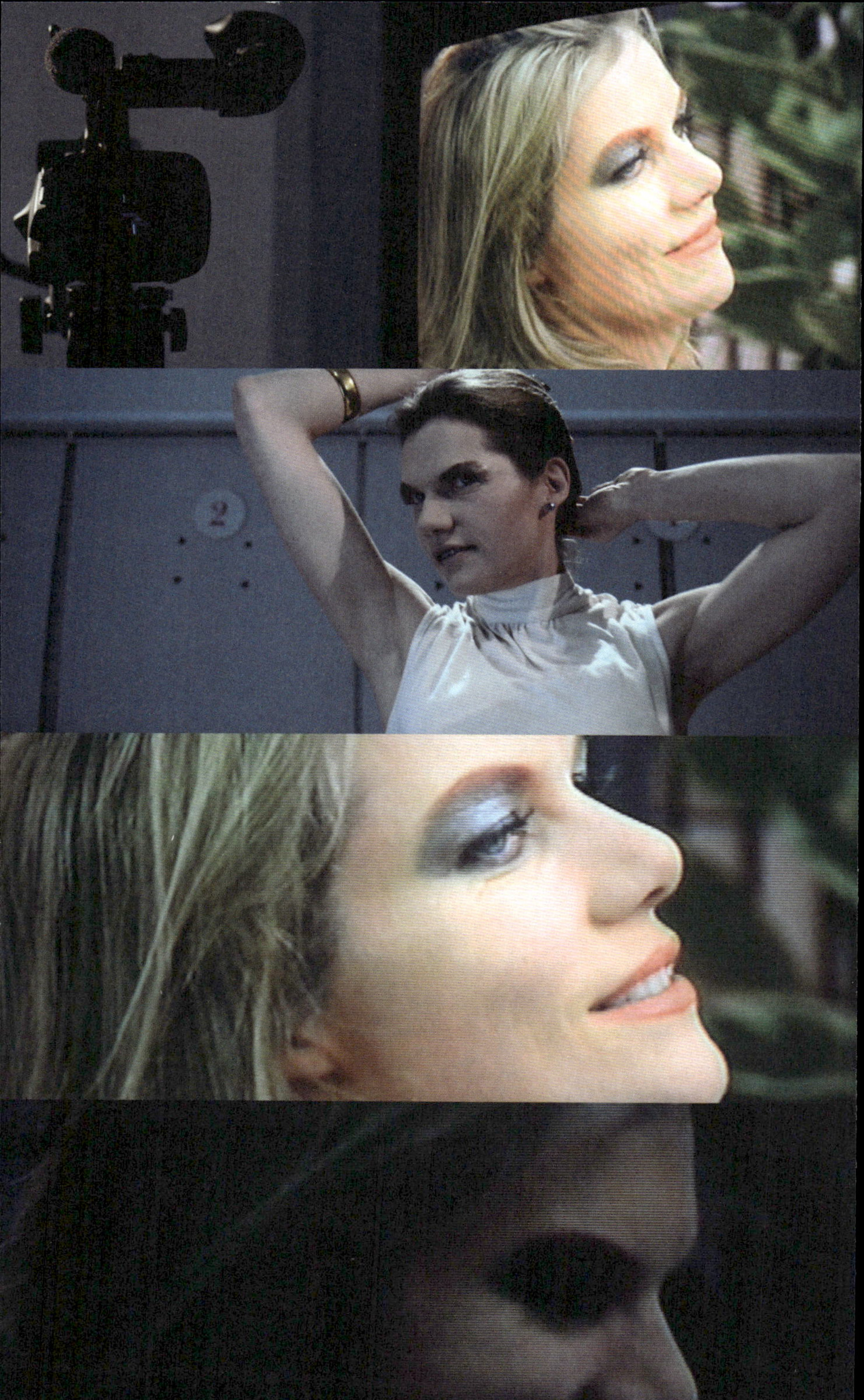
2

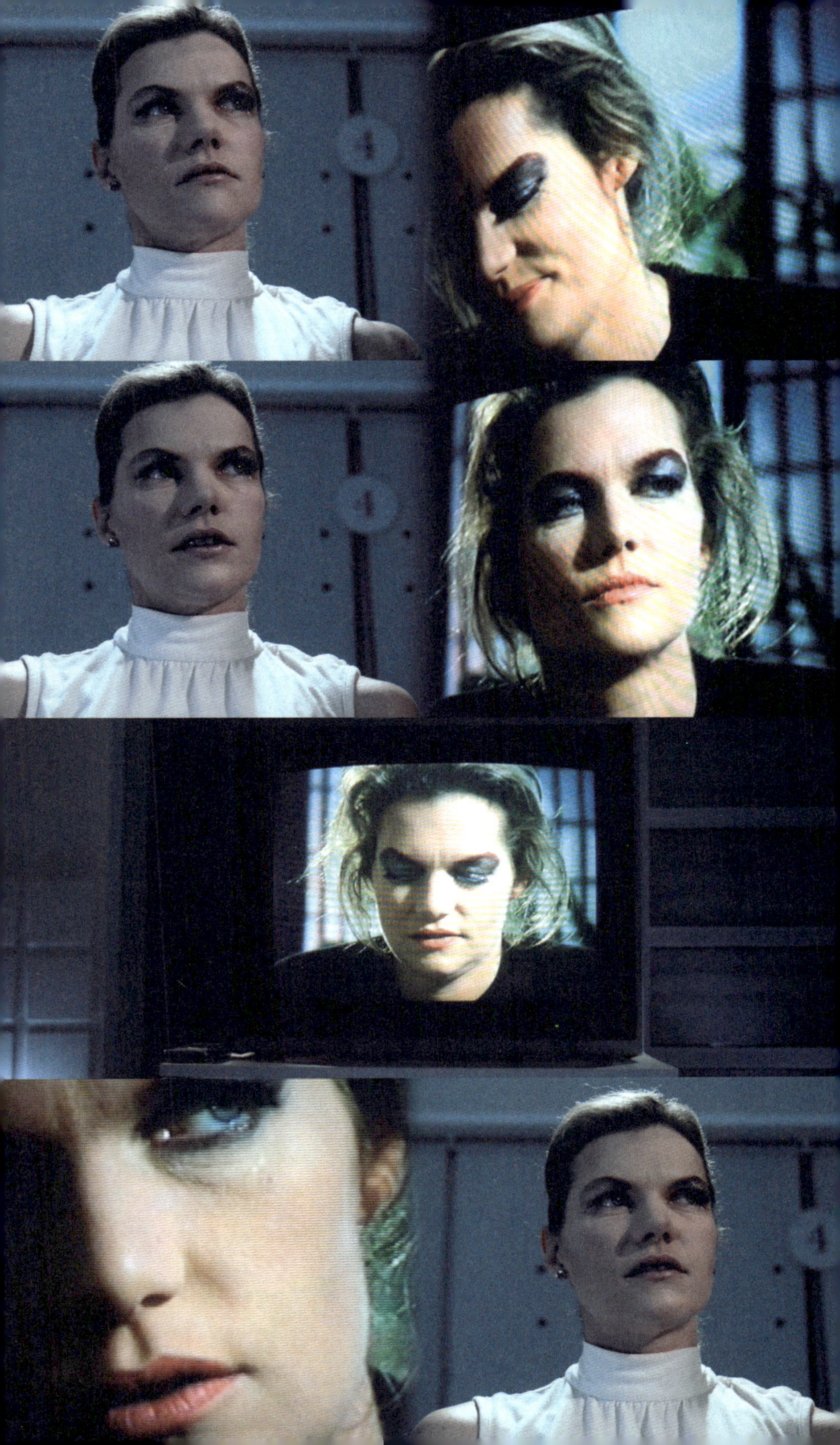

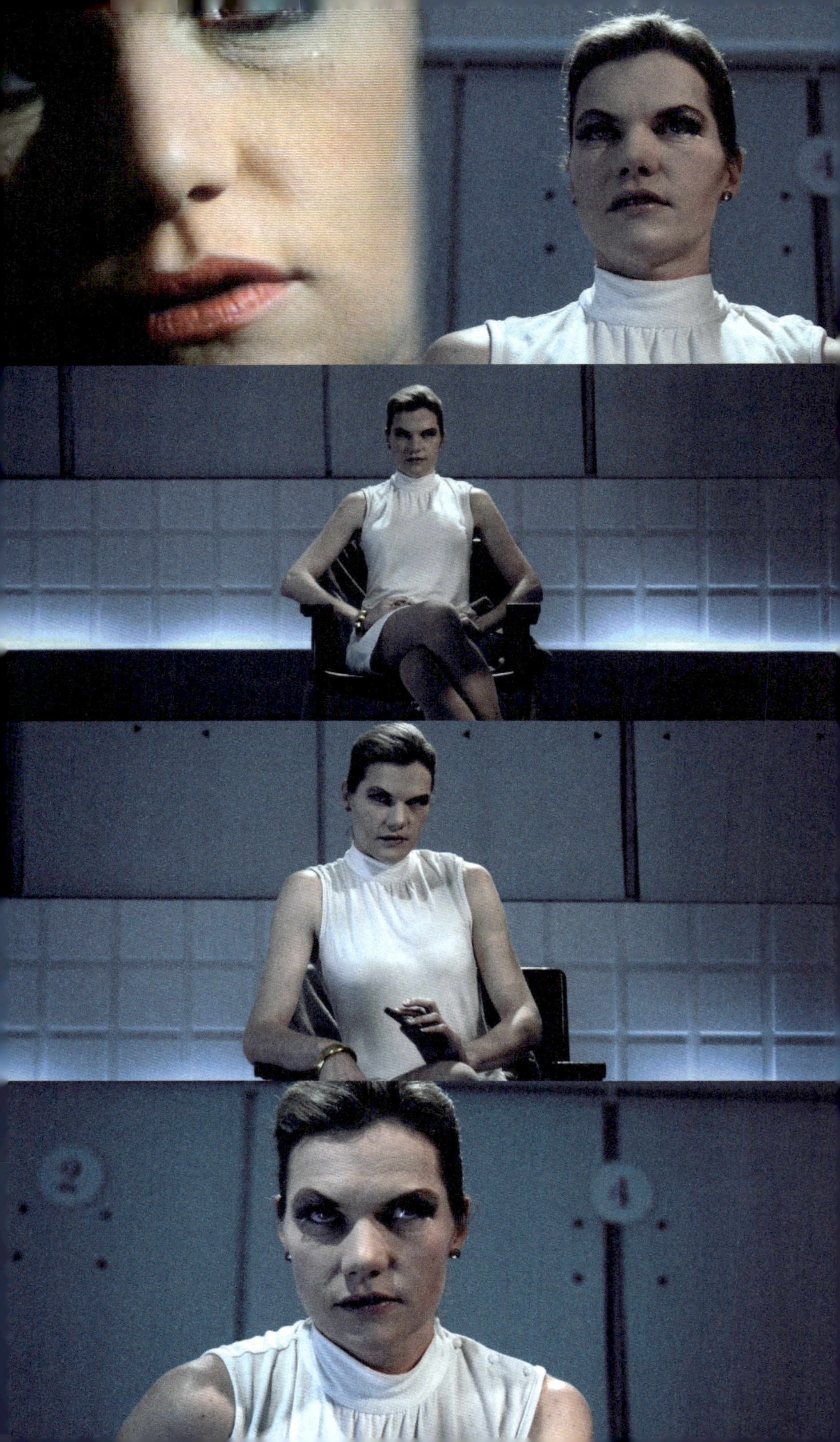

BODY DOUBLE XXXII

11'02"
AFTER BRIAN DE PALMA'S CARRIE (1976)
2017

CAST
ALEX WETTER

IMAGES
LOÏC BOVON

EDITING, SOUND DESIGN
& SPECIAL EFFECTS
BRICE DELLSPERGER

FIRST ASSISTANT DIRECTOR
& SCRIPT
QUENTIN GOUJOUT

SOUND DESIGN
DIDIER BLASCO

MAKE-UP DESIGN
MELODIE DOUGNAC-MOYEN

SET MANAGER
GILLES MARTINEZ

ASSISTANT CAMERA
COLIN CHEVILLOTTE, XI NING,
CLEMENT PIRES

SET DESIGN, CONSTRUCTION
& TECHNICAL TEAM
JOY CHARPENTIER, COLIN
CHEVILLOTTE, ANAIS DOCTEUR,
MELODIE DOUGNAC-
MOYEN, MATHIAS MOREAU,
NINA QUEISSNER, XI NING,
CLEMENT PIRES, JORDAN
ROGER, LÉA TISSOT, AMELIE
VAVASSEUR, ELISE VOET

PRODUCTION
FNAGP, FRANCE; ENSA
BOURGES, FRANCE; FIRST
IDEA, NMNM - NOUVEAU
MUSÉE NATIONAL DE
MONACO; AIR DE PARIS

EXECUTIVE PRODUCTION
BEAU BIZARRE (NICOLAS
PERGE, DAVID LAVIALLE,
ARNAUD OLIVIER)

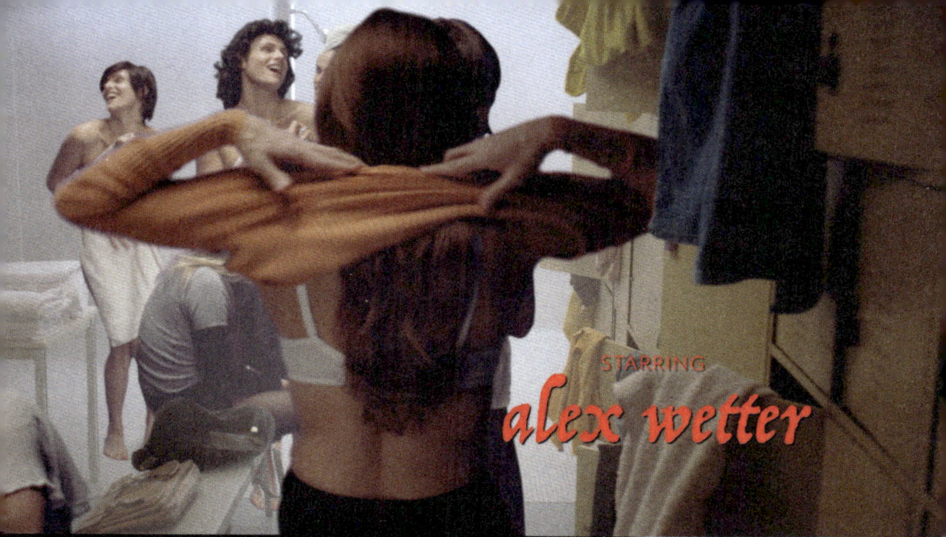
STARRING
alex wetter

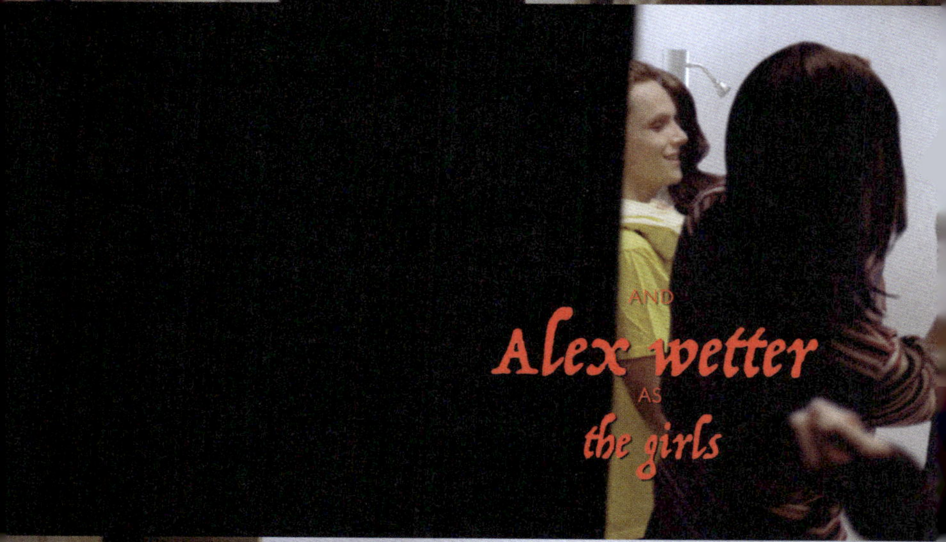
AND
Alex wetter
AS
the girls

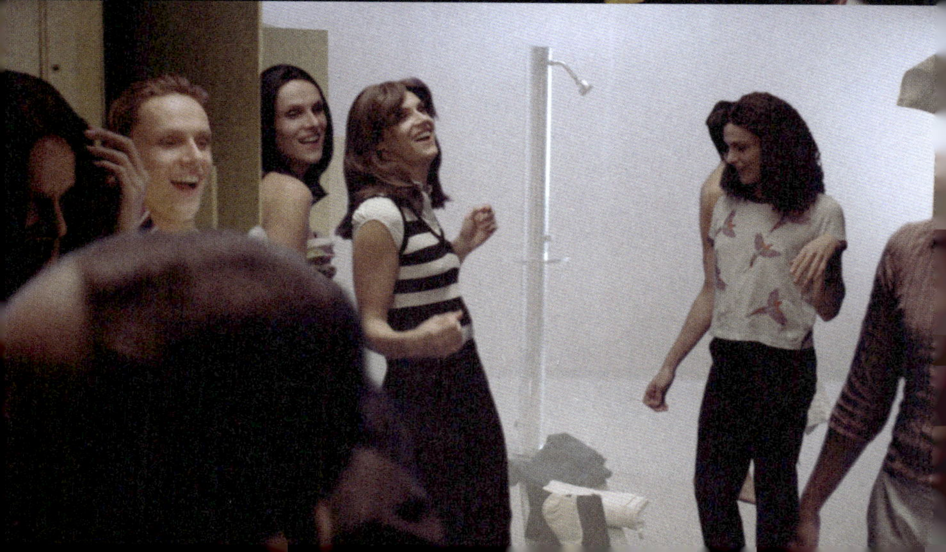

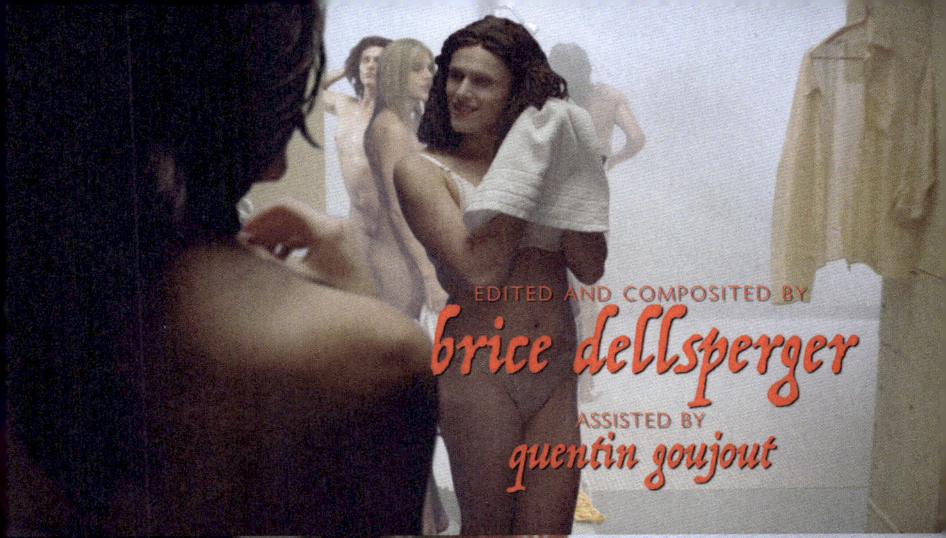
EDITED AND COMPOSITED BY
brice dellsperger
ASSISTED BY
quentin goujout

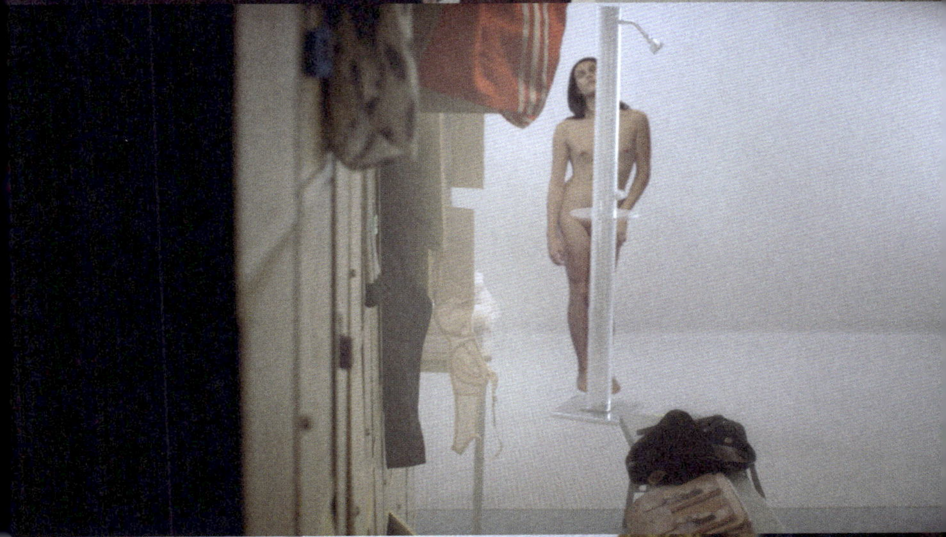

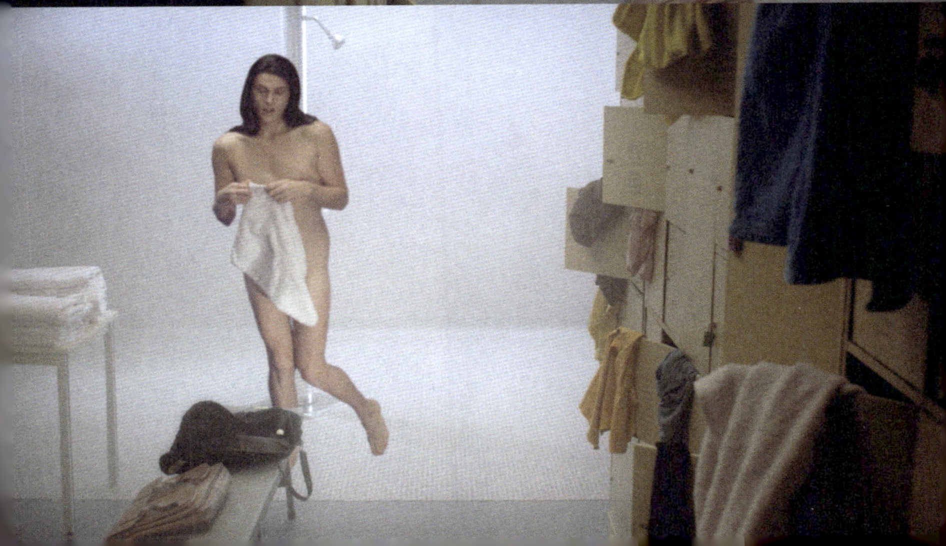

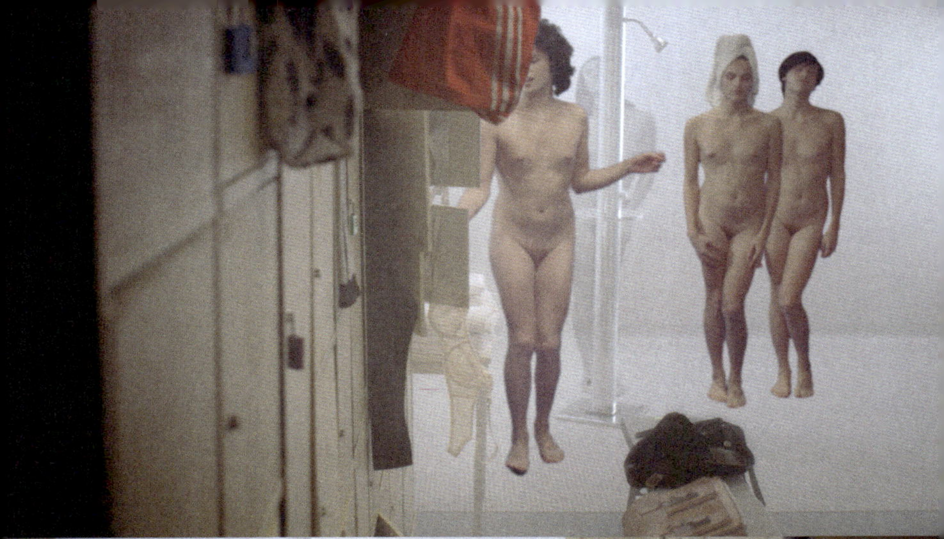

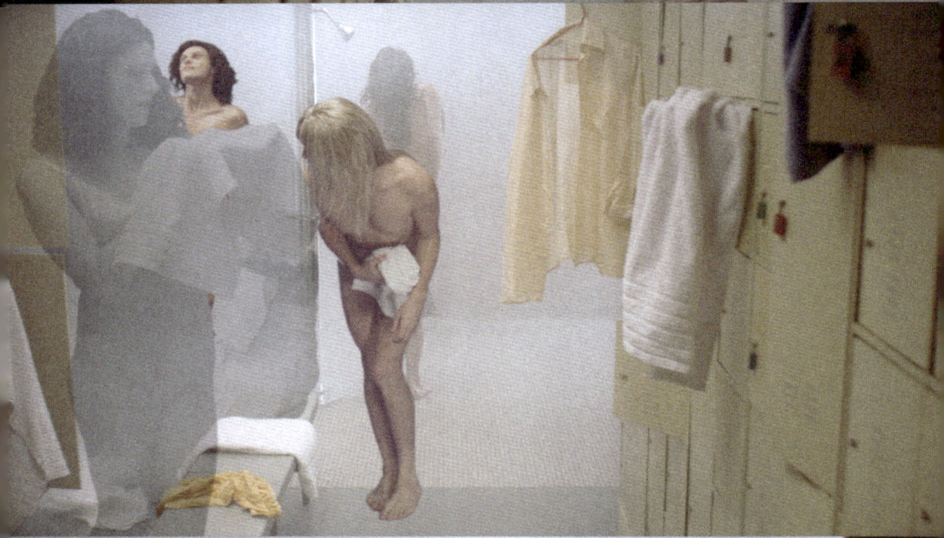

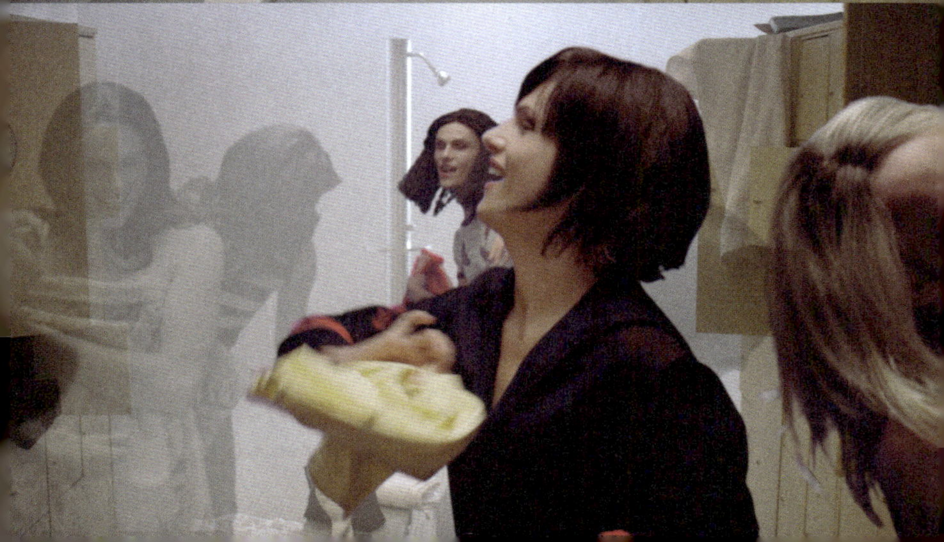

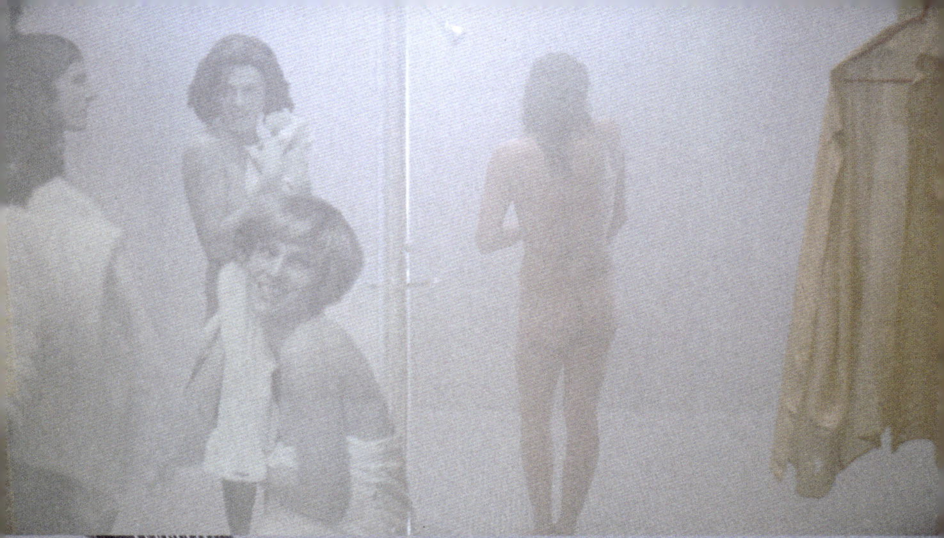

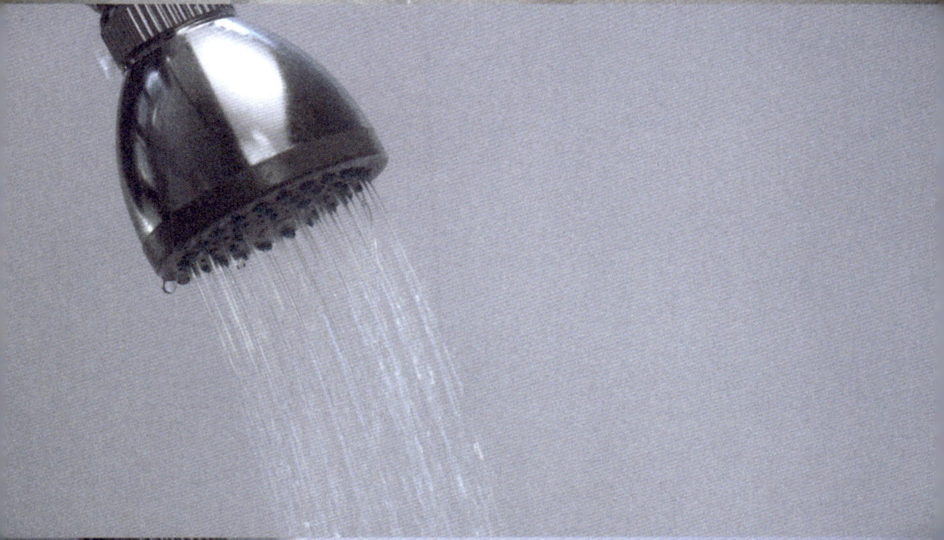

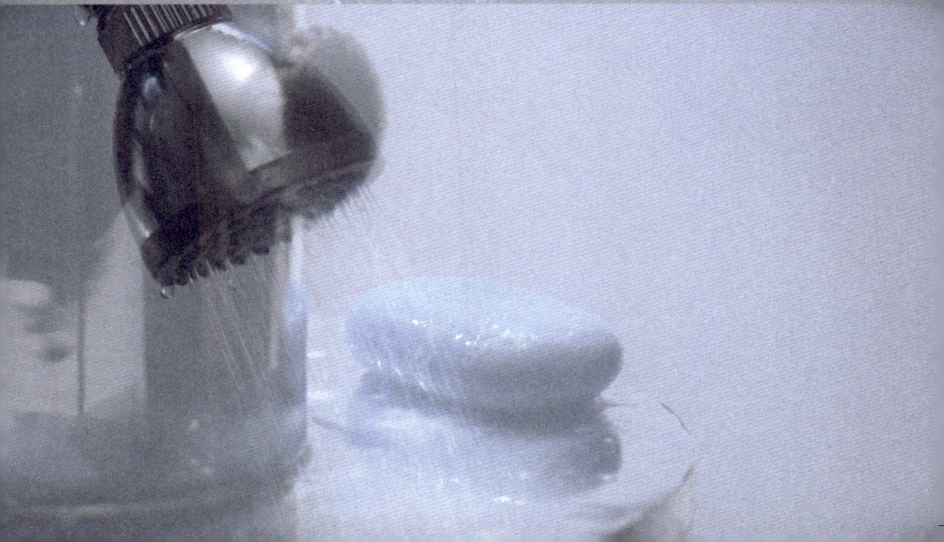

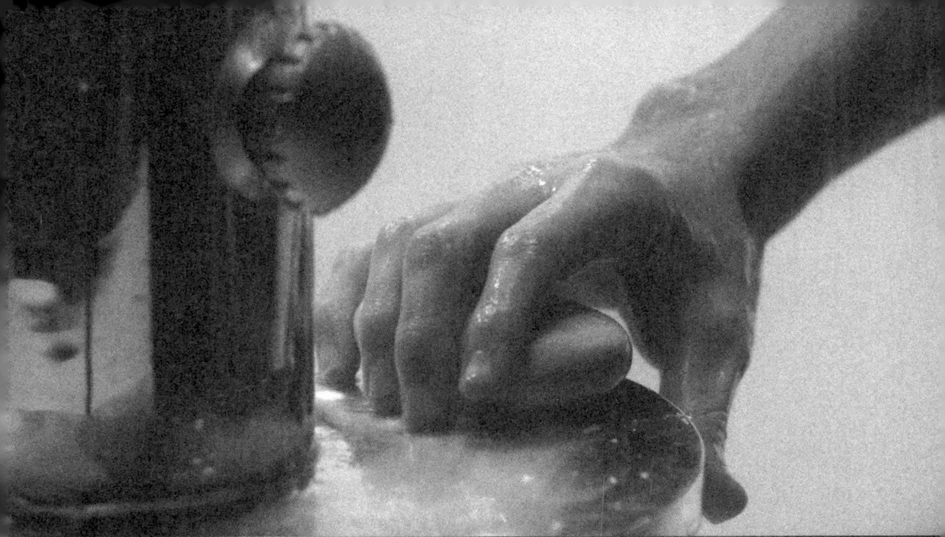
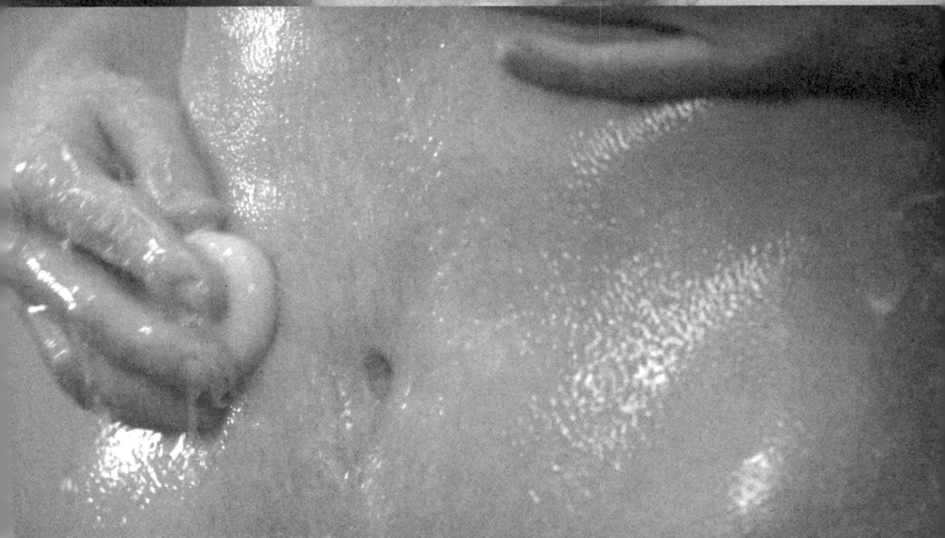
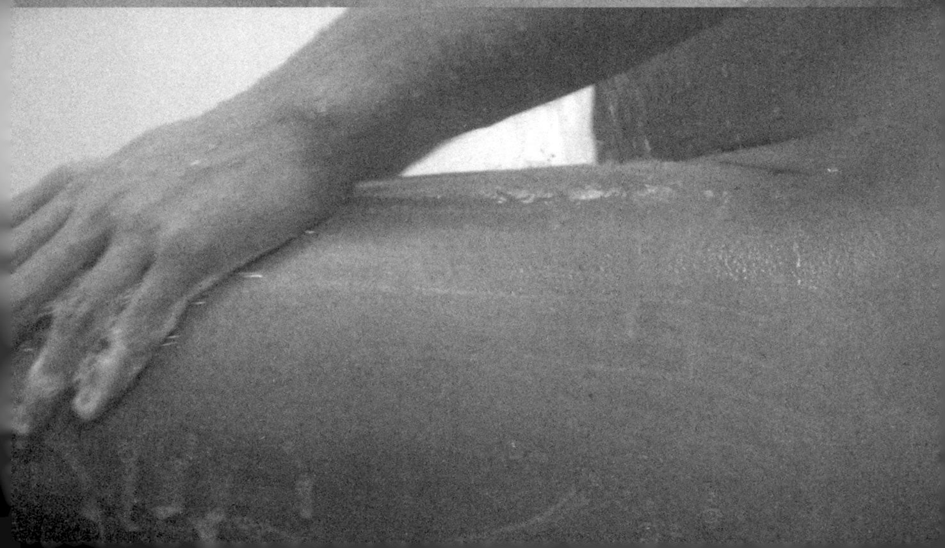

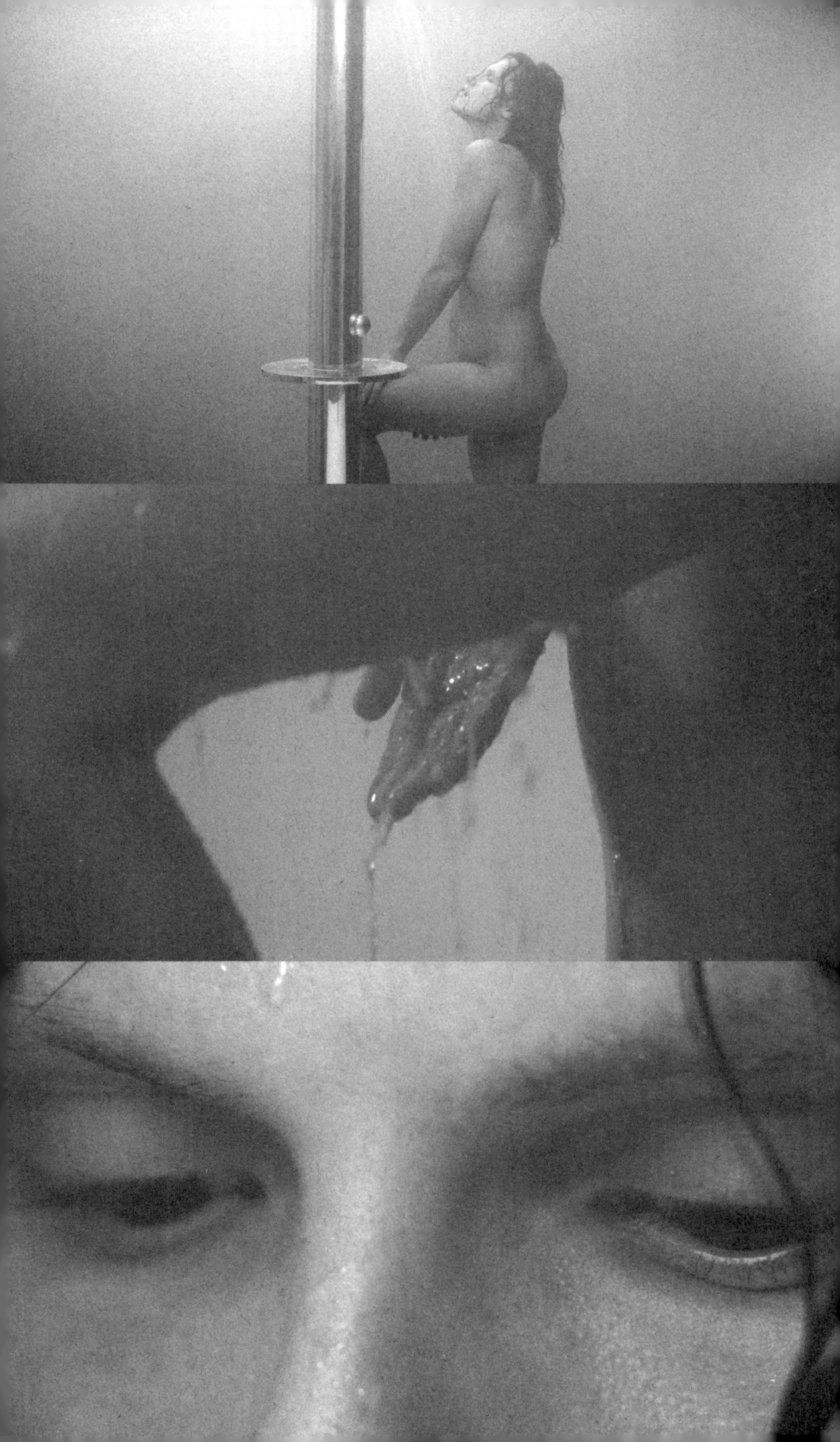

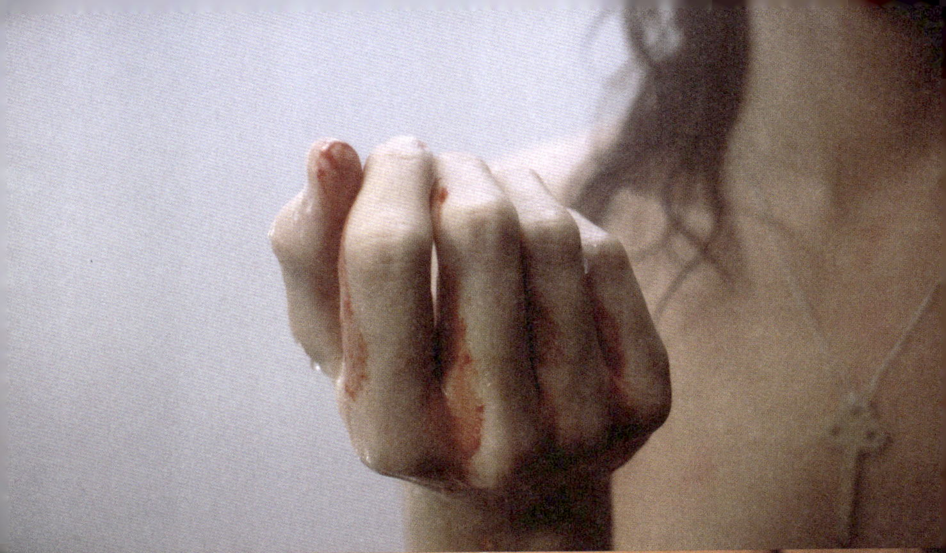
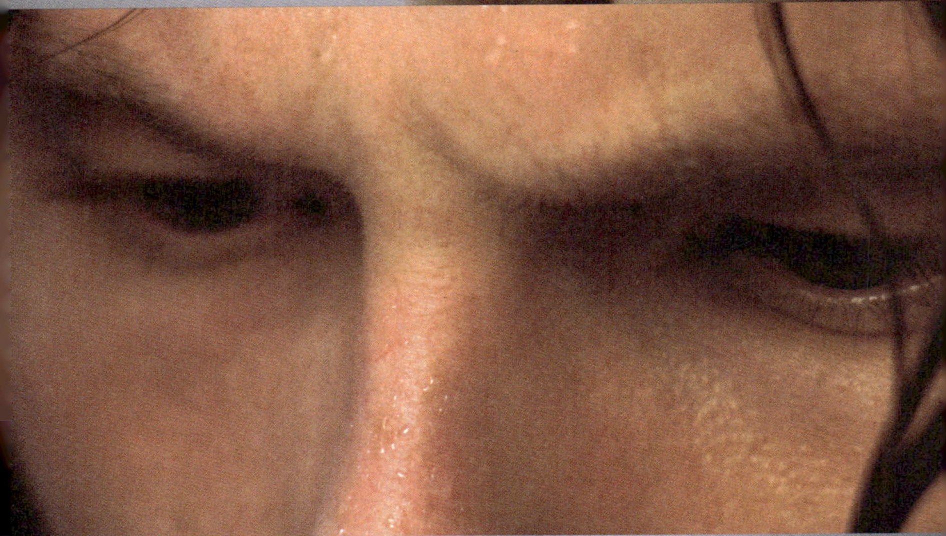
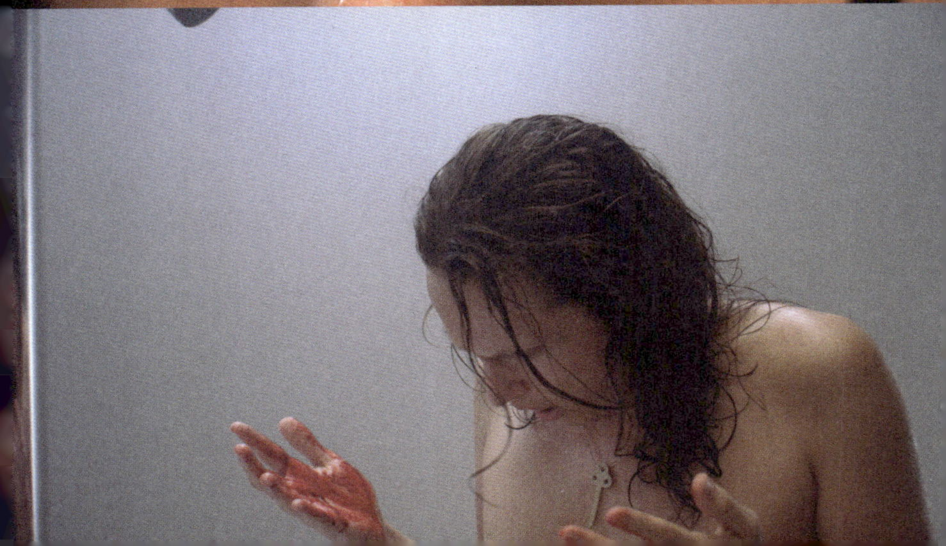

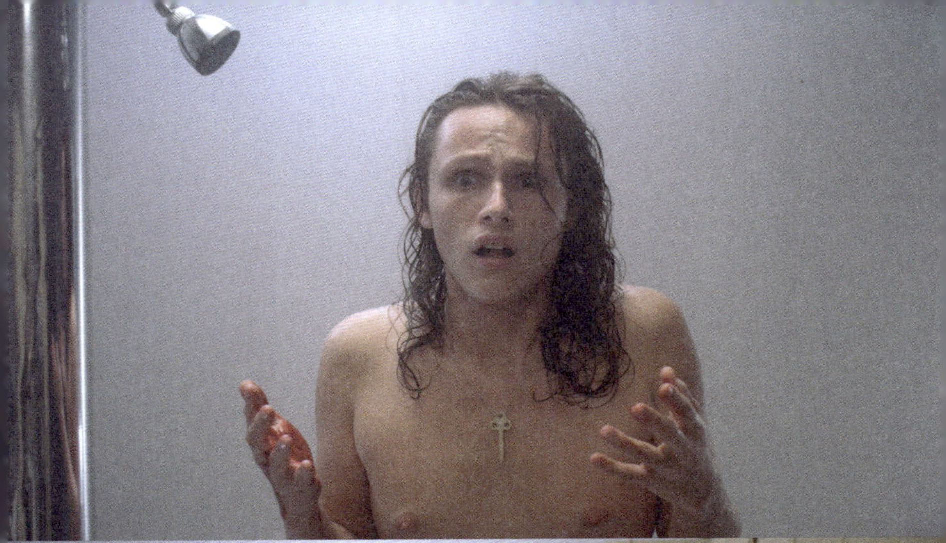

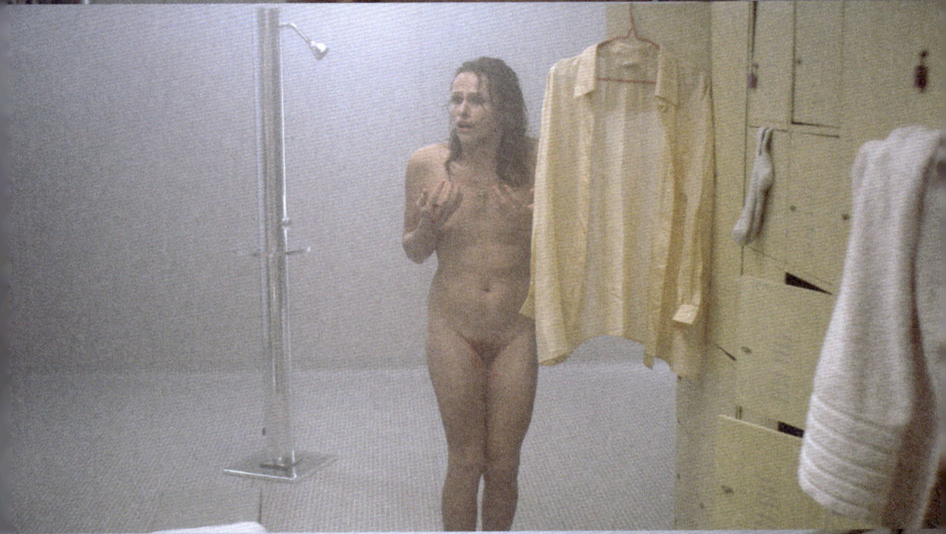

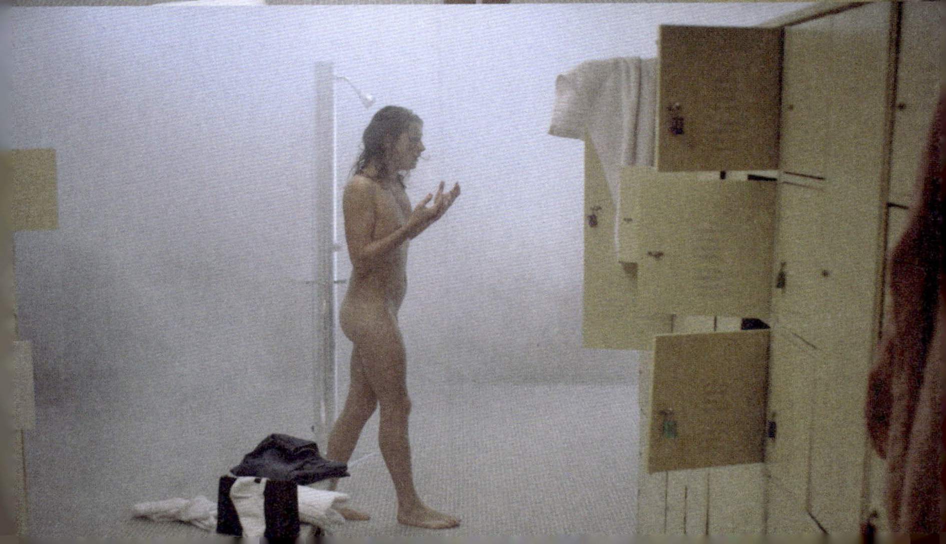

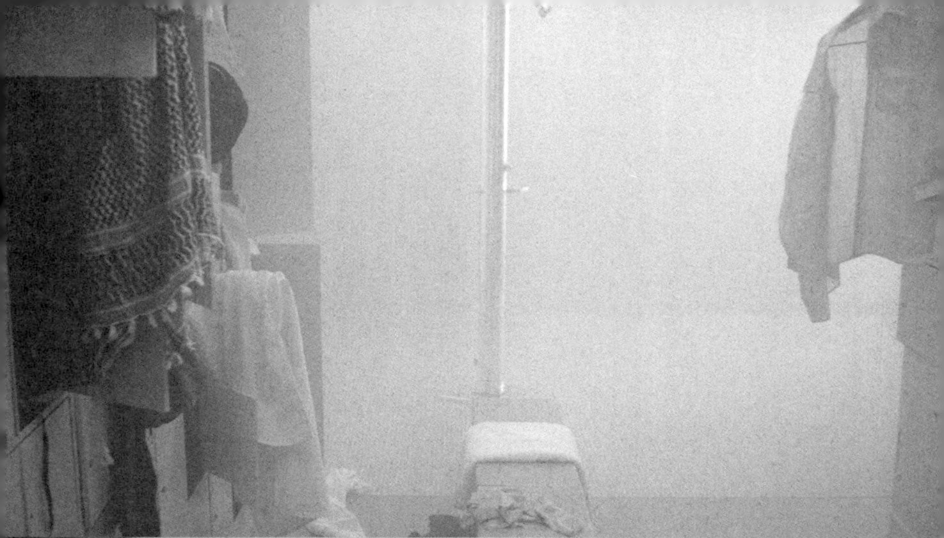

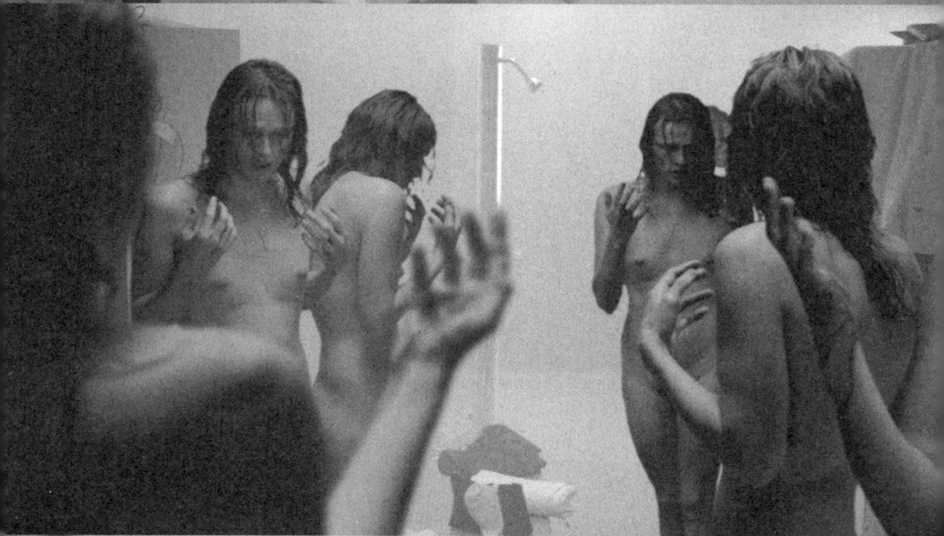

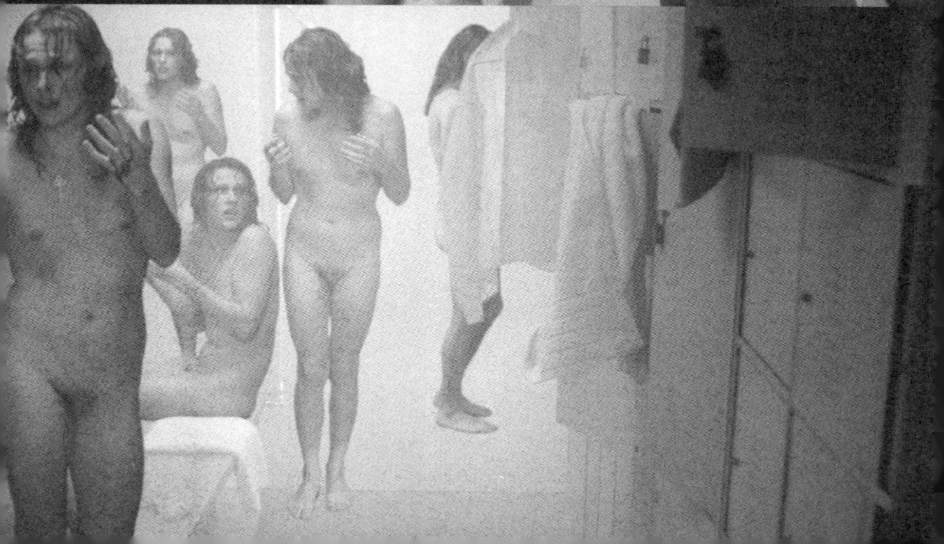

BODY DOUBLE XXXIII

5'05''
AFTER BRIAN DE PALMA'S PASSION (2012)
2014

CAST
BRICE DELLSPERGER

IMAGES
NICOLAS PERGE

EDITING, SOUND DESIGN
& SPECIAL EFFECTS
BRICE DELLSPERGER & NICOLAS PERGE

PRODUCTION
BRICE DELLSPERGER; AIR DE PARIS

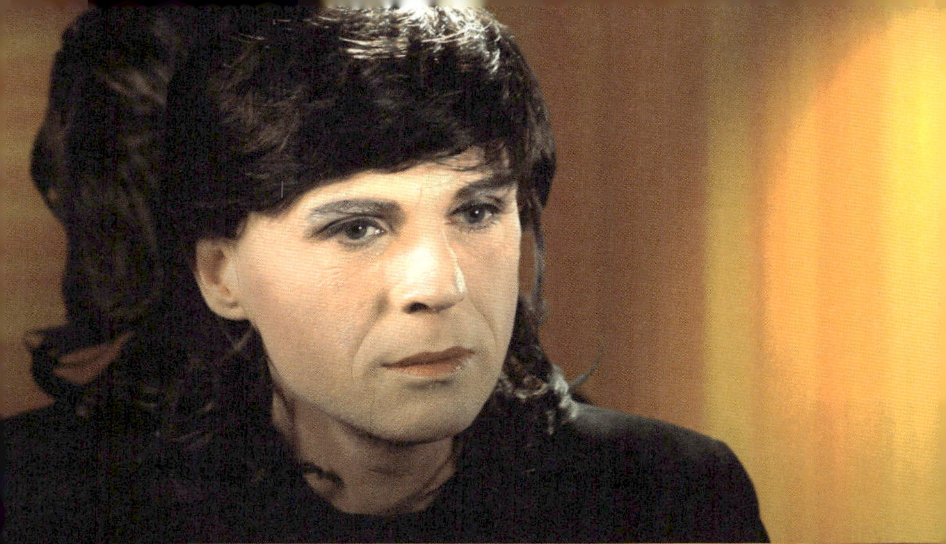
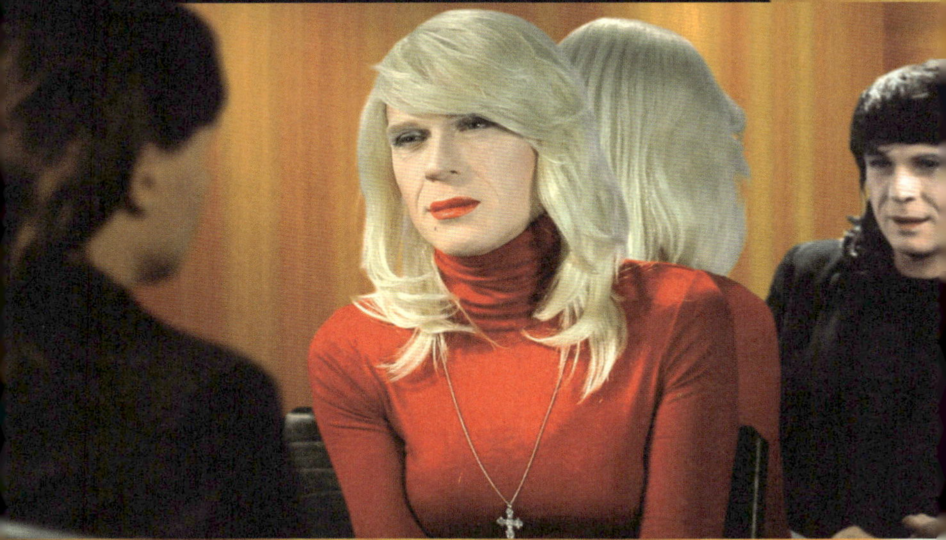
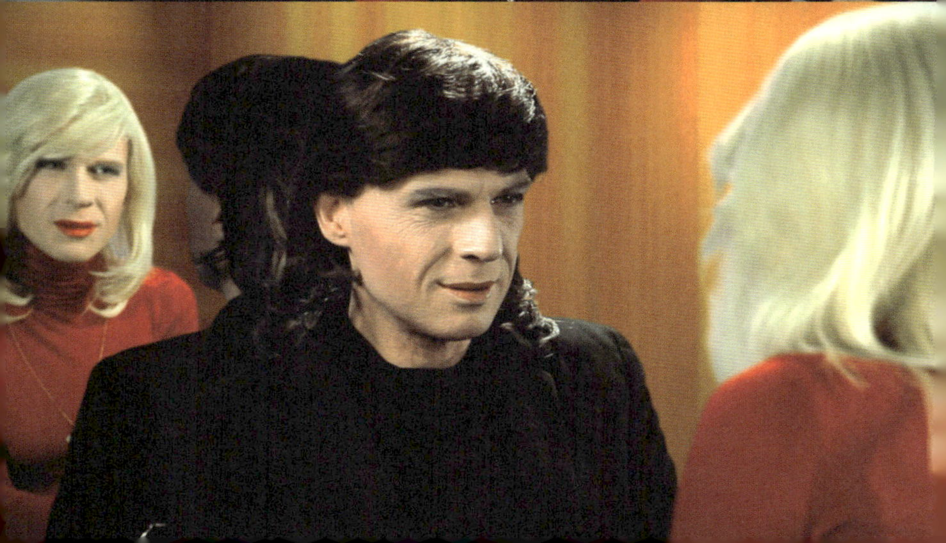

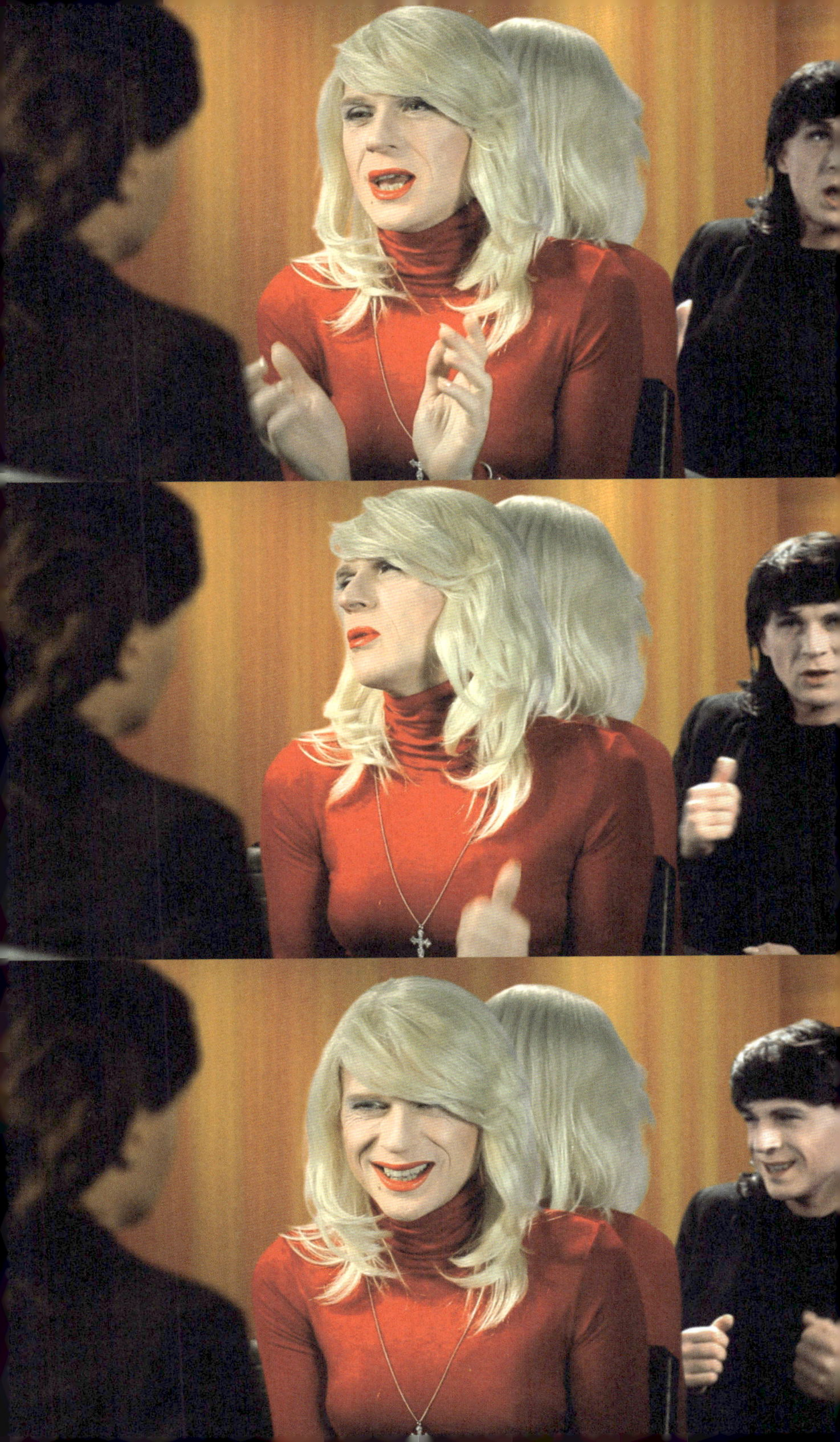

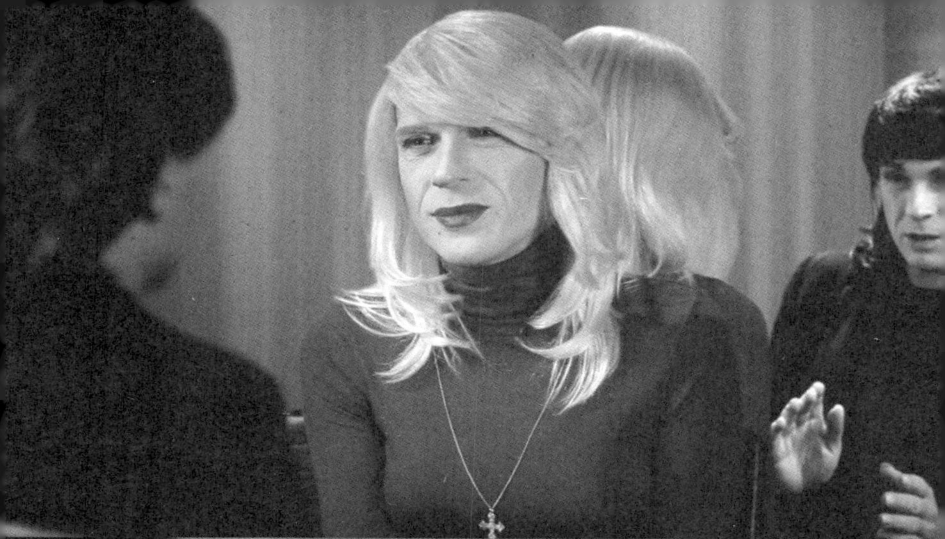
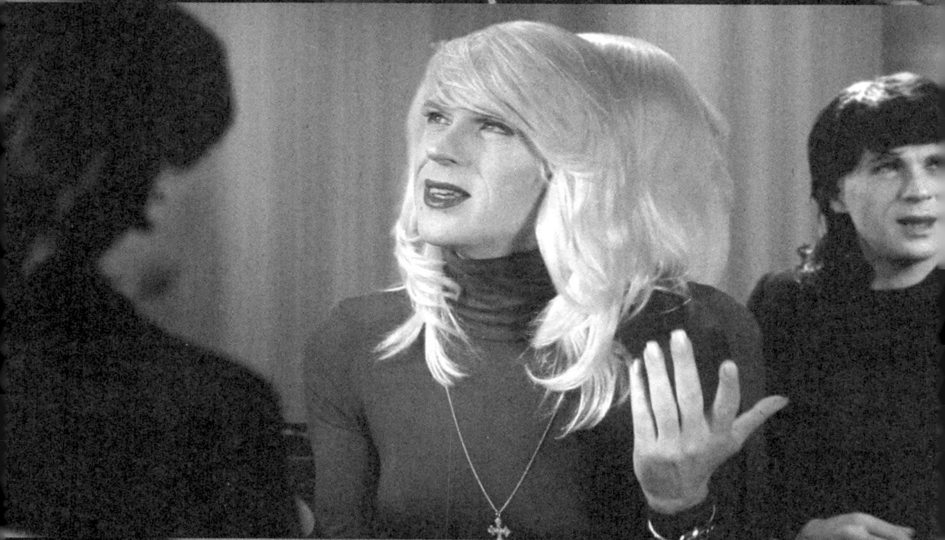
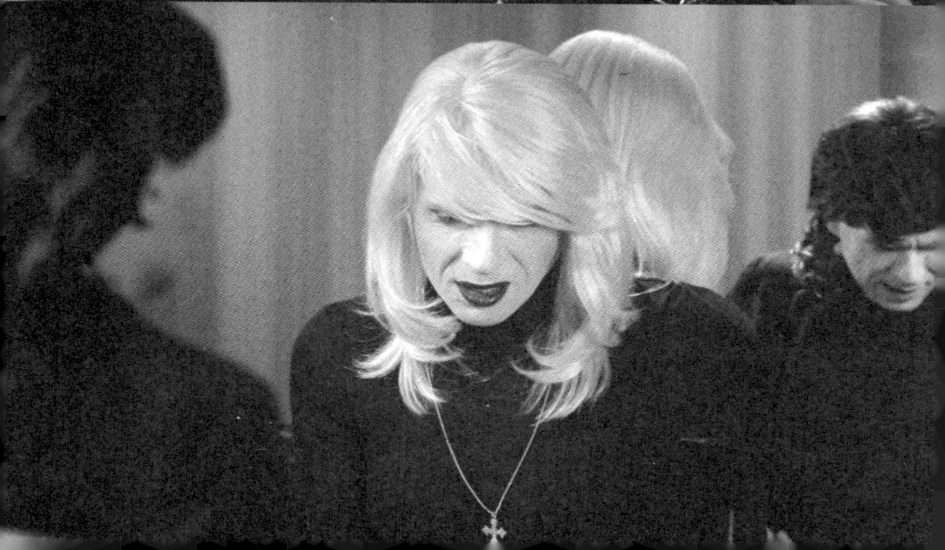

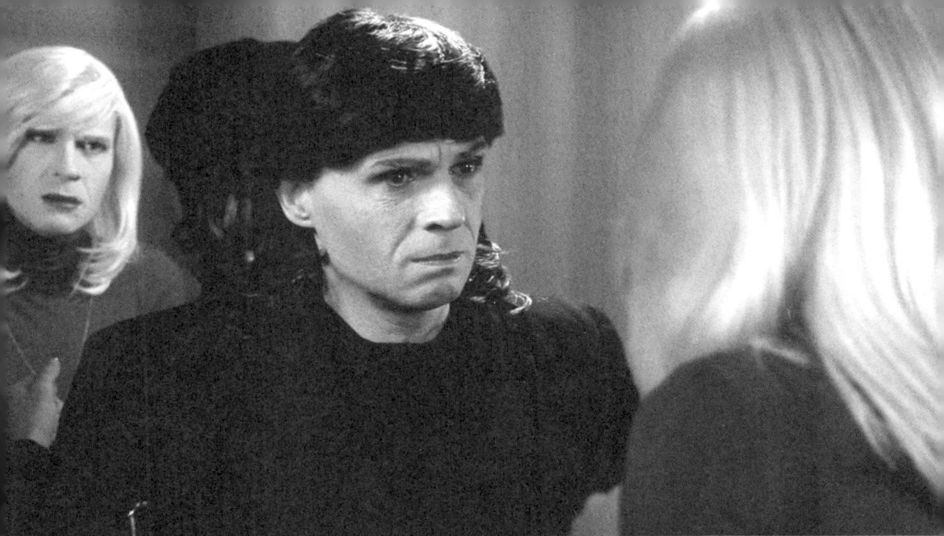

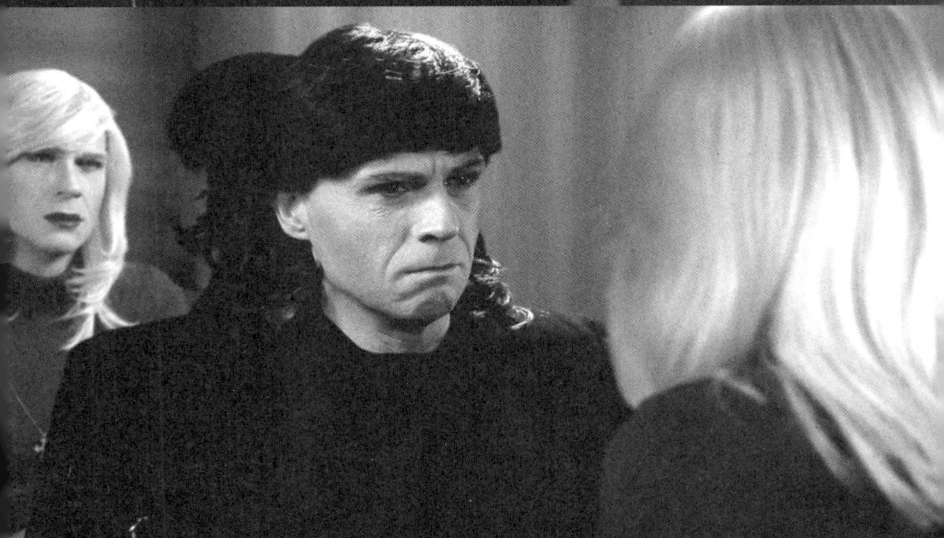

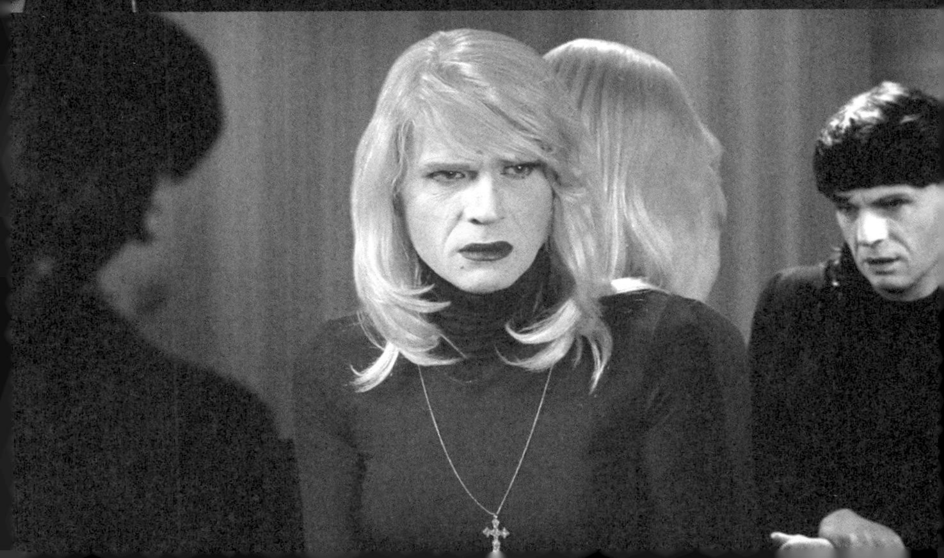

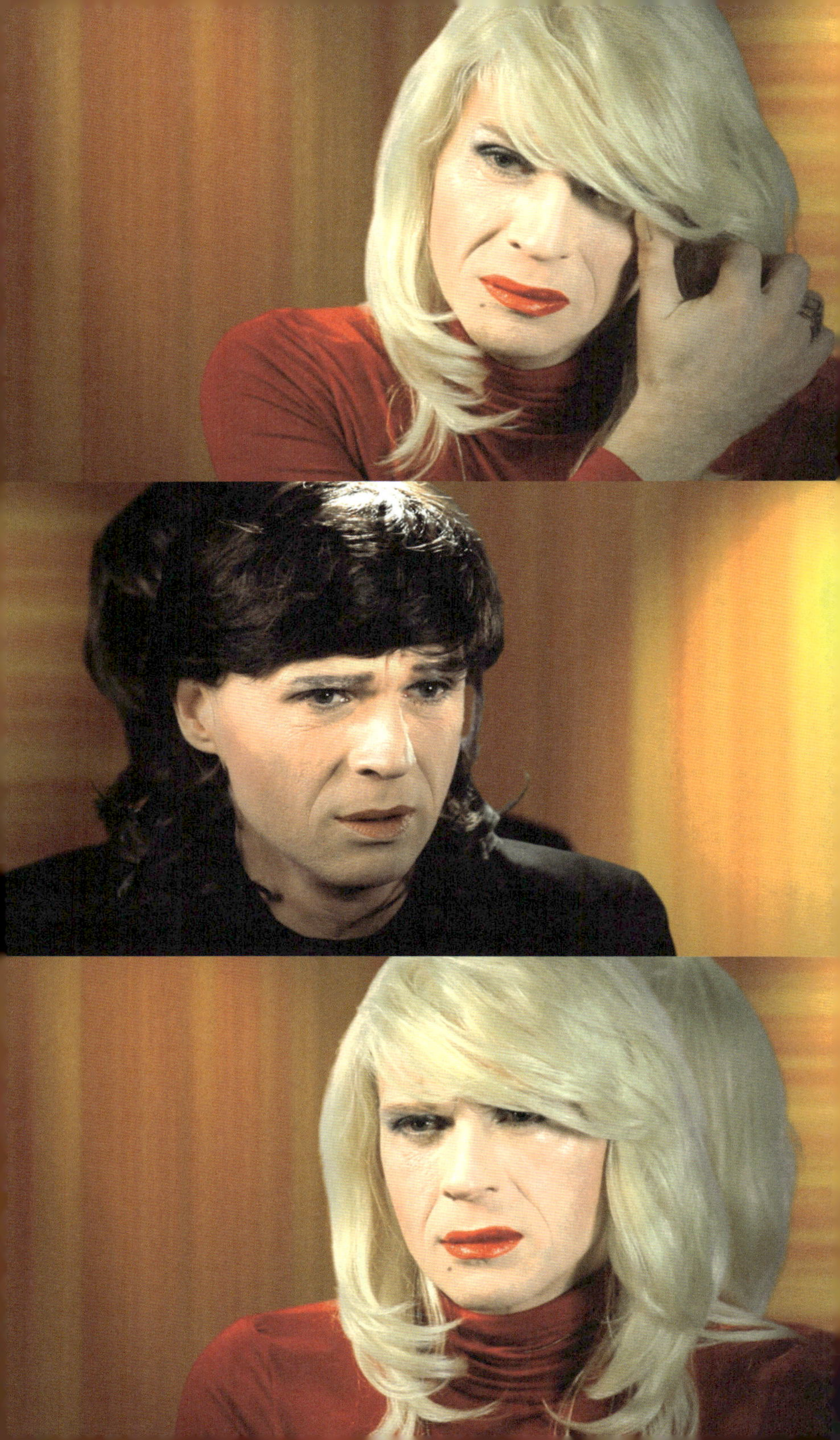

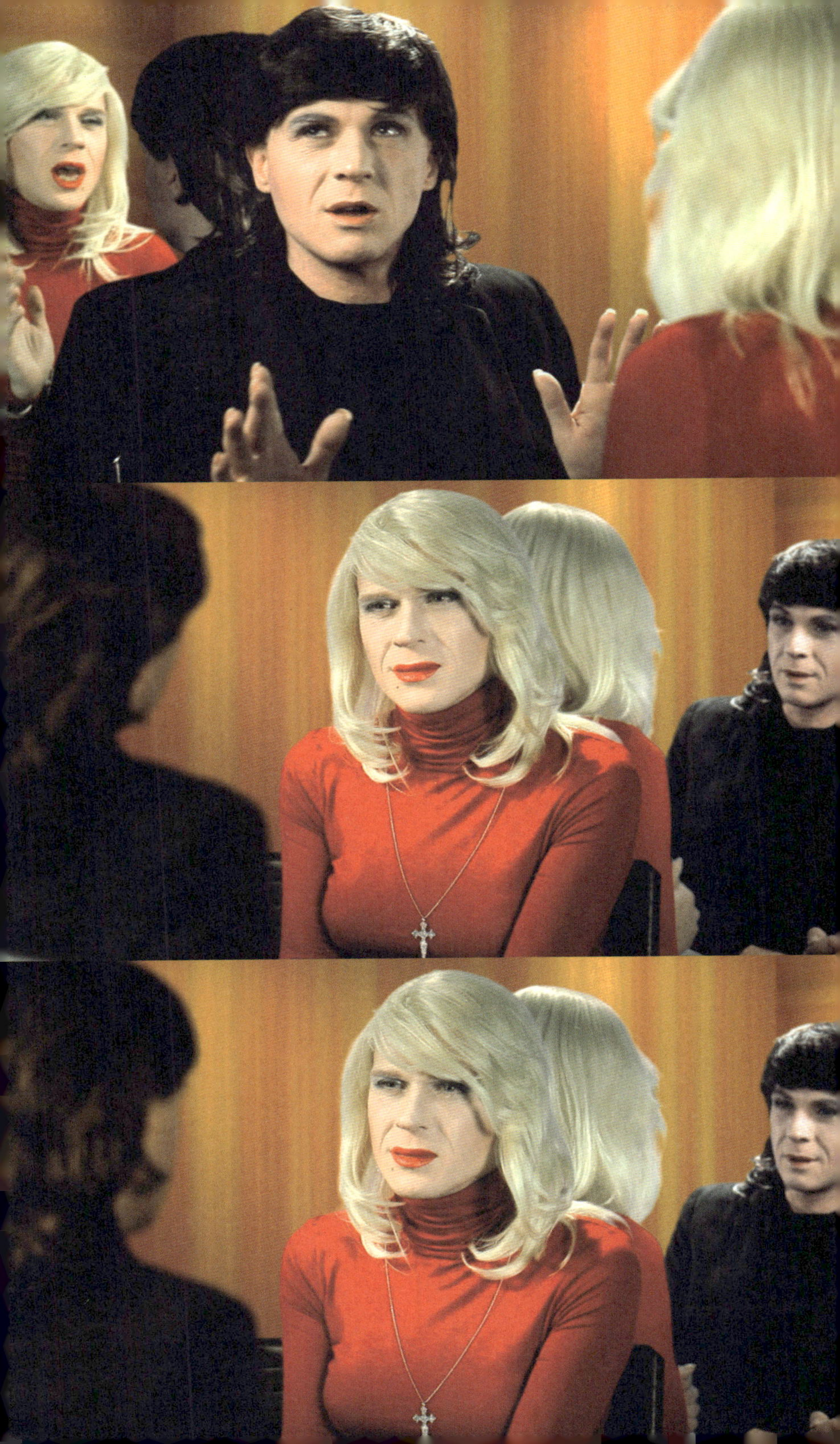

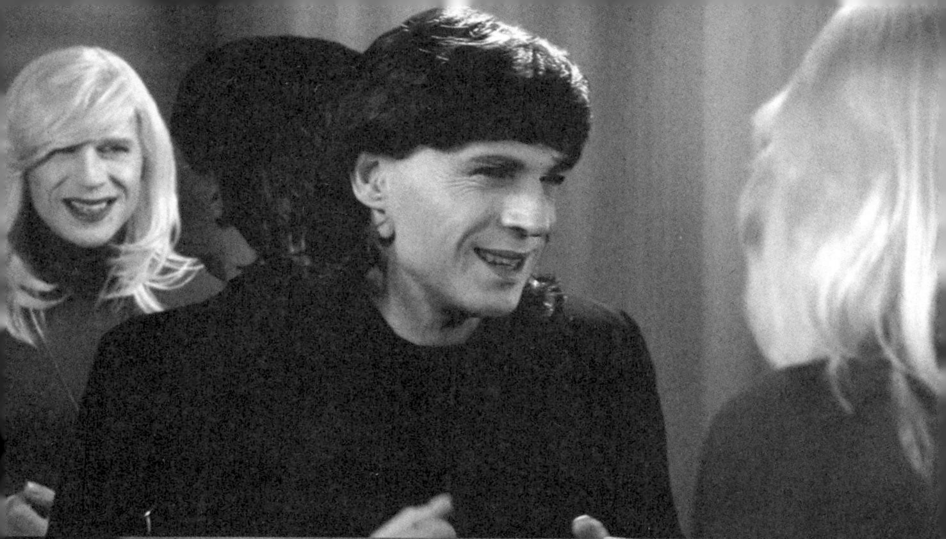
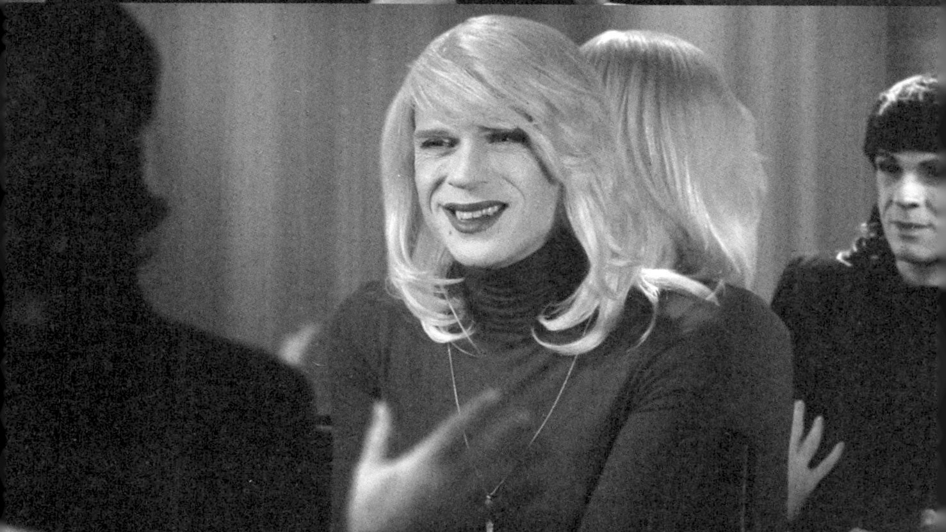
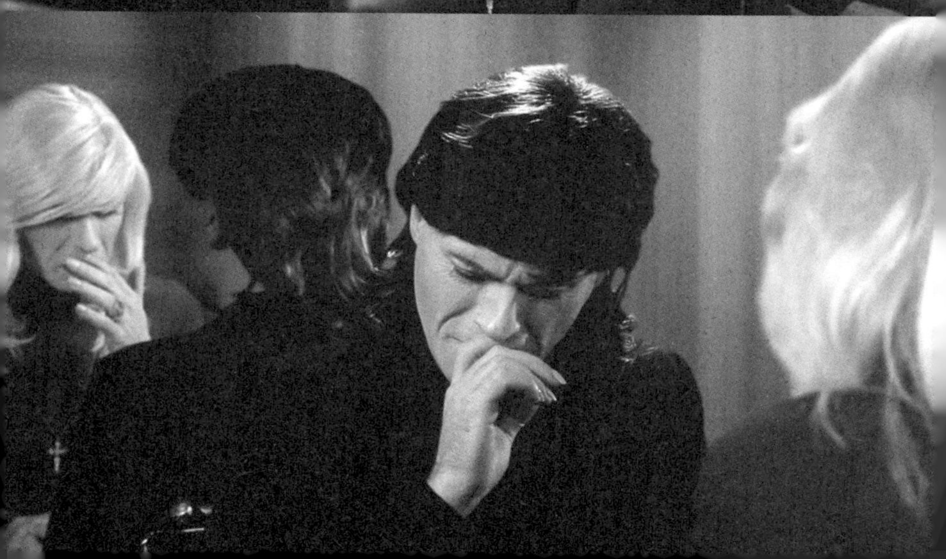

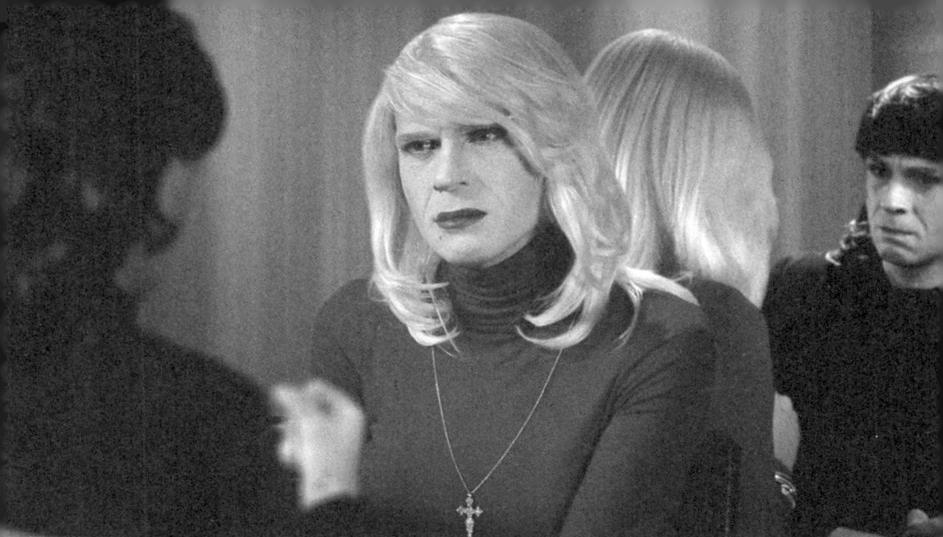
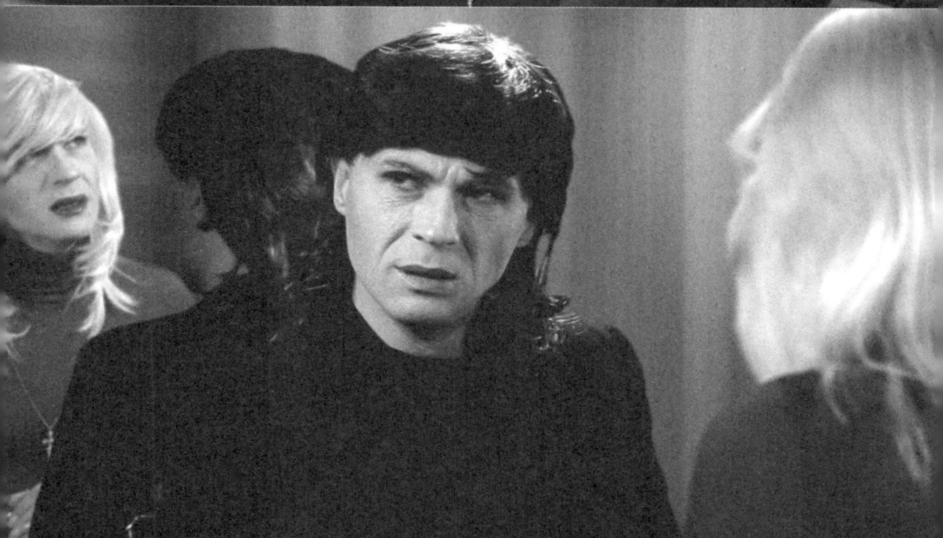
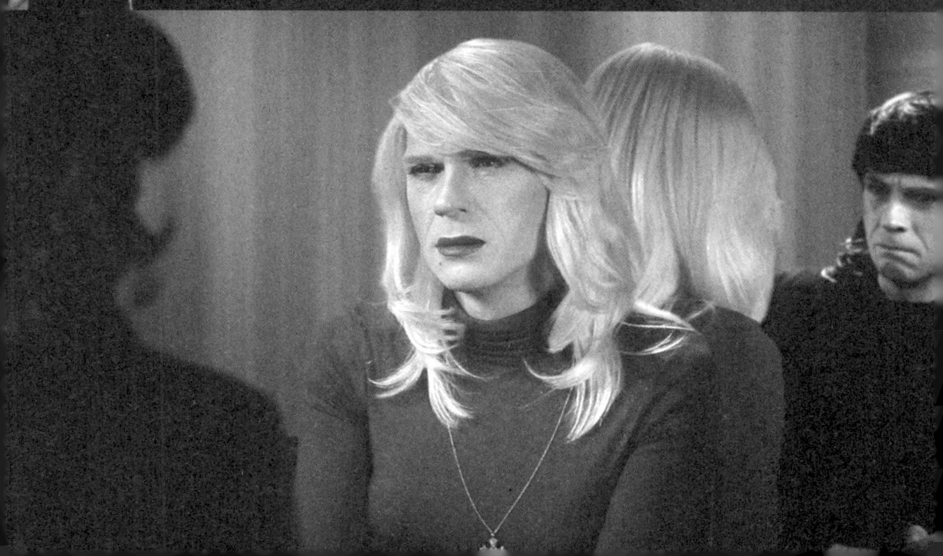

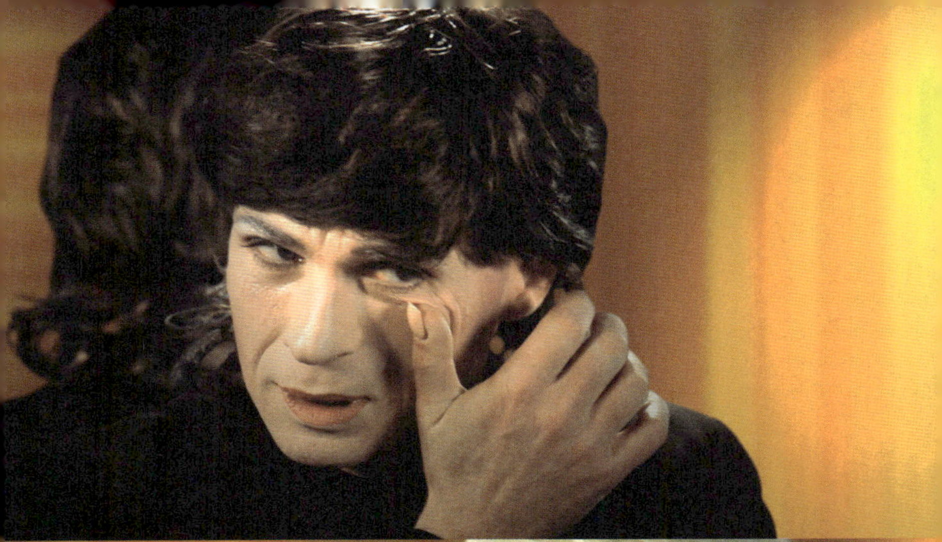
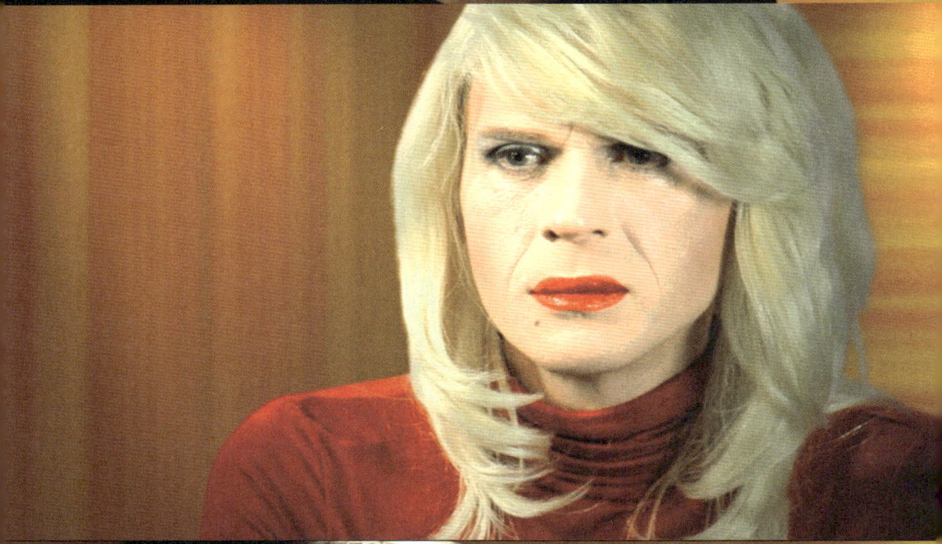
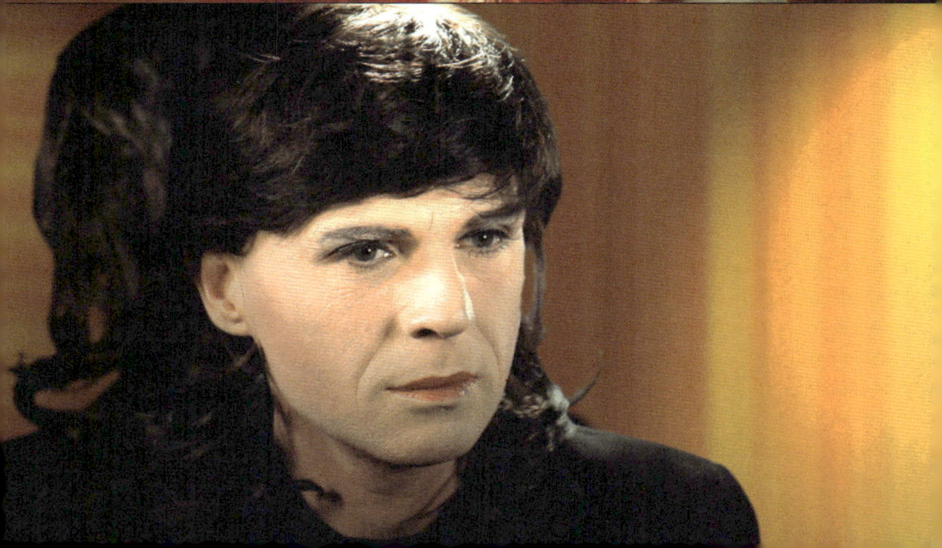

BODY DOUBLE XXIV

10'21"
AFTER GUS VAN SANT'S MY OWN PRIVATE IDAHO (1991)
2015

CAST
ALEXANDRE COLLET, CAMILLE CORNILLON, OPHÉLIE DEMURGER, FLORIS DUTOIT, ADRIANE EMERIT, ROMAIN GANDOLPHE, QUENTIN GOUJOUT, ALEX HUTHWOHL, ARTHUR MISEREZ, AXELLE PINOT, ADRIEN ROCCA, MILEVA TESTAS, EUGÉNIE ZELY

IMAGES
NICOLAS PERGE

EDITING & SPECIAL EFFECTS
BRICE DELLSPERGER

GRAPHIC DESIGN
ADRIEN ROCCA

TECHNICAL TEAM
JULIEN BENOIT, PAUL BOURDONGLE, ALEXANDRE COLLET, GARANCE COQUART POCZTAR, CAMILLE CORNILLON, OPHÉLIE DEMURGER, FLORIS DUTOIT, ADRIANE EMERIT, ROMAIN GANDOLPHE, PAULINE GHERSI, QUENTIN GOUJOUT, ALEX HUTHWOHL, ARTHUR MISEREZ, AXELLE PINOT, ADRIEN ROCCA, VALENTIN ROLOVIC, MILEVA TESTAS, EUGÉNIE ZELY

PRODUCTION
LE CONFORT MODERNE, POITIERS, FRANCE; ENSBA, LYON, FRANCE

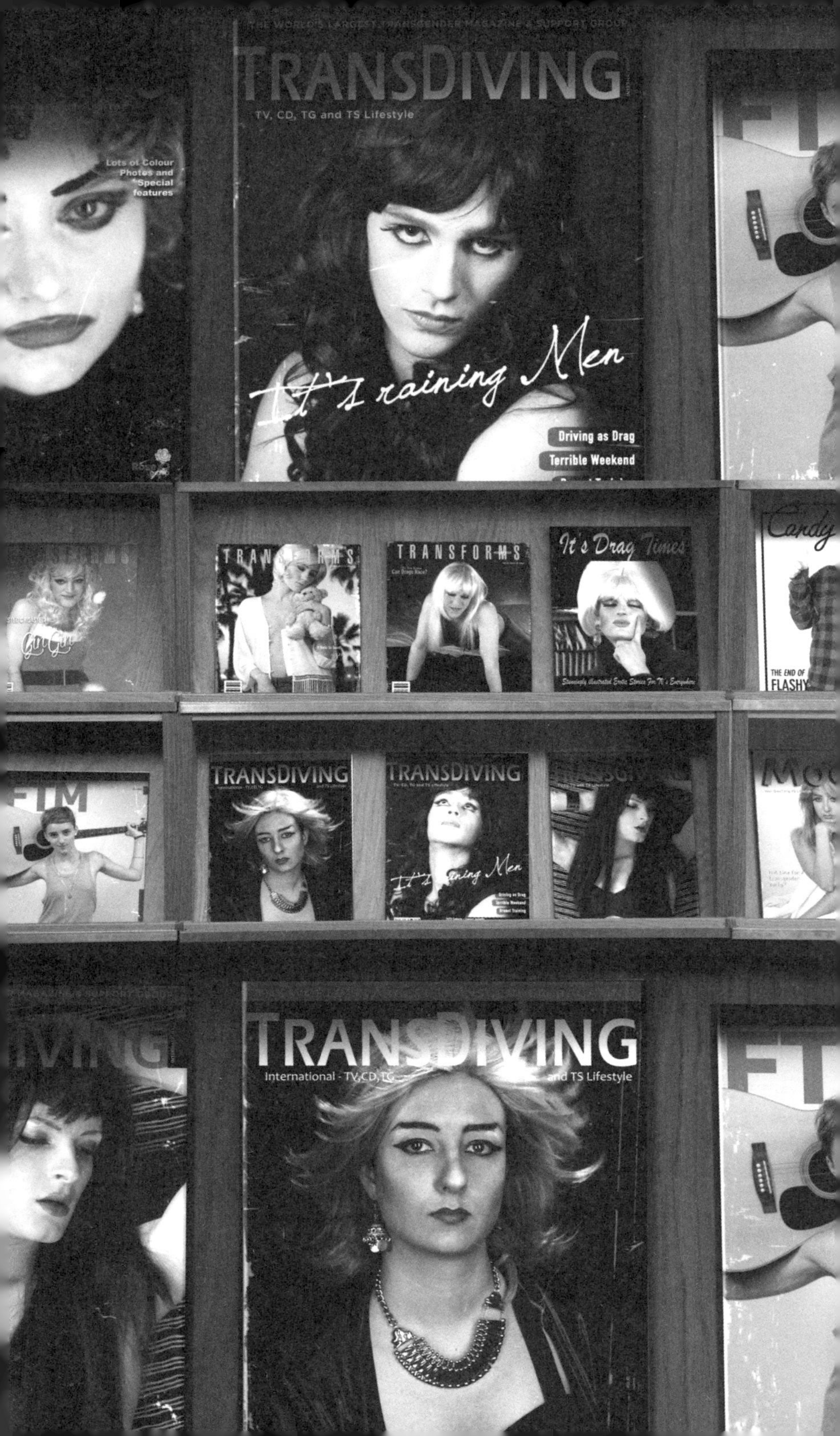
THE WORLD'S LARGEST TRANSGENDER MAGAZINE & SUPPORT GROUP
TRANSDIVING
TV, CD, TG and TS Lifestyle
It's raining Men
Driving as Drag
Terrible Weekend
Lots of Colour Photos and Special features
TRANSFORMS
TRANSFORMS
It's Drag Times
Candy
THE END OF FLASHY
FTM
TRANSDIVING
TRANSDIVING
It's raining Men
TRANSDIVING
International - TV,CD,TG and TS Lifestyle

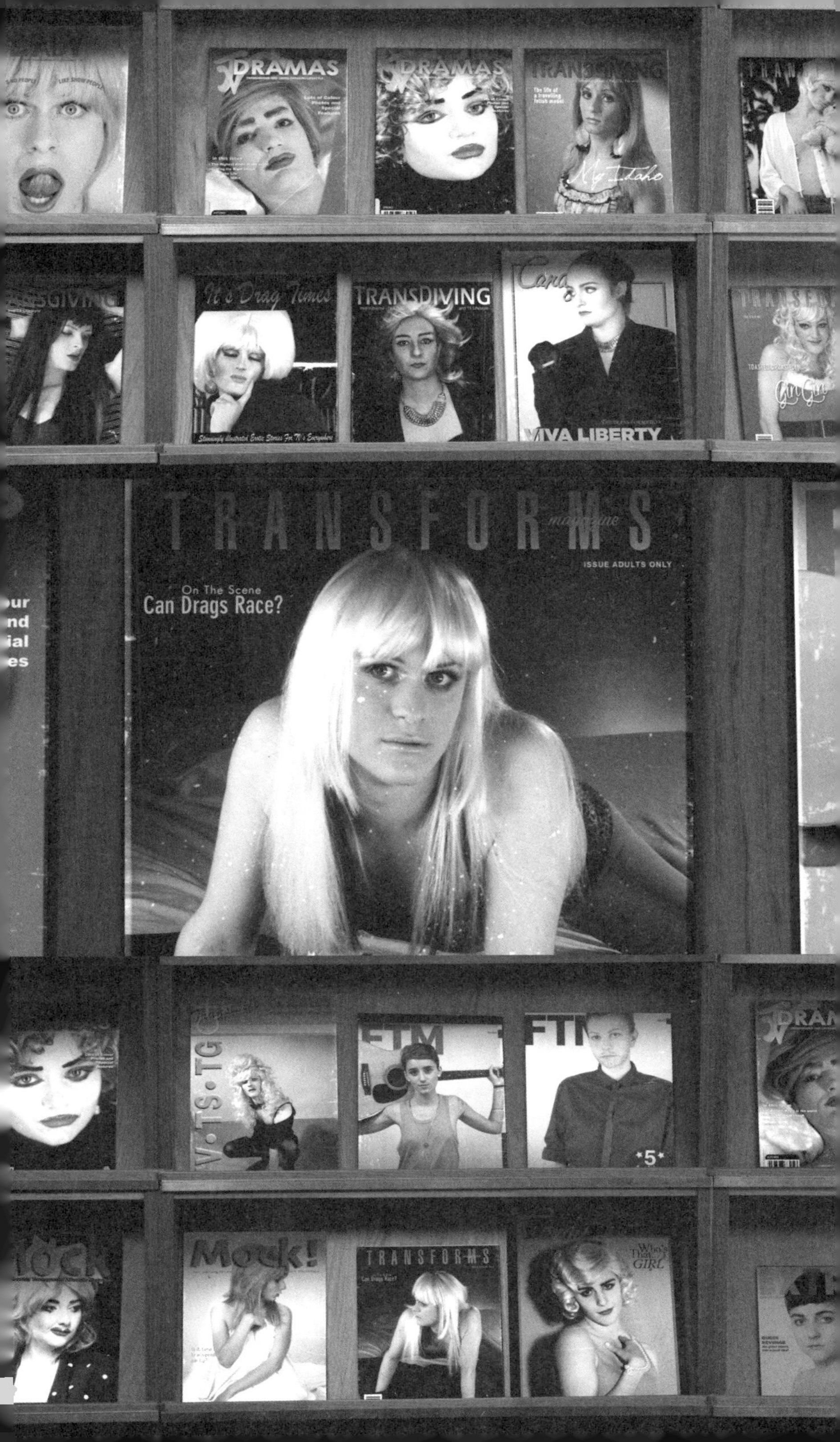
DRAMAS
DRAMAS
It's Drag Times
TRANSDIVING
VIVA LIBERTY
TRANSFORMS
ISSUE ADULTS ONLY
On The Scene
Can Drags Race?
FTM
Mock!
TRANSFORMS
Who's That GIRL

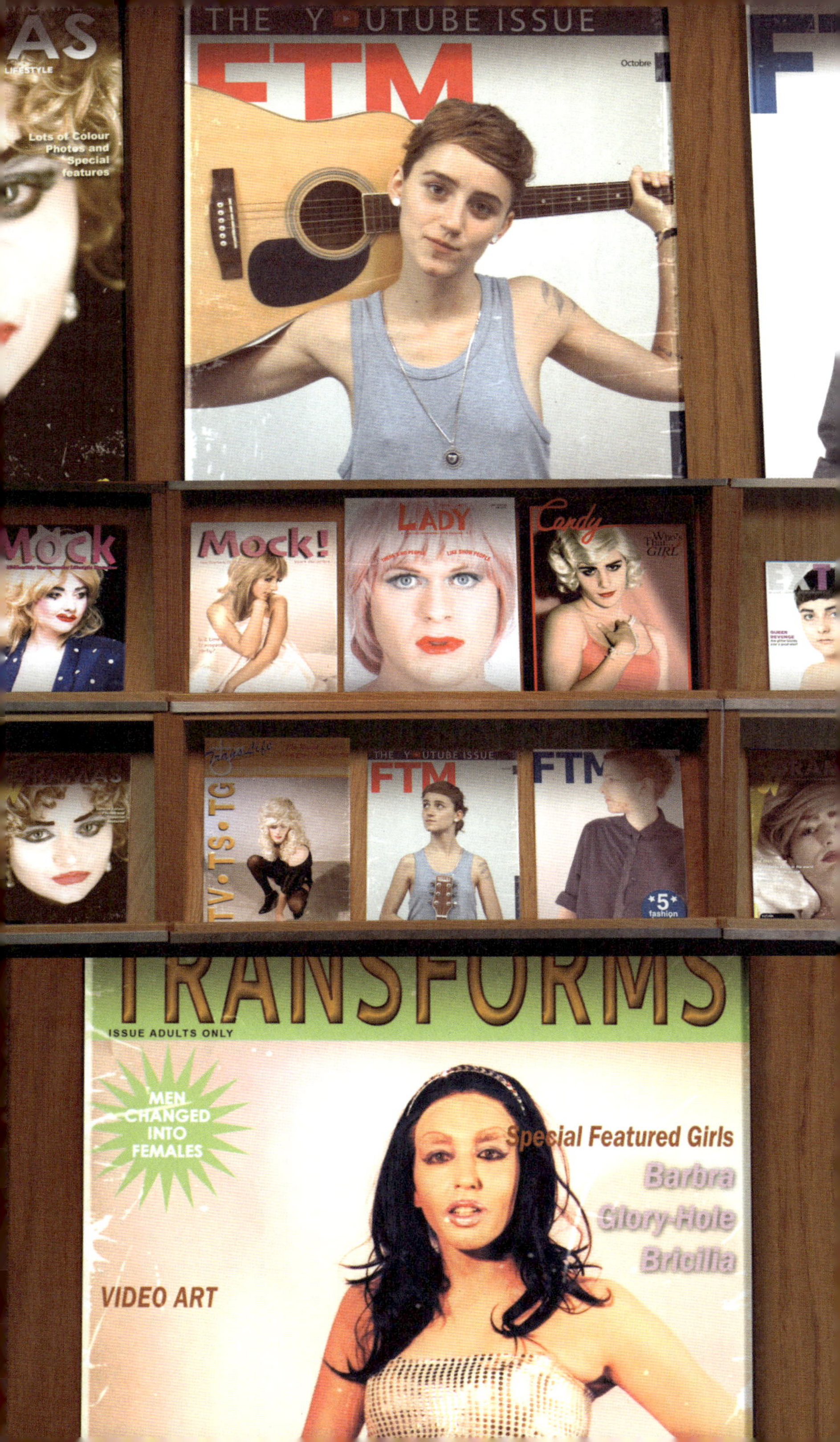
THE YOUTUBE ISSUE
FTM
Octobre
AS
LIFESTYLE
Lots of Colour Photos and Special features
Mock
Mock!
LADY
Candy
Who's That GIRL
TV • TS • TG
THE YOUTUBE ISSUE
FTM
FTM
5 fashion
TRANSFORMS
ISSUE ADULTS ONLY
MEN CHANGED INTO FEMALES
Special Featured Girls
Barbra
Glory-Hole
Bricilla
VIDEO ART

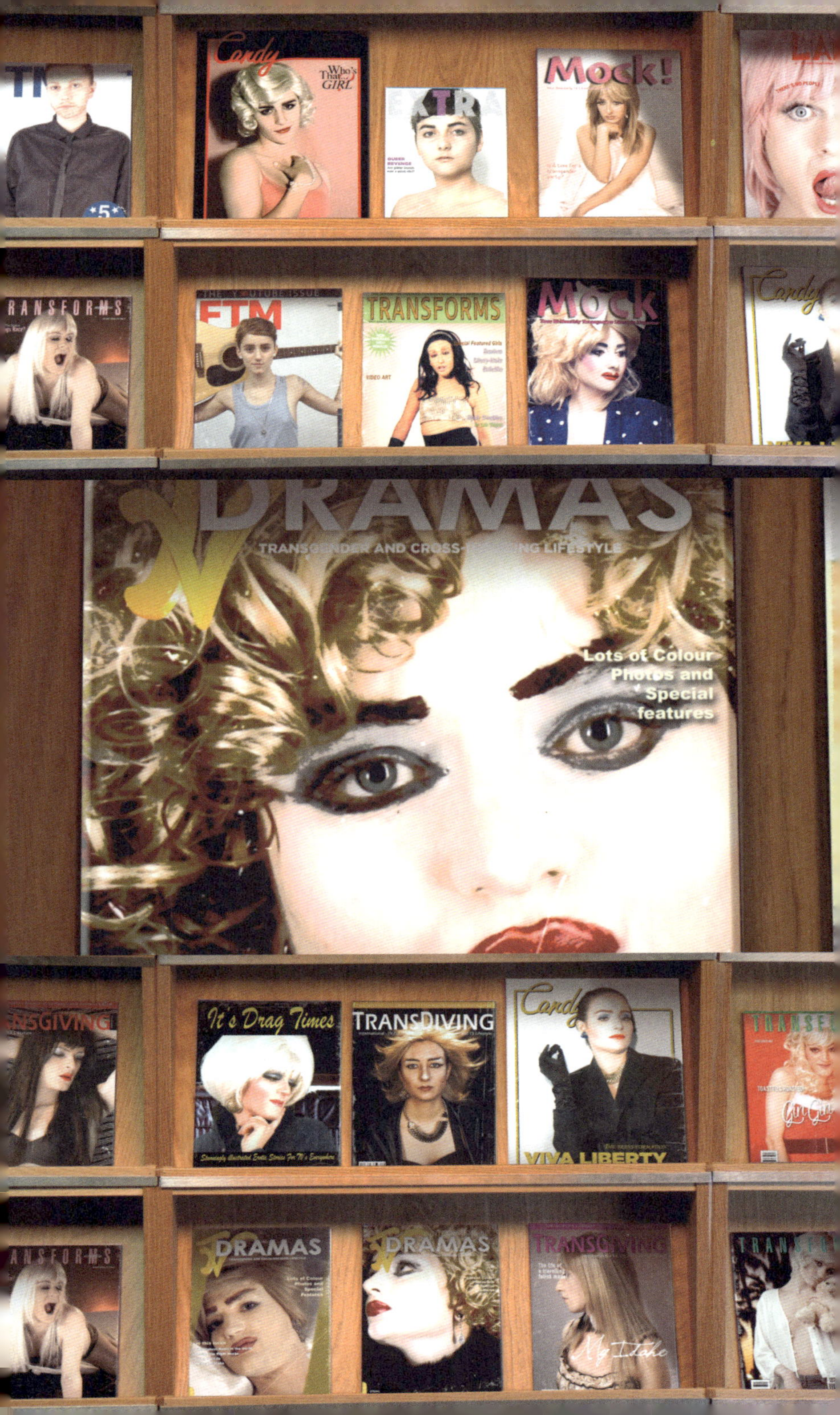
Candy
Who's That... GIRL
EXTRA
Mock!
FTM
TRANSFORMS
VIDEO ART
Mock
Candy
DRAMAS
Lots of Colour
Photos and
Special
features
It's Drag Times
TRANSDIVING
Candy
VIVA LIBERTY
DRAMAS
DRAMAS

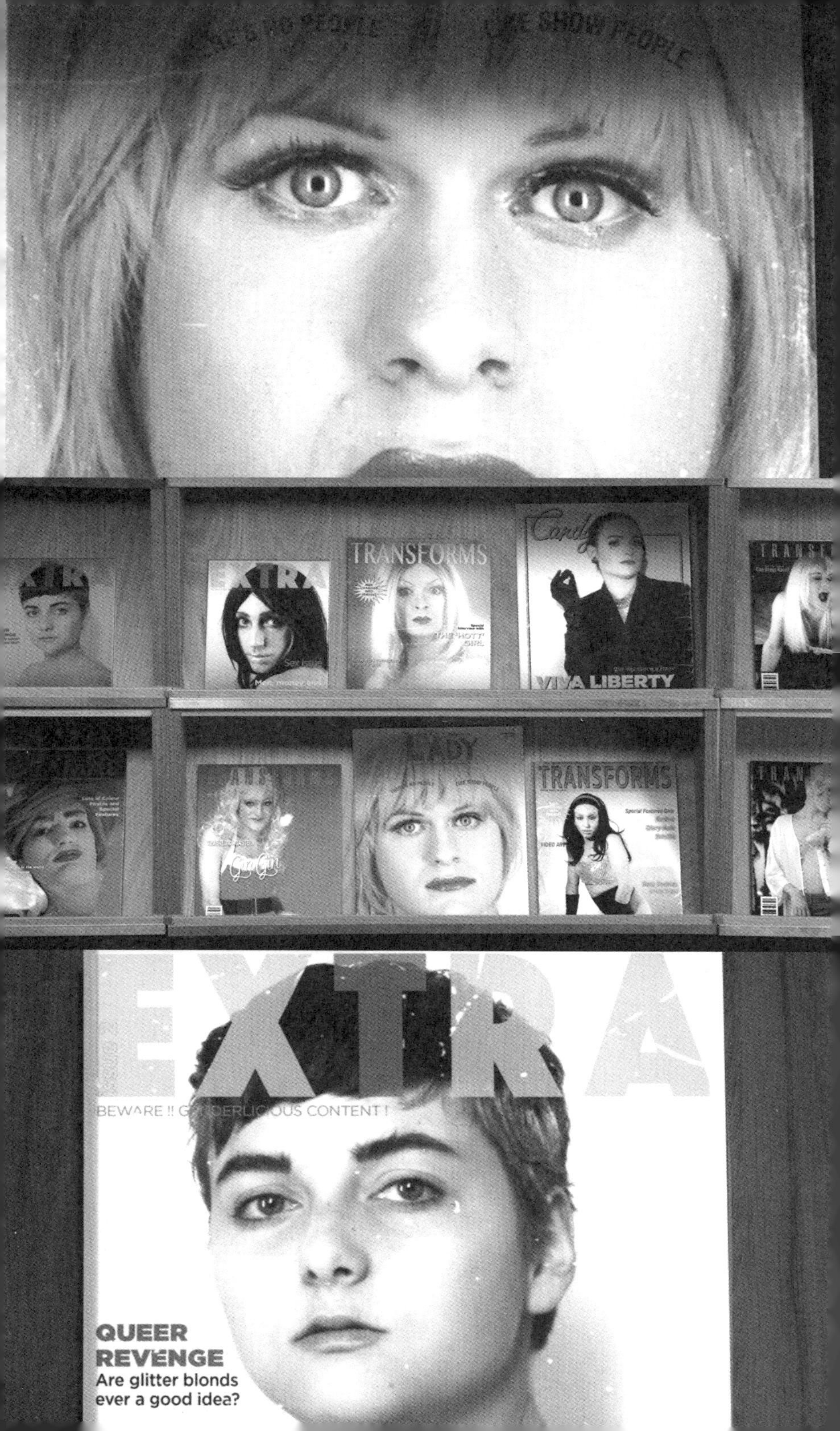

THE SHOW PEOPLE
EXTRA
Sex Issue
Men, money and
TRANSFORMS
THE 'HOTT' GIRL
VIVA LIBERTY
LADY
TRANSFORMS
EXTRA
ISSUE 2
BEWARE !! GENDERLICIOUS CONTENT !
QUEER
REVENGE
Are glitter blonds
ever a good idea?

BODY DOUBLE XXXV

4'15''
AFTER ROBERT GREENWALD'S XANADU (1980)
2017

CAST
FRANÇOIS CHAIGNAUD

IMAGES
LOÏC BOVON

EDITING & SPECIAL EFFECTS
BRICE DELLSPERGER

FIRST ASSISTANT DIRECTOR & SCRIPT
QUENTIN GOUJOUT

ASSISTANT CHOREOGRAPHER
SYLVAIN DECLOÎTRE

FABRIC DESIGN
MARC-CAMILLE CHAIMOWICZ

COSTUME DESIGN
SUKKI HO

MURAL
FLOYD SIMMONS

MUSIC
LES DUPONT, I'M ALIVE (YELLOW MIX FEAT. JULIEN LOKO); ORIGINAL SCORE JEFF LYNNE; SOUND DESIGN DIDIER BLASCO; SOUND MIXER IVAN GARIEL

TECHNICAL TEAM
SELIM BIBI MOREAU, FLORA AUSSANT, OLIVIER AUSSEDAT, THOMAS DEMURE, VICTOIRE EOUZAN, CLARA FAYE, JOSSELIN GERVAL, THÉO JOLLET, BARBORA KRIZOVA, BAPTISTE LAVIGNE, GUILLAUME THOMAS

PRODUCTION
CENTRE POMPIDOU, PARIS, FRANCE; SWISS INSTITUTE, NYC; TEAM GALLERY; AIR DE PARIS

COLLECTIONS
MUSÉE NATIONAL D'ART MODERNE, MNAM, CENTRE POMPIDOU, PARIS, FRANCE; NMNM - NOUVEAU MUSÉE NATIONAL DE MONACO

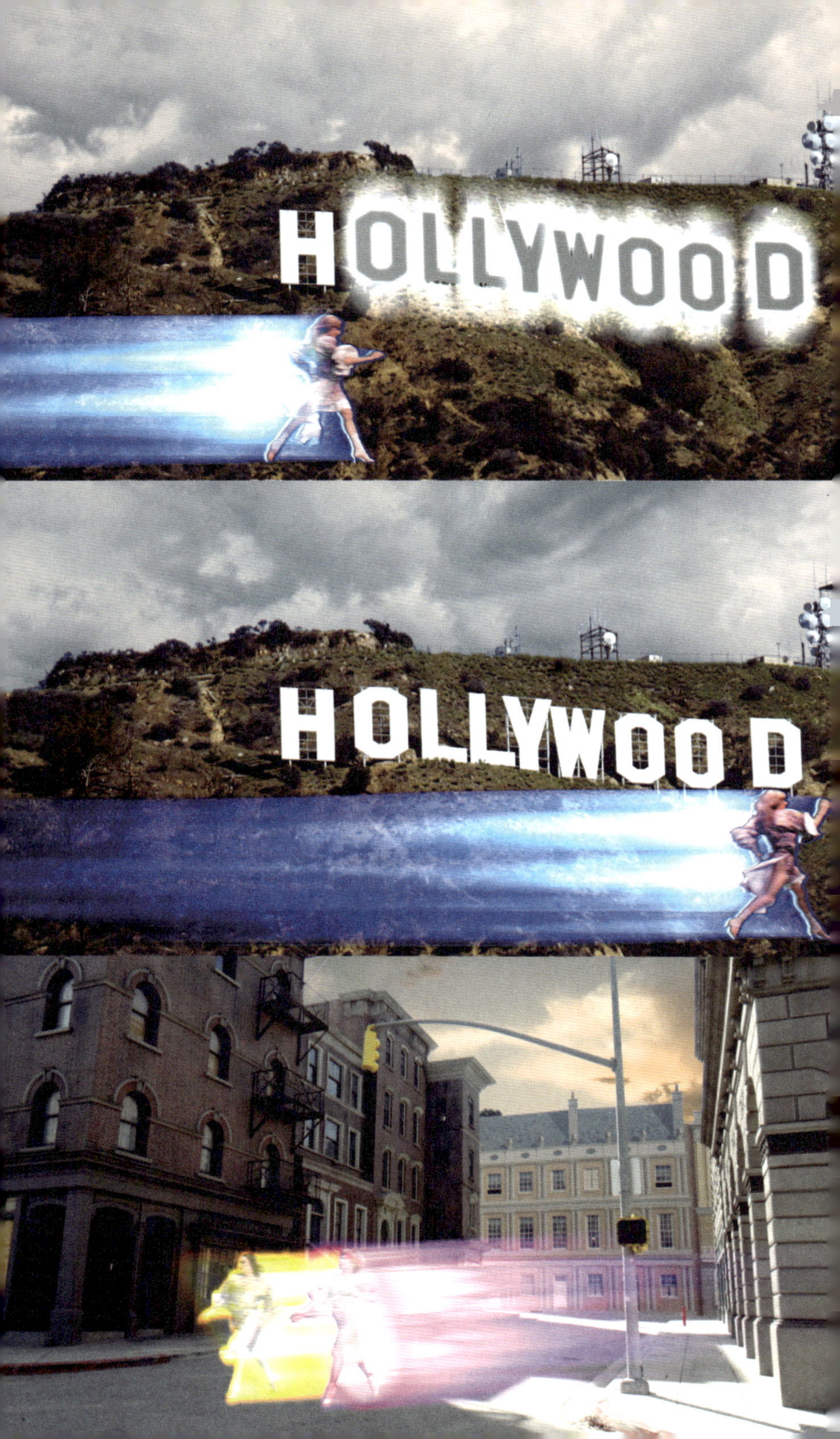
HOLLYWOOD
HOLLYWOOD

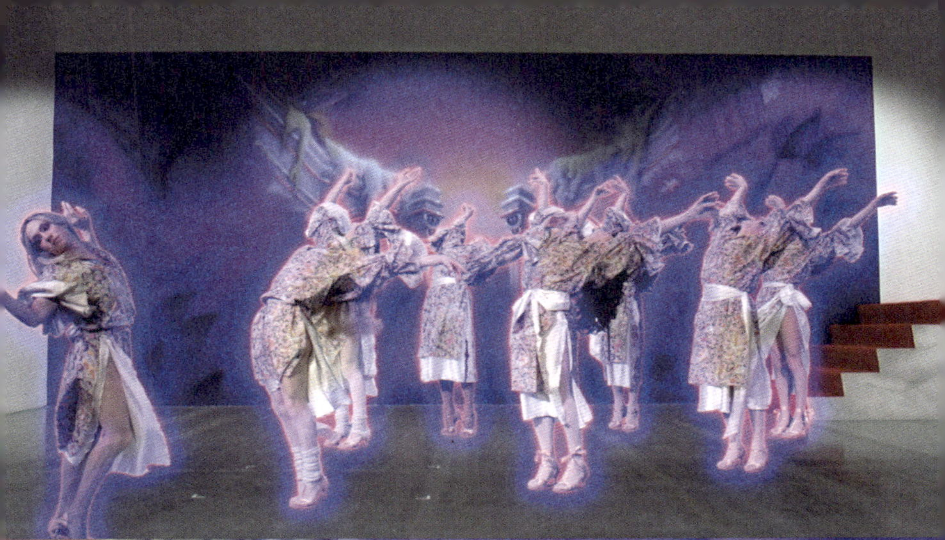

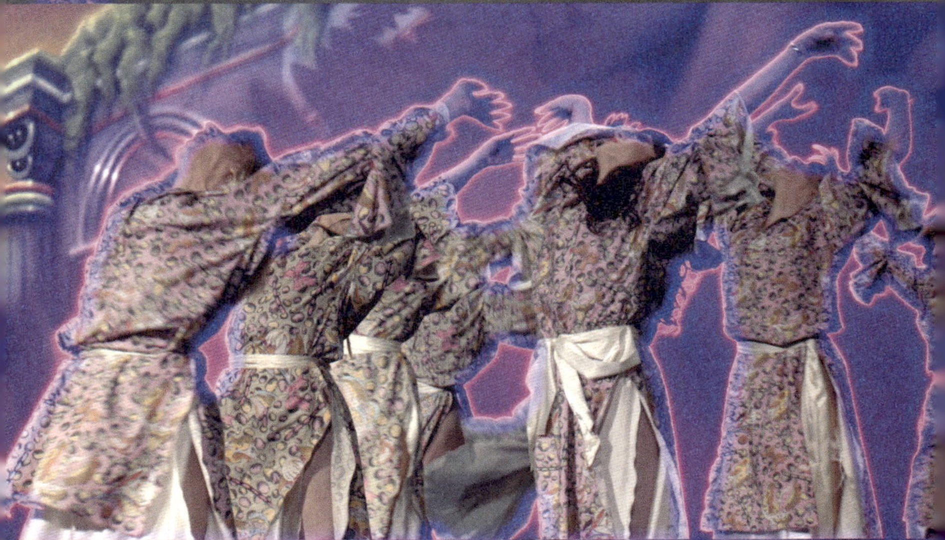

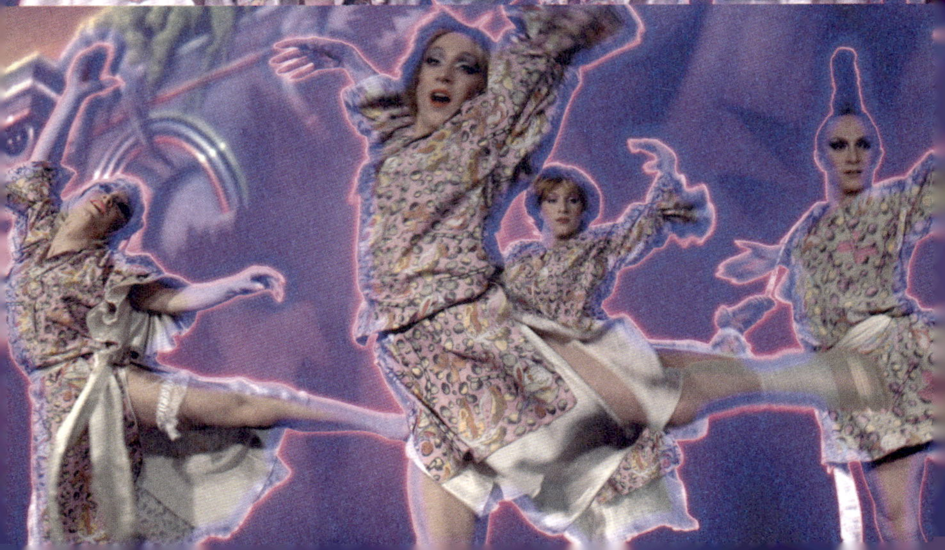

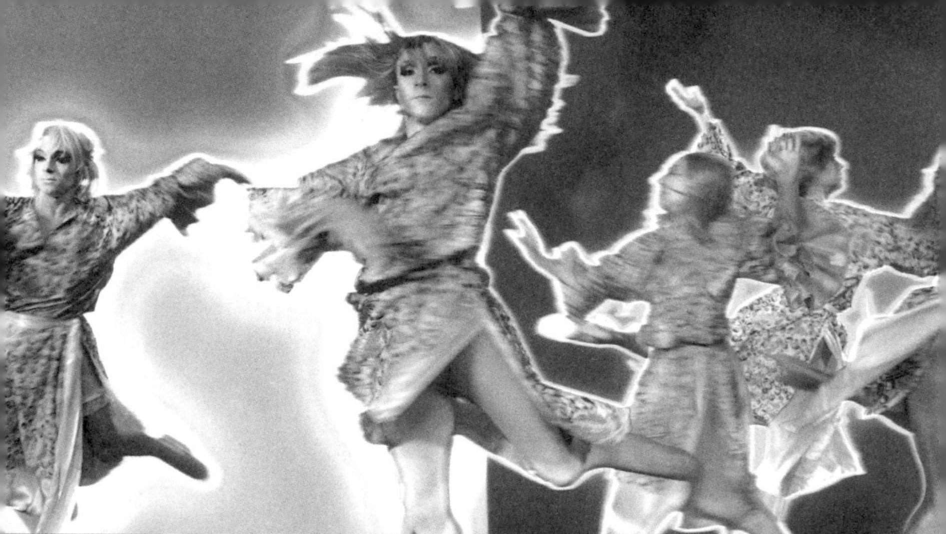
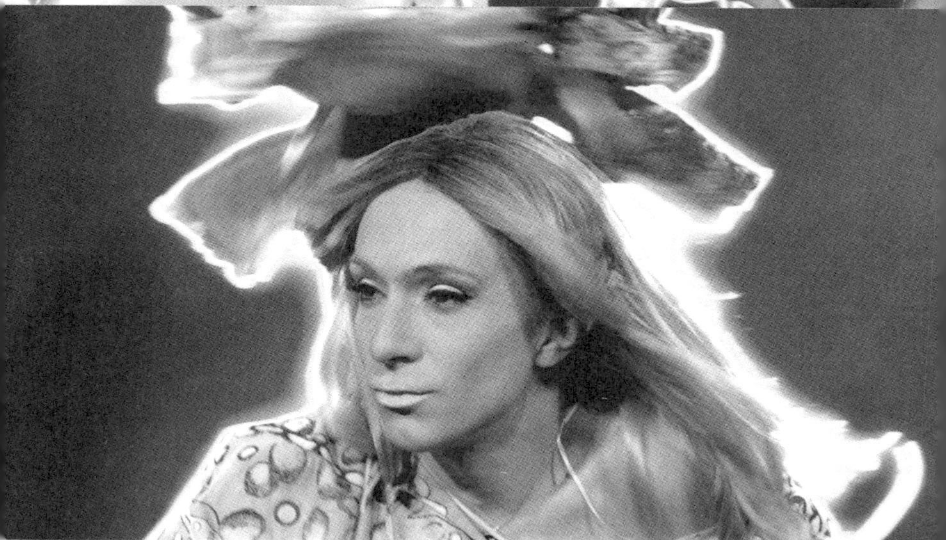
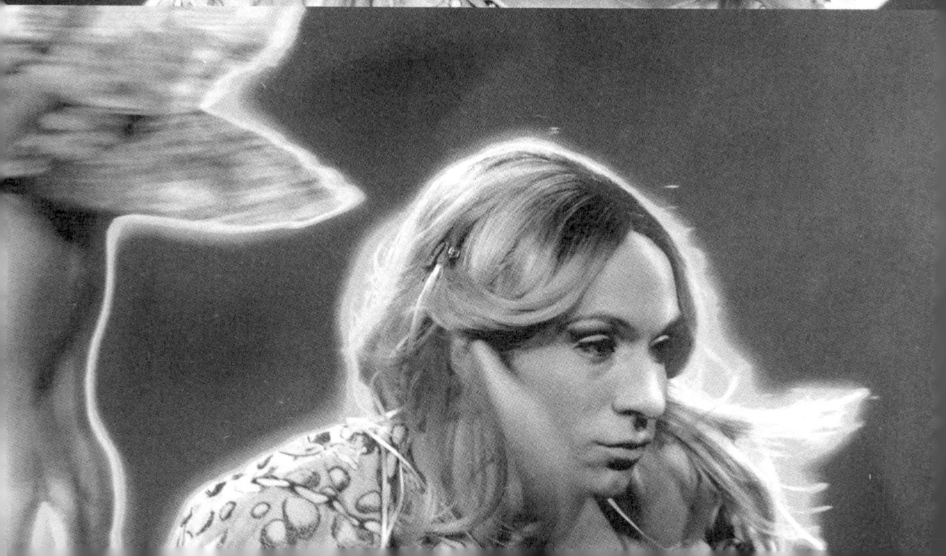

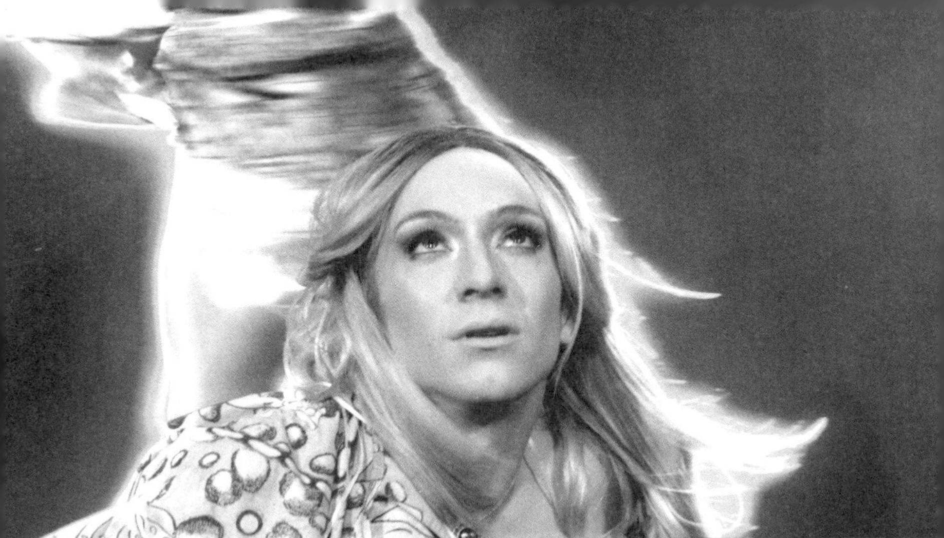
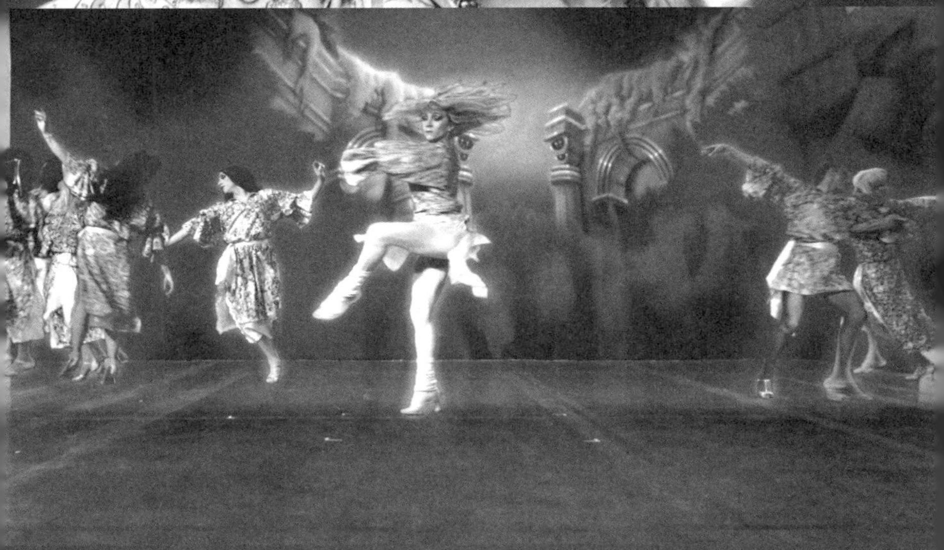
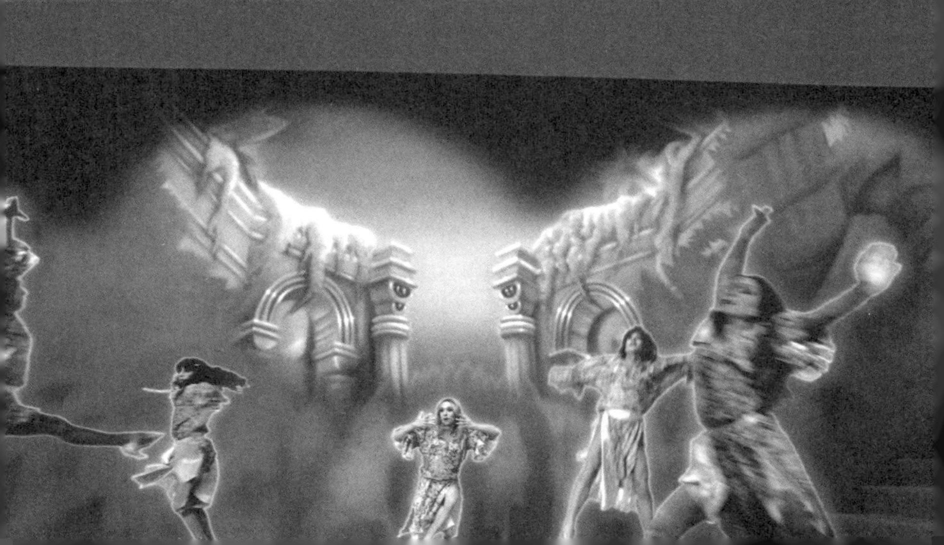

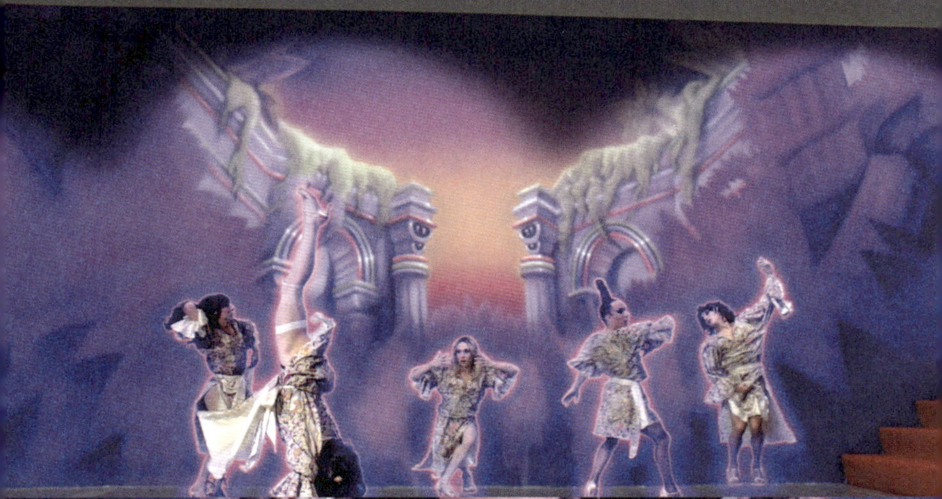

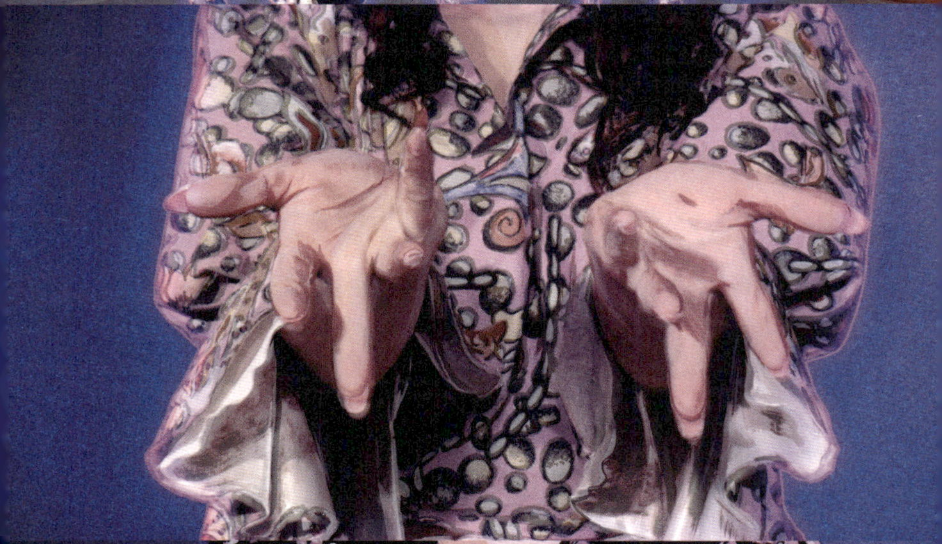

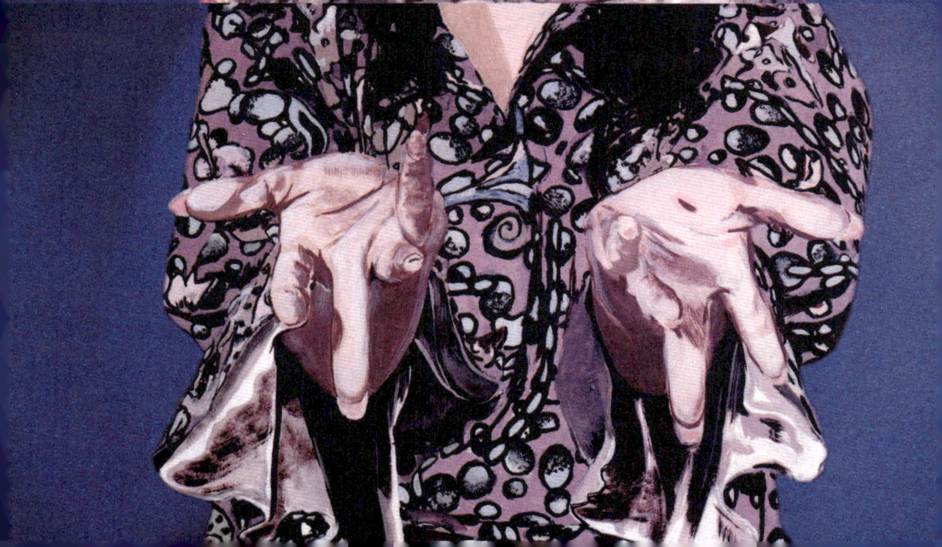

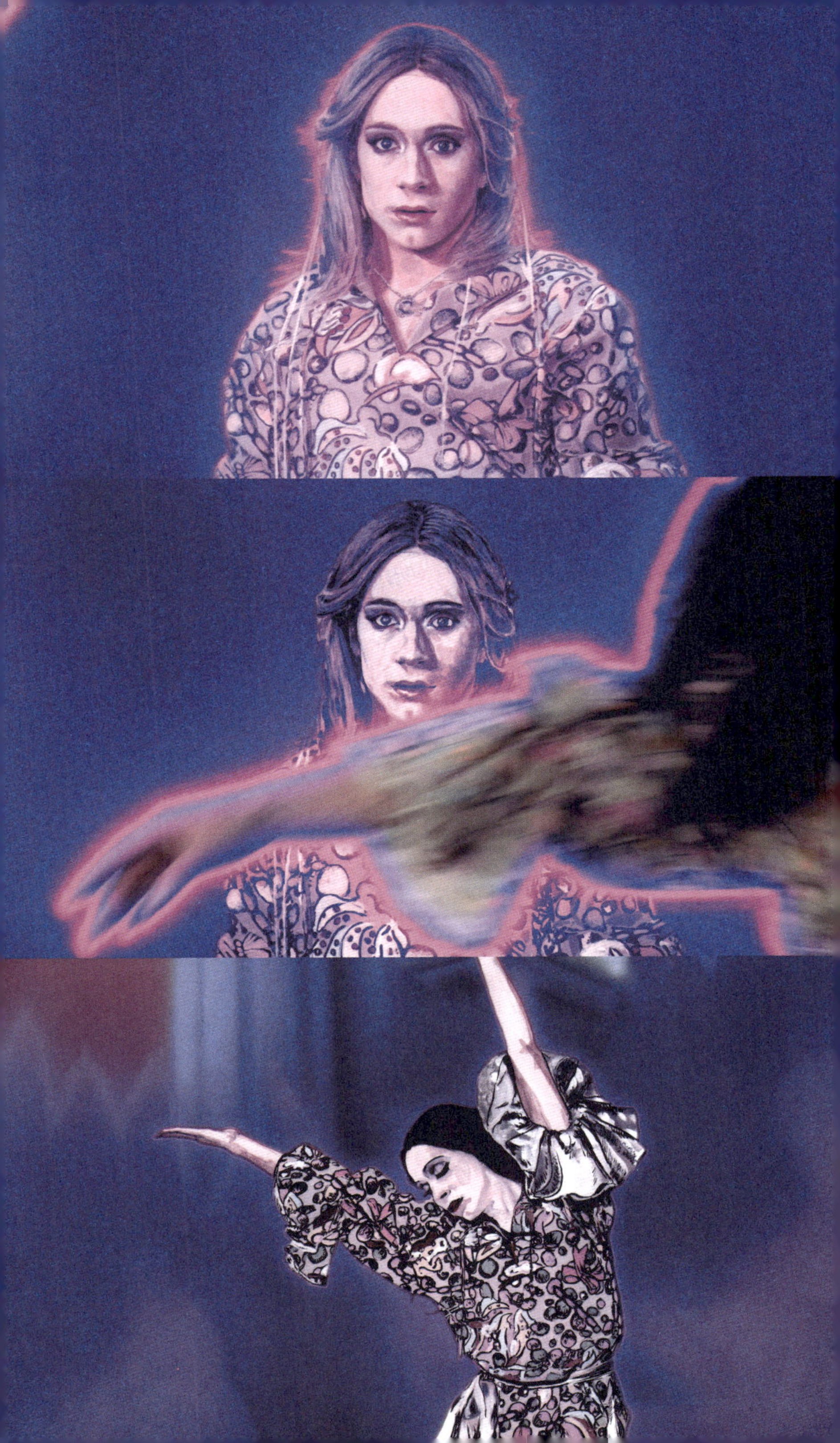

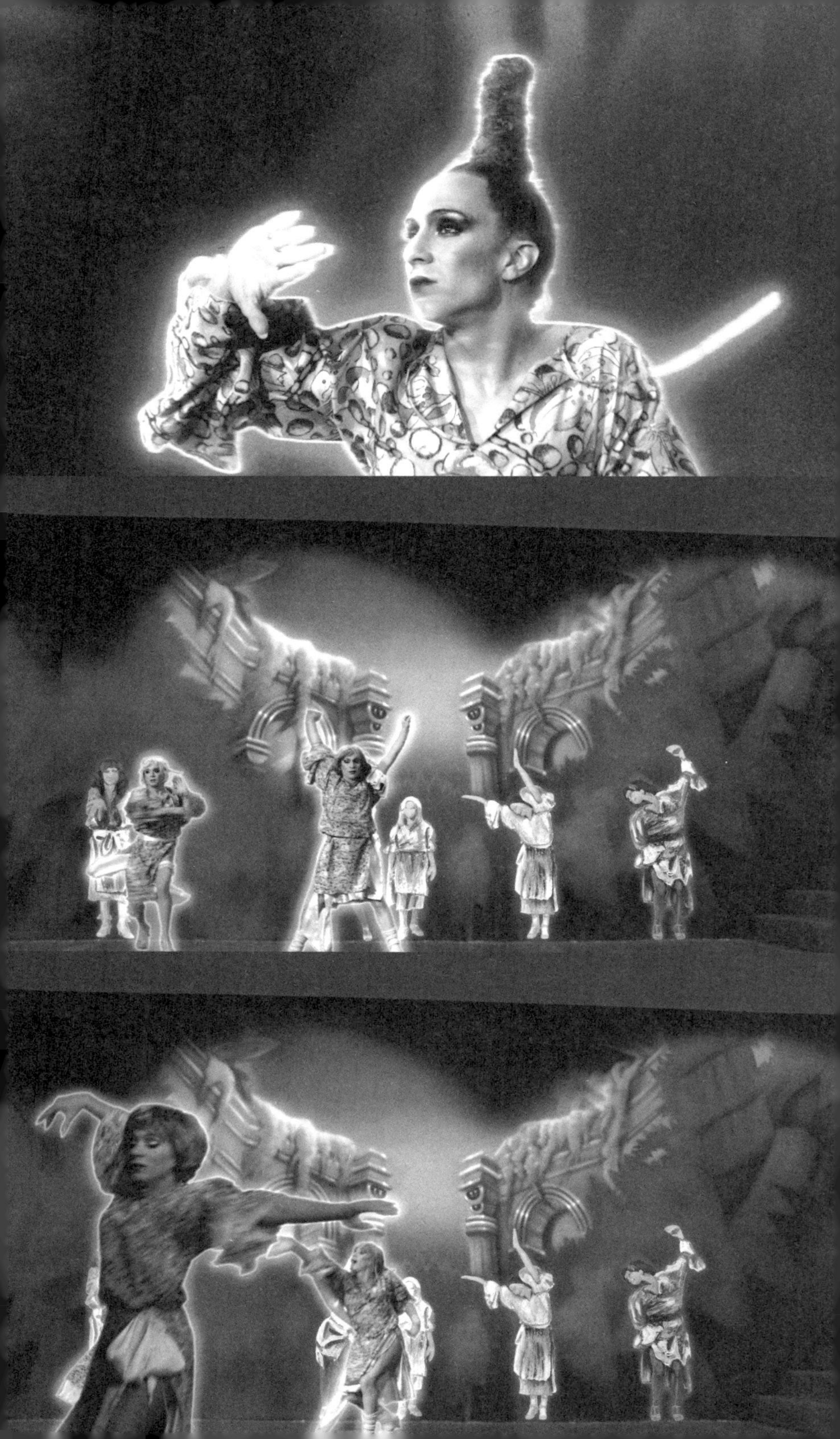

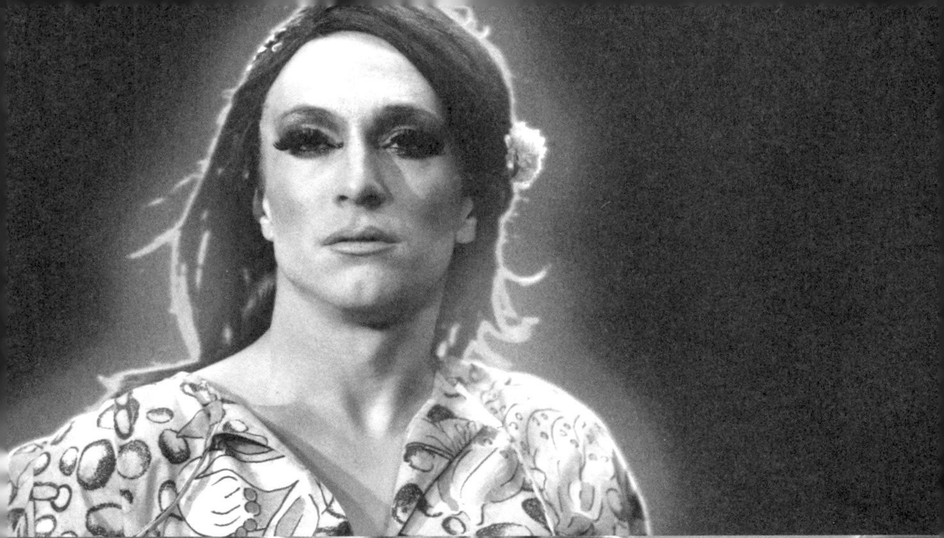
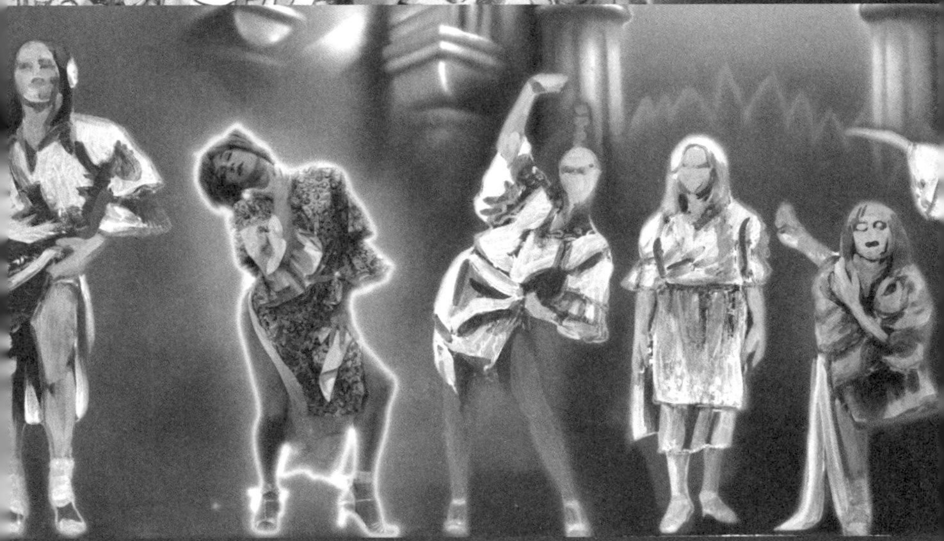
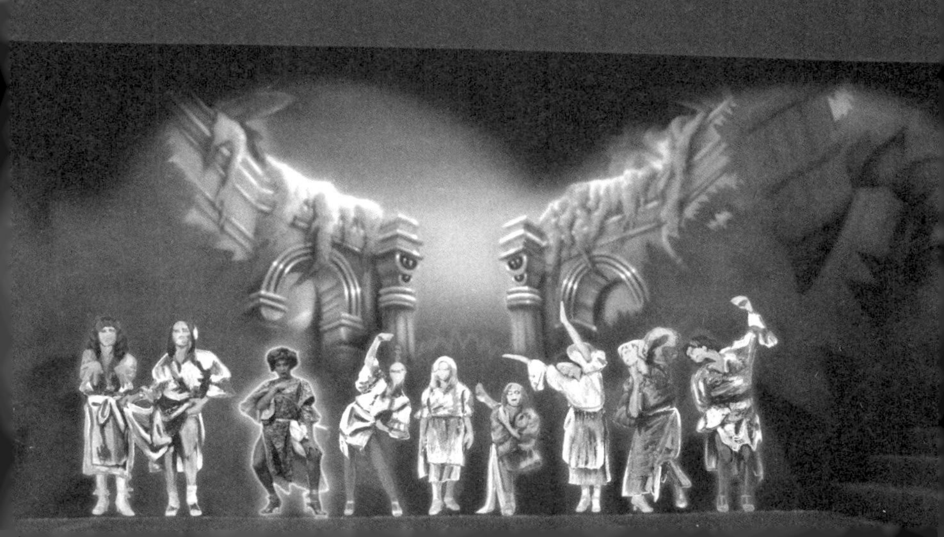

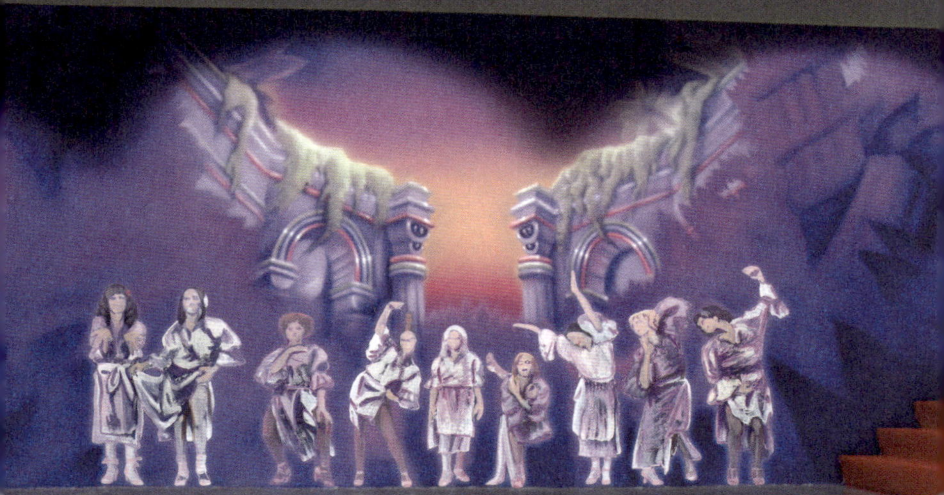
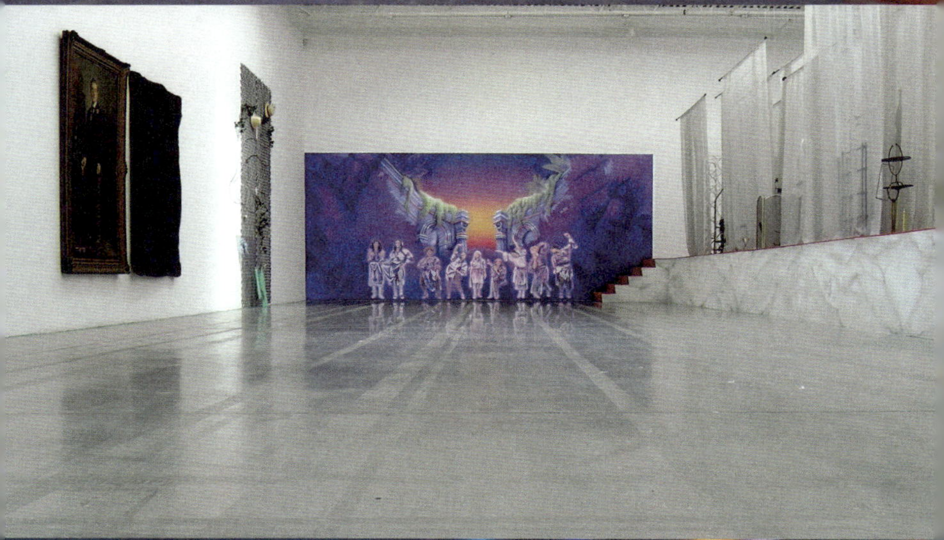
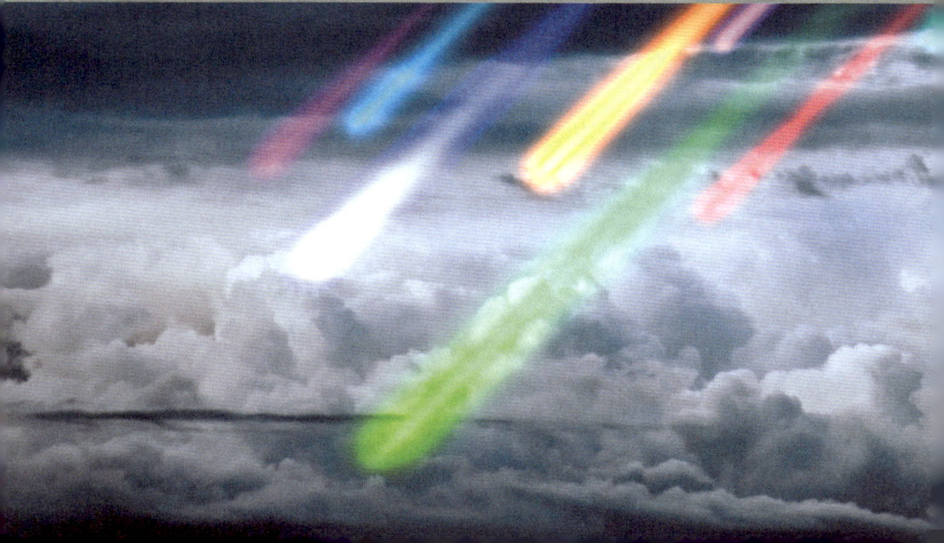

BODY DOUBLE XXXVI

8'58''
AFTER JAMES BRIDGES' PERFECT (1985)
2019

CAST
JEAN BICHE

IMAGES
LOÏC BOVON

EDITING & SPECIAL EFFECTS
BRICE DELLSPERGER

FIRST ASSISTANT CAMERA
ALEXANDRE BERRY

SOUND DESIGN
DIDIER BLASCO

TECHNICAL TEAM
VINCENT BERGER, ANTOINE CONDE,
LÉA DOUSSIÈRE, MATTHIEU
MAYTRAUD, HAYOUNG KIM

SUPPLIER
RVZ, PARIS; DIACOSMIE, CENTRE DE
PRODUCTION DE L'OPÉRA DE NICE

PRODUCTION
VILLA ARSON, NICE, FRANCE

EXECUTIVE PRODUCTION
BEAU BIZARRE

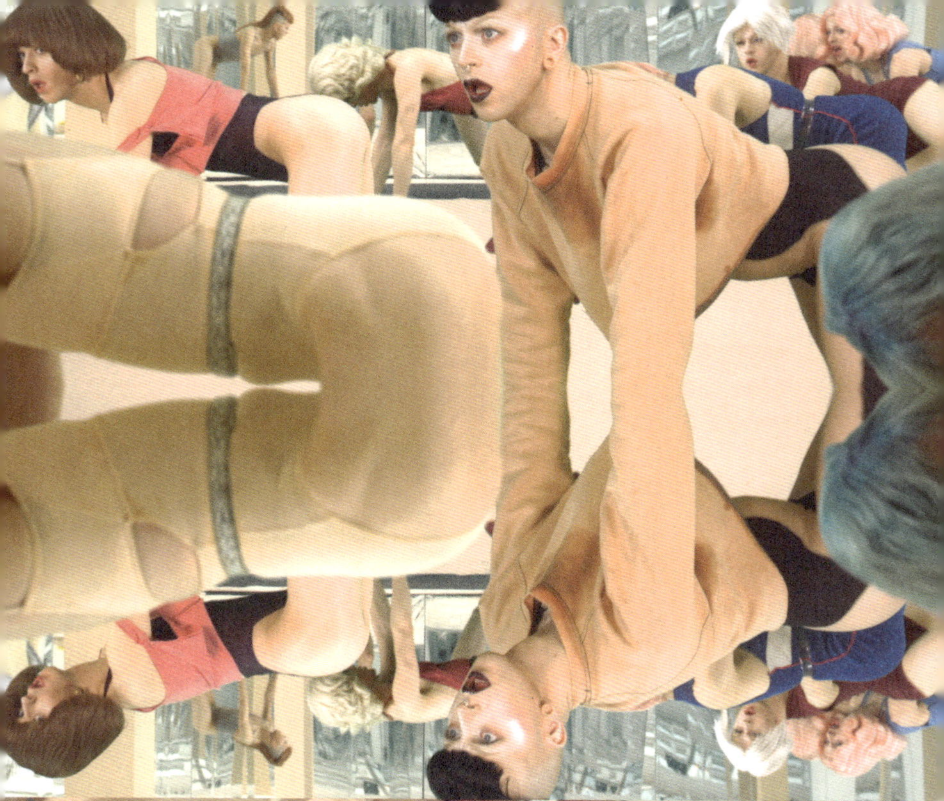

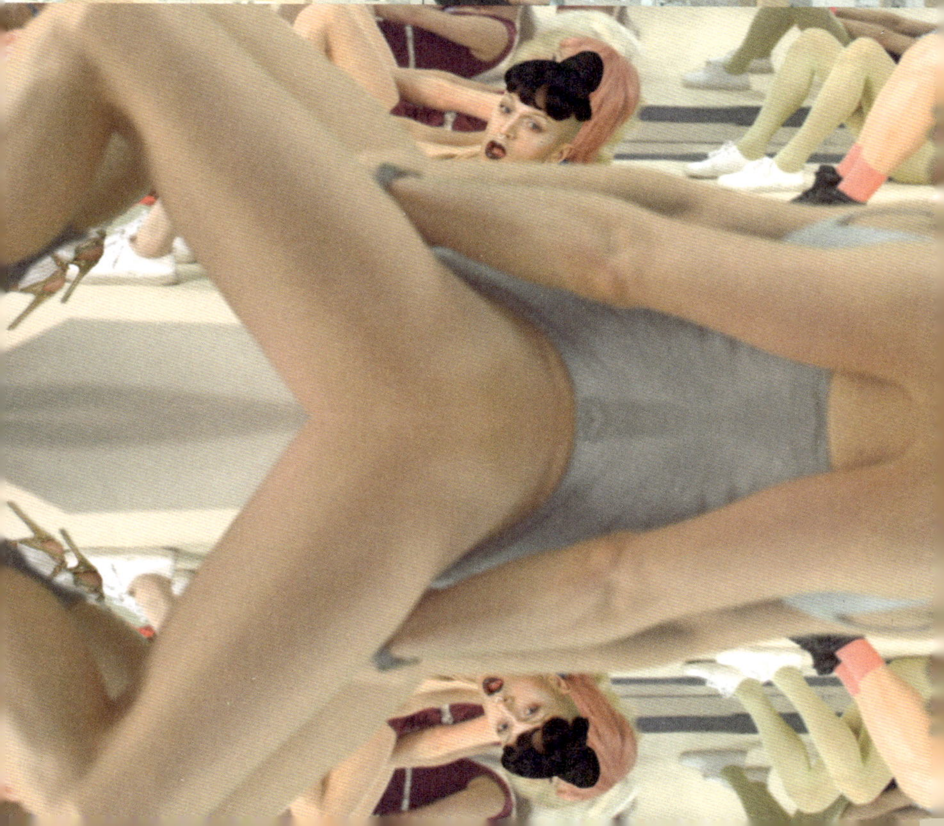

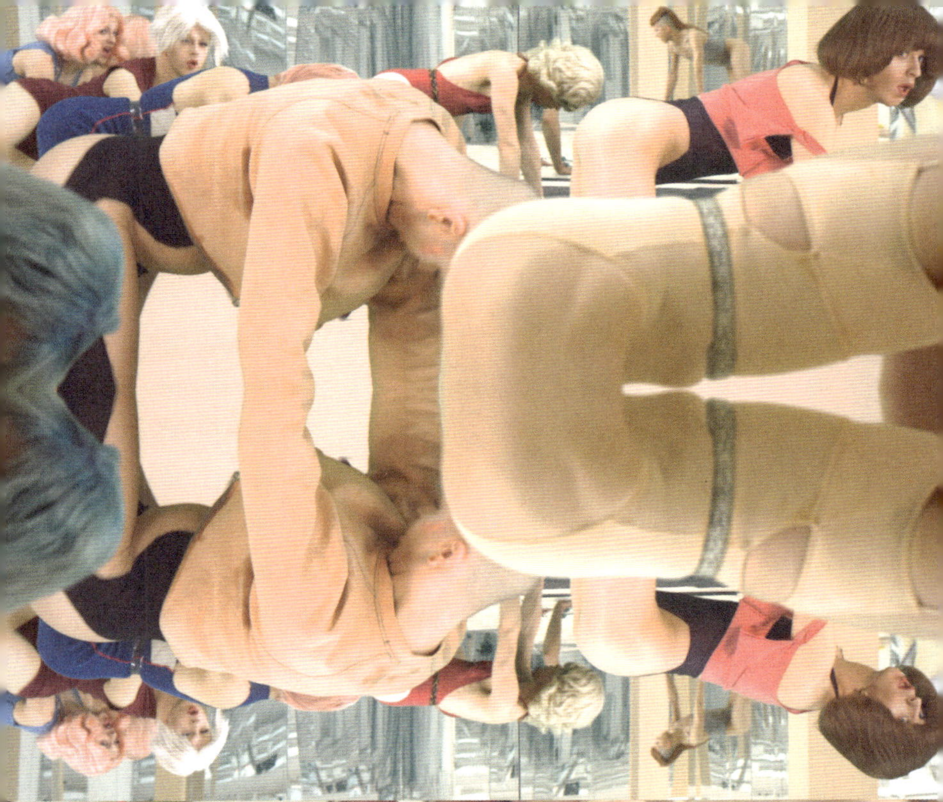

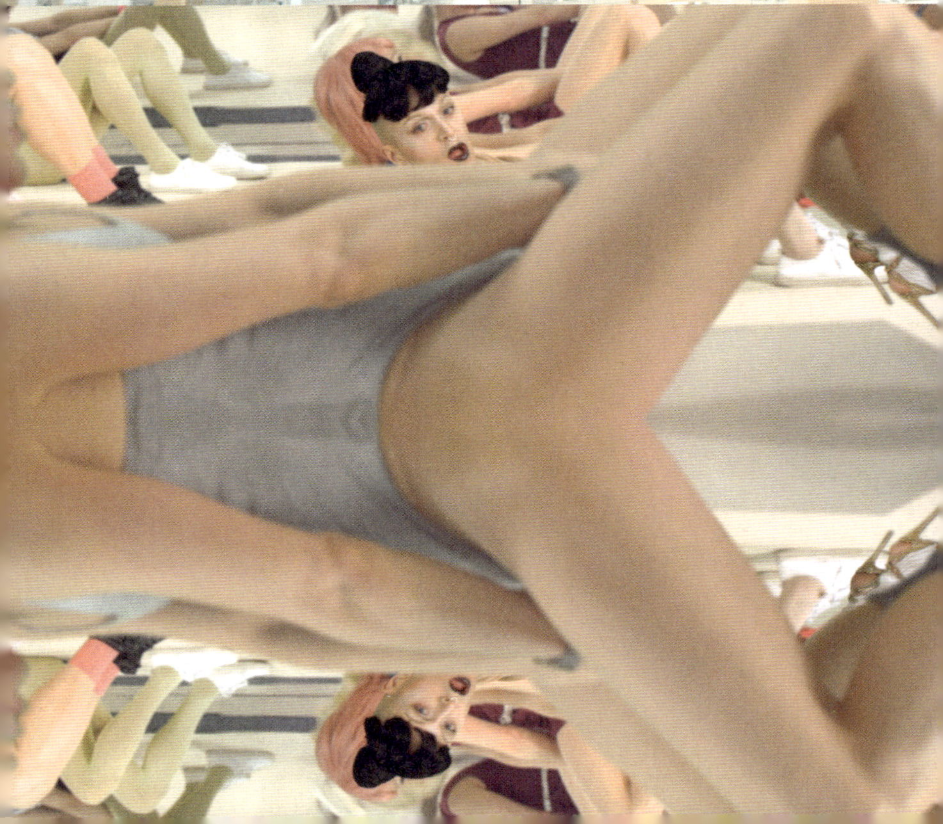

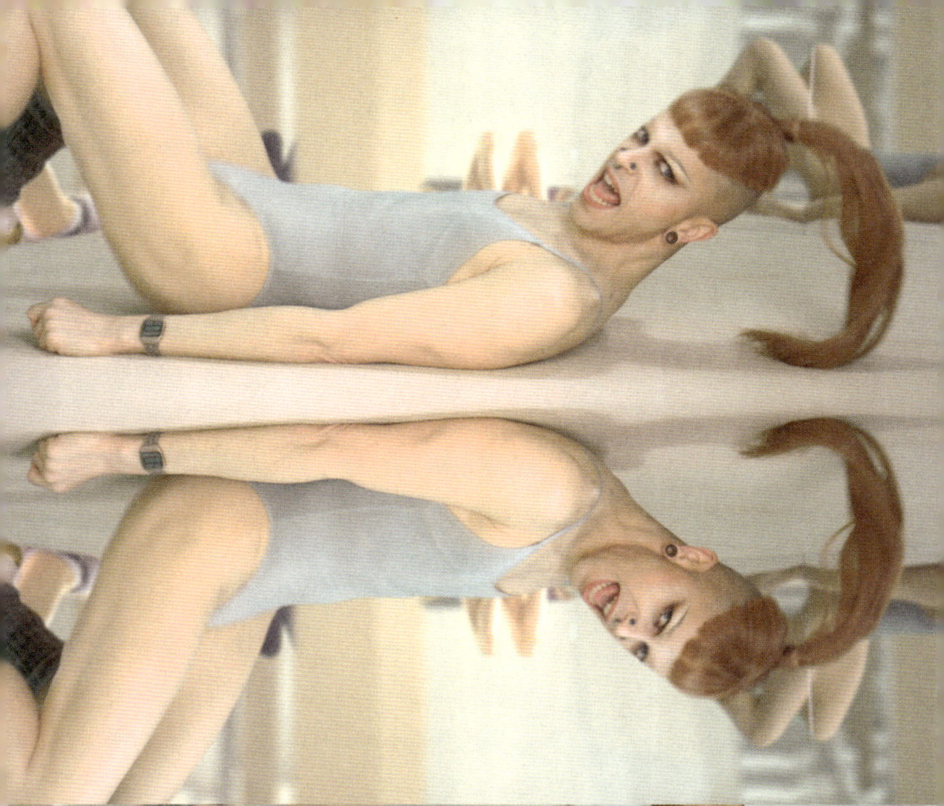

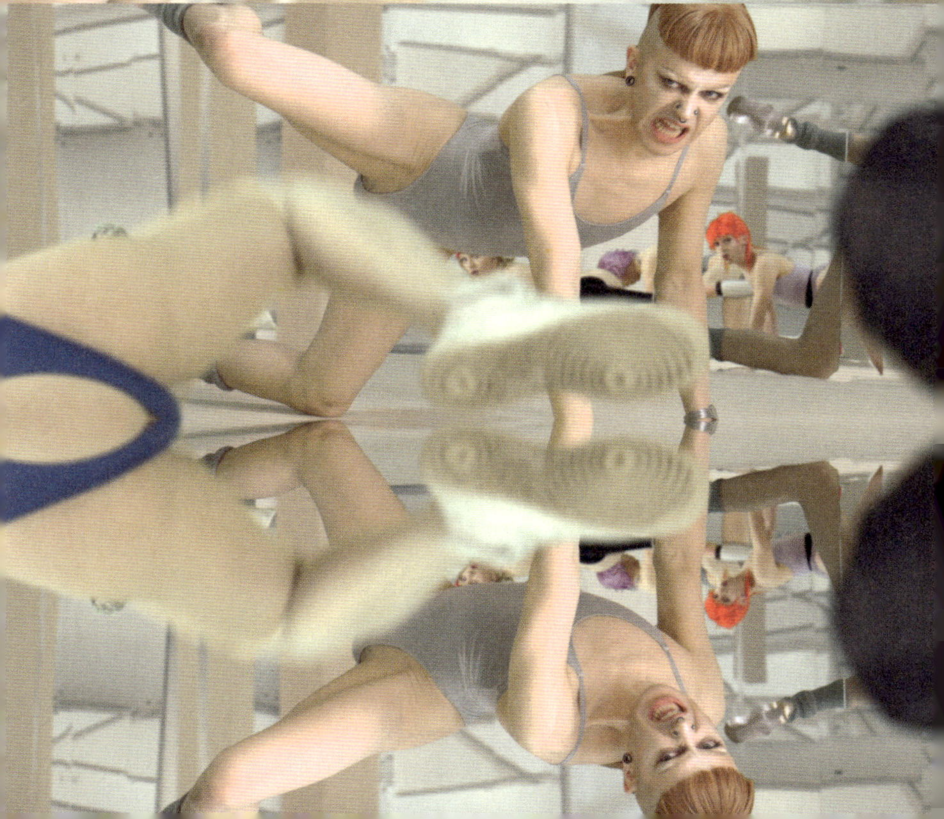

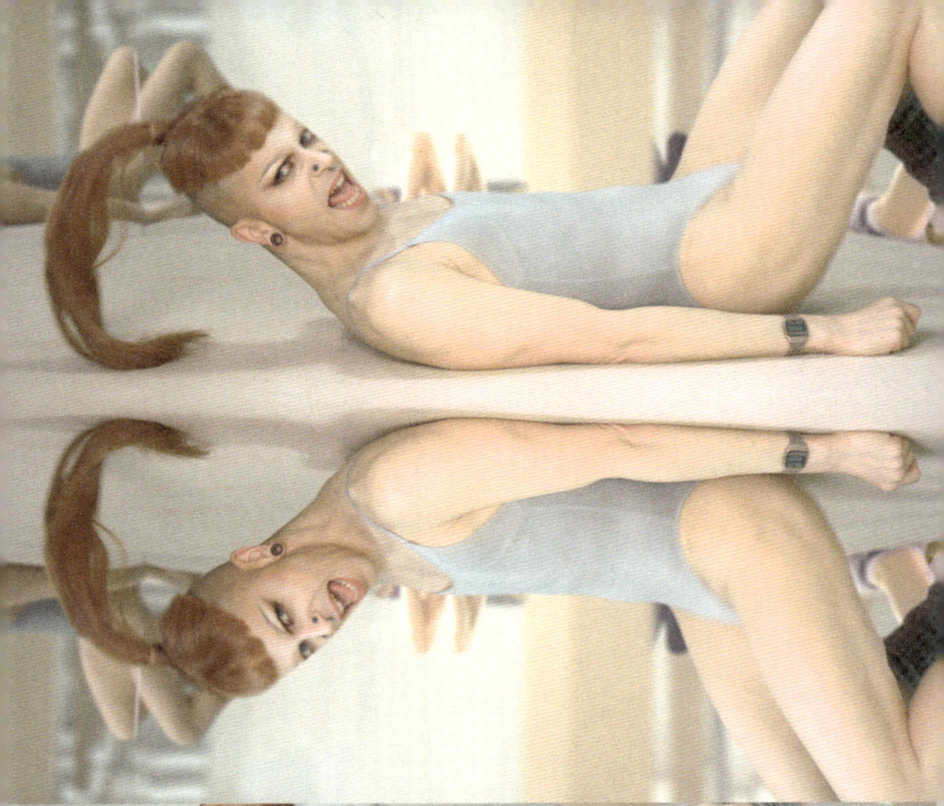

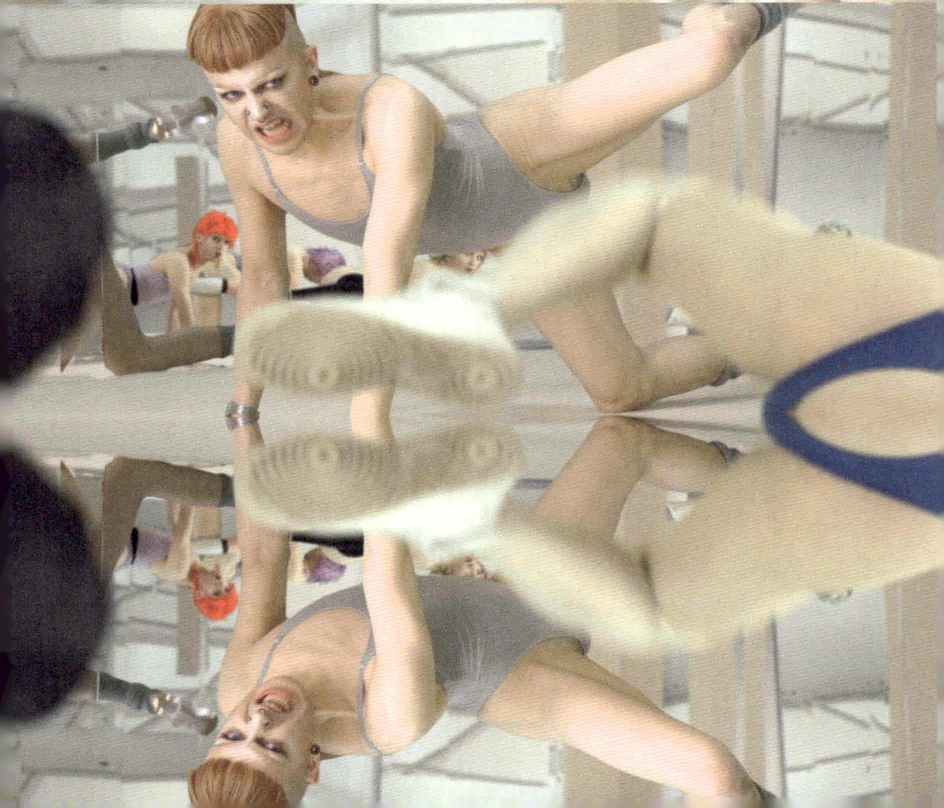

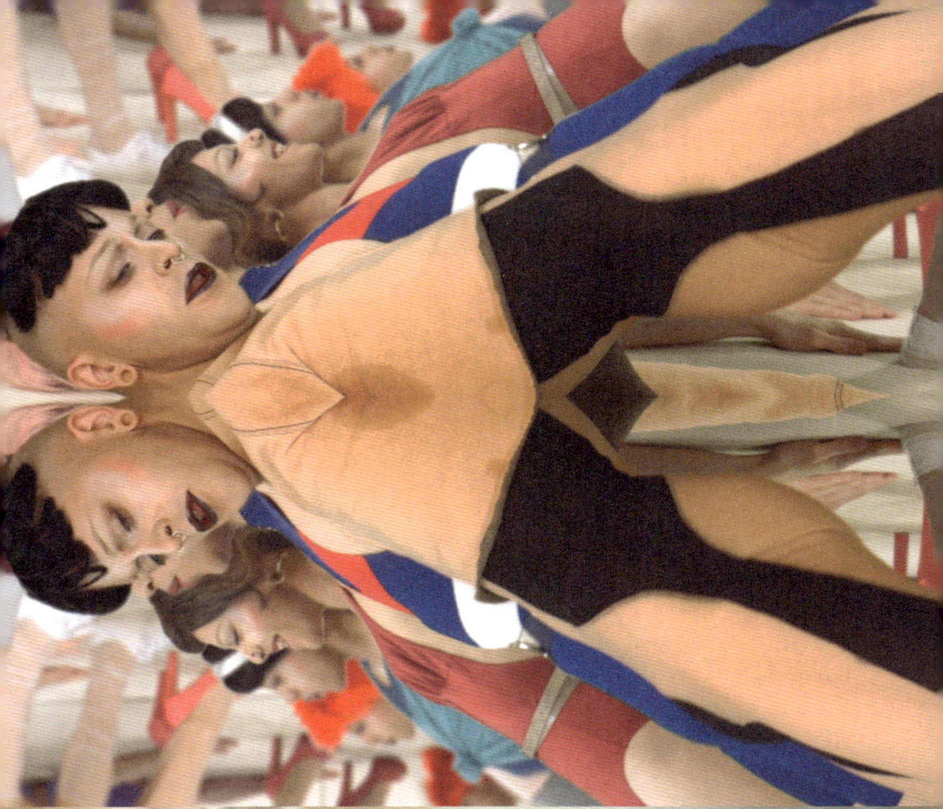
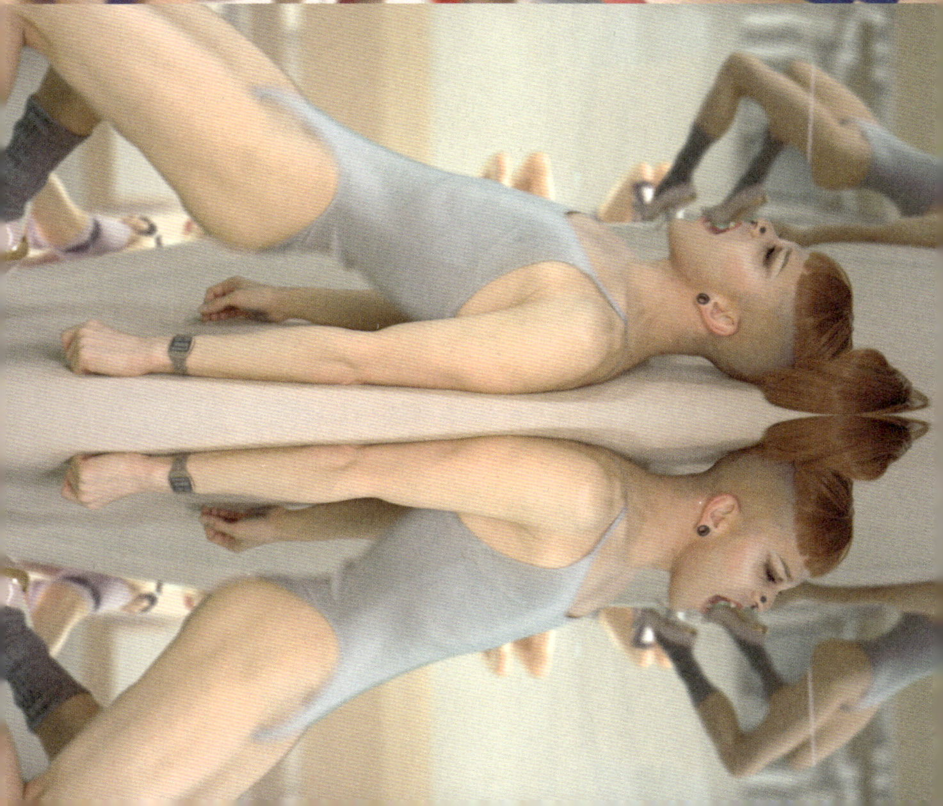

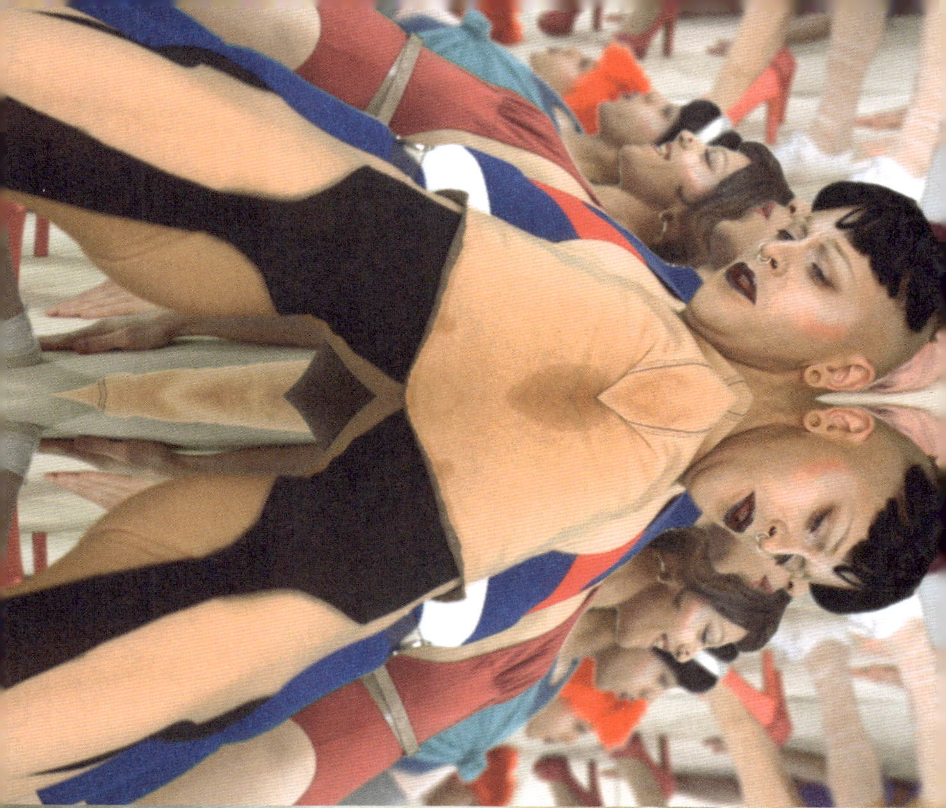
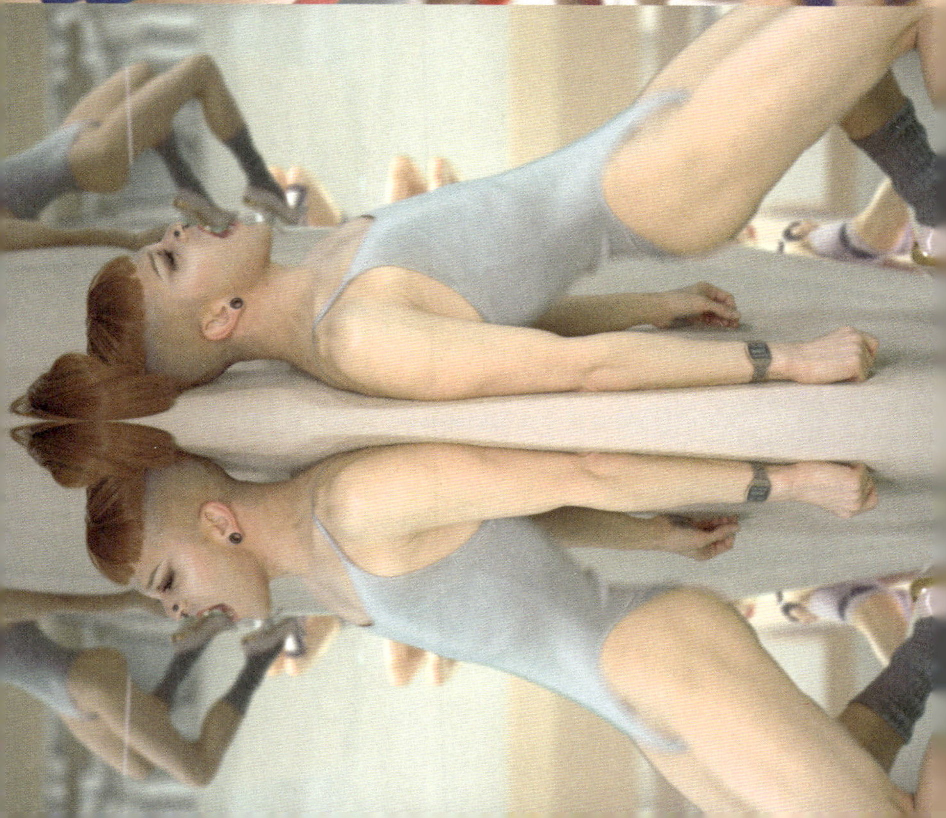

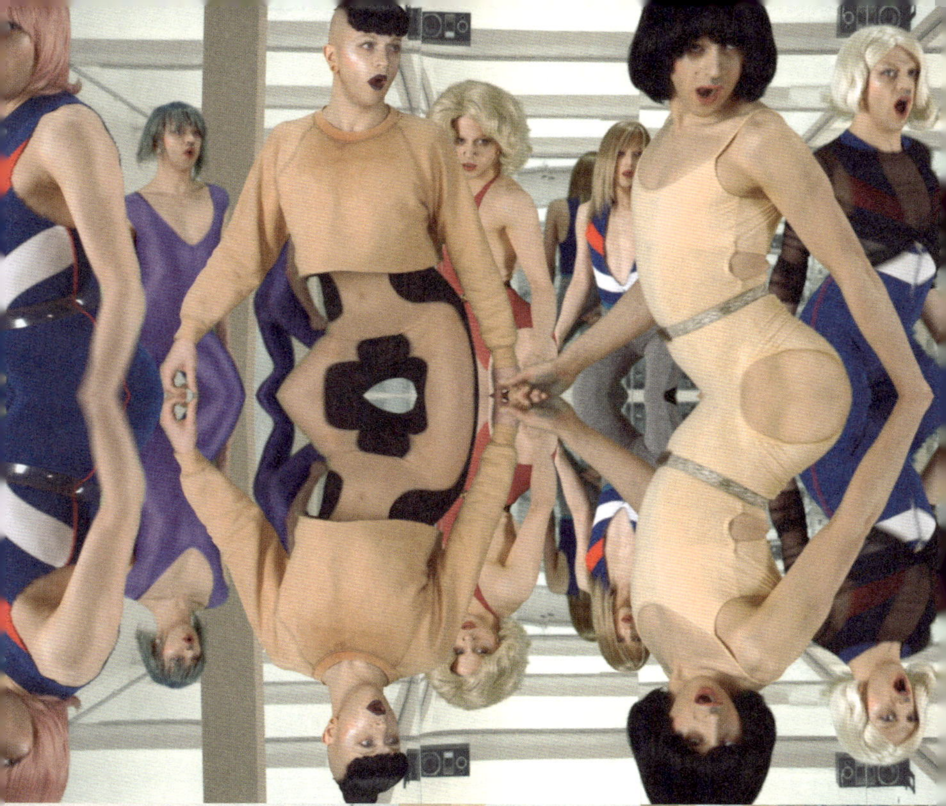

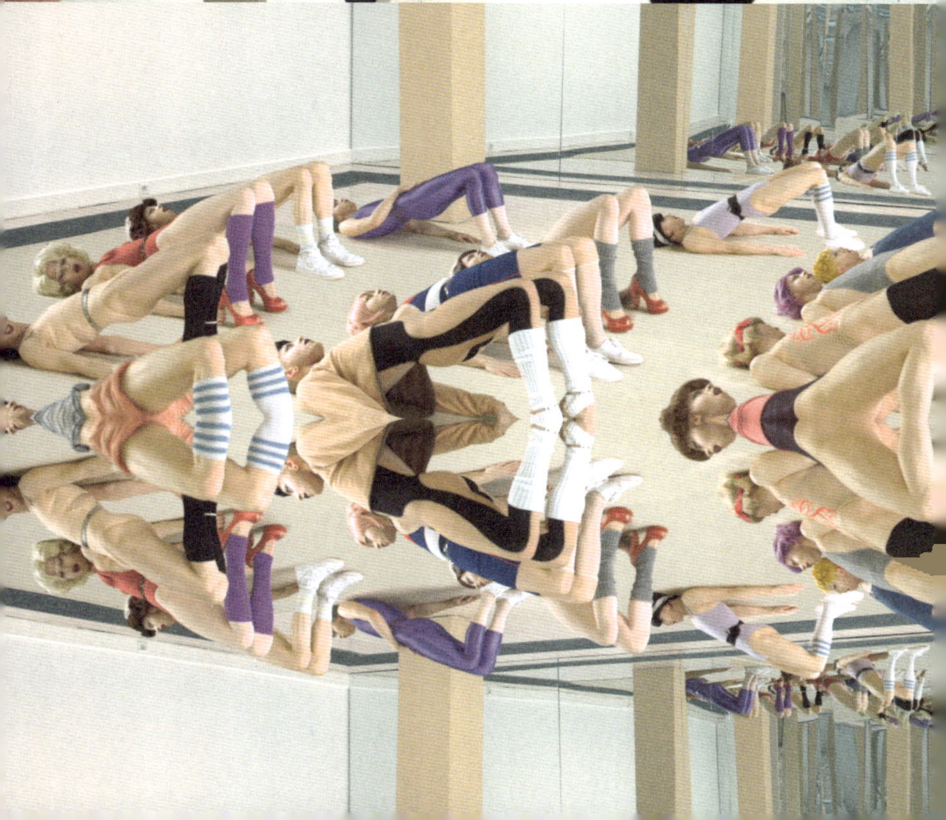

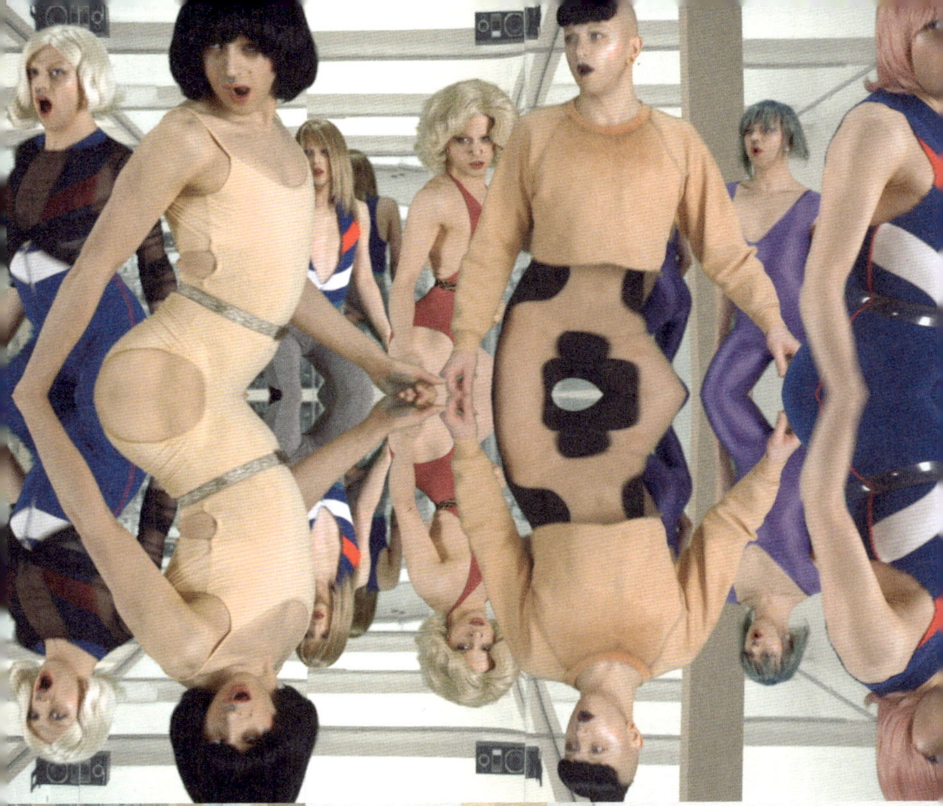

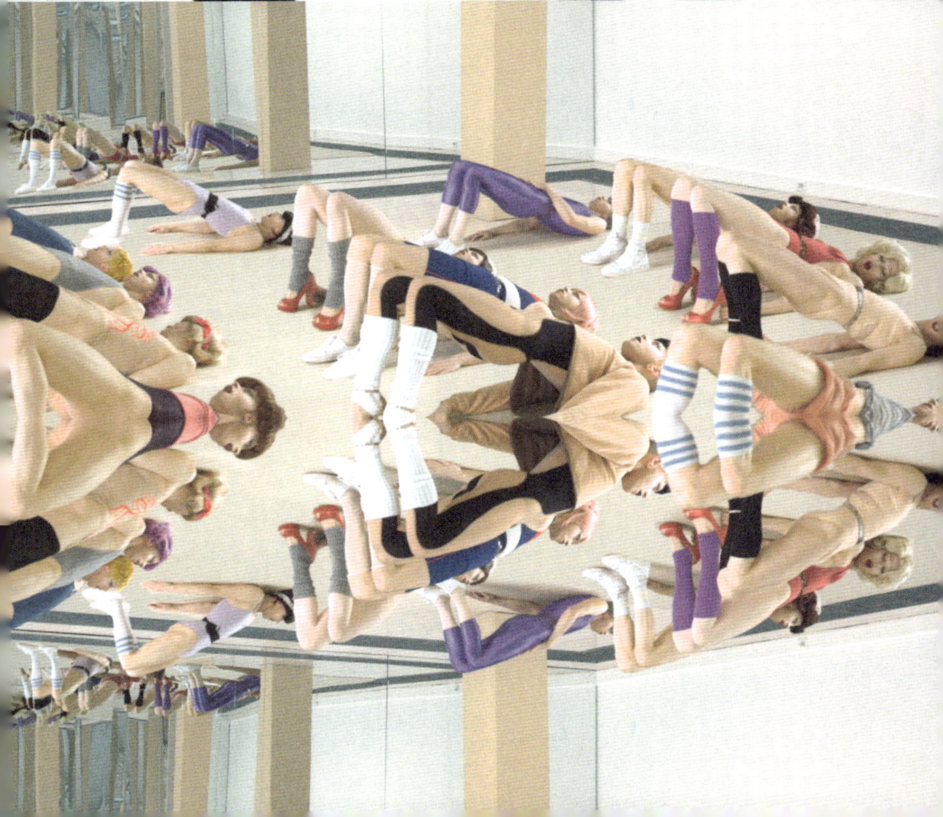

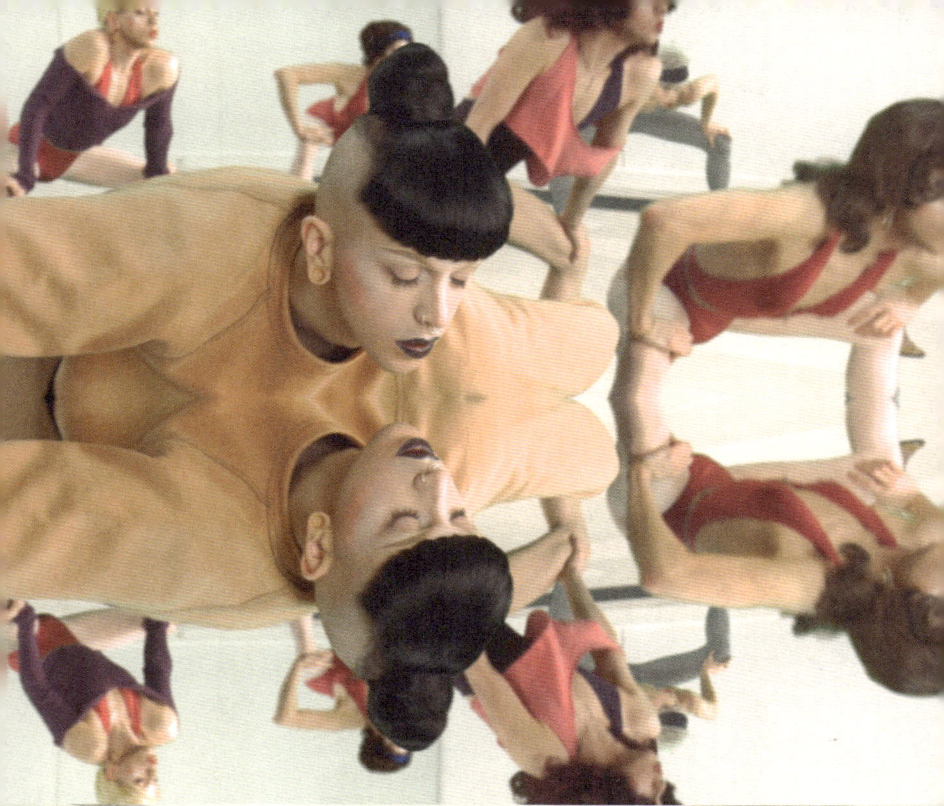

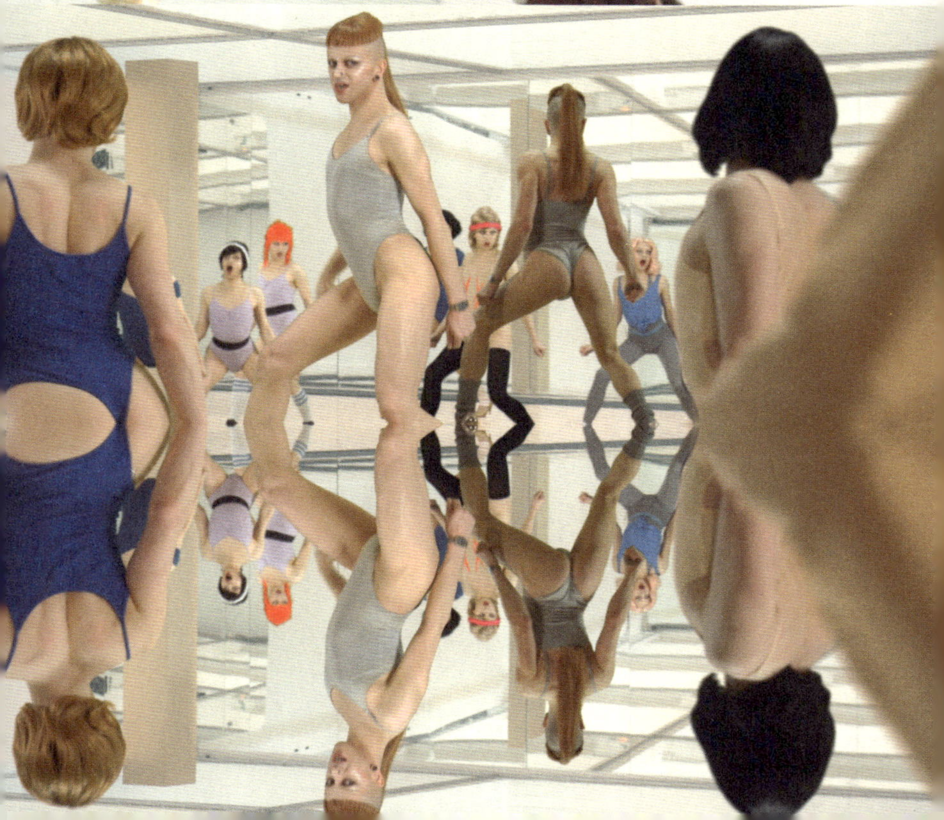

BODY DOUBLE XXXVII

3'55''
AFTER BRIAN DE PALMA'S DRESSED TO KILL (1980)
2020

CAST, IMAGES, EDITING & SPECIAL EFFECTS
BRICE DELLSPERGER

PRODUCTION
BRICE DELLSPERGER

COLLECTION
MUSÉE NATIONAL D'ART MODERNE, MNAM,
CENTRE POMPIDOU, PARIS, FRANCE

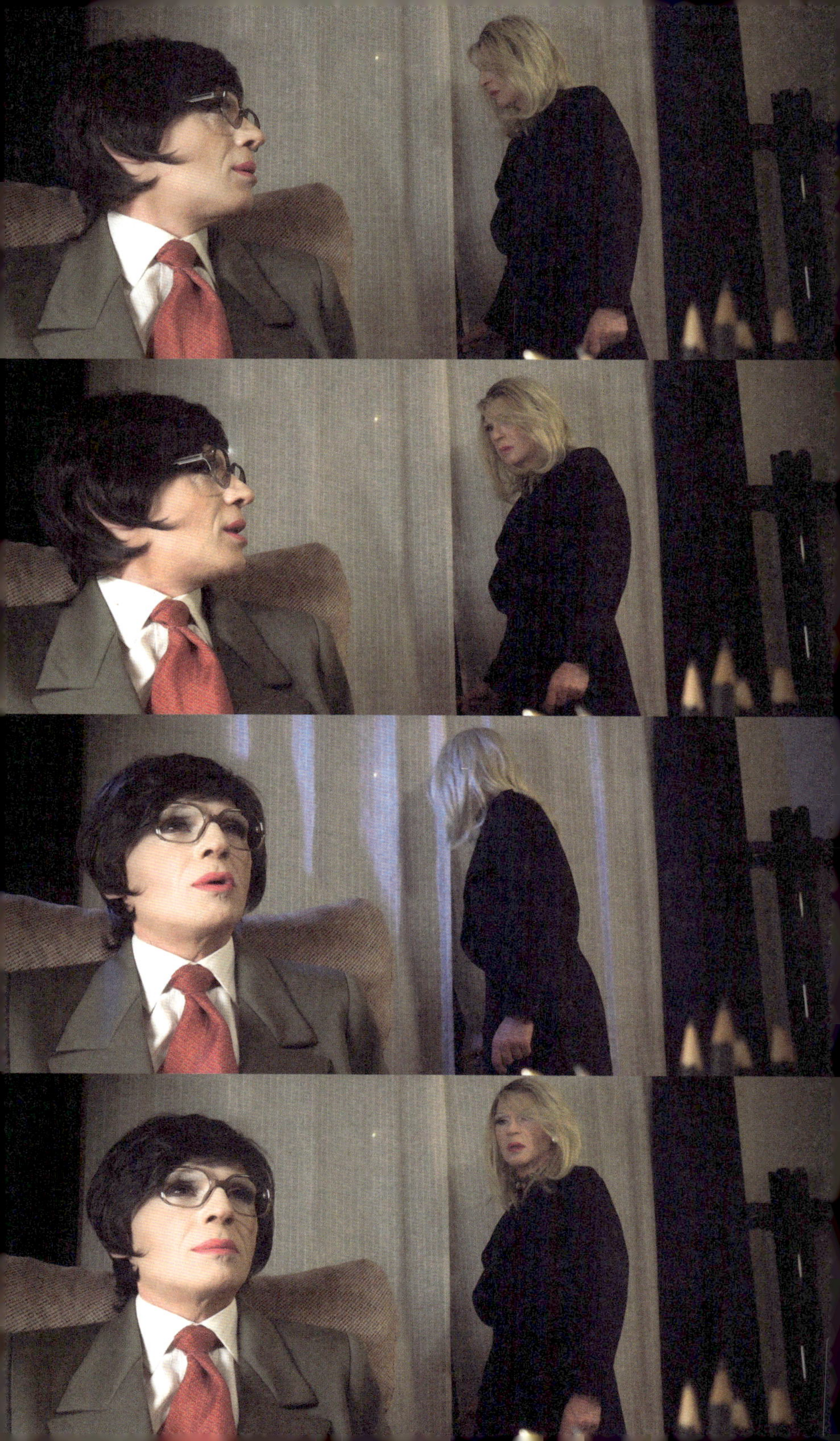

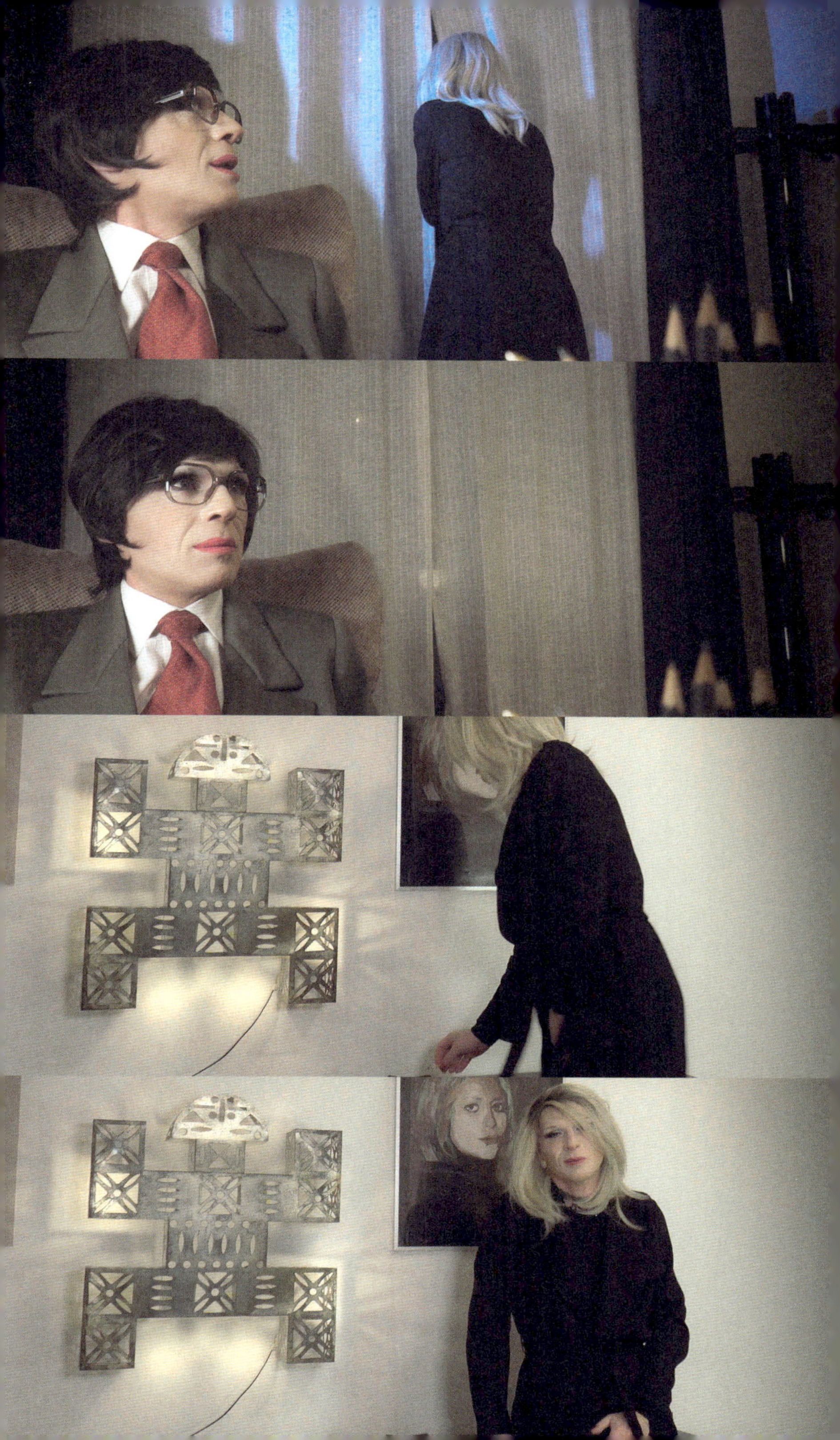

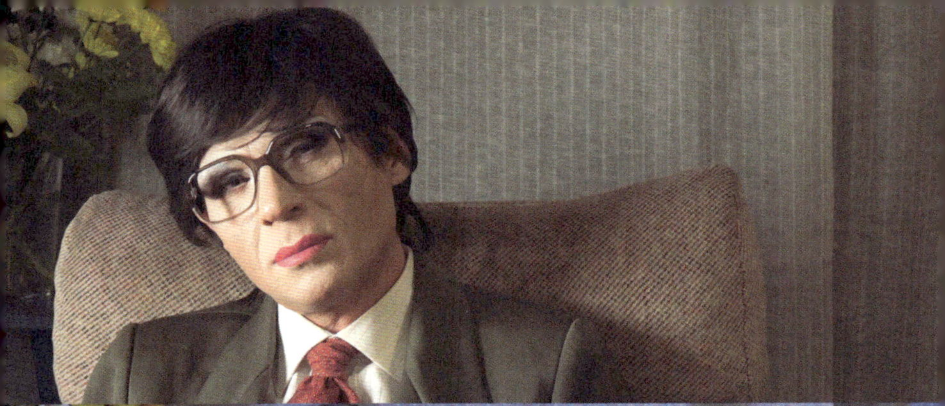

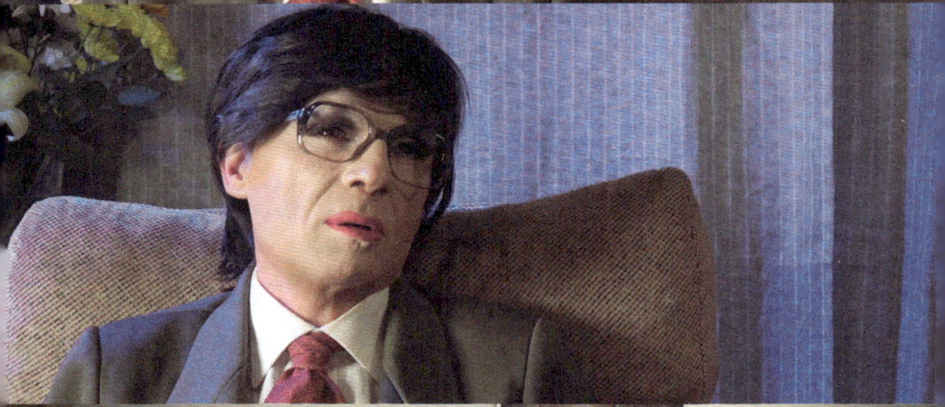

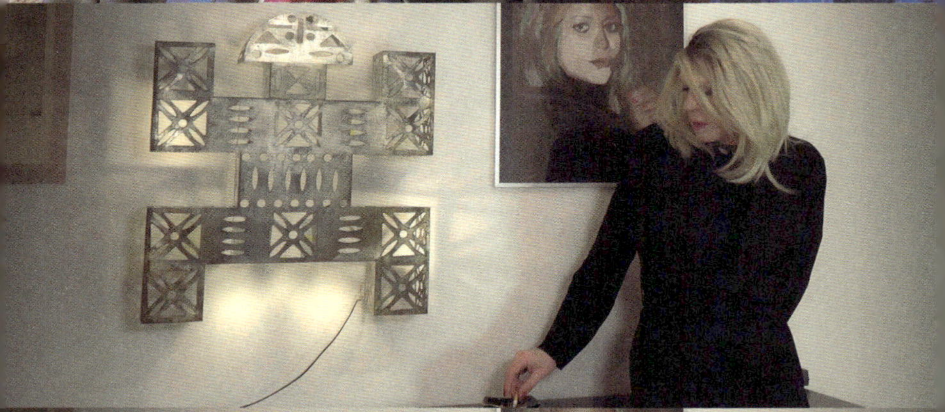

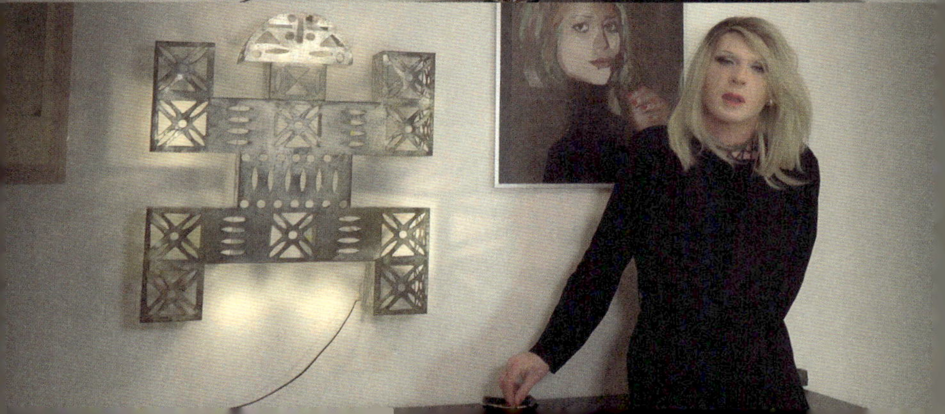

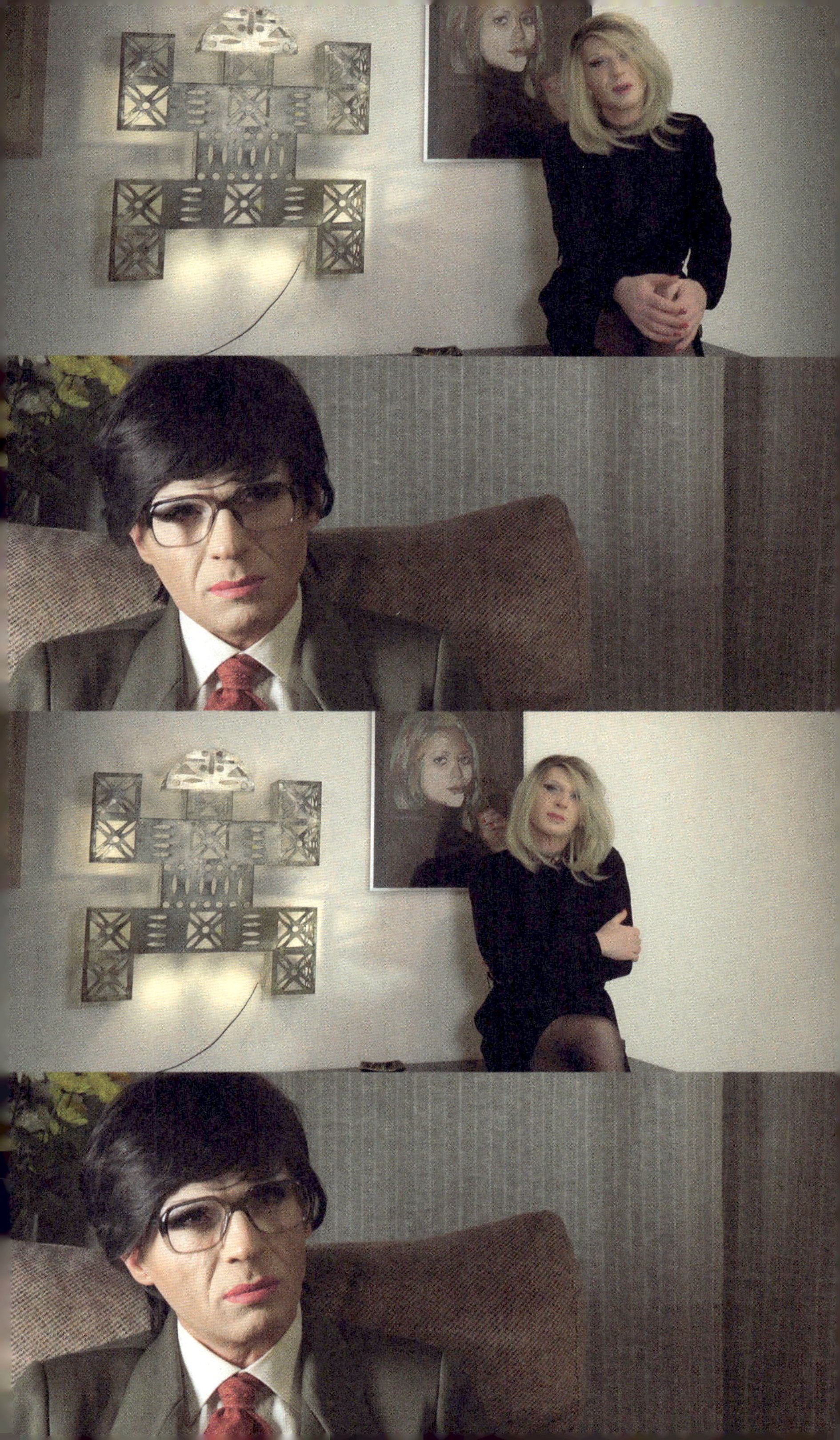

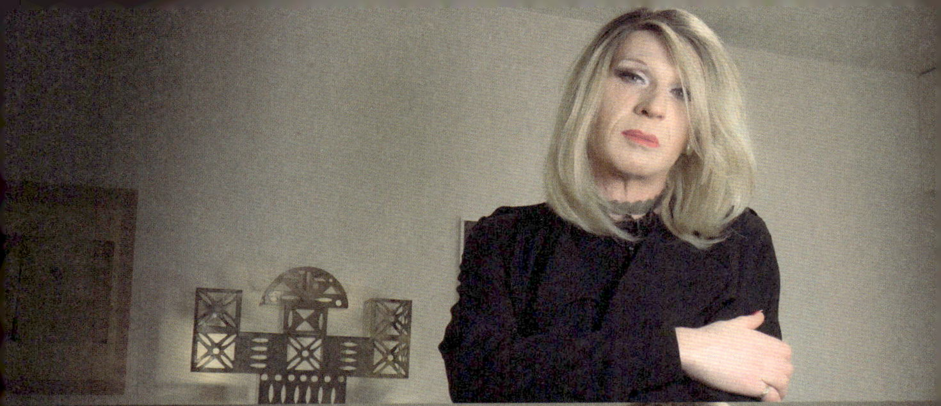
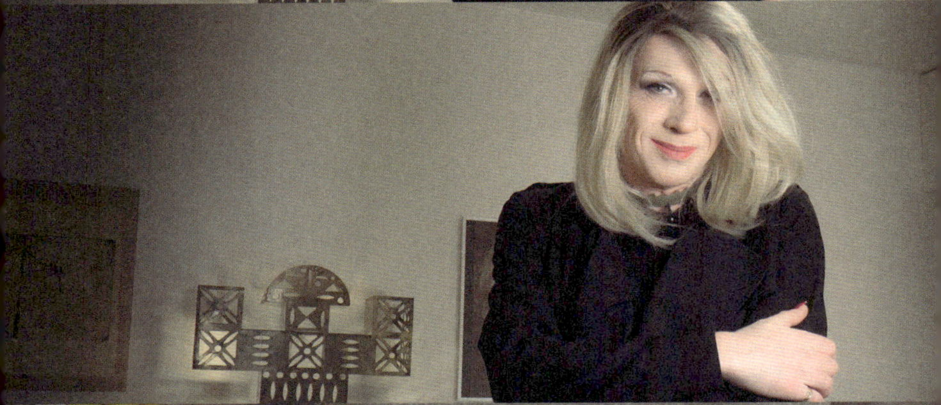
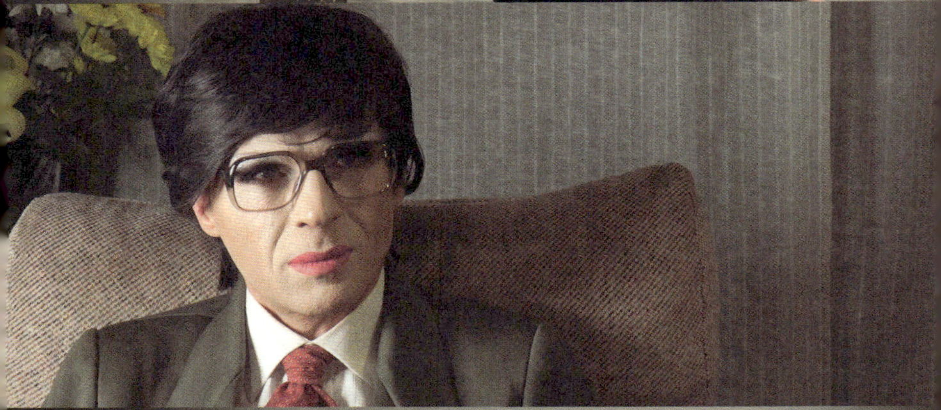
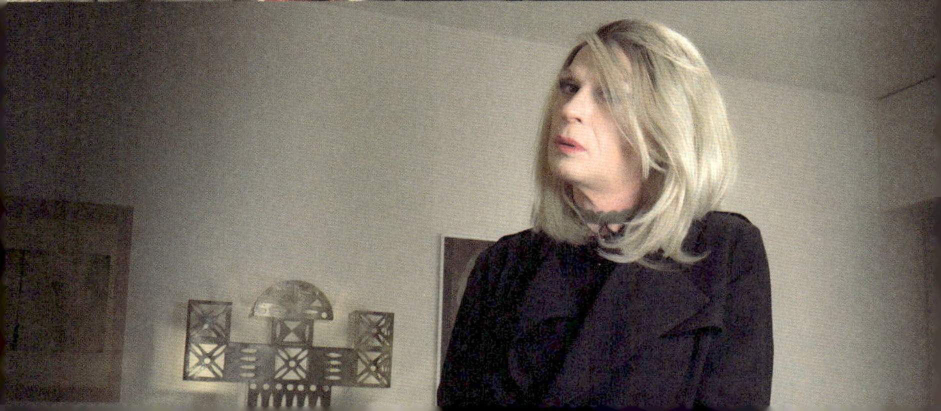

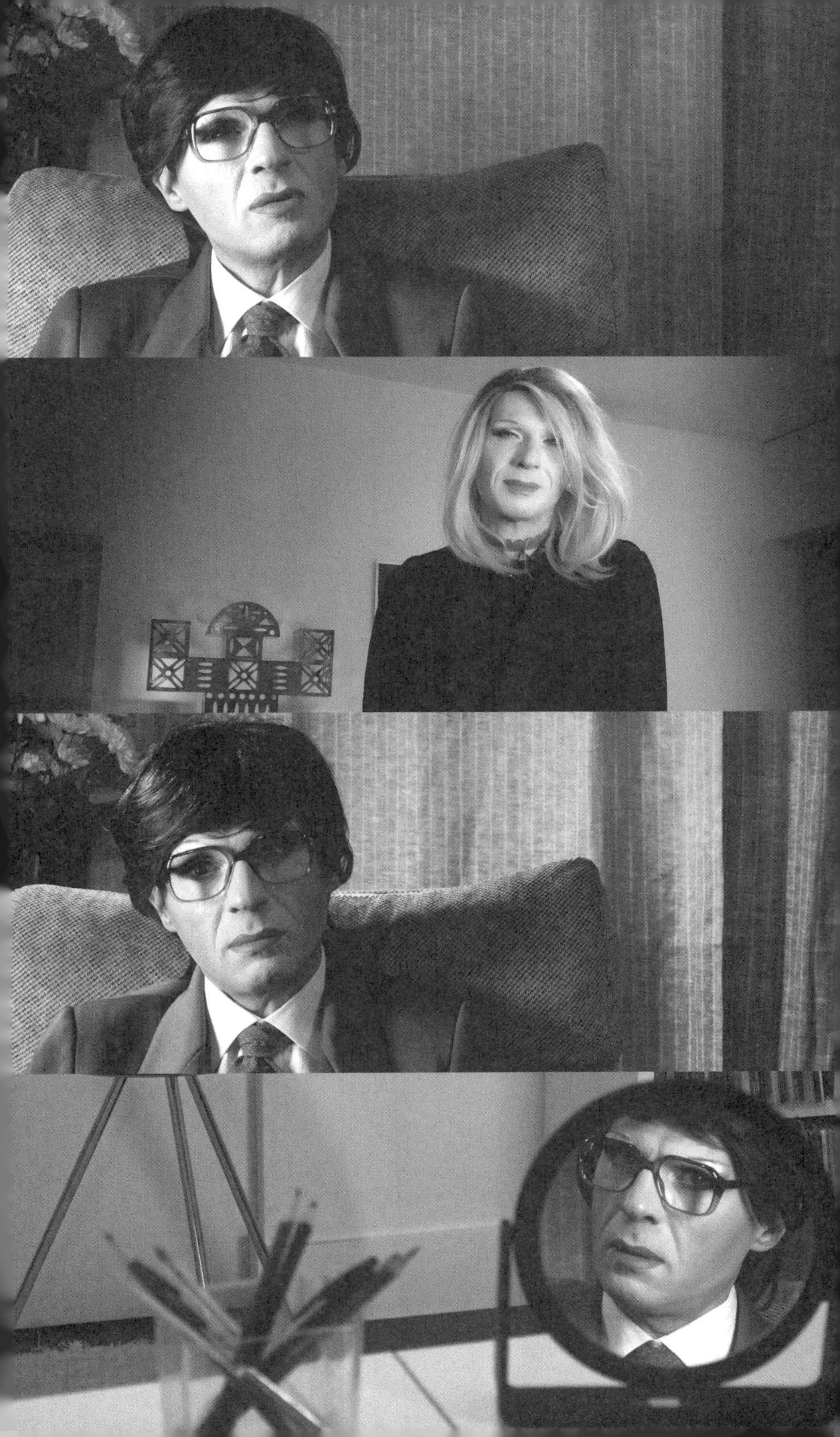

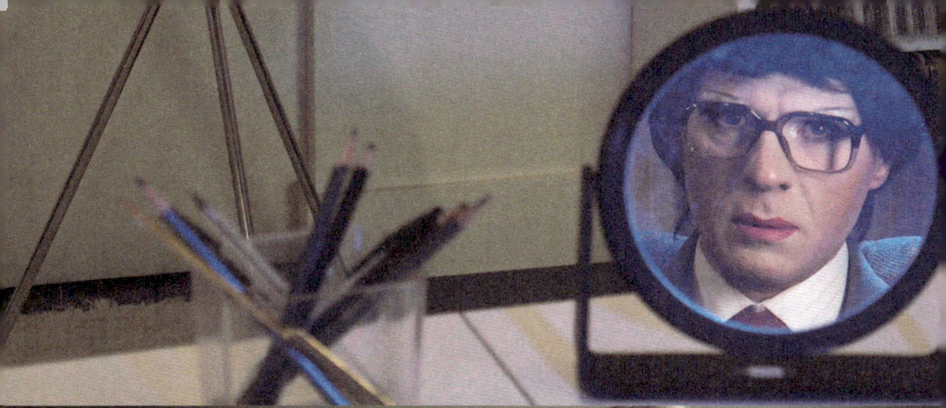

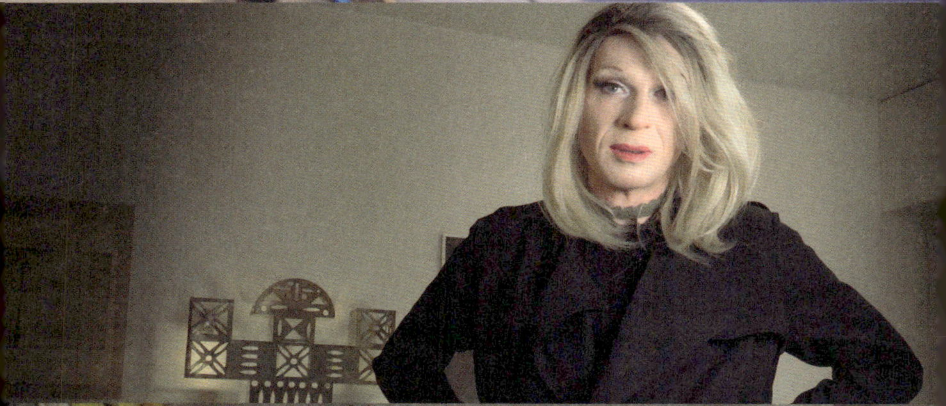

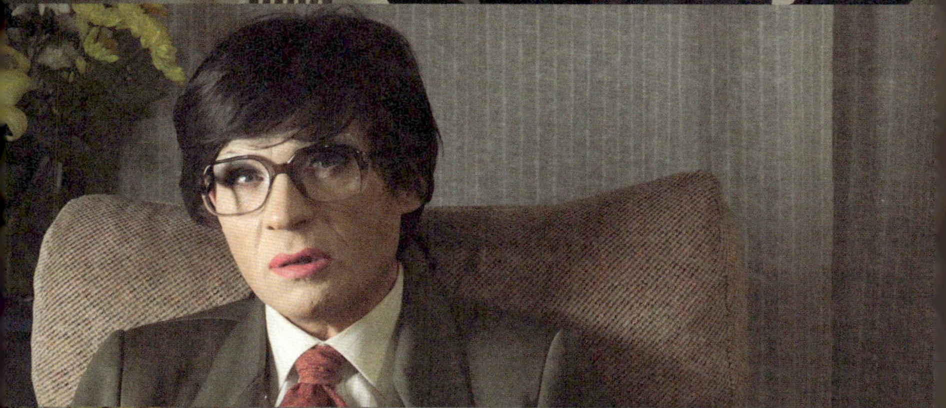

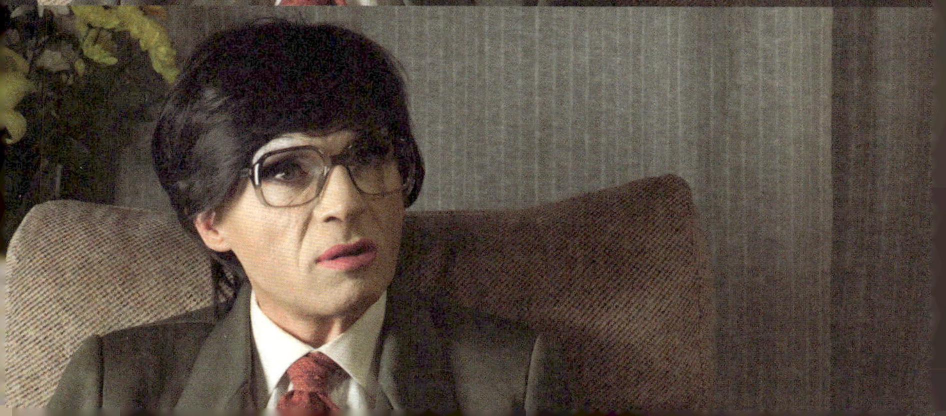

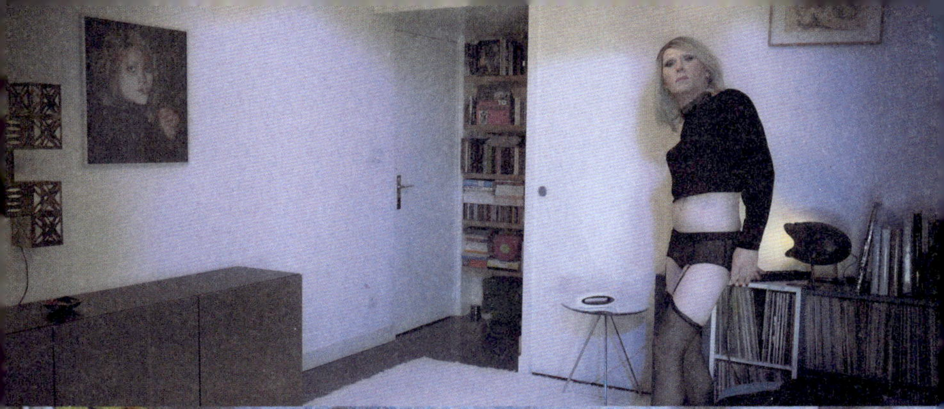
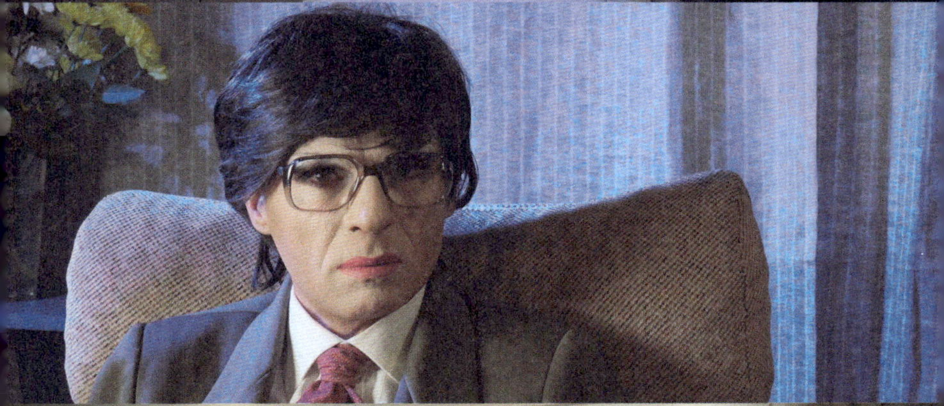
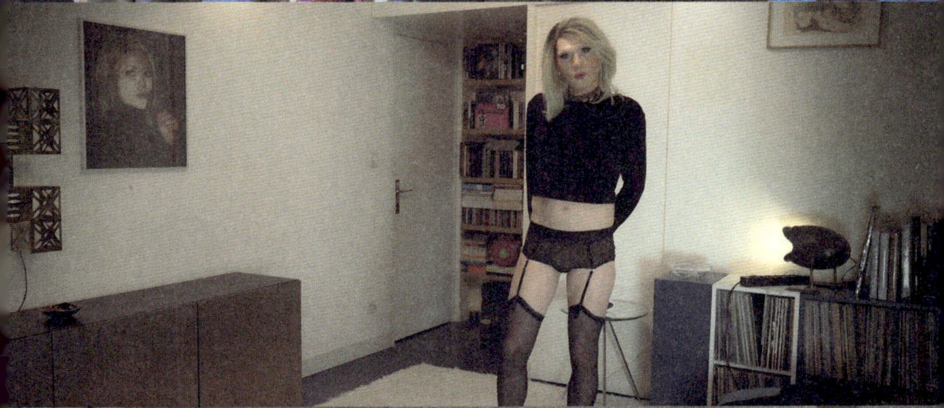
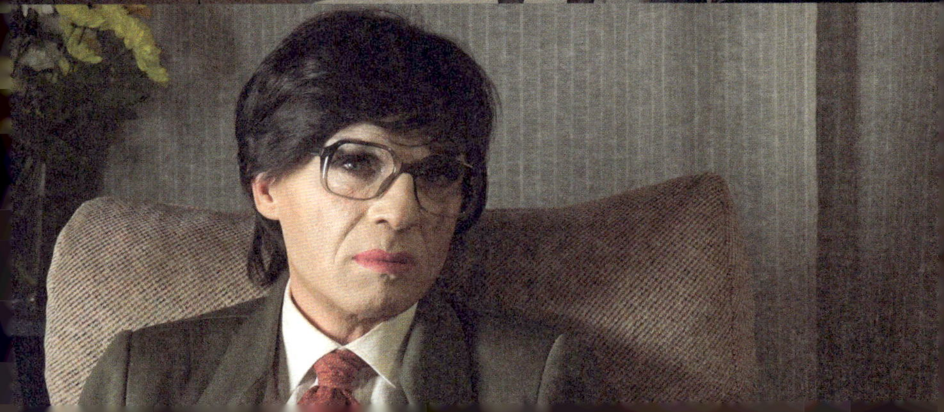

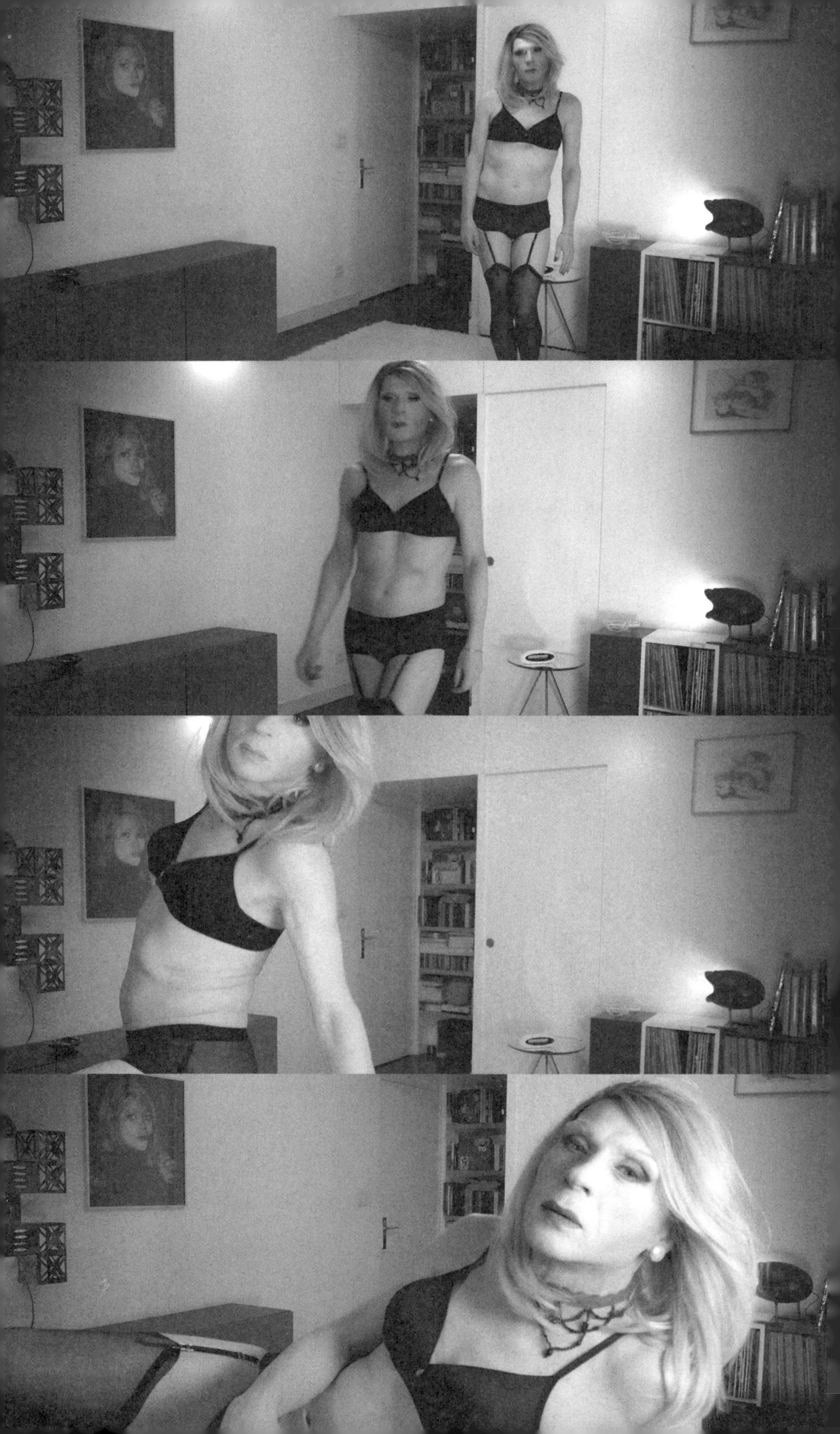

BODY DOUBLE XXVIII

6'43"
AFTER KENNETH ANGER'S PUCE MOMENT (1949) & DARA BIRNBAUM'S TECHNOLOGY/TRANSFORMATION: WONDER WOMAN (1978-79)
2022

CAST
EVA SVENNUNG

IMAGES
LOU FAUROUX

SECOND CAMERA
GABRIEL CALAIS

EDITING, SOUND DESIGN & SPECIAL EFFECTS
BRICE DELLSPERGER

FIRST ASSISTANT DIRECTOR
ROBIN LADIER

COSTUME DESIGN
CHLOTHILDE DU MUR
& BRICE DELLSPERGER

MAKE-UP DESIGN
ALONA MATETSKAYA

STILL PHOTOGRAPHER
GINA FOLLY

PRODUCTION
LA GALERIE, CENTRE D'ART CONTEMPORAIN
DE NOISY-LE-SEC, FRANCE
BRICE DELLSPERGER

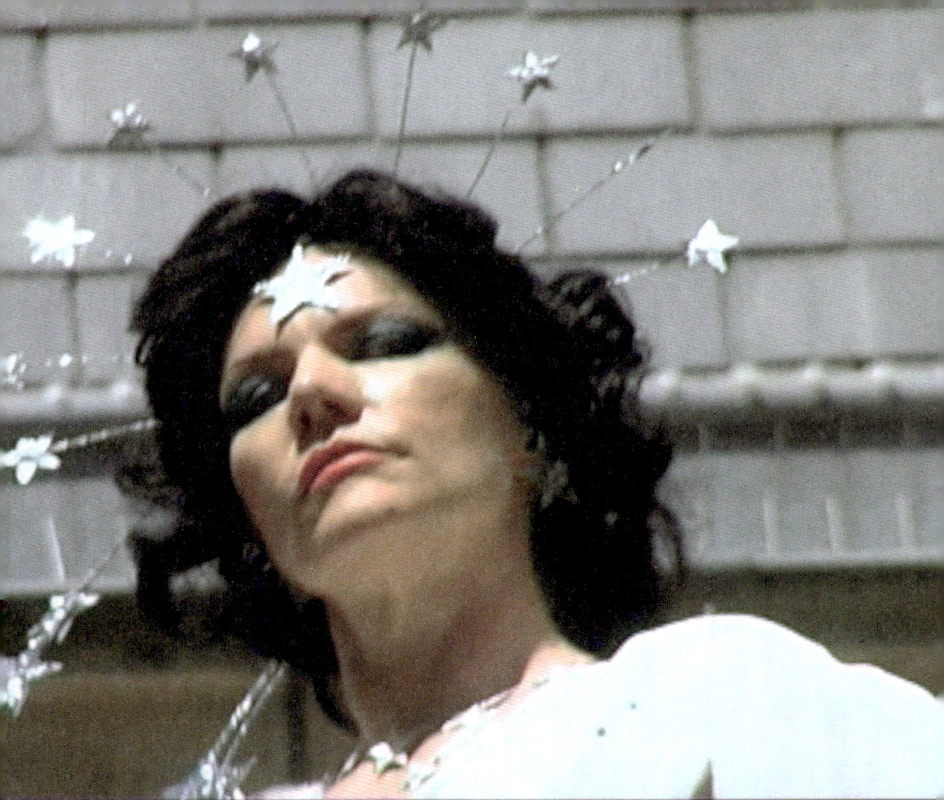
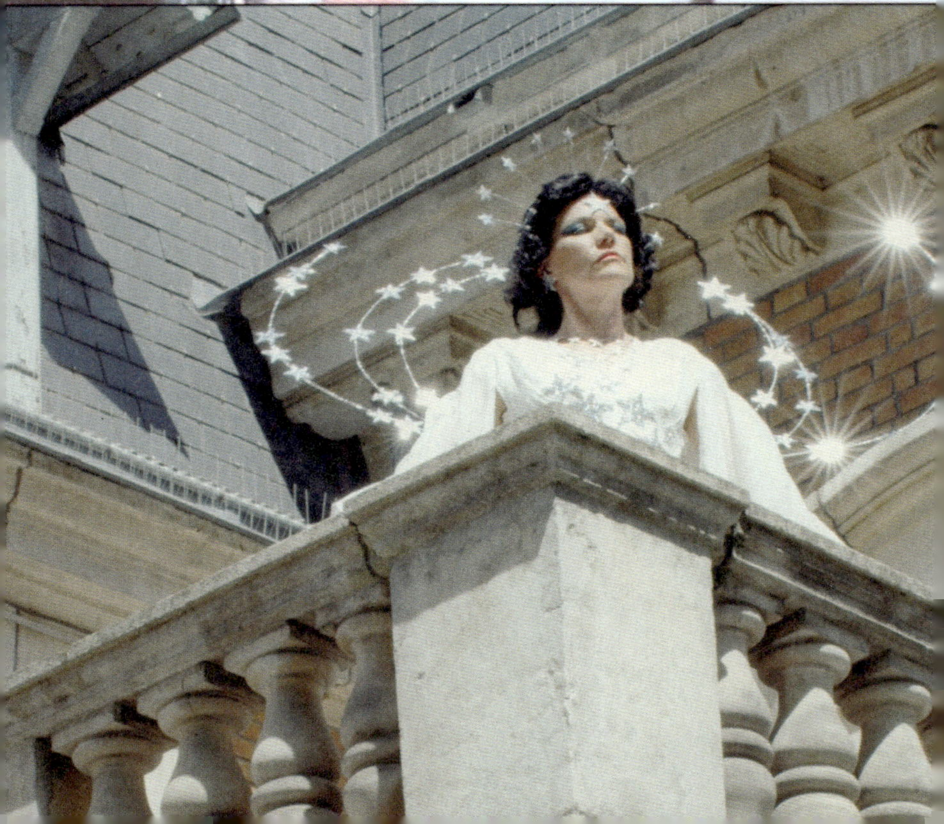

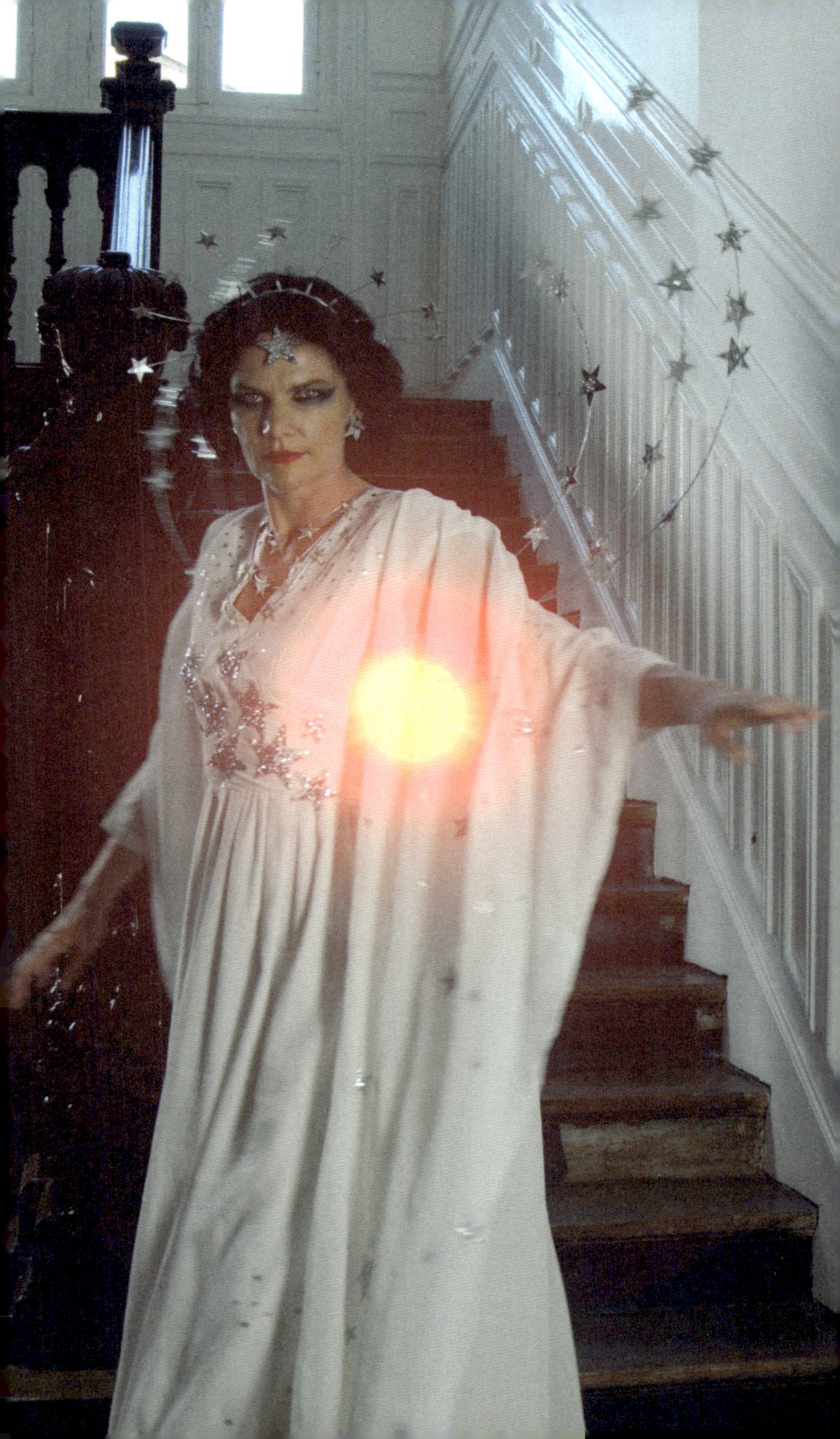

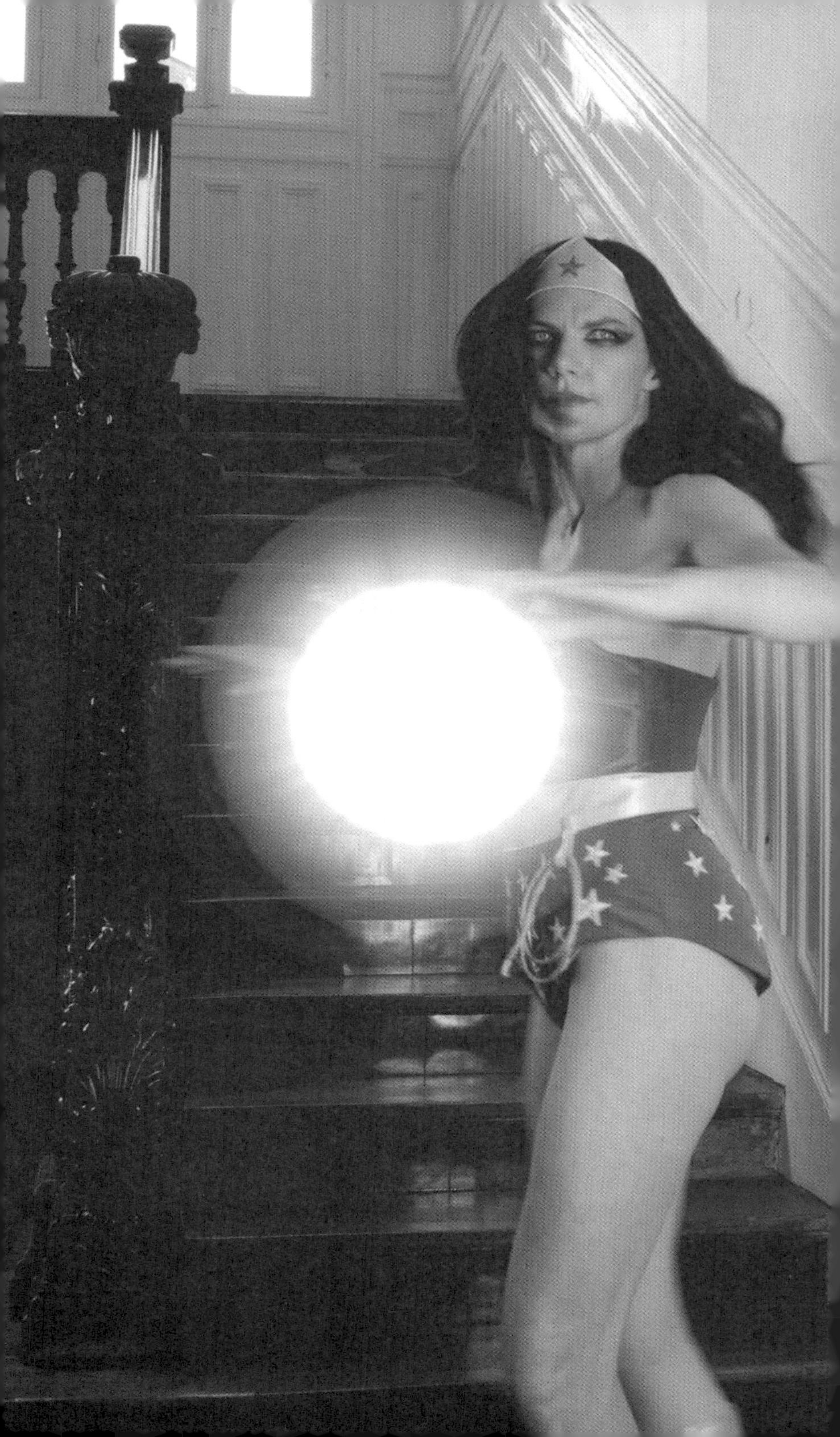

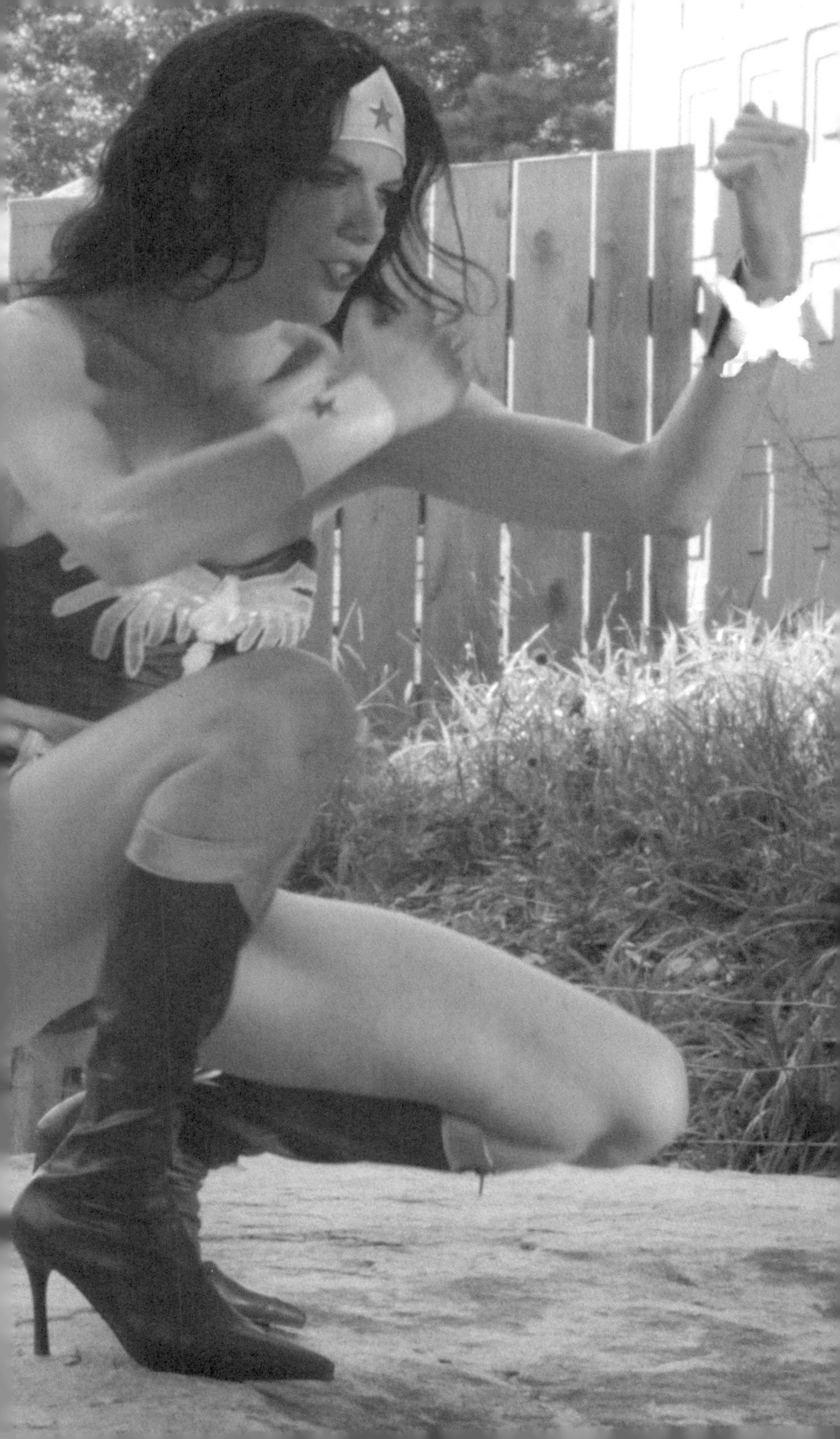

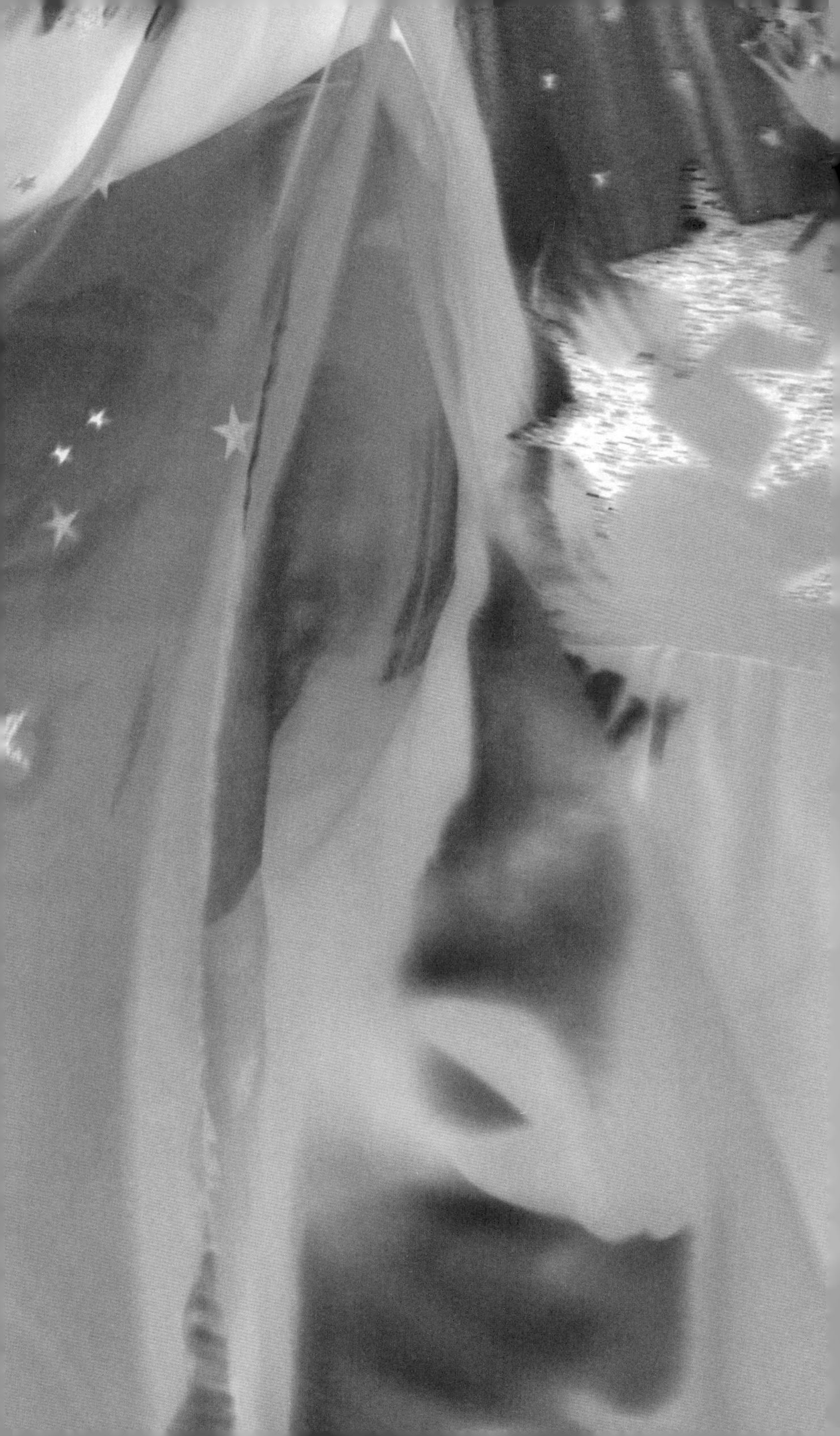

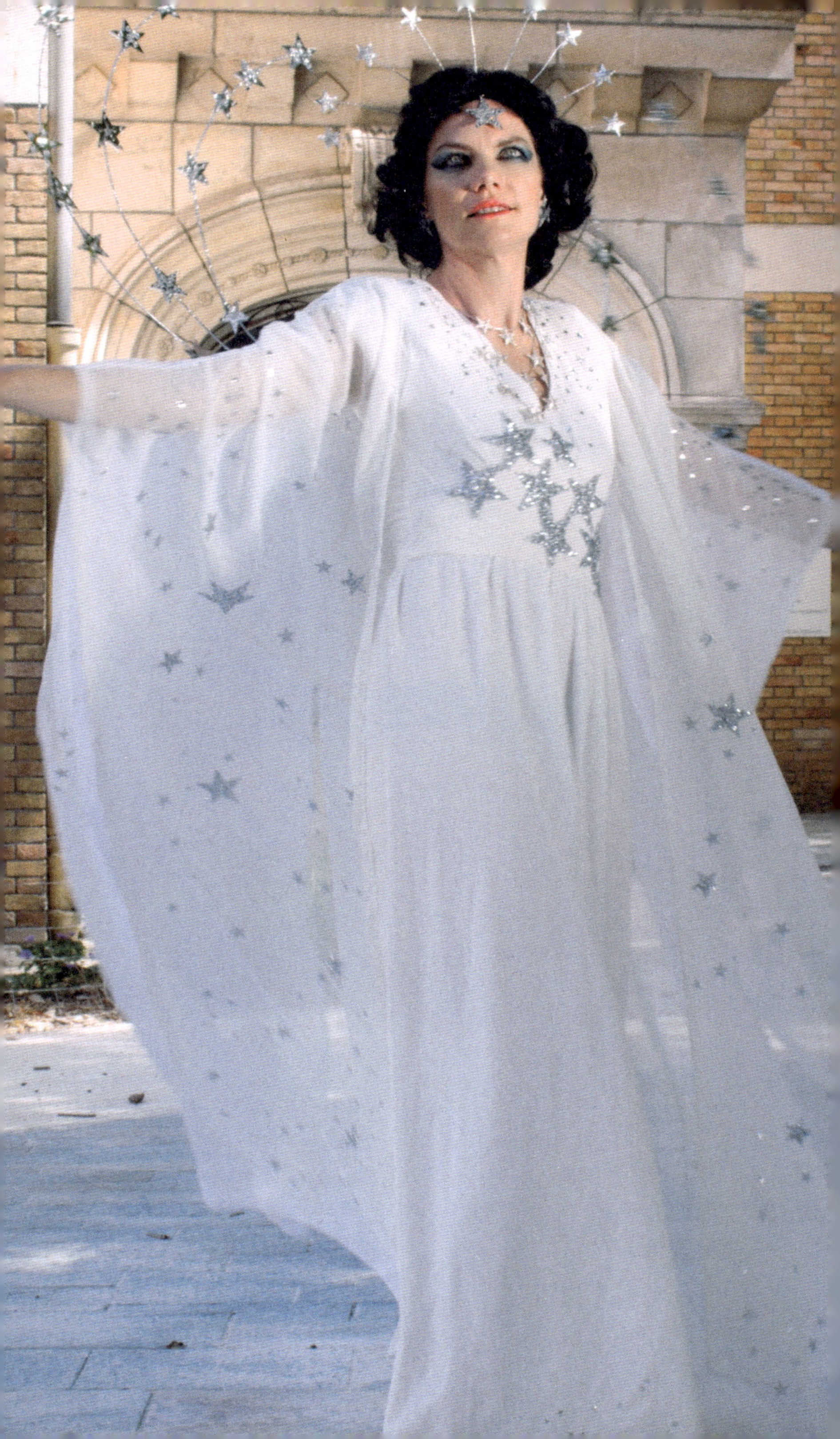

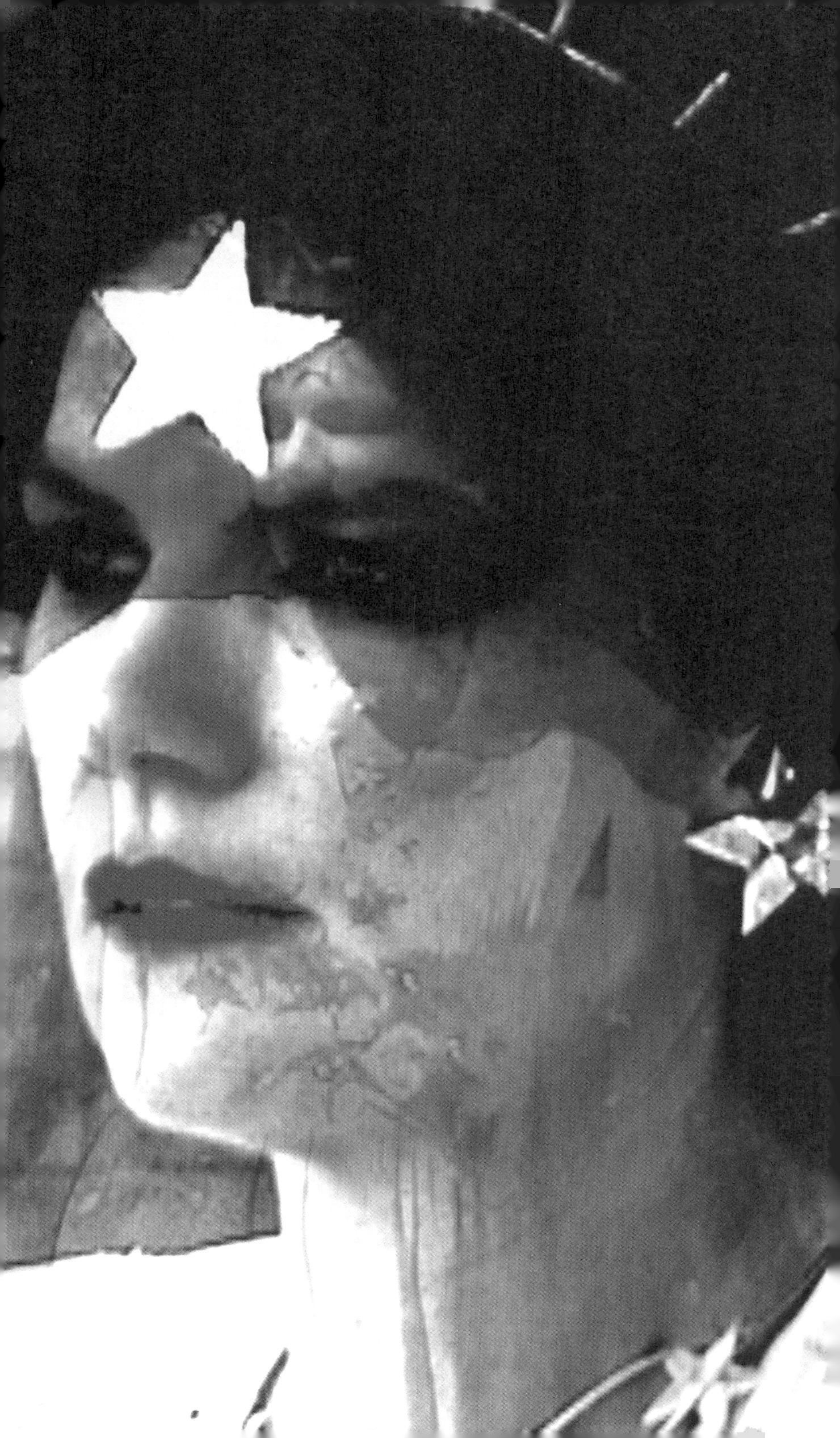

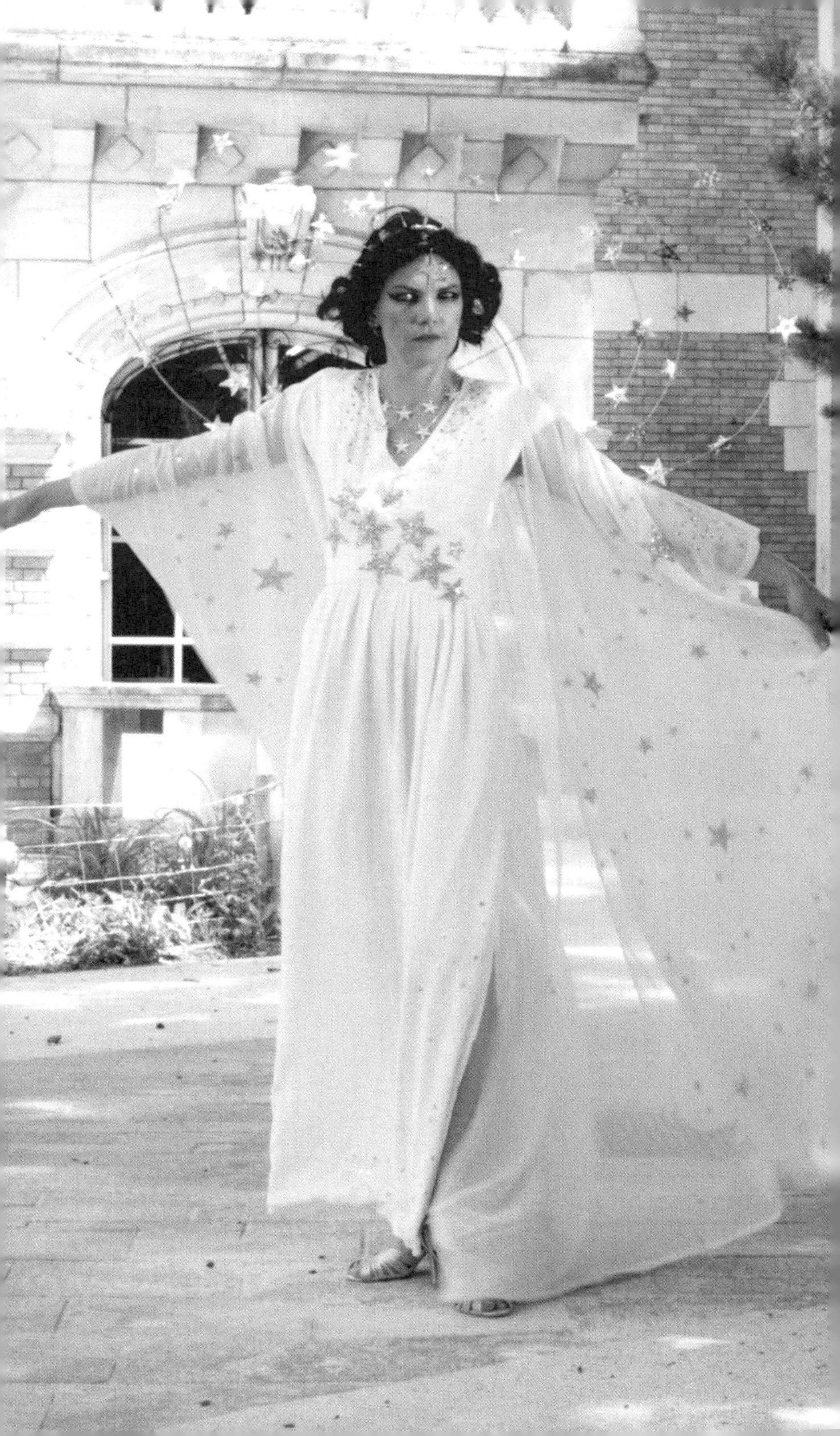

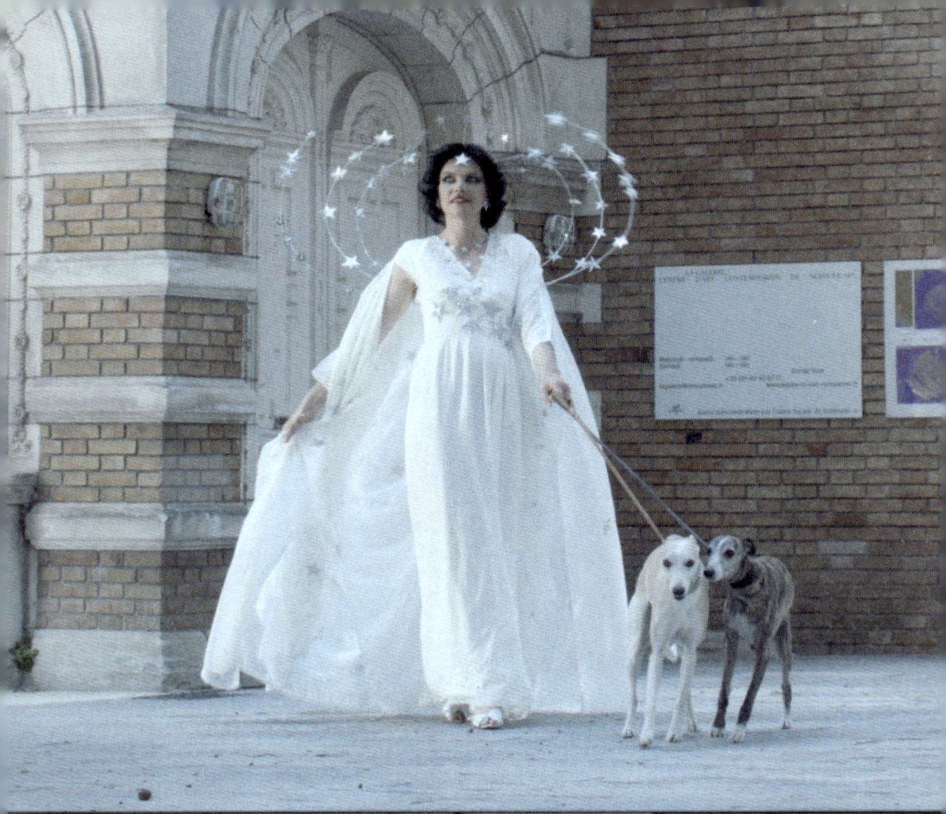

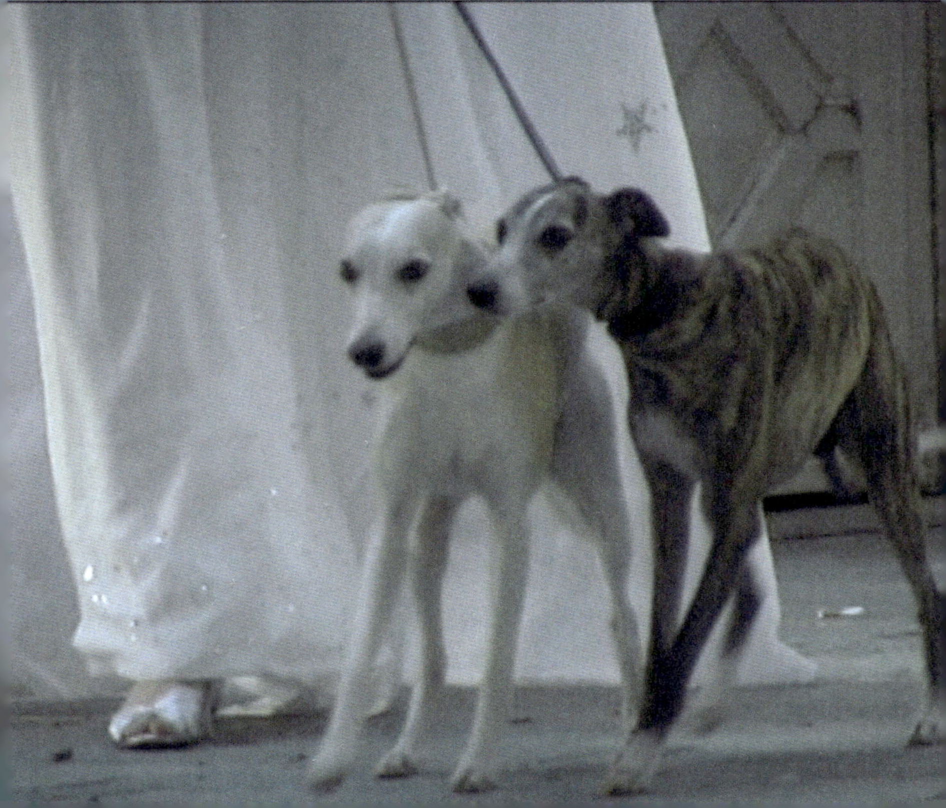

BODY DOUBLE XXXIX

12'44"
AFTER DAVID CRONENBERG'S DEAD RINGERS (1988)
2024

CAST
JEAN BICHE, FRANÇOIS CHAIGNAUD, ALESSANDRO DE MARINIS, GIN GIN MEZZANOTTE

IMAGES
LOÏC BOVON

FIRST ASSISTANT CAMERA
LARA MZAYEK

EDITING & SPECIAL EFFECTS
BRICE DELLSPERGER

FIRST ASSISTANT DIRECTOR
ROMANE DEAL

MUSIC
SEELAND BY NEU! (1975)

COSTUME DESIGN
SUNNY BÉZY

COLORIST
JACKY LEFRESNE

GAFFER
LEO ROUSSEL

HEAD CARPENTER
ROBERT FERNYS

SUPPORT SET DECORATORS
STEFFEN MISCHKE, MARC SUSKI

DRIVER
ALEXANDRE AYED

CATERING
MATTHIAS FABRY

PRODUCTION
BRICE DELLSPERGER; AIR DE PARIS; CENTRE NATIONAL DES ARTS PLASTIQUES, CNAP; FONDATION DES ARTISTES; TRAMPOLINE ASSOCIATION, FRANCE; DORTMUNDER KUNSTVEREIN, GERMANY

EXECUTIVE PRODUCTION
BEAU BIZARRE

SUPPLIER PANAVISION FRANCE

COMMISSIONED BY
DORTMUNDER KUNSTVEREIN
(REBEKKA SEUBERT)

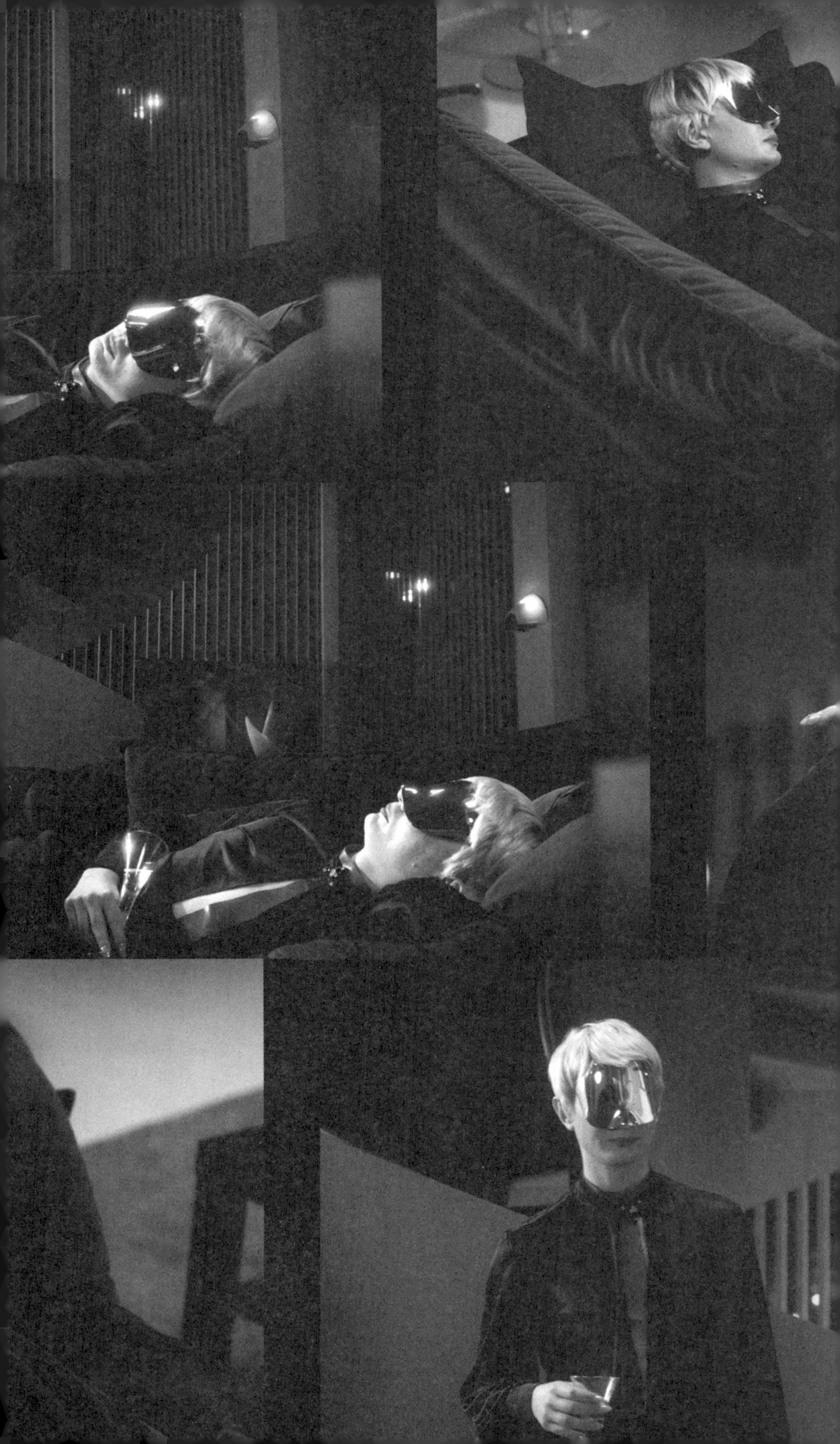

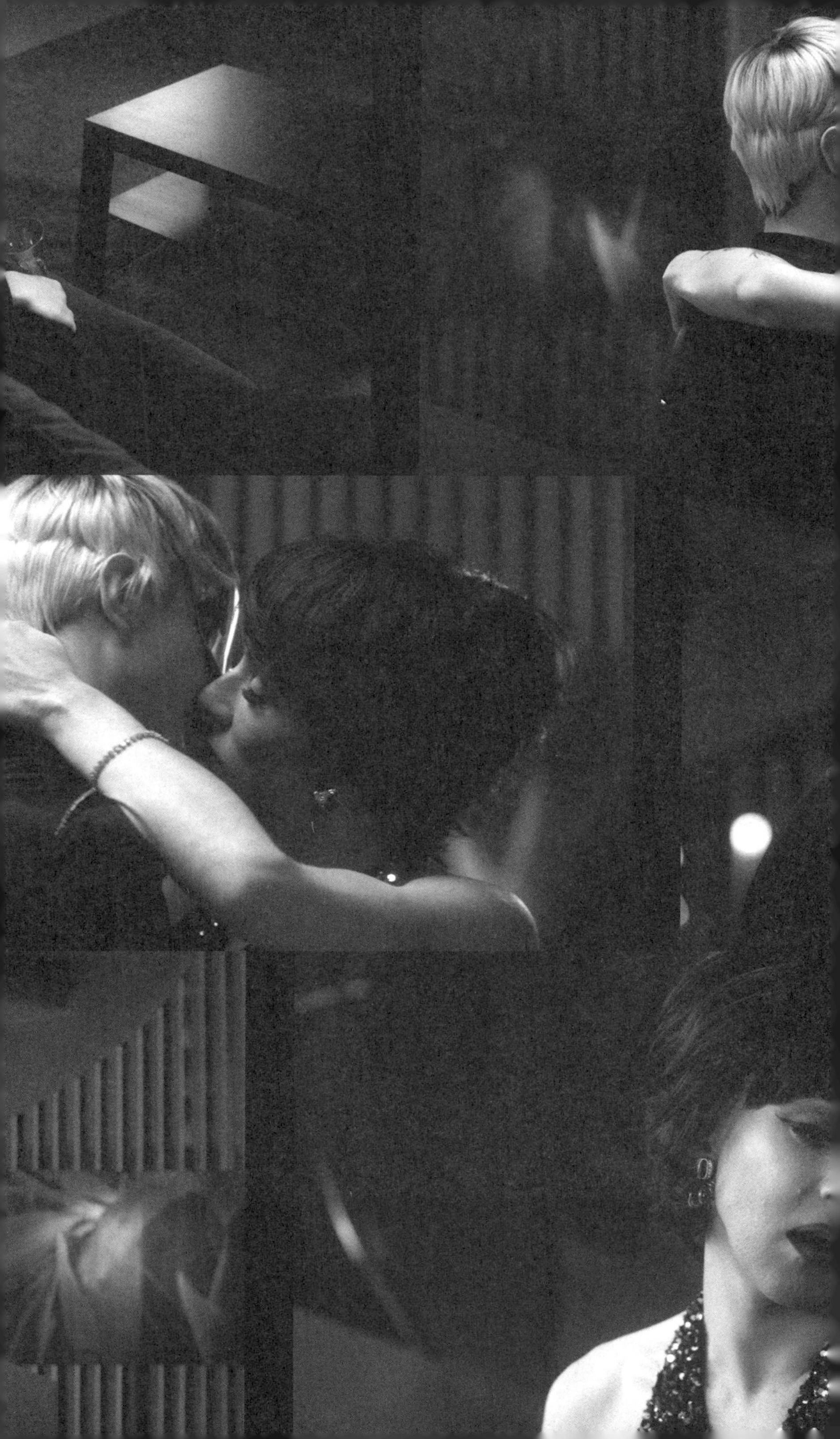

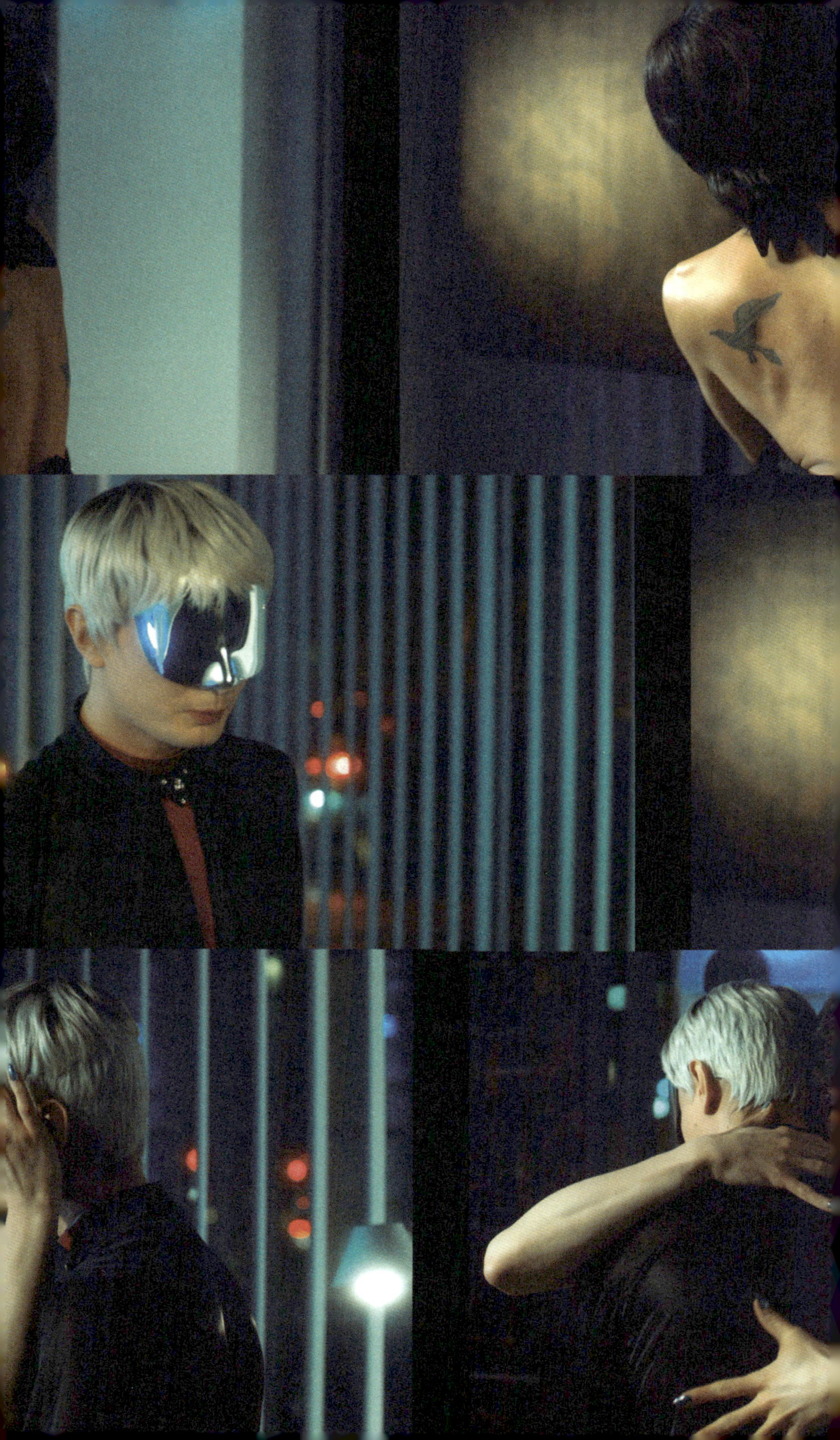

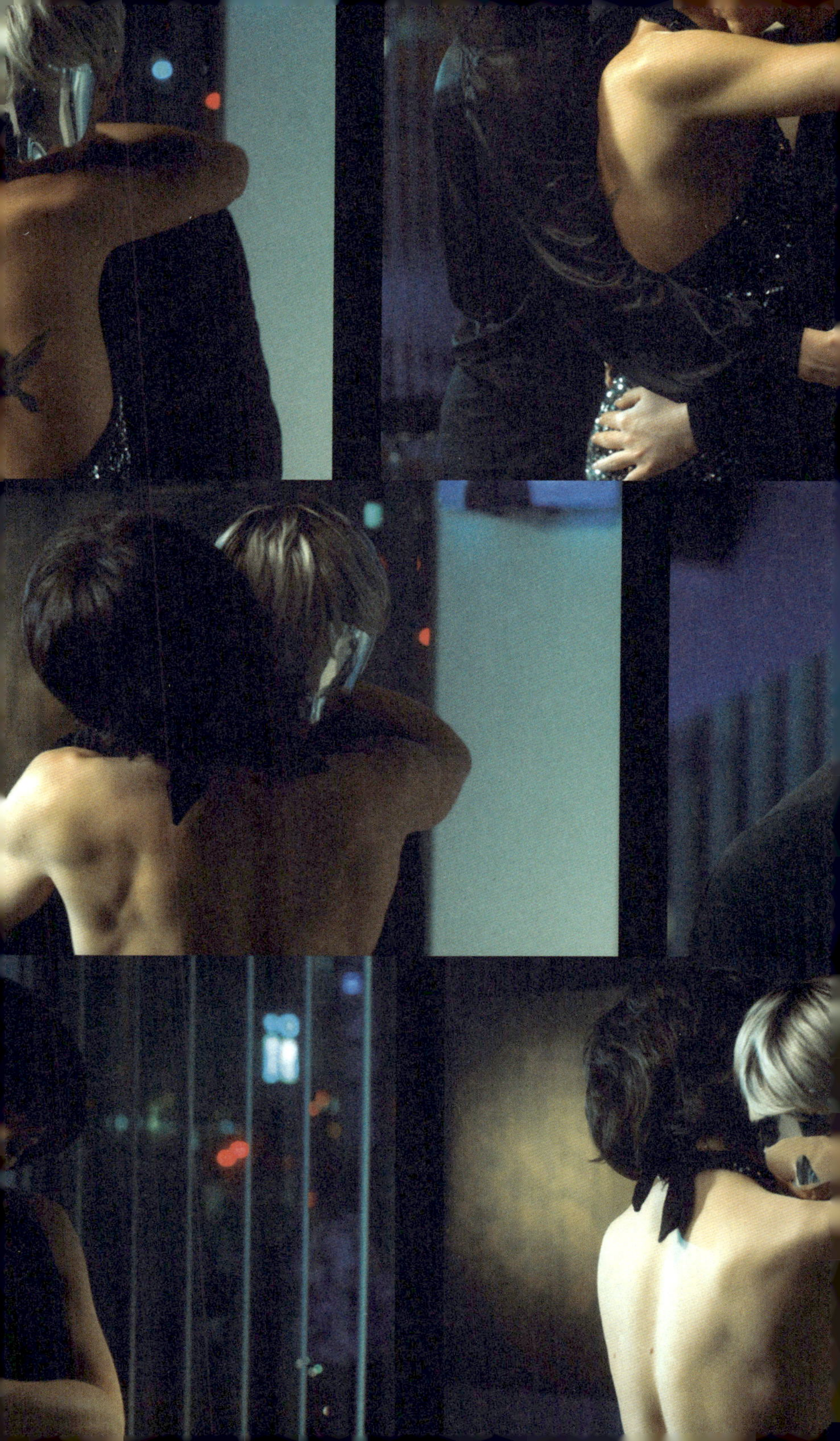

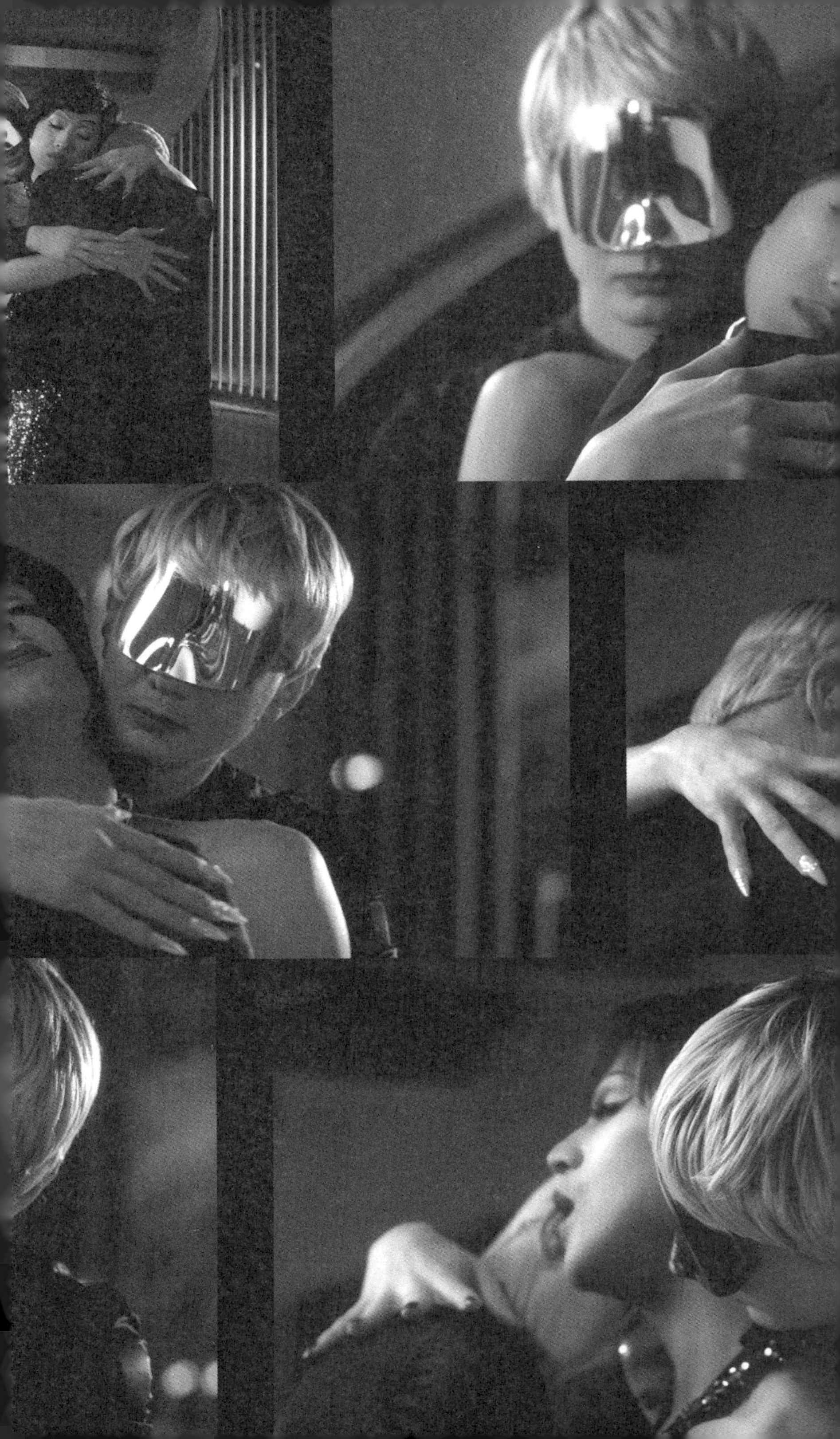

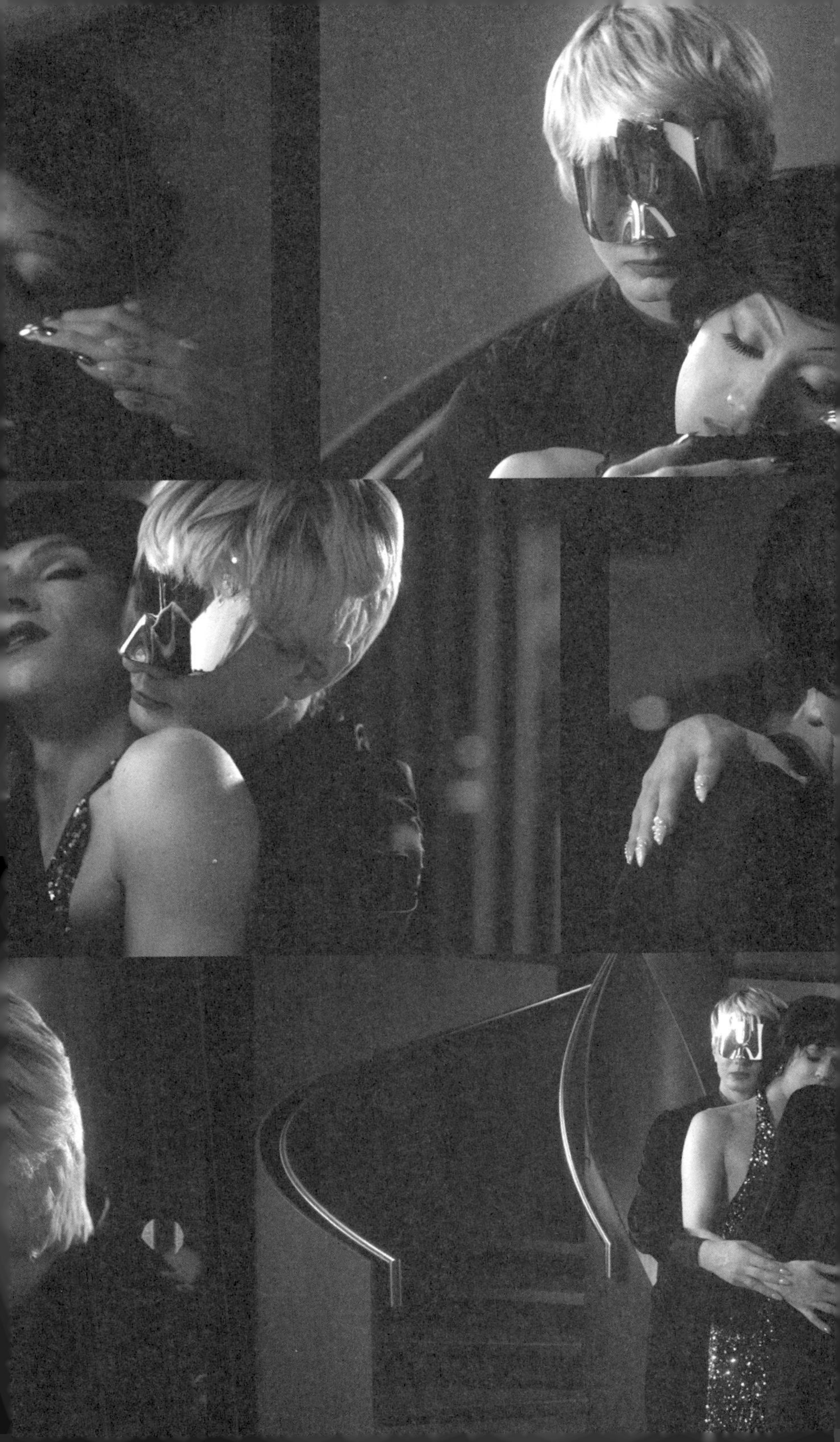

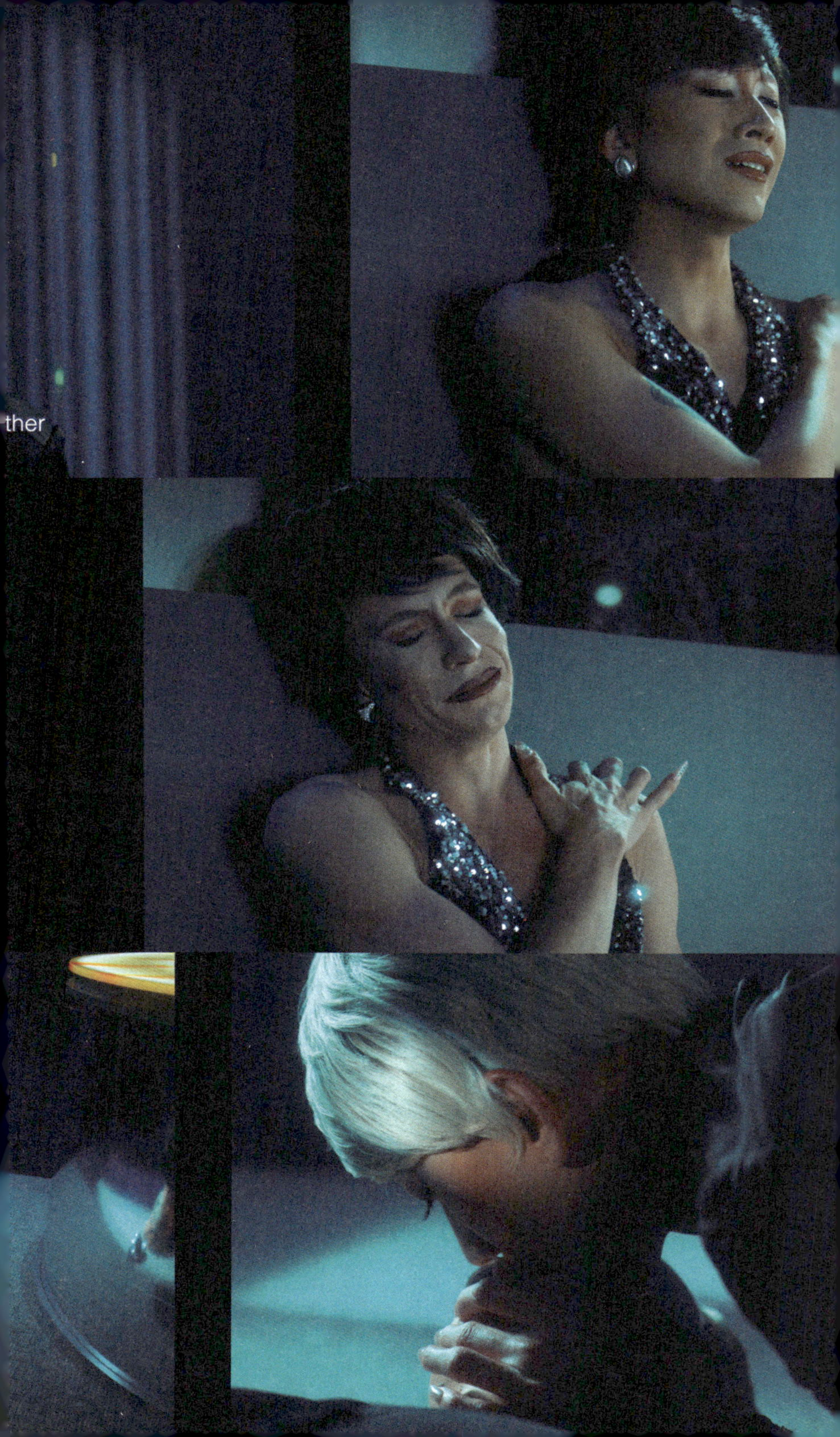

ther

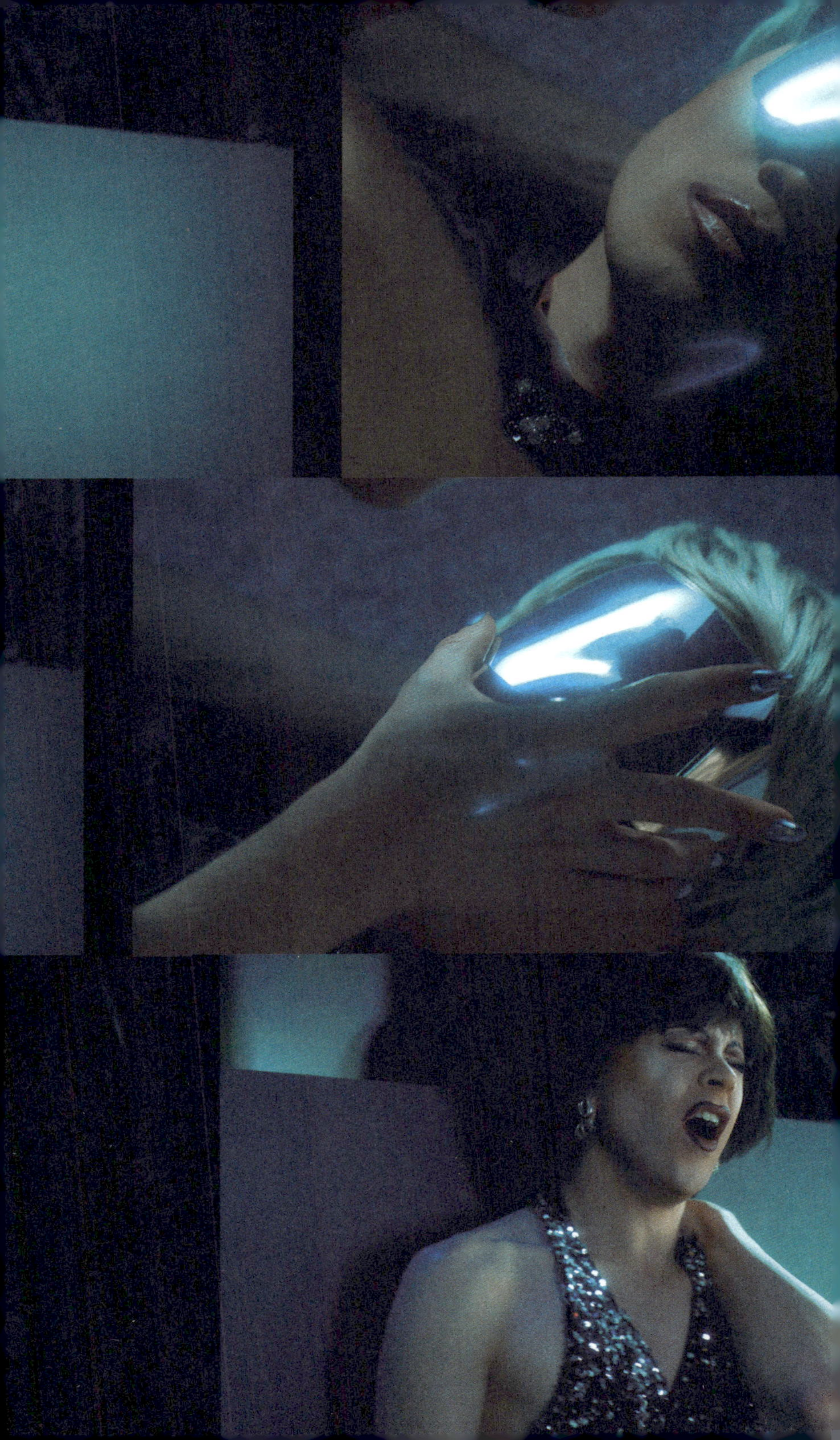

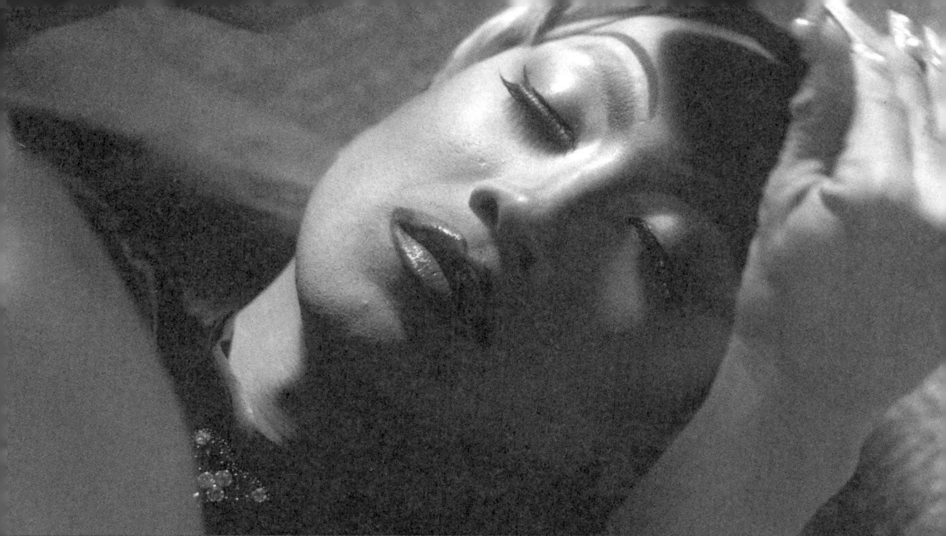
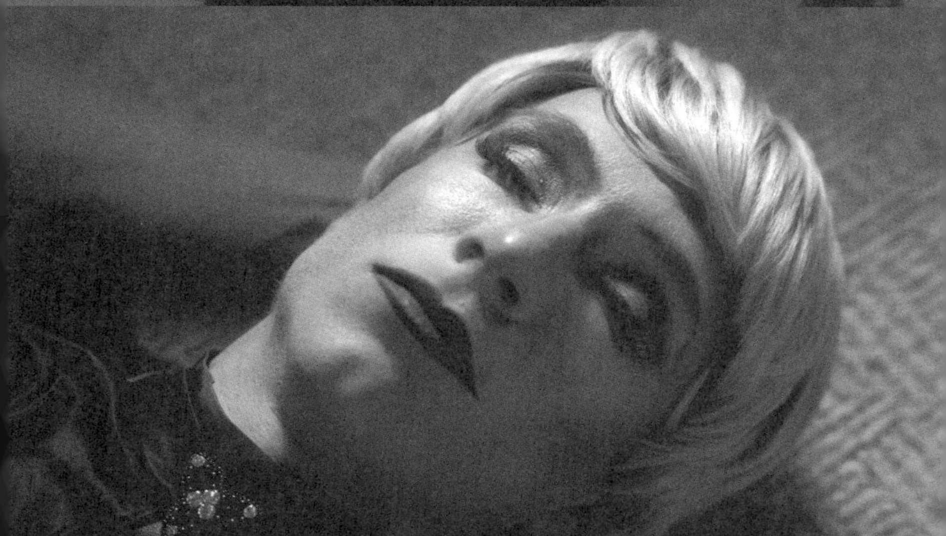
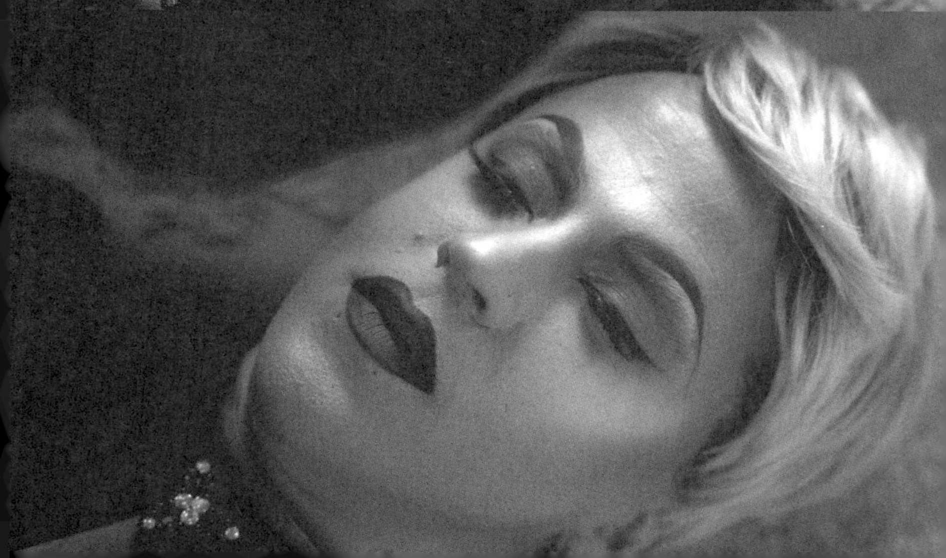

BODY DOUBLE XL

1'45''
AFTER BRIAN DE PALMA'S BLOW OUT (1981)
2024

CAST, IMAGES, EDITING & SPECIAL EFFECTS
BRICE DELLSPERGER

FIRST ASSISTANT DIRECTOR
ROBIN LADIER

PRODUCTION
BRICE DELLSPERGER

COLLECTION
FRAC OCCITANIE MONTPELLIER, FRANCE

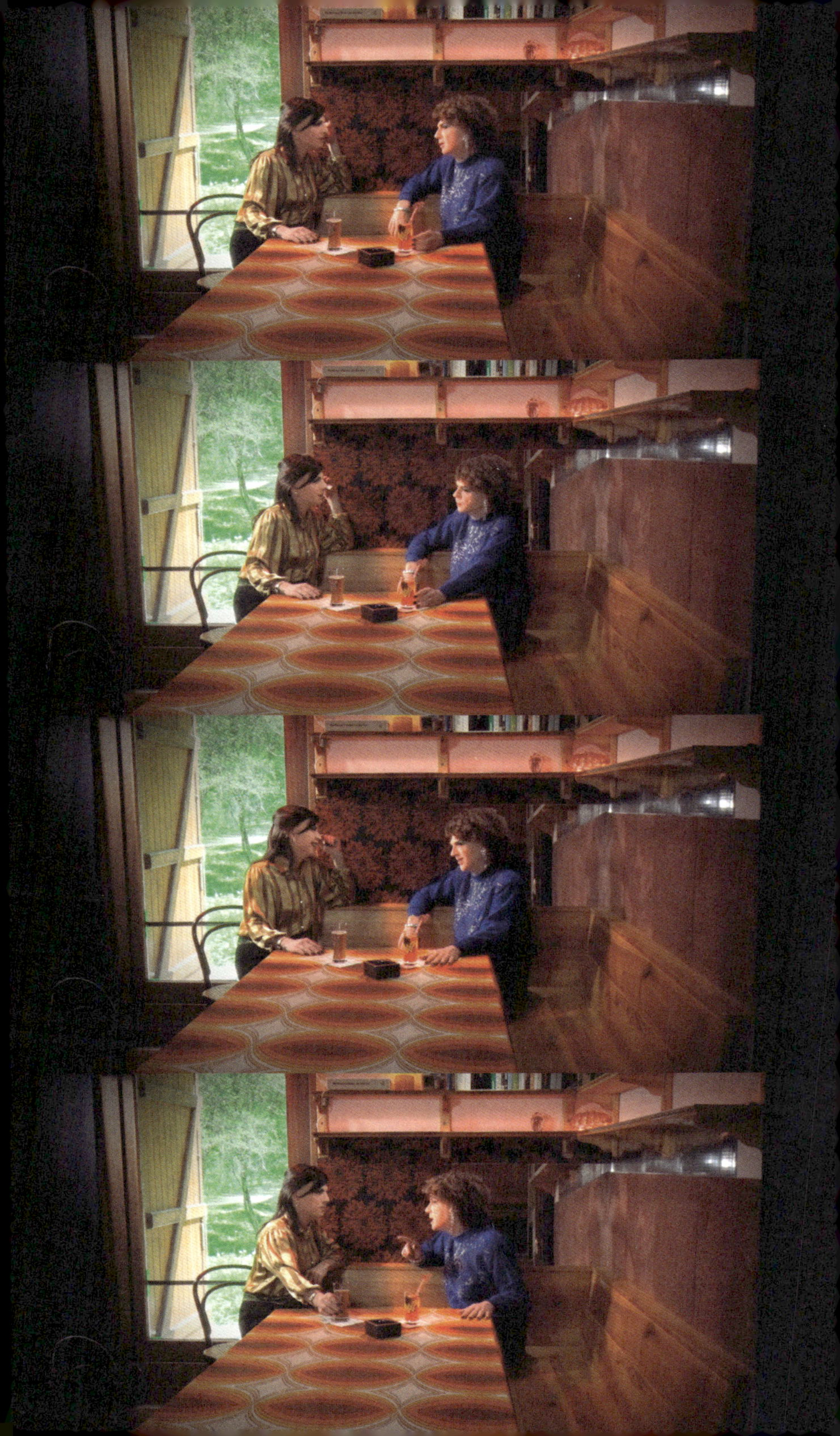

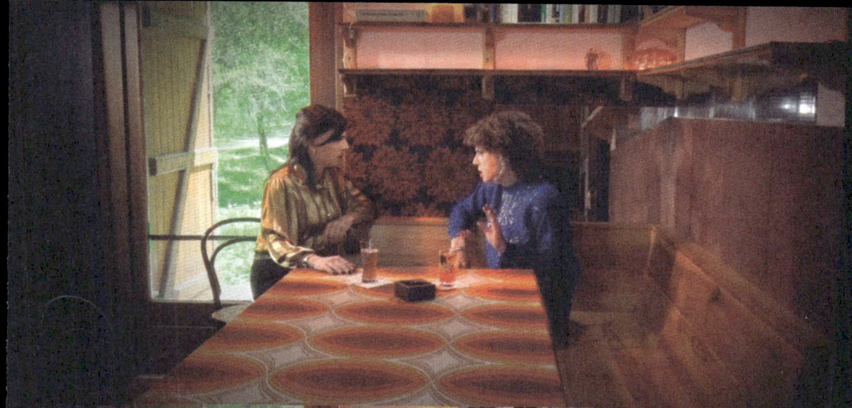

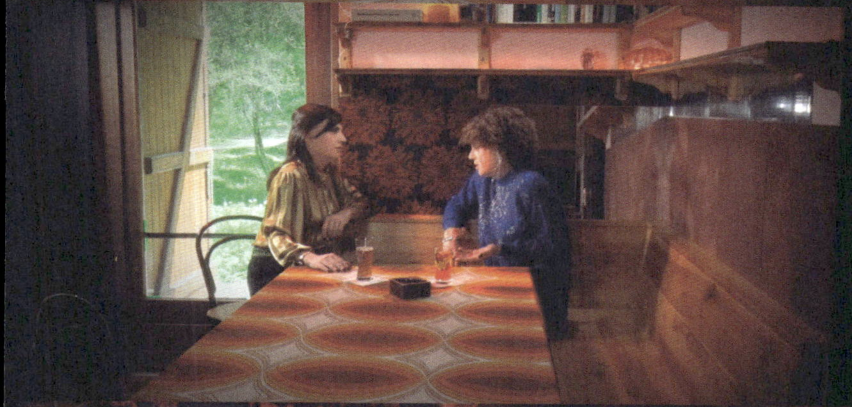

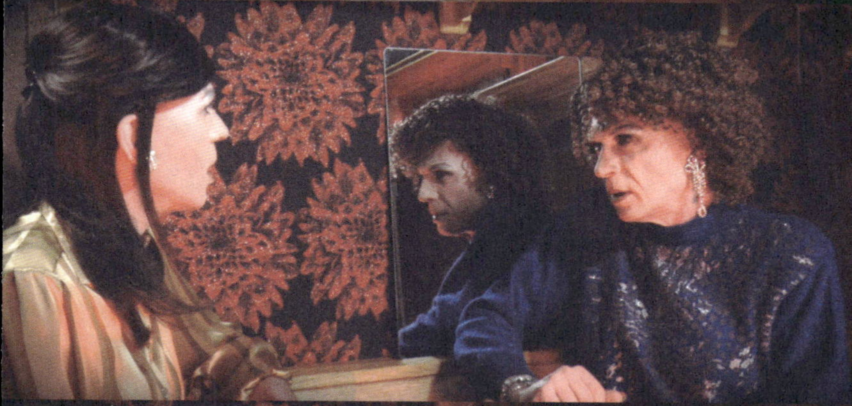

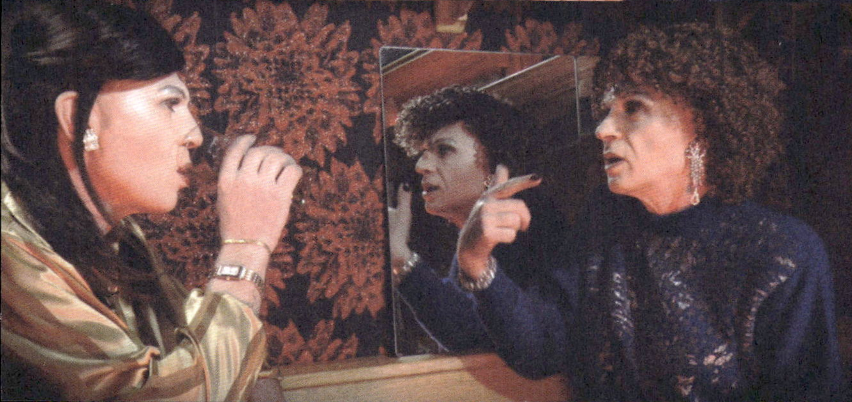

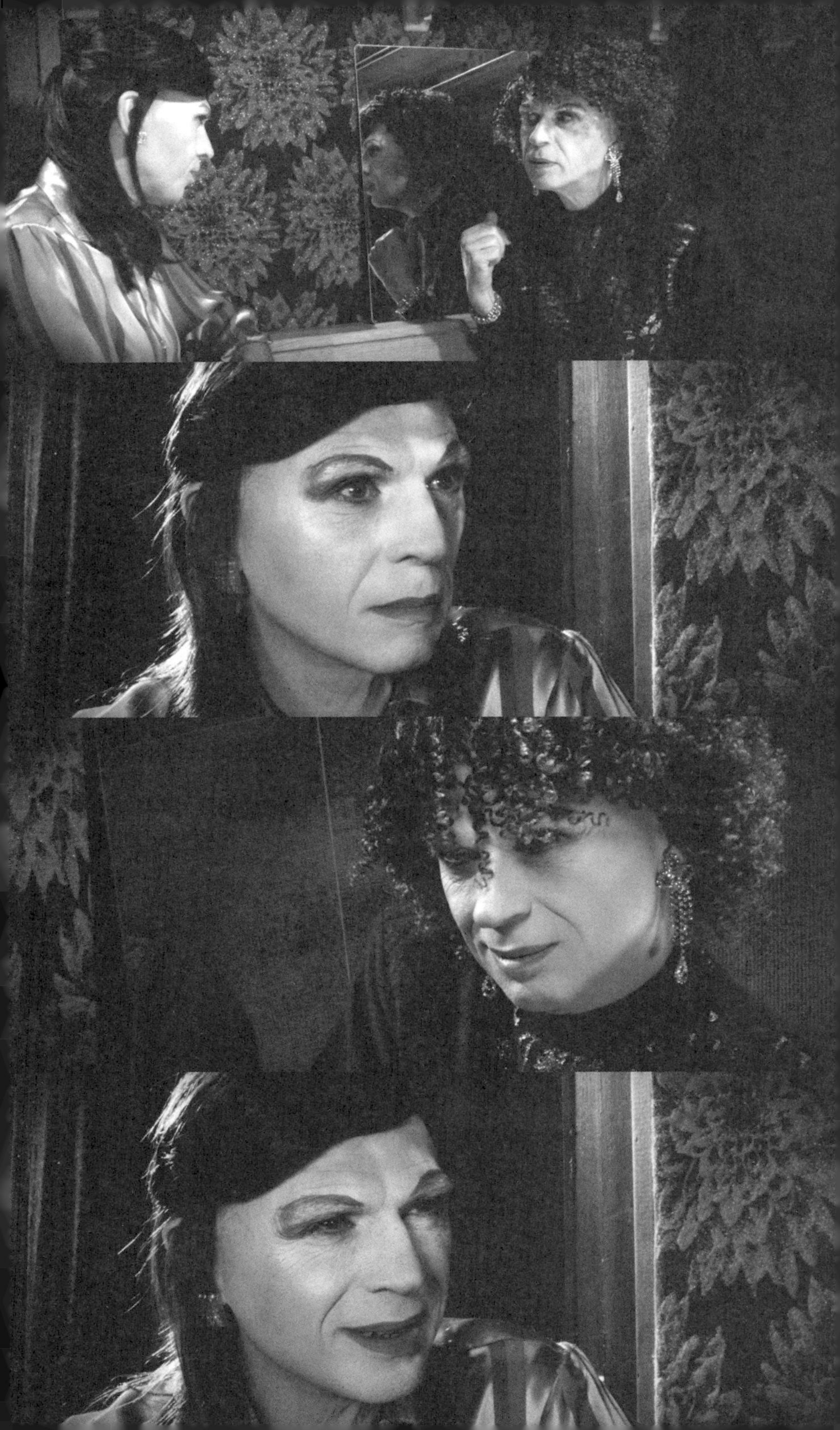

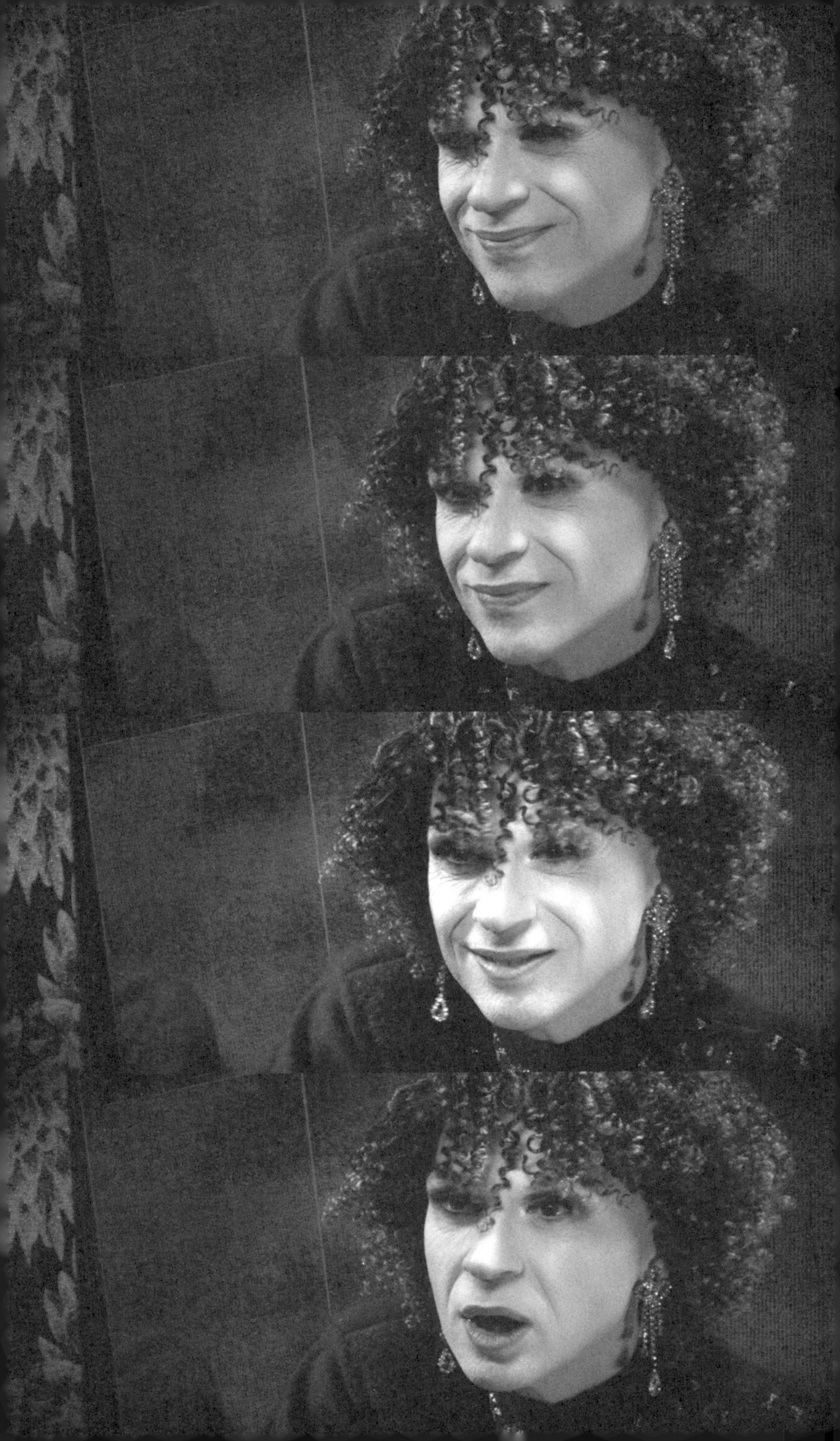

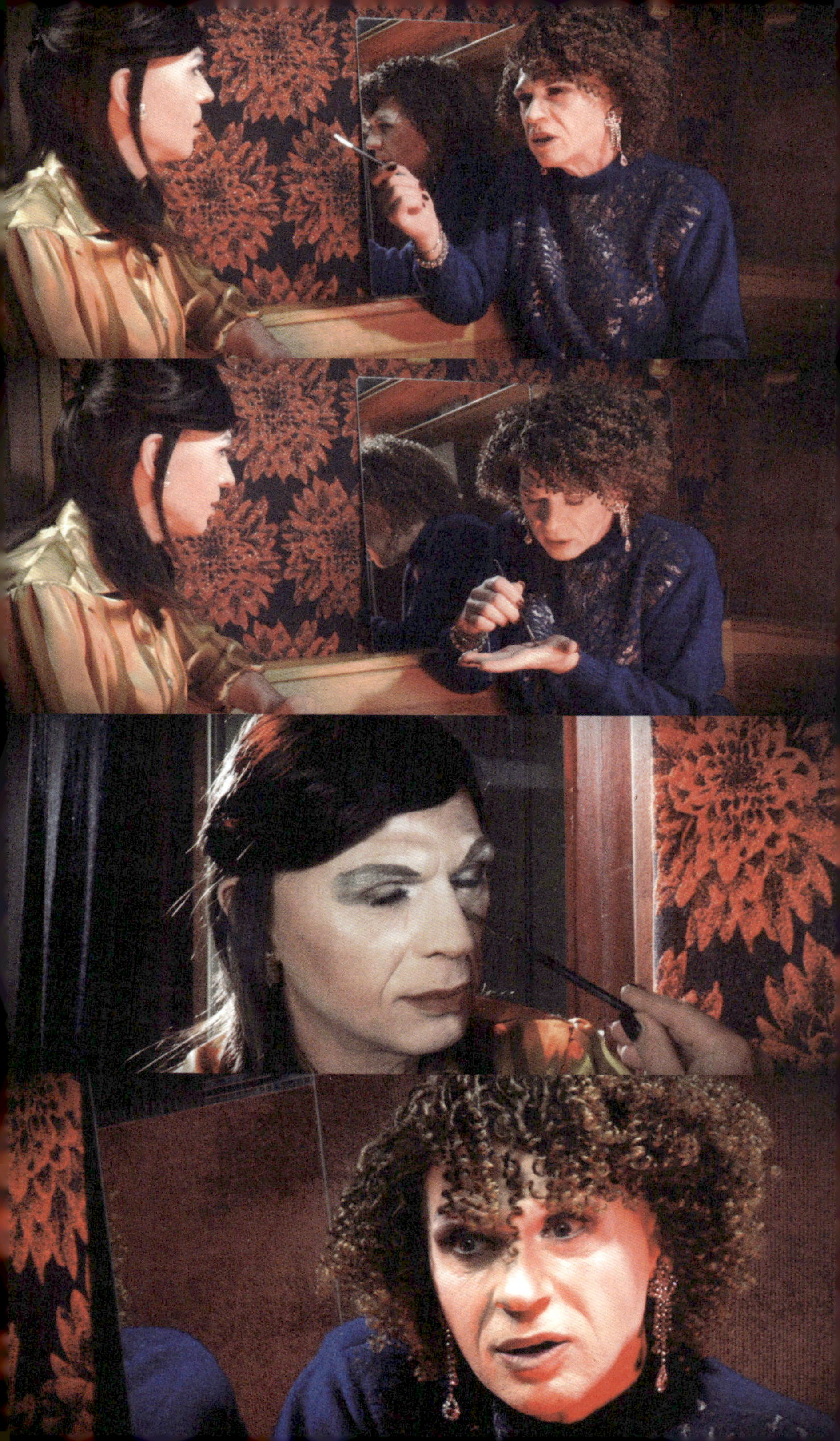

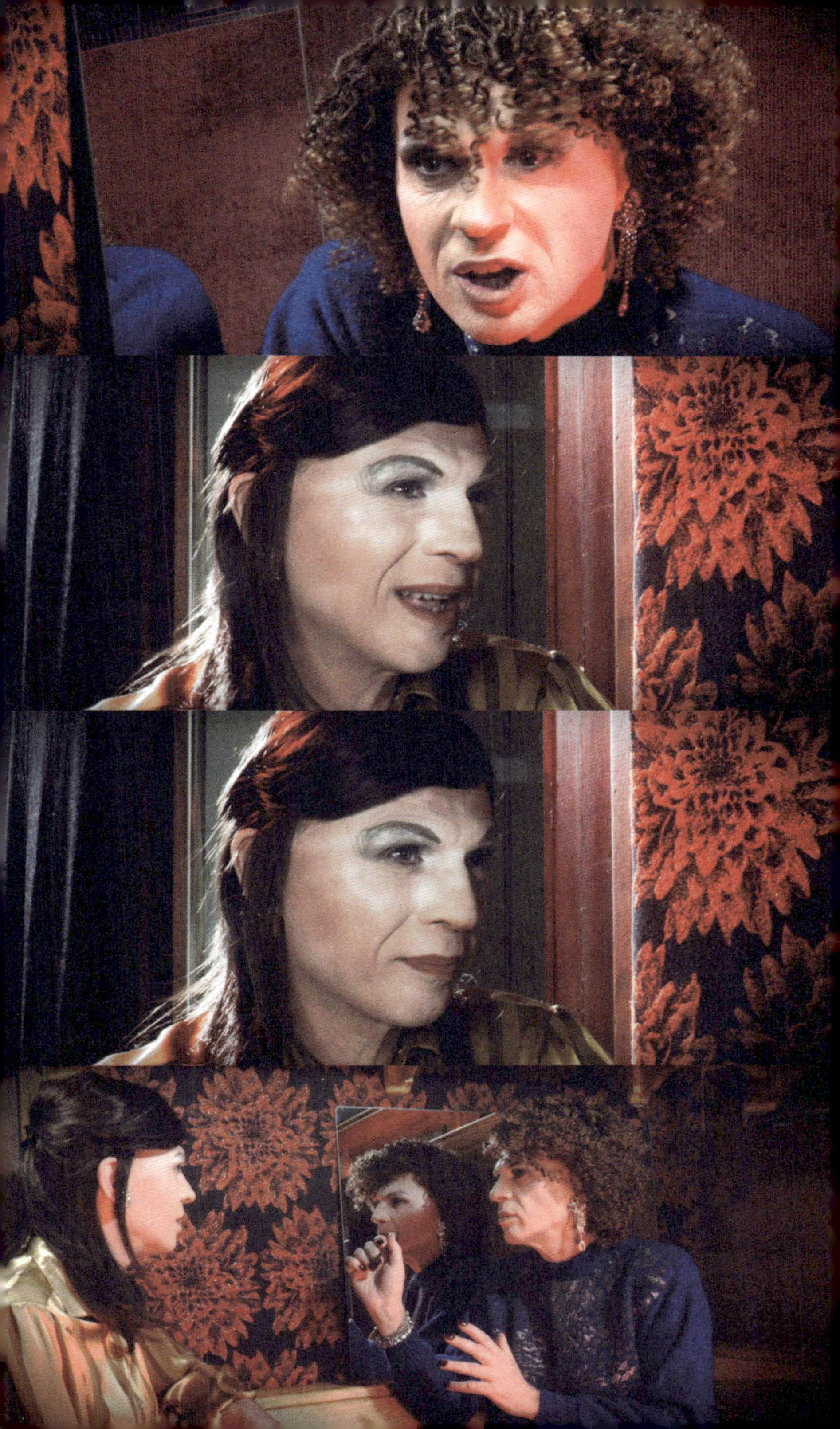

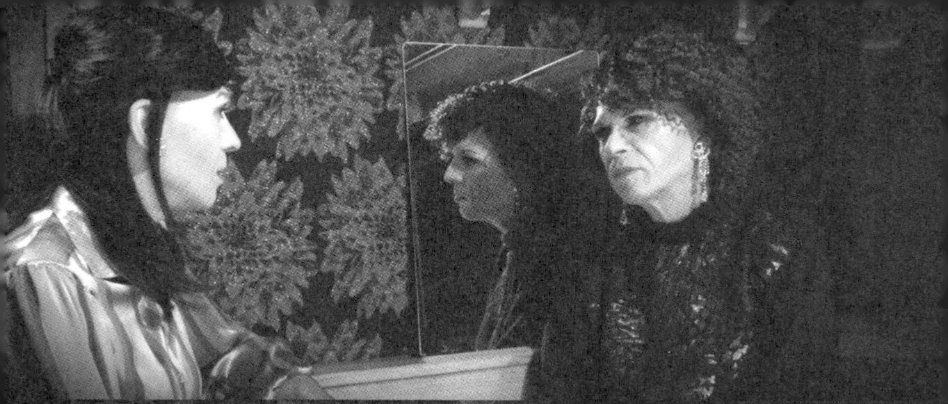

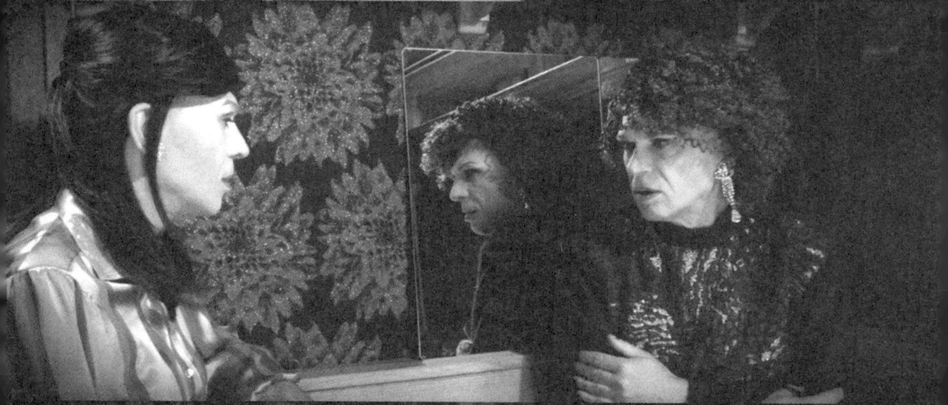

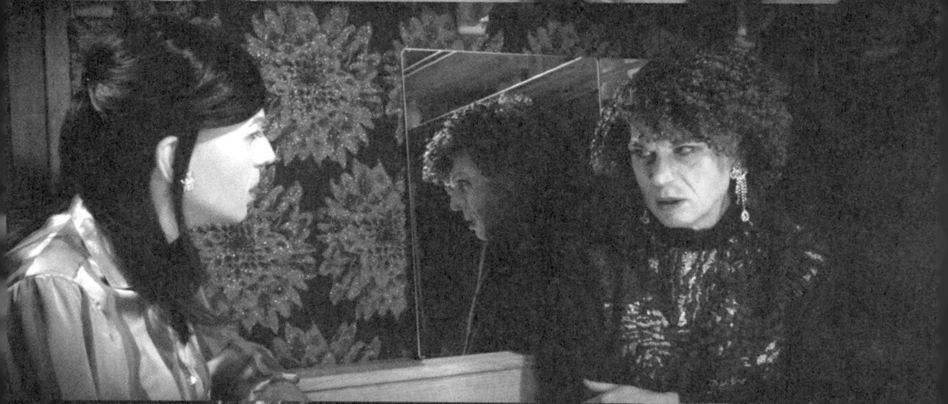

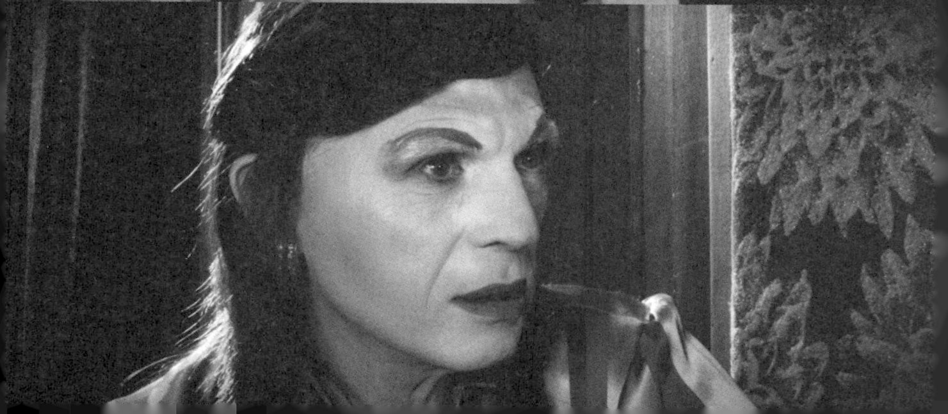

DOUBLE TROUBLE

BY EVAN MOFFITT

The essay *Double Trouble; Brice Dellsperger according to Evan Moffitt* was originally commissioned by TextWork, the editorial platform of the Fondation Pernod Ricard, supported by the French Ministry of Culture, and published in 2025.

INT: ELEVATOR – NIGHT[1]

In closeup, a finger anxiously jabs button number six. It belongs to a fashionably dressed woman in a white blouse and cream trench coat, her dark red lipstick matching the color of her feathered hair. We see her through a fish-eye lens placed roughly where the button should be. She seems like she's in a hurry. Then, the camera cuts to the elevator door as it slowly opens, and this time we see through her eyes: on the landing, a blonde woman in a black leather coat and gloves, her eyes shielded by dark glasses, approaches menacingly with a razor. Cut, cut, cut, cut—we switch abruptly back and forth between blond and redhead, foreshadowing the fatal blows. Finally, the door closes on them both, entombing killer and victim in a flying steel coffin.

But something is wrong here. It isn't the presence of a homicidal maniac, nor the strangely impassive expressions on both women's faces. It's the fact that redhead and blonde, victim and slasher, are the same woman, which is to say, one man: the artist Brice Dellsperger, who plays both roles in drag. Cinephiles may recognize the scene in his *Body Double 1* (1995) as the first murder in Brian De Palma's 1980 thriller *Dressed to Kill*. In the spirit of a lip-sync, Dellsperger has even used the film's original audio for his reenactment. De Palma's preposterous melodrama is perfectly suited for the camp ventriloquism of a drag queen sashaying across a nightclub stage, and so we might be forgiven for thinking this is all an elaborate comedic routine. Dellsperger's vaudevillian vamp makes us laugh until we suspect the joke may no longer be funny.

Metaphorical cracks start to show in the mirrors which line the interior walls of the elevator. The final frames of Dellsperger's video, in which we see both women reflected together, could only have been possible with the aid of a body double standing in for one of the roles played by the actor-director—a trick that gives the work and ensuing series its name. In De Palma's original, we see the lethal stab reflected in a convex mirror mounted in the upper corner of the carriage; in Dellsperger's version, that mirror has become the camera. The artist quite literally sends us through the looking glass, a move he has repeated almost obsessively in the three decades since. His forty "Body Doubles", painstaking recreations of scenes from his favorite movies with genders swapped and key details subtly altered, are self-reflexively turned in on themselves. That deceptively simple act of dress-up from 1995—like the very best art, a difficult thing made to seem easy—is part of a monumental undertaking the artist continues to this day.

> As soon as Dellsperger's vast archive of "Body Doubles" starts to cohere into a vision of the world, the reel sputters. Gender glitches. Identity malfunctions, its image repeated until rendered almost meaningless. We watch in bemused horror as the semiotics of cinema self-implode. Dellsperger reperforms scenes until they start to fall apart. Endless copies only prove that their sources are simulacra. As Judith Butler has argued, this is itself a hallmark of drag, which "constitutes the mundane way in which genders are appropriated, theatricalized, worn, and done; it implies that all gendering is a kind of impersonation and approximation."[2]

Duly disguised, Dellsperger has snuck into the projectionist's booth and swapped out all the parts for poorer ones, heightening our awareness of the medium's technological illusionism. For those like him born in the twentieth century, film (along with TV) bears a singular responsibility for what Eve Kosofsky Sedgwick called our "subjectivation," or the way we understand ourselves and others, such as our notions of masculine and feminine.[3] Like Dellsperger's sometimes confounding edits, those notions no longer make sense—if indeed they ever did. In Dellsperger's hands, straight blockbuster cinema becomes an absurd, unworkable thing, much like heterosexuality itself. "If heterosexuality is an impossible imitation of itself, an imitation that performatively constitutes itself as the original," Butler continues, "then the imitative parody of 'heterosexuality'—when and where it exists in gay cultures—is always and only an imitation of an imitation, a copy of a copy, for which there is no original."[4]

Perhaps nowhere is heterosexuality more grotesquely caricatured than in the films of Brian De Palma. Like his 1984 neo-noir satire *Body Double*, *Dressed to Kill* is a camp mash-up of the Alfred Hitchcock classics *Psycho* (1960) and *Rear Window* (1954), two films that conflate bloodlust with the cross-dressing and voyeurism at the heart of Dellsperger's project. Men are aloof, women are lascivious, and a psycho-killer psychiatrist murders because they are both—or neither. De Palma pathologizes dysphoria by repeatedly presenting it to us in a mirror: while the surfaces of those mirrors are unbroken, the subjects we see in them are all cracked up. But in Dellsperger's reenactments, which expose all their cracks, those subjects are made whole. Every role is inverted, and every actor, whether cisgender or gender-non-conforming, performs in drag. It's all too fitting that the murder in *Body Double 1* happens in a space that resembles a closet, that architecture of queer and trans subjectivation. A space which, according to Sedgwick, was constructed around the binaries of inside/out that attended to early twentieth-century stereotypes of "sexual inversion".[5] By killing himself—or rather, his double's body double—Dellsperger had found a way to break free.

INT. CANNES – LATE 1970S

A film plays on a living room TV. "Why, I'm all dressed up and ready to fall in love!" purrs Babs Johnson, played by the actress and drag queen Divine. Her silver polka dot halter and angular brows are in soft focus, her movements strangely glitchy. The film is John Waters' *Pink Flamingos* (1972), and Brice Dellsperger is enraptured. Of course, this isn't my memory, nor is it precisely Dellsperger's, who can't recall the exact date he first saw Waters' notorious film on a degraded bootleg VHS. Like the copy itself, the details are blurry. It may have been years later—but he remembers that the tape passed from one friend to another, its magnetic Mylar gradually losing luster. This was par for the course back then: "My generation was copying all the time," he says.[6] Tapes recorded from the radio, illicit dupes of Cocteau Twins and Sisters of Mercy albums, were made and given as precious tokens. Copying something was a way of holding onto it.

Cannes may be a seasonal destination of the film industry, but it was hardly the center of the cultural universe during Dellsperger's childhood there, and like any gay kid, the budding artist hoarded whatever media could offer him a vision of himself, however distorted—and by extension the promise of escape. He would annotate the TV Guide at his parents' home to find the reruns of films and TV shows he liked, especially those with strong female leads. He loved the divas of *Dynasty*, *Charlie's Angels*, and *The Bionic Woman*, and was fascinated that these series used wigged men as their stunt doubles.[7] How fabulous to don long blonde tresses and go flying through the air!

The first female TV action stars were a departure from the oppressive gender ideology of the postwar era, even if they were stereotypically feminine in appearance. Dellsperger describes this as the "washing machine of gender" where everything is always turning and nothing is ever "right-side up"; from an early age, he refused to get clean. Instead, through his practice, he became the women he idolized, using a medium of projected light to project himself onto the identities of others. "I'm trying to play with identification," Dellsperger has said. "I believe that we identify with the characters that we like, up to the point of wanting to resemble them."[8] Indeed, as Butler notes, "identification and desire can coexist, and…their formulation in terms of mutually exclusive oppositions serves a heterosexual matrix."[9] As a very gay man knows, you can both want to be someone and want to fuck them at the same time.

> According to José Esteban Muñoz, "identifying with an object, person, lifestyle, history, political ideology, religious orientation, and so on, means also simultaneously and partially counteridentifying, as well as only partially identifying, with different aspects of their social and psychic world."[10] Dellsperger's "Body Doubles" recreate and reroute the identification he felt for those TV divas into something much more psychologically entangled. Rather, they recall James Baldwin's having recognized himself as a young boy in Bette Davis, with her "pop-eyes popping", when he first saw her in a movie matinee: "I was held…by the tense intelligence of the forehead, the disaster of the lips: and when she moved, she moved just like" a Black woman.[11] This famous white actress thousands of miles away from young Baldwin in real space and a million more in social standing was nonetheless proof that someone like him, which is to say an effeminate man with big eyes like hers, could command the stage. "I had discovered that my infirmity might not be my doom," he writes; "my infirmity, or infirmities, might be forged into weapons."[12]

Muñoz describes this move, which is both a projection onto the Other and a simultaneous turn away from them, as "disidentification", and it is a crucial element of Dellsperger's films. Disidentification "is a strategy that works on and against dominant ideology" such as gender: "Instead of buckling under the pressures of dominant ideology (identification, assimilation) or attempting to break free of its inescapable sphere (counteridentification, utopianism)" it "tries to transform a cultural logic from within".[13] More importantly, for Dellsperger, as "for Baldwin, disidentification is more than simply an interpretive turn or a psychic maneuver; it is…a survival strategy."[14]

> In 2017, more than two decades after his first *Body Double*, Dellsperger staged his own version of a

scene from another Brian De Palma film, *Carrie* (1976), for *Body Double 32*. Rather than the memorable prom night bloodbath from the climax of the film, he chose a more innocuous scene from the beginning of the movie because he says it reminded him of getting bullied in the locker room as a young boy. By this point, Dellsperger had long stopped starring in all of his videos; the nonbinary actor Alex Wetter plays Carrie, along with all the other girls in the locker room—some nearly three dozen of them. With a soapy synthesizer score composed for the project by Didier Blasco, a collaborator on several "Body Doubles", Dellsperger has drawn out De Palma's tracking shot into an absurd, slow-motion titillation. When Carrie gets her period in the shower, we see her first reflected in the pipes; then, suddenly, she is everywhere. All the other girls, who previously had their own hair and makeup and personalities—if also identical faces—are now unmistakably Carrie too, their hands simultaneously covered in the same blood. "It's a curse," Dellsperger explains.[15] A revenge spell? Perhaps: De Palma's version is even harder to watch, as Carrie's shame becomes an excuse for the other girls to torment her. Unlike her, they've all been through this before. But the incessant repetition of *Body Double 32* goes further: it multiplies identity like a virus, one that inoculates those it infects. Revisiting a site of childhood trauma by reworking a camp classic from the artist's youth, the video is an example of disidentification as survival strategy. It reminds us that because of—not *in spite of*—our differences, we are all essentially the same.

INT. NIGHTCLUB – 1995

Brice Dellsperger takes the stage. Which is to say the concrete floor and whitewashed wall of the open studios at Nice's Villa Arson, repurposed for his very first live performance, *Ladies and Gentlemen* (1995). Dressed in a black corset, heels, stockings with garters, and a red feather boa, the artist begins a sultry strip-dance before his assembled classmates. Massive Attack's "Be Thankful for What You've Got (feat. Tony Brian)" (1992) plays from a boombox. Dellsperger memorized the routine from the single's music video, in which a woman performs an acrobatic strip-tease on the stage at Raymond Revuebar, a famous burlesque club in London's Soho district. There's already a subtle gender-bend to her lip-sync of Brian's male falsetto, but in his re-performance, Dellsperger added a new twist, putting *on* his clothes instead of taking them off. The big reveal is an act of self-transformation, one that locates erotic pleasure in the social construction of gender rather than its biologically essentializing conception. It's even more fitting that in the Massive Attack video, the star dancer performs in the set of an elevator, a cubicle the same shape and size as a closet—where Dellsperger would go on to film his very first *Body Double* later that year.

Dellsperger was a regular at the drag clubs in Nice before moving to Paris in 1995. "I was fascinated by these impersonators: the show is very frontal, meant to be seen from the front as an image, but the image has depth and relief," he has said.[16] In this sense, drag recalls what Erwin Panofsky famously observed of baroque art, such as Bernini's *Ecstasy of St. Teresa* (1647-52): viewed frontally, sculptural tableaux are a kind of painting come to life.[17] Perhaps the performances Dellsperger saw were statuary come to life—the animation of an impossible ideal, like Pygmalion's Galatea. Exaggerated drag make-up certainly suggests an unachievable femininity. As for the performers themselves, Dellsperger admired their bravery: "I was fascinated with transformation," he says. "I found it very daring… the biggest adventure, like going to the moon."[18]

With his "Body Doubles," begun shortly before he moved to Paris, Dellsperger sought to exert greater control on his work than could ever be possible in a live performance, though the spirit of performance remains in all of them. "For me, film is the result of a performance," he has said. "In fact, the first videos in contemporary art were often recordings of performances."[19] This may be a reference to conceptual art practices of the 1960s and '70s, though Dellsperger's work bears closer relation to the "Untitled Film Stills" of Cindy Sherman and the work of the 1980s Pictures Generation, whose appropriations critiqued the power of media in postmodern culture. Sherman used photography to recreate cinema's mythologizing atmosphere; we know all of her women, whether or not we have seen them before.

In such a project, the characters are more real than the stage. "I conceive my work as a sum of artificialities—even if we are talking about performances taking place in the real world, they are then transposed into an imaginary world: what I call aesthetic flutter for my characters, which highlights a loss of reference points," says Dellsperger. "Thus, my work contains the idea that the characters must come into tension with the artificial world into which they are inserted."[20] The artist's avatars reclaim for themselves the power to define what is real and what is fake, flouting those who would set the terms of their identity. When they cut loose from the heteronormative world, the results can be dizzying.

Body Double 1 was the first of many De Palma homages. It was also not the last scene that Dellsperger would reconstruct from *Dressed to Kill*. *Body Double 5* (1996) invokes the moment when Kate Miller loses all her reference points: while sitting before a portrait of a woman in an art museum, a mysterious, handsome man in dark sunglasses silently joins her. She smiles at him, but he doesn't smile back; when he gets up, she follows him through a maddening labyrinth of Old Master paintings. Like so many of Dellsperger's sources, this one is almost preposterously queer-coded, a cruising scene gone wrong. Art serves to literally scramble desire. But it's difficult to recognize in *Body Double 5* because the artist chose to re-perform it in a quiet corner of Disneyland Paris, that museum of the masses. And in the video, he cruises himself: we watch as two women with brown bobs, dressed in black suits—identical twins, digitally stitched together—sit side-by-side on a park bench. Their failure to recognize each other seems absurd; but Dellsperger's video is a mirror which has transformed the self into an Other.

Body Double 5 also marked Dellsperger's increasingly ambitious use of technology to duplicate and synchronize his videos. He was able to time his movements perfectly to the sounds of De Palma's film by hiding a portable Hi8 player screening *Dressed to Kill* between his legs. The doubling of his image, accomplished with a simple split-screen in some shots and a more complicated post-production collage in others, presages the methods he would employ in subsequent "Body Doubles". But technological precision, like the costuming of a drag queen, can only highlight its flaws the more it apes for perfection. And so too with Disneyland: until they are scheduled to perform, the actors in demented bodysuits who greet children at the "Happiest Place on Earth" are never allowed to be seen out of costume, but rather move about unseen behind the false facades of ancient architecture and snow-capped mountain ranges painted on wooden boards. Synchronization is a contractual requirement of the job. Like museums, theme parks strap us into their absorbing fictions. In them, gender is less a "washing-machine" than an endless roller-coaster ride.

The precise alignments of Dellsperger's videos are no more important than the moments when they jump off the tracks. In 1997, he began experimenting with three-channel videos whose frames perform the same movie scene in sync with one another. In *Body Double 8*, three actors play Luke Skywalker and Princess Leia at the moment in *Star Wars: Episode VI—Return of the Jedi* (1983) when they discover they are siblings. In each channel, the actors have incestuously swapped roles. Once again, verisimilitude is not Dellsperger's aim: even with the same clothing and makeup, these actors don't resemble one another, and the cuts don't always line up. This simultaneous multiplication serves to reinforce the notion that each copy has no original. These roles exceed the limits of their frames.

In his multi-channel videos of 1997, Dellsperger also began working with actors other than himself. He street-cast men and queens from Blueboy, a favorite gay club in Nice, and later met Sophie Lesné, whom he cast in *Body Double 14* (1999)—a re-enactment of the campfire scene from queer classic *My Own Private Idaho* (1991)—at Le Pulp, a legendary lesbian club in Paris.[21] He also initiated a decades-long collaboration with artist and punk-rock chanteuse Jean-Luc Verna, who in 2000 would star in Dellsperger's most sweeping project to date: a painstaking recreation of all 102-minutes of Andrzej Zulawski's *L'important c'est d'aimer* (That Most Important Thing: Love, 1975), in which Verna plays every single character. The choice of Zulawski is instructive, for the Polish emigre's film follows a down-on-her-luck actress plucked from a soft-core porn shoot and cast in a stage play. The film's opening scene breaks the fourth wall, inducing a Brechtian *Verfremdungseffekt*—that way of making the medium and its illusions suddenly seem strange. In *Body Double (X)*, we watch as a dragged-up Verna comes horrified upon his own corpse, before a film crew of his clones intrude and reveal it all to be a performance for the camera. Dellsperger traced the bodies of every actor in the original film onto a transparency, laid atop a monitor, so he could tell Verna precisely where to stand. (In later Body Doubles, these positions would be mapped with gridded coordinates, like the choreography of a ballet.) All of these Vernas were then stitched together into a head-spinning composite, each haunted by a digital glow. Dellsperger's film is not simply a representation of a representation, but rather a film about a film about a film, so referentially coiled it can send us in circles forever.

But then cinema is always a tangled affair. If it is continuous, that is because it loops back on itself. As much as they have grown in ambition, Dellsperger's methods cycle in a similar way. Just as soon as he had completed the gargantuan task of digitally editing *Body Double (X)*, the artist returned to his roots in performance, directing actors before a screen projection of David Lynch's *Twin Peaks: Fire Walk with Me* (1992) for *Body Double 17* (2001). Lynch's actors have been edited out of the original frames, so the actors were free to perform under stage lights whose colored gels approximated the hues of the original production. There's something deeply unsettling—Lynchian, perhaps—about the fact that Dellsperger has spirited Laura Palmer away and replaced her with a doppelganger. With its unique methods, *Body Double 17* may be more realistic than other Dellsperger videos, but like the dark pools in *Body Double (X)*, it is haunted by the graininess of its background image, as though Lynch's film about a case of spiritual abduction has itself begun to disappear.

Until *Body Double 21*, Dellsperger always used the original sound from films to score his videos. In that work, a reaction of the bathtub suicide from *Rules of Attraction*, Harry Nilsson's "Without You" (1971) from the original soundtrack has been distorted so it sounds submerged in bloody water. If Dellsperger's precisely coordinated lip-syncs had "the ability to collapse the boundaries of self and other…suggesting a singularity between performing body and the voice of the track,"[22] then his subsequent audio manipulations, which mimic but do not replicate the original soundtracks, underscore the difficulties of articulating one's identity in any representational medium. What's more, they often tease out subtext to perverse extremes.

In recent years, Dellsperger has collaborated with the director and composer Didier Blasco to create new scores for his videos, including *Body Doubles 32*, *35* and *36*. On a practical level, this may have been a way of circumventing copyright issues, but it also invokes the long history of cinematic dubbing, common practice for foreign films and TV shows in France. We might consider Dellsperger's films themselves to be dubs, rather than doubles—translations, not copies, which add just as much to their sources as they take from them. The gaps of meaning introduced by translation are also fundamental to the way cinema functions on a representational level. "Because the spectator and the actor are never in the same place at the same time, cinema is the story of missed encounters," Kaja Silverman has argued. "Moreover, unlike theater, which employs real actors to depict fictional characters, film communicates its illusions through other illusions; it is doubly simulated, the representation of a representation."[23] In Dellsperger's "Body Doubles", there's no telling where this hall of mirrors ends.

INT. DANCE STUDIO – DAY

A woman swings her head to the beat of the music, cracking her high ponytail like a whip. At first, we see only her head and shoulders, mirrored in the video's adjacent channel. As the sequence continues and the camera begins to pan out, we realize the mirroring is more than just a post-production effect: this woman is in a dance studio with mirror-paneled walls where she—along with her students, who are also herself—are reflected in a kind of infinite regression. Dellsperger staged the campy aerobics class from James Bridges' 1985 rom-dram *Perfect* over one arduous week at his alma mater, Villa Arson, for *Body Double 36* (2019). Jean Biche dances every role; as in so many of Dellsperger's videos, all the men in the room—including the film's male lead, played by John Travolta—have become women. In his musical adaptation, Didier Blasco has given the scene's original soundtrack, Whitney Houston's "Shock Me (with Jermaine Jackson)", a slightly manic, hyperpop feel. As it drags on more than twice the length of the original scene's 4-minute run, we start to notice that not everything adds up:

the mirrors in the studio don't always reflect the bodies before them. The two mirrored channels are likewise not always the same. Repeatedly, Jean Biche's lock-stepped avatars fall out of sync with one another, and even with their own reflections. If the mirror image has lost its fidelity to truth, then so, too, have the representations in Dellsperger's cinema—a medium whose technological apparatus depends upon the use of such mirrors to reflect light. When the work was installed at Villa Arson, both channels were projected onto a 17-meter screen atop a mirrored floor, placing viewers within a cinematic kaleidoscope. Pulsating bodies folded symmetrically around a central focal point, like endlessly contracting labia. The display suggested that both the interior and exterior architecture of cinema can serve to amplify its self-referential illusionism. Similarly, the dislocations in Dellsperger's video remind us that we shouldn't always believe what we see.

In this sense, *Body Double 36* implodes its source material, folding those titular, athletically "perfect" bodies in on themselves. The video sends identity, or more precisely self-image, back through the mirror in which it was originally constituted. Lacan's famous mirror stage, that crucial moment of childhood subjectivation when we learn to recognize our own reflections, is complicated by our identification with actors on the silver screen. We may know we're not looking at ourselves in a film, but that doesn't prevent us from imagining ourselves up there, living out all the same actions. That quality of cinema is what makes it such a powerful propaganda tool—and conversely, in Dellsperger's work, such an effective mechanism of critique. As the Lacanian psychoanalyst and film theorist Christian Metz observed, cinema is a "chain of many mirrors" like "the human body, like a precision tool, like a social institution."[24] All three of these aspects come together in Dellsperger's videos, only to subsequently fall apart. His works are not representations but deconstructions of the way identity functions in a world shaped by cinematic fictions.

Recently, mirrors have assumed an even more central role in Dellsperger's videos, abandoning any pretense that their reworking of cinematic references are not also a reflection of the viewers themselves. In Dellsperger's *Body Double 39* (2024), three actors across three channels swap roles as the twin gynecologists and their lover in David Cronenberg's *Dead Ringers* (1988), with the twins wearing eyeless, mirrored masks. As the channels fall in and out of sync with their audio track, the masks suck in all our attention, warping not just their surroundings but also the camera's gaze. Dellsperger calls the mask a "black hole," which seems fitting, not just for the way it structures the image but also the way it erases the actors' expressions, key narrative indicators. If before, Dellsperger's videos mostly cast the same actors as different characters, here different actors are presented as identical. The mask literalizes that process by which we project our shifting desires and (dis)identifications onto cinematic characters, momentarily collapsing the space between self and Other. As with all of Dellsperger's work, meaning is quite literally in the eye of the beholder; by the same token, a young gay boy can see himself in the eyes of a female diva. This is cinema as a reflective void—one in which we may find ourselves and perform how we want to be.

1
Note to reader: the subtitles in this essay are formatted as scene introductions, also known as sluglines, in a film script. They were adapted from the script of *Dressed to Kill* (1980). "INT" here signifies "interior."

2
Judith Butler, "Imitation and Gender Insubordination," *The Lesbian and Gay Studies Reader*, ed. Henry Abelove, Michele Aina Barale, and David M. Halperin (New York: Routledge, 1993), 313.

3
Eve Kosofsky Sedgwick, "Introduction: Axiomatic," *The Epistemology of the Closet* (Berkeley: University of California Press, 1990), 1-66.

4
Ibid, 314.

5
Ibid, 46.
6
Conversation with the artist, Paris, 12 March 2025.
7
Conversation with the artist, Paris, 14 March 2025.
8
Marie-France Rafael, *On Gender Performance* (Floating Opera Press, 2020), 44.
9
Butler, 314.
10
José Esteban Muñoz, *Disidentifications: Queers of Color and the Performance of Politics* (Minneapolis: University of Minnesota Press, 1999), 8.
11
Ibid.
12
Ibid, 9.
13
Muñoz, 11.
14
Ibid, 18.
15
Conversation with the artist, Paris, 14 March 2025.
16
Marie-France Rafael, *On Gender Performance* (Floating Opera Press, 2020), 22.
17
Erwin Panofsky, "What is Baroque?", *Three Essays on Style* (Boston: MIT Press, 1997).
18
Conversation with the artist, Paris, 14 March 2025.
19
Marie-France Rafael, *On Gender Performance* (Floating Opera Press, 2020), 26.
20
Ibid, 33.
21
Conversation with the artist, Paris, 14 March 2025.
22
Jacob Mallinson Bird, "Touching Synchrony: Drag Queens, Skins, and the Touch of the Heroine," *Ethnomusicology Review*, 23 July 2017, https://ethnomusicologyreview.ucla.edu/content/touching-synchrony-drag-queens-skins-and-touch-heroine
23
Kaja Silverman, *The Acoustic Mirror: The Female Voice in Psychoanalysis and Cinema (Theories of Representation and Difference)* (Bloomington: Indiana University Press, 1988), 3.
24
Christian Metz, *The Imaginary Signifier: Psychoanalysis and the Cinema* (Bloomington: Indiana University Press, 1982), 51.

A COLLECTIVE DOLL HOUSE

BY REBEKKA SEUBERT

A few days before the opening of *Jalousies*, premiering *Body Double 39* and *Body Double 40* (both 2024), Brice Dellsperger and I were sitting in the office of Dortmunder Kunstverein, taking joy in writing some personal postcard invites and emails to dear friends. One of Brice's addressees was the artist Marc Camille Chaimowicz (1947–2024), who had made the costumes for *Body Double 35* (2017). Brice sent him an email with a scanned drawing he had made for him on the Kunstverein's headed note paper. A day later, during our press preview, we learnt that Marc Camille had died that same morning. It came to us like a shock and the idea that he may still have seen the drawing was a thought to hang on to. However, this experience made me sensitive for an aspect of Brice Dellsperger's work that becomes visible over time, as the series of videos progresses: the personal relationships that his works register from 1995 to 2025, as a collective endeavour of going through life together. Almost in passing, Brice documents a group of friends, a queer scene and its changing societal context that get inscribed into the work. His performers and their non-fictional real-life characters leave their mark, enable the work and ground it with credibility. This relational—or documentary—aspect of the work makes it possible to combine thoughts on performance, embodiment and representation with a sense of time, age and loss that becomes traceable with the appearance and reappearance of his cast in different roles throughout his video work.

It is this sense of gravity reflecting the relationship of life and death in all its symbolic layering that plays the powerful baseline to the *Body Double* reenactments. The *Xanadu*[1] scene used for *Body Double 35* stands as enigmatic for this thought: Nine muses in a painting start to move and come to life, leaving the frame to dance through Hollywood. It's a camp scene, full of joy, excitement and weirdness. In Brice Dellsperger's version, all the muses are enacted by Frannie aka. François Chaignaud dancing in the said costumes designed by Marc Camille Chaimowicz to the remixed version of

ELO's *I'm alive* (1980). The lyrics provide a string to which to attach the thoughts that I wish to develop more deeply in this text:

(I'm alive) And the world shines for me today
(I'm alive) Suddenly, I am here today

Seems like forever (and a day)
Thought I could never (feel this way)
Is this really me? [...]

concluding with the words:

Suddenly came the dawn (from the night)
Suddenly, I was born (into light)
How can it be real?

The lyrics and the acting are as much fun and camp as the slightly cheesy and dreamy musical style of the arrangement. The lyrics announce transformation, accompanied by fears, doubt and eventually the joy of being reborn differently—a narrative that echoes with the embodiments in Brice Dellsperger's series of *Body Double* videos while at the same time also reminding us of the trope of the butterfly symbol that the transgender community likes to use to celebrate transformation.

A FILM IS A SORT OF PHANTASM, NOT AN ACT OF CREATING A NEW REALITY

Born in 1972, Brice Dellsperger grew up in Cannes at the Côte d'Azur, a site that has informed his work on various levels: On one hand, Cannes connected him from an early age to the world of international cinema, its storytelling and role writing—mostly marked by lacking queer characters. It also made him aware of cinema's fan culture, the red carpet, the stars and the glitches to the screen roles that their personal presence can produce when they attend the festival. Lastly,

Cannes is a small town of some 30,000 inhabitants that counted as many as three gay clubs in the 1990s which Brice liked to frequent. With its many weekend visitors and fairs of the creative industries, Cannes had great potential for clients looking for queer life and adventure. It comes as no surprise that Cannes also was home to the first known gay club in Europe, The Zanzibar (1885–2010) that is, with its 125-year history, also the longest continuously operating gay club in the world. Trans barmaids and performers were part of that scene, figures who—back then and still often today—were much associated with being characters of the night, when the daytime rules are set aside and the whole world plays a different game. *How can it be real?*

For the "Body Double" videos, Brice Dellsperger worked mainly with his own body and collaborated with his circle of friends from Villa Arson art school. However, from as early as *Body Double 8* (1997) he also included his wider queer surroundings and nightlife encounters. Together with his friend Maggy Hue (1950–2019)—who worked with him on the production of many videos from the series—he started approaching drag performers, scouting for them at the Cannes clubs. Brice soon created his own business card saying "I do art films, would you like to act in them?" With Maggy, Brice approached Alexia, a transwoman and *entraîneuse* from a Cannes nightclub, who later starred in *Body Double 9–12*. Apart from the nightclub, she was also a sex worker in the streets—a job with high risk potential, especially for trans people. However, when it came to playing a scene from Brian de Palma's *Blow Out* for *Body Double 12* in which a 'hooker' is killed by a client in the toilet of a train station, Alexia was more than excited to play both parts—thinking it would mean acting them at the same time, running from one position to the next to create the interaction fluently. Her humour, so full of sexual allusions, marked the team spirit of the *Body Double* productions for many years: she would touch a person's clothes around their private parts and say "Is this textile?"—which became a running joke during much of the filming.

Around the same time in 1997, alongside his close friend Bruno Pélassy (1966–2002) and Jean-Luc Verna, Brice spent three months in Nice for a short residency at Villa Arson. He met Joy Falquet, a transformist performer from Nice's Blue Boy Club (1980–2013) starring in the *Body Doubles 9, 10* and *11*. He also met Dominique, starring in *Body Doubles 9–10*, who at their first encounter gave Brice a business card that you could flip, offering the female or male contact information.

Working with characters from European nightlife has since become a common thread in Brice Dellsperger's video work over the last decade: glamorous or cheeky, punk or fairylike, they are dancers like François Chaignaud, multimedia artists like Jean-Biche or glamorous drag performers like GinGin Mezzanotte, who was born in Taiwan and who now lives in Milan. To this day, the "Body Double" videos are a result of an encounter, starting with Brice finding a scene to re-enact, creating a set of handmade decor, sculptures, lamps and costumes: "a sort of dolls' house where I invite other people's dolls to play."[2] While re-enacting Hollywood cinema scenes, he also gives the performers the space to leave their individual choices and marks within the role. "Everybody brings something personal into my personal artistic proposition. A film is a sort of phantasm, not an act of creating a new reality."[3] In this sense, Brice Dellsperger's "Body Double" videos are a collective creation of a piece of fiction—but over time the inexplicit mirroring of the performers' realities seem to create a relational aspect to the work that becomes relevant when thinking about the "Body Double" series as a life project—both on narrative and conceptual levels.

APPLYING ANOTHER TRUTH

Brice Dellsperger's "Body Double" series isn't just quoting a title of a movie of the same name by

Brian de Palma.[4] The title also points literally to the use of body doubles for Dellsperger's re-enactments—either by working with different actors for the same role—such as, in this catalogue, *Body Double 29, 34* and *39*—or with the same actor for different roles—such as in *Body Double 30, 31, 33, 32, 35, 36, 37* and *40*. In the film industry, body doubles are generally used when something is required of an actor that she or he cannot perform, either physically (like playing twins, or doing a stunt) emotionally (a kiss, a touch) or aesthetically (when an actor physically doesn't fulfil the aesthetic image a director would like to produce and gets replaced by body part doubles). Thus, re-enacting Hollywood scenes with real drag performers and queer night life characters is like adding elements to those Hollywood movies that the Hollywood directors and actors are not able to perform, like a gap that needs to be filled with a different perspective, a different experience from reality to complete the narration—potentially adding a layer of documentary to the fiction of those blockbuster narratives that globally nourish our subconscious conceptions of society and gender roles. It's the narrative gap in Hollywood movies reproducing a dominant perspective on what is considered natural, fixed and inescapable, without proposing a counter-perspective, another truth that could be applied to it. Queer re-enactments create the possibility to "go back in the history of a production of knowledge about bodies and their emotions, affects and desires—to pursue traces of history and to work out alternatives at the same time—precisely because drag means retracing processes of construction on one's own body. Costumes, wigs, make-up props, posed photographs and film scenes staging and (possibly) fraudulent narrations connected to 'appearances' reflect expectations, evidence, stereotypes and violent histories without facilitating their repetition."[5]

The multiplication of embodiments through representation—the enactment of another actor playing a Hollywood film role—is part of Brice Dellsperger's multi-layering that he doubles and triples with the recurring mirror motif and his interest in twin roles, where the very root of the word 'identity' as related to 'identical' gets properly twisted. Twinning, doubling and mirroring are all strategies in a game of muddling categories, while at the same time allowing Brice Dellsperger to add another layer to them—that of ambivalence: confusing not only the male and female categories, but also those of fiction and documentary, professionalism and amateurism, good and evil, day and night, life and death. *I'm alive.*

1
Xanadu, musical film, USA (1980), 96 min, dir. Robert Greenwald, starring Olivia Newton-John, Gene Kelly and Michael Beck.

2
Conversation with the artist, 30 August 2025.

3
Ibid.

4
Body Double, erotic noir film, USA (1984), 114 min, dir. Brian de Palma, starring Craig Wasson, Gregg Henry and Melanie Griffith.

5
Renate Lorenz, "Drag-radical, Transtemporal, Abstract", in: *Queer Art*: A Freak Theory, trans. Daniel Hendrickson (New Brunswick: Transaction, 2012) p. 20–23.

EXHIBITION VIEWS

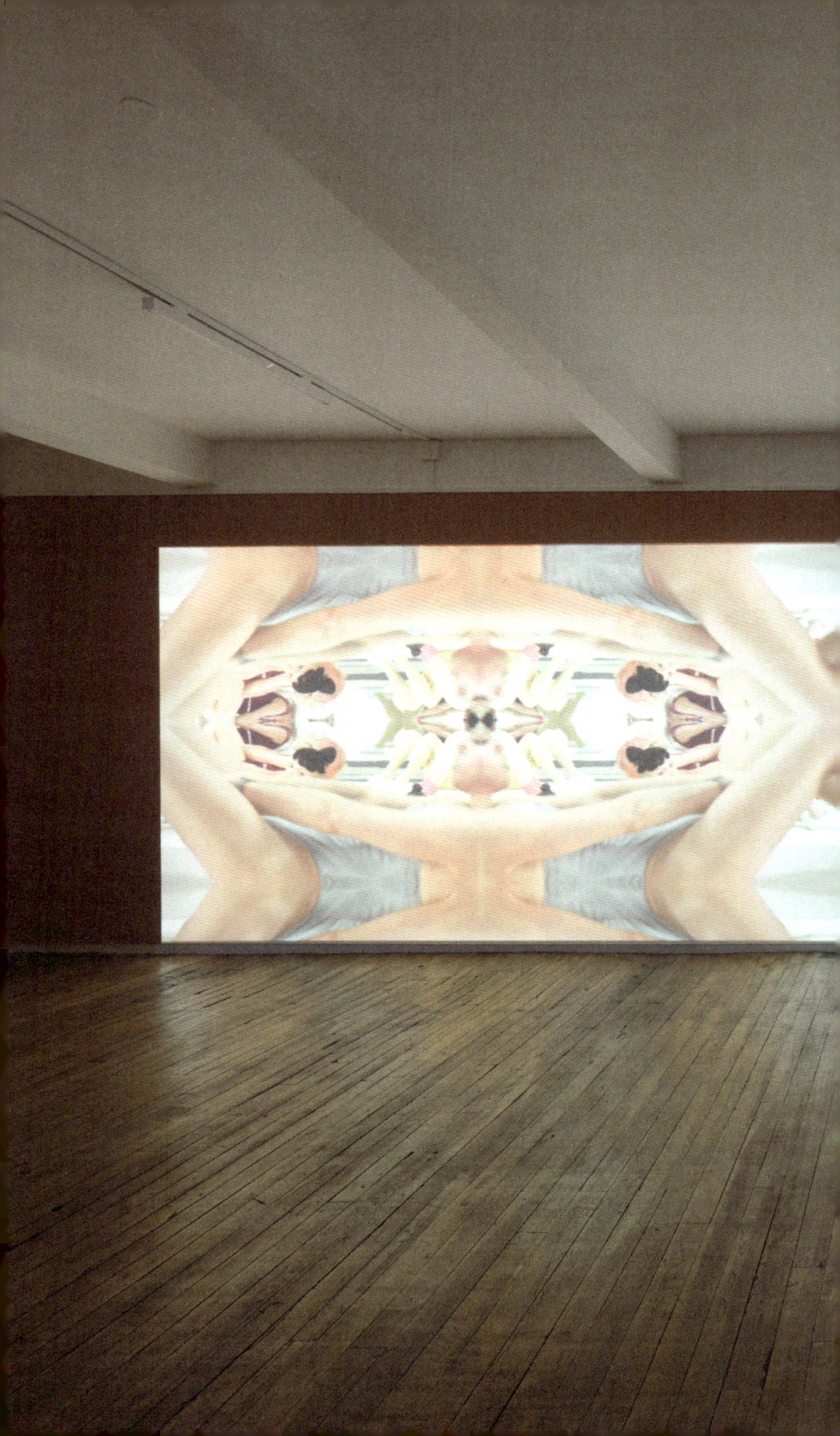

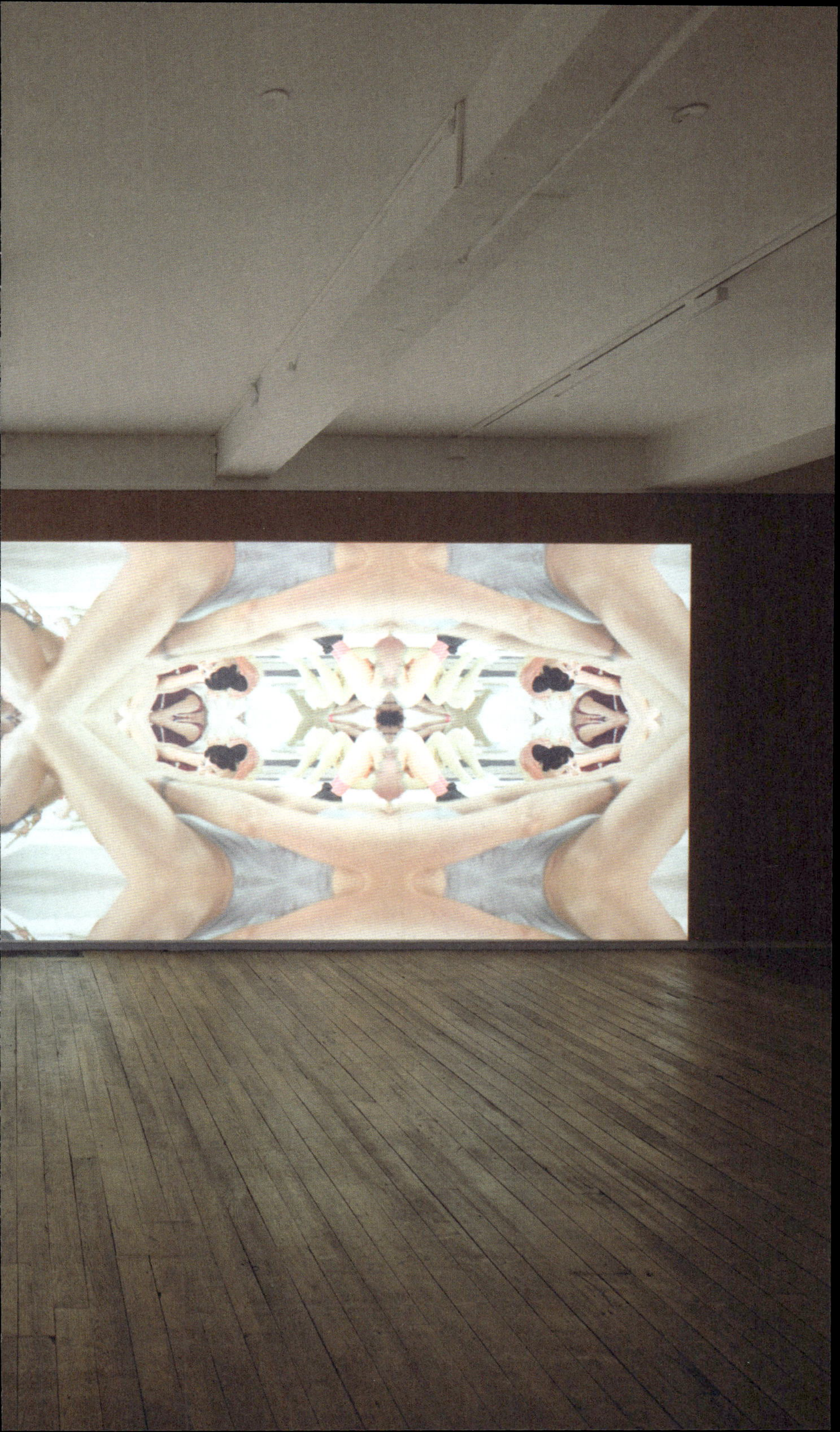

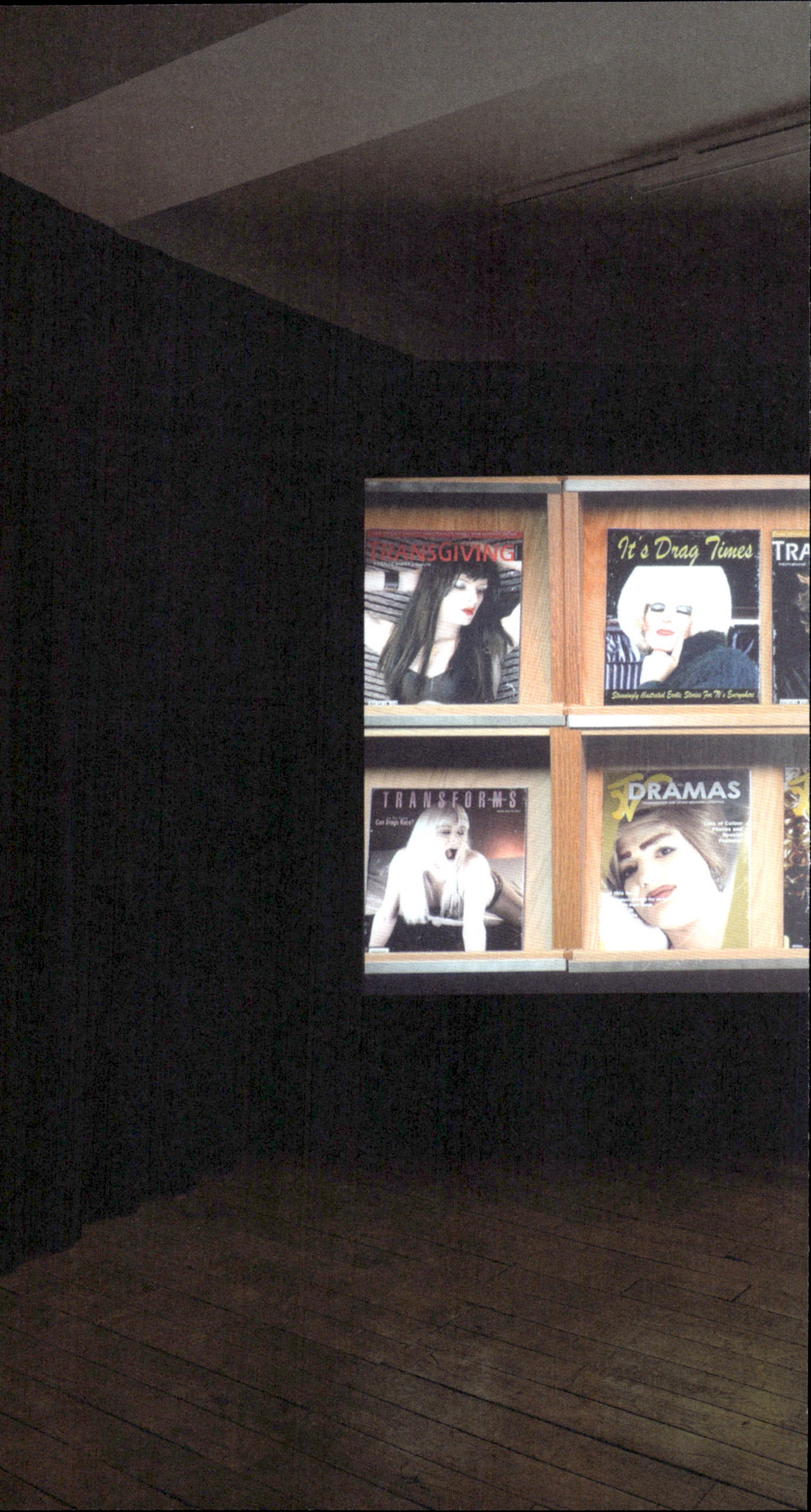
TRANSGIVING
It's Drag Times
Stunningly Illustrated Erotic Stories For TV's Everywhere
TRANSFORMS
Can Drags Race?
DRAMAS

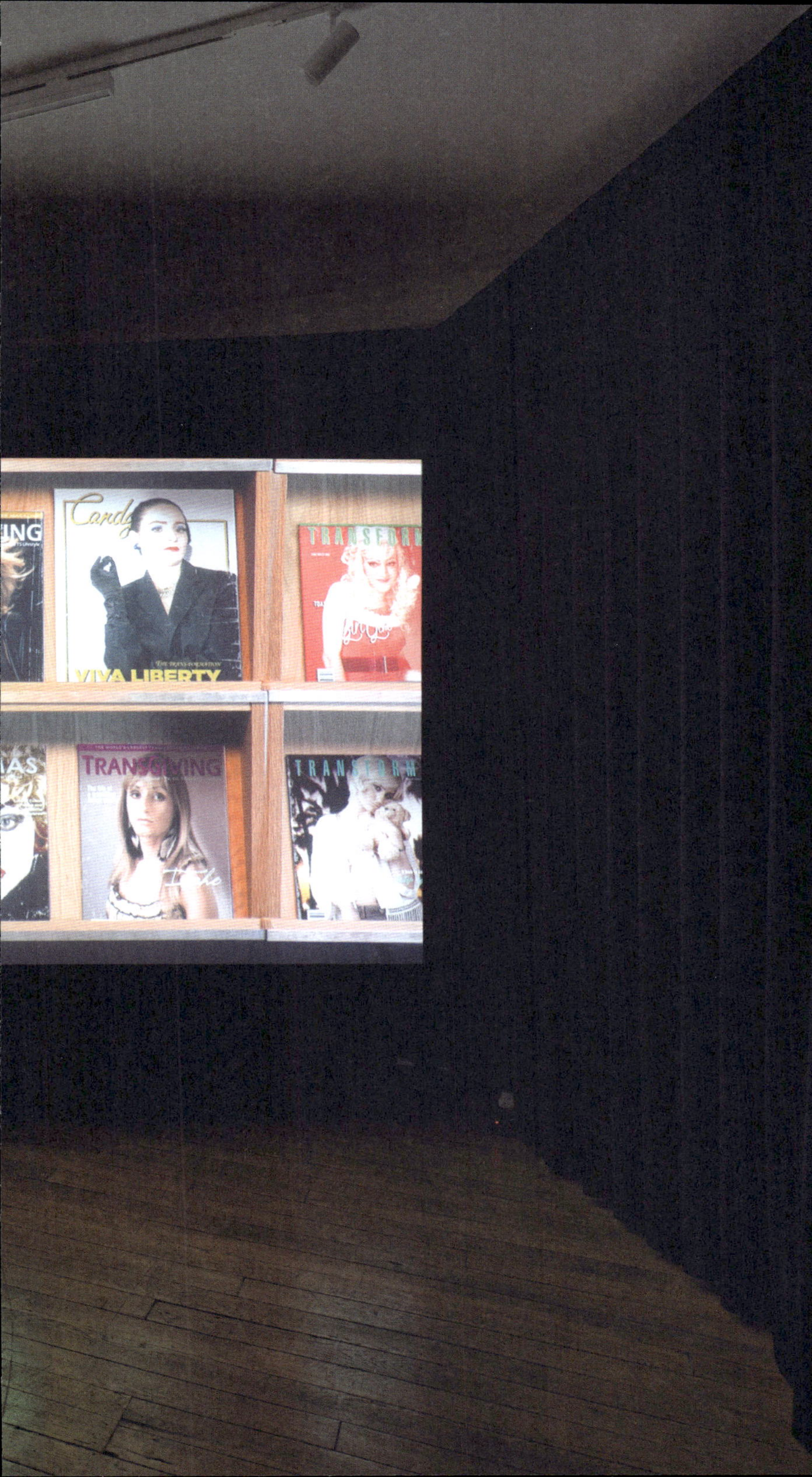
VIVA LIBERTY
TRANSGIVING

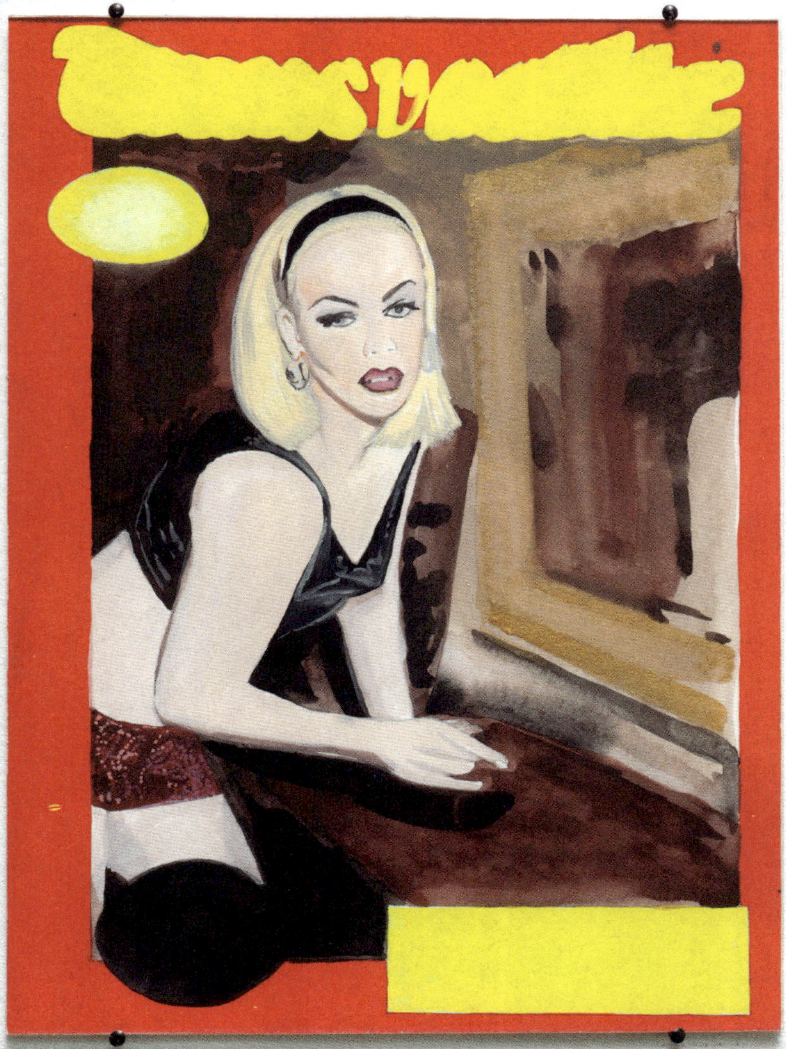

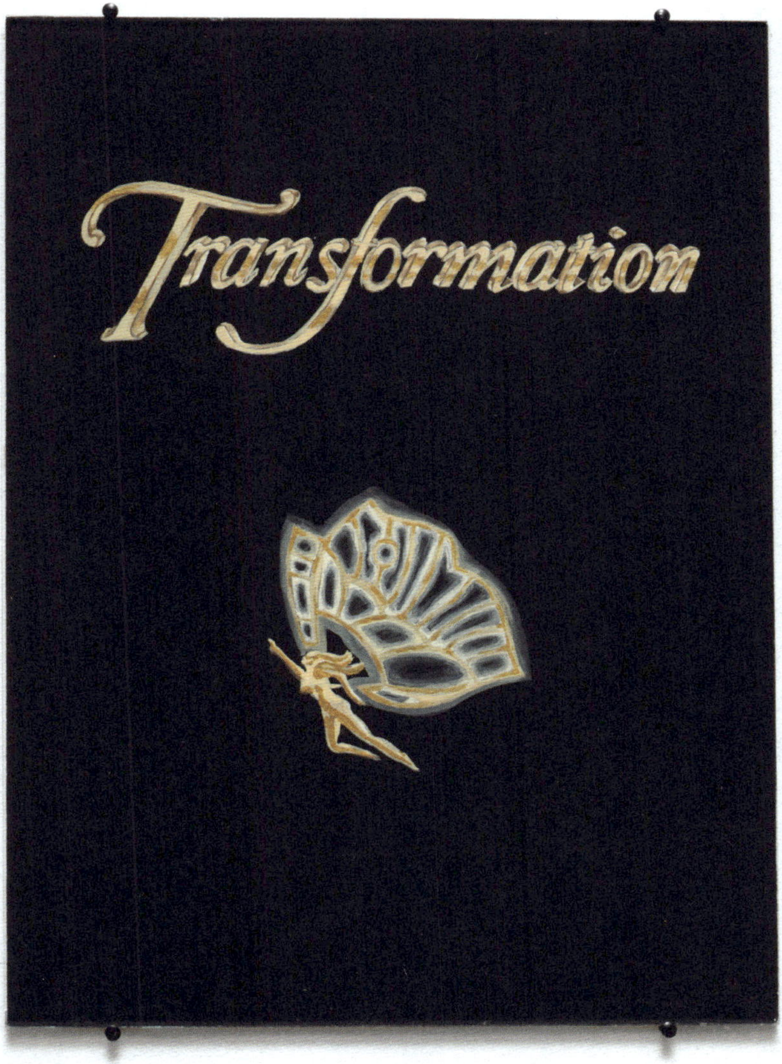
Transformation

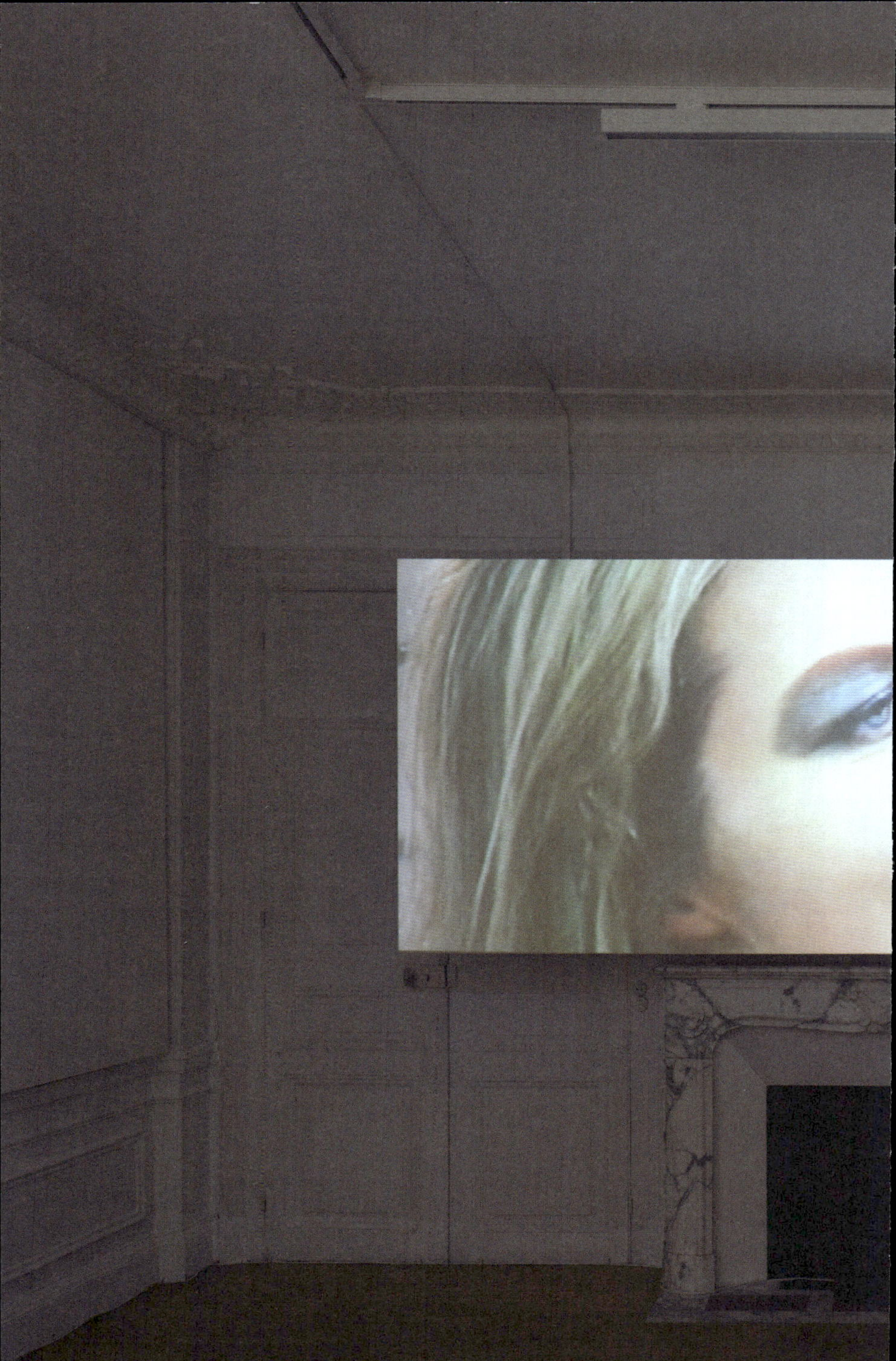

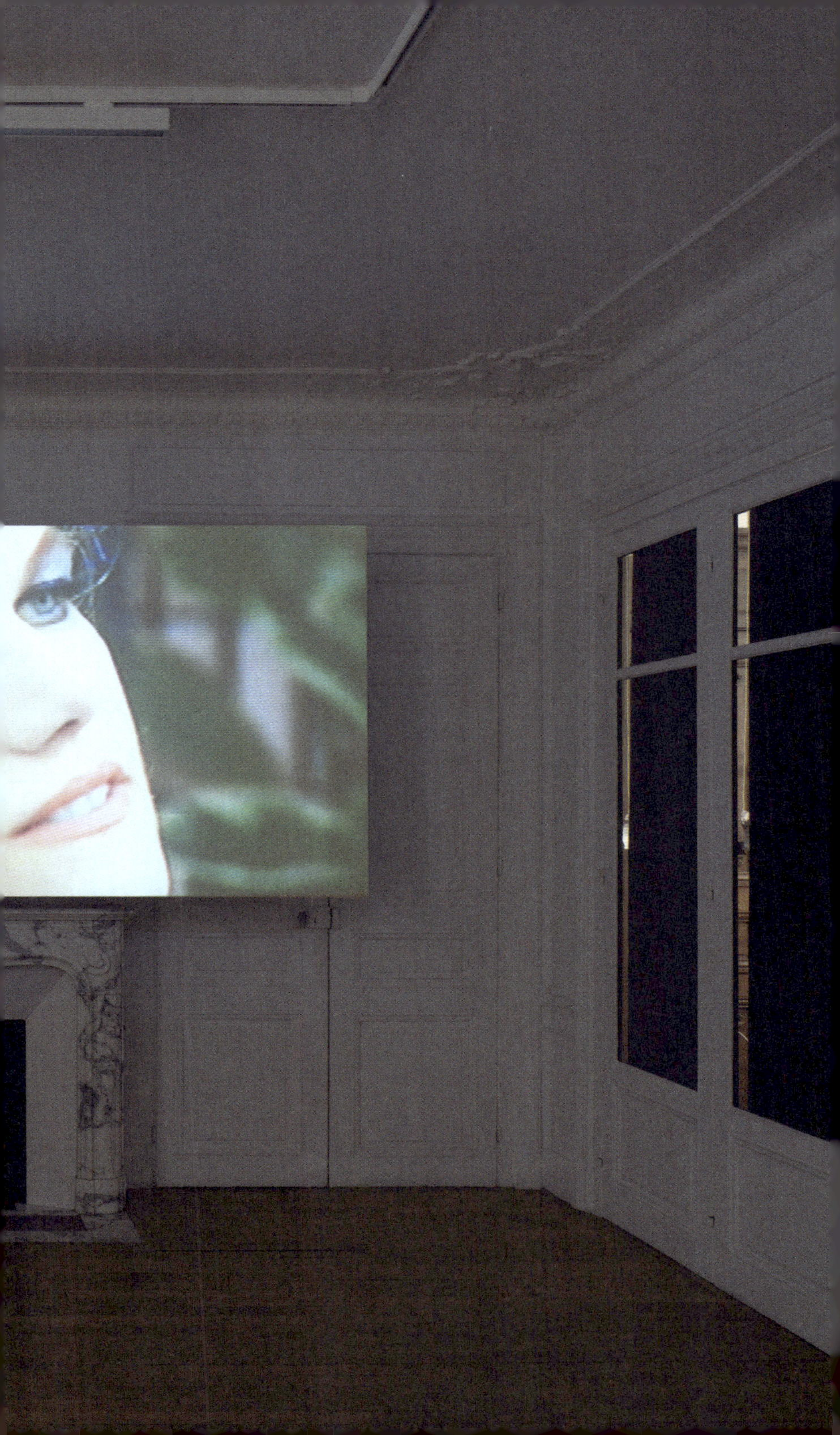

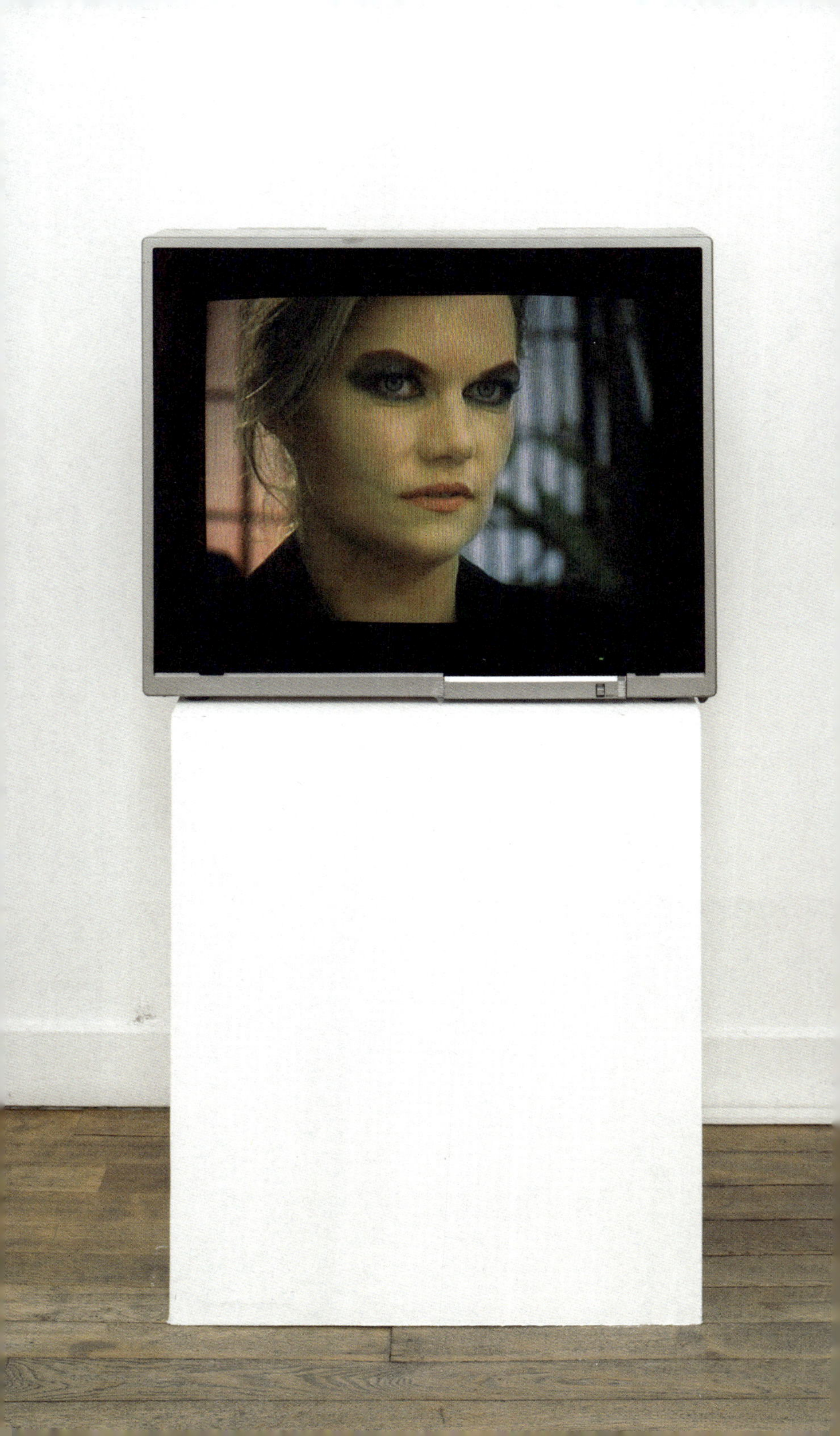

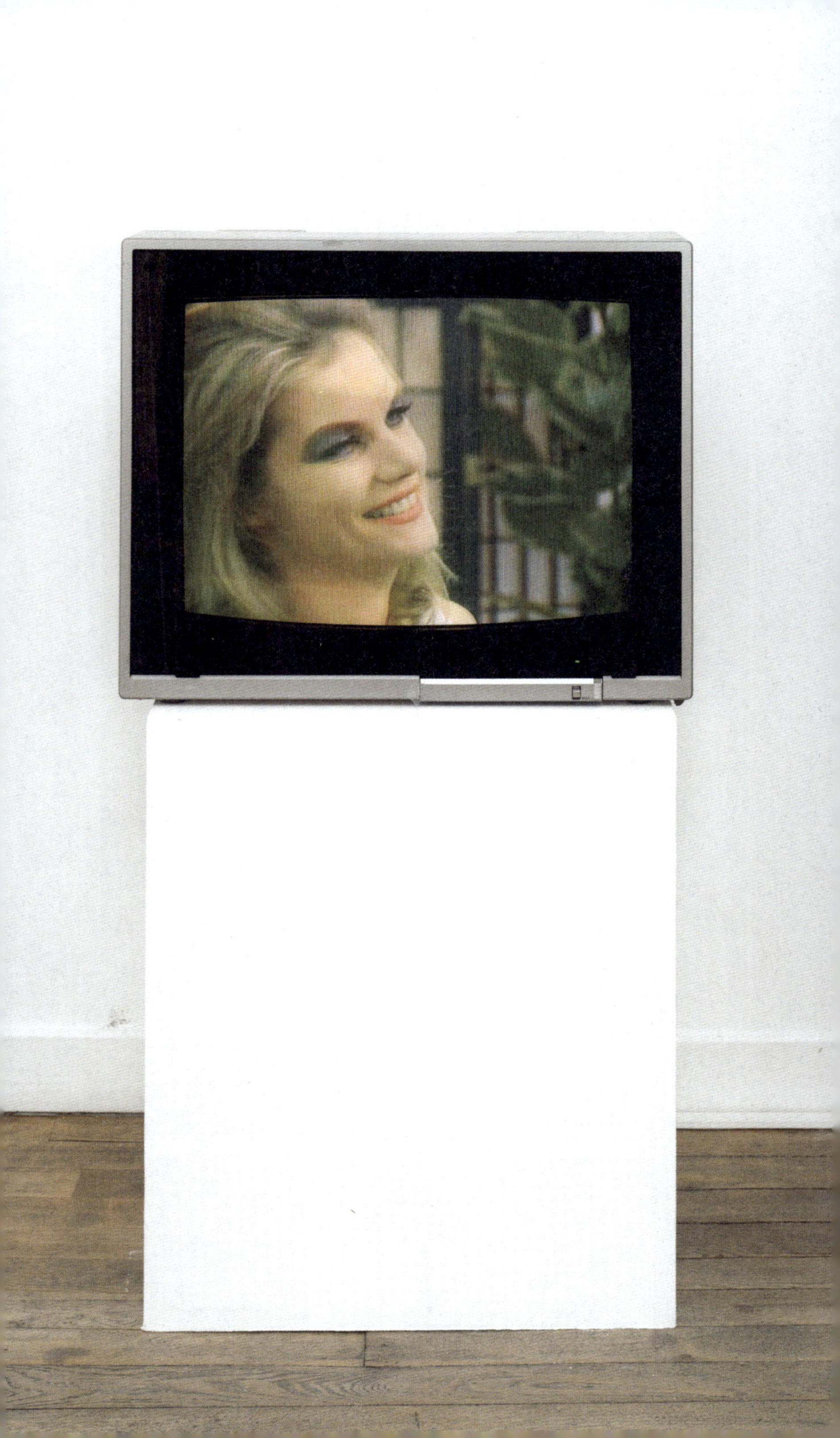

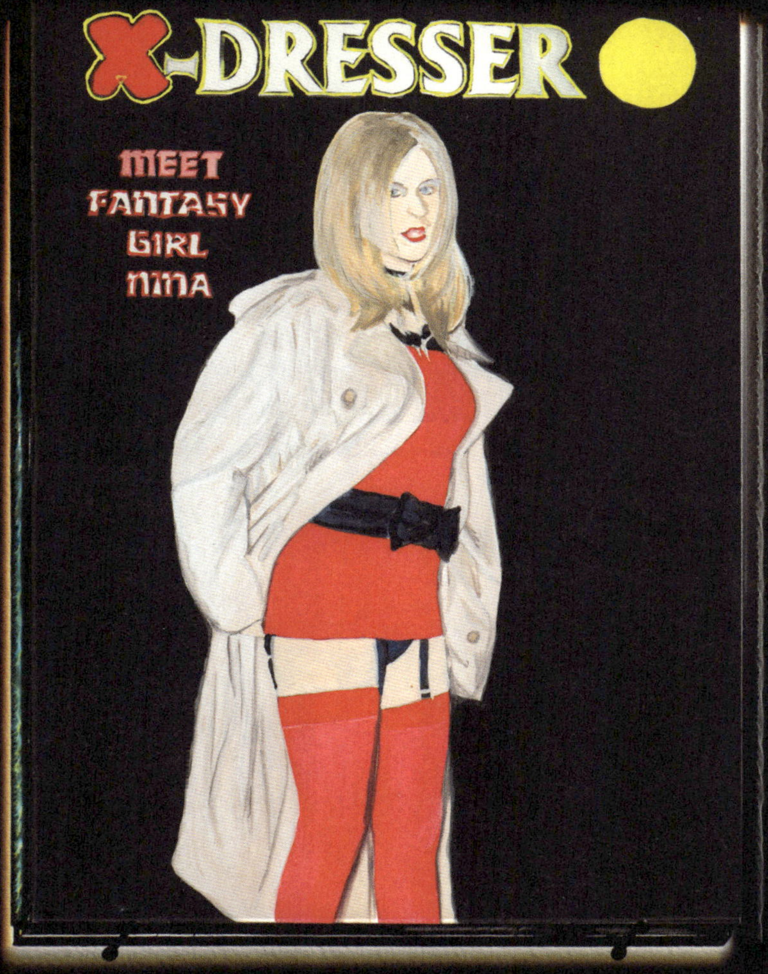
X-DRESSER
MEET
FANTASY
GIRL
NINA

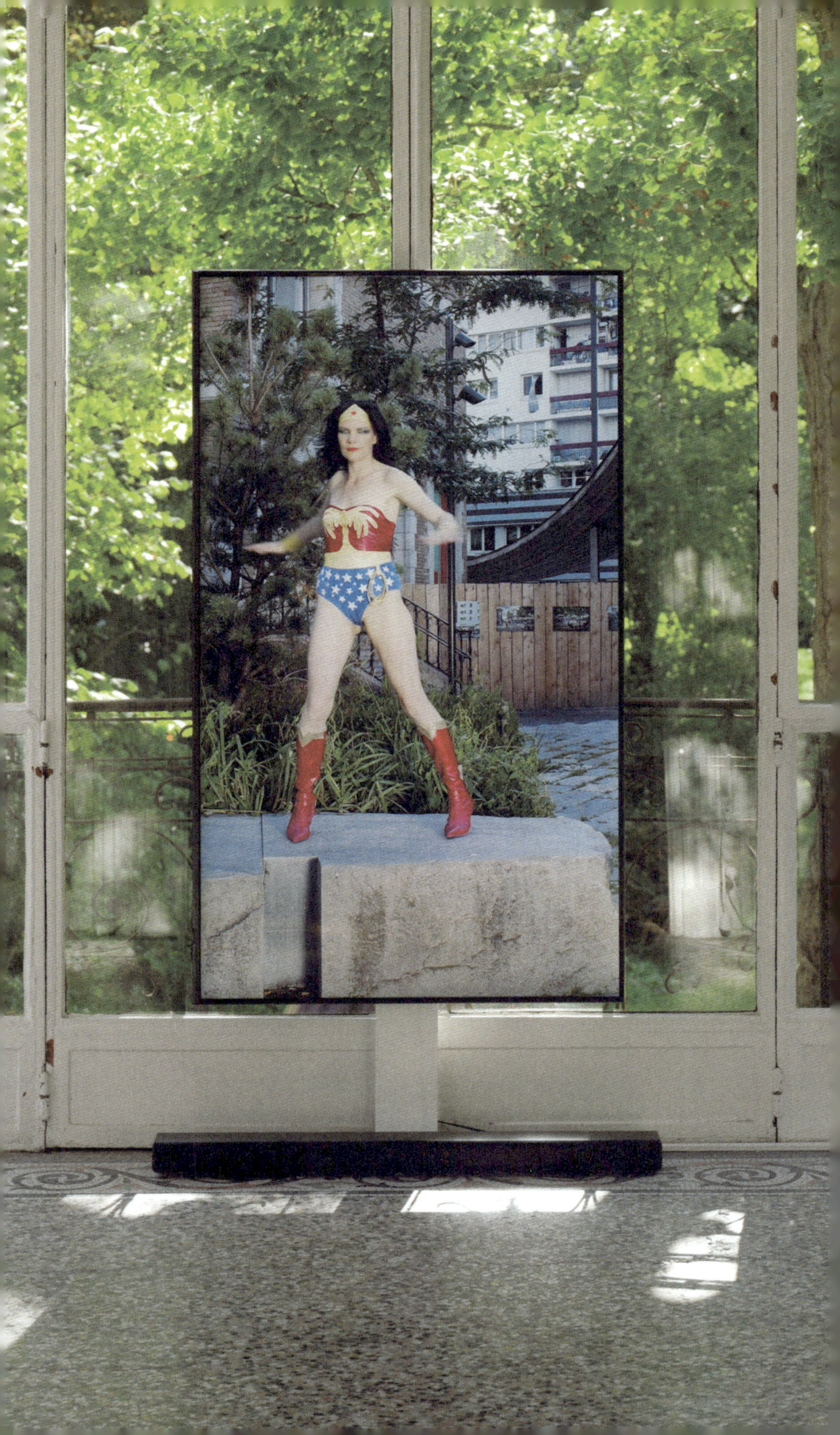

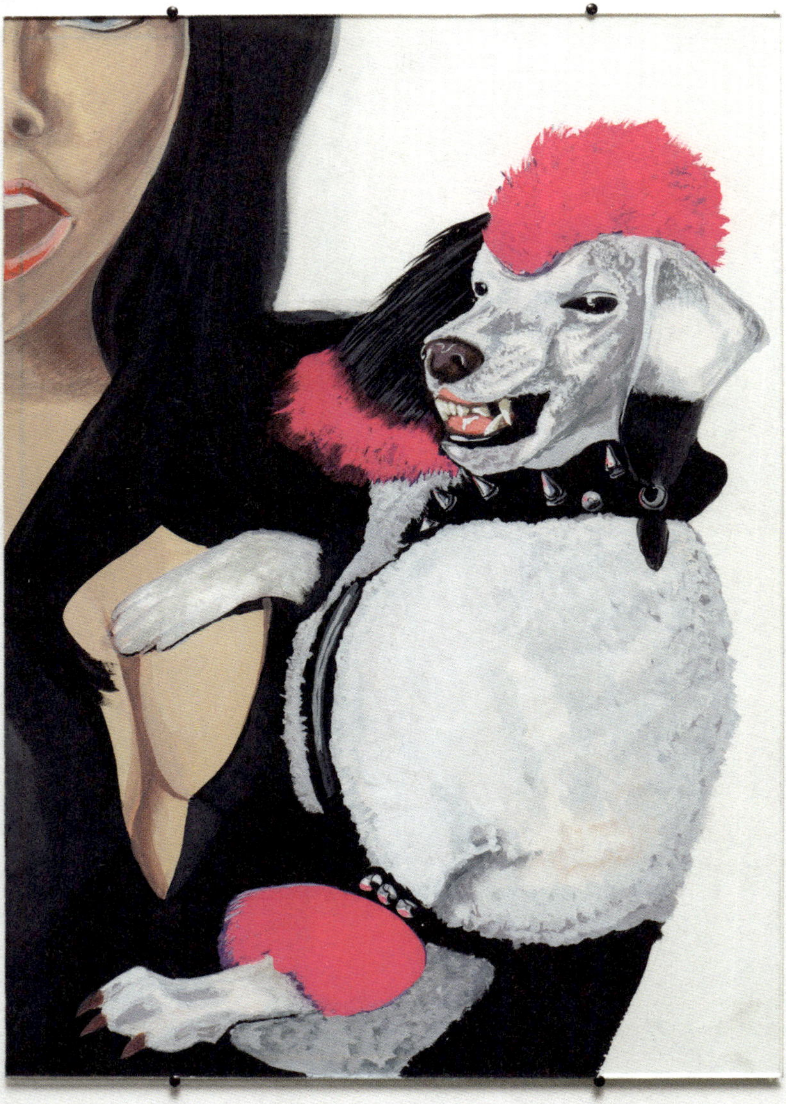

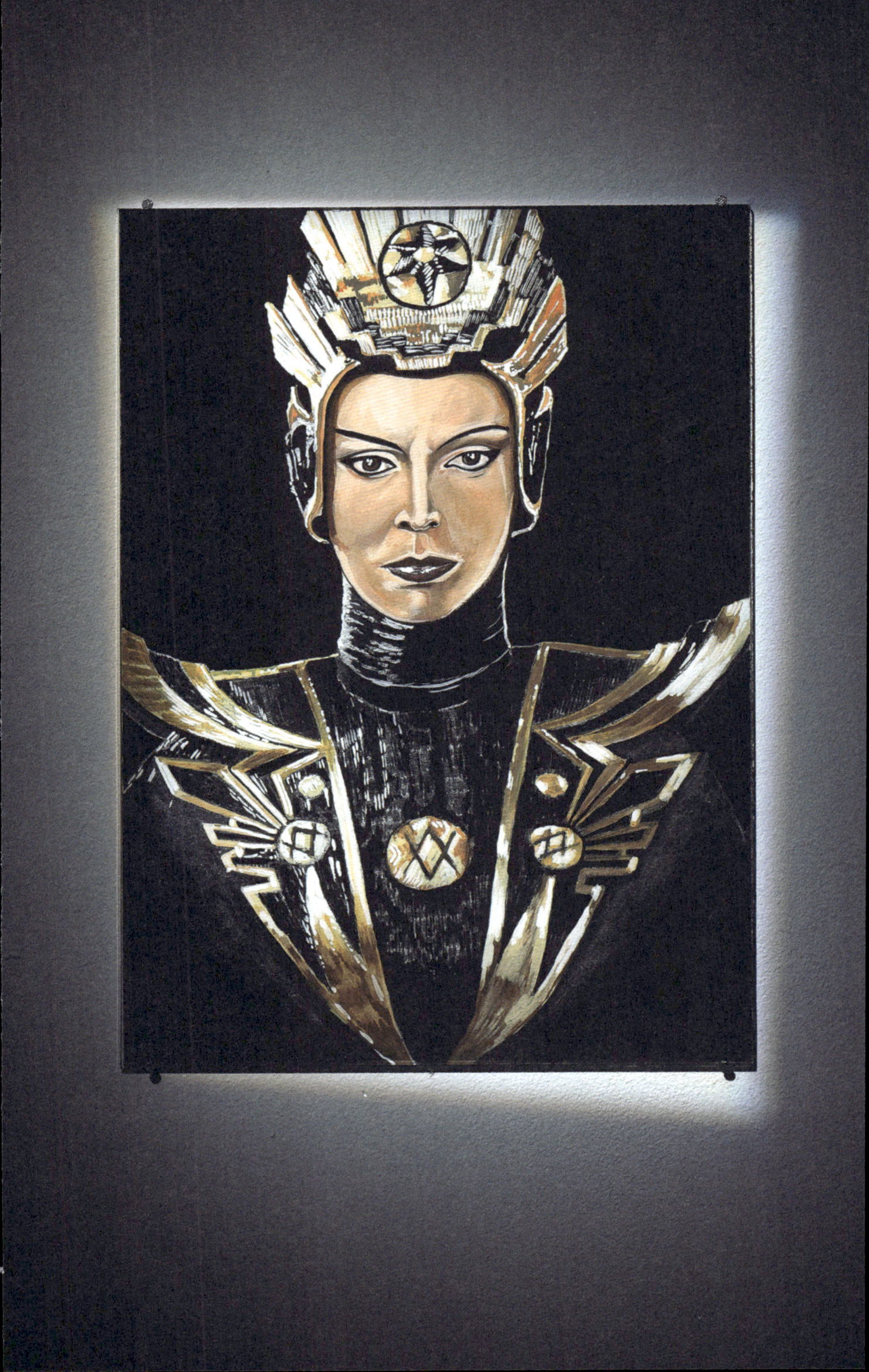

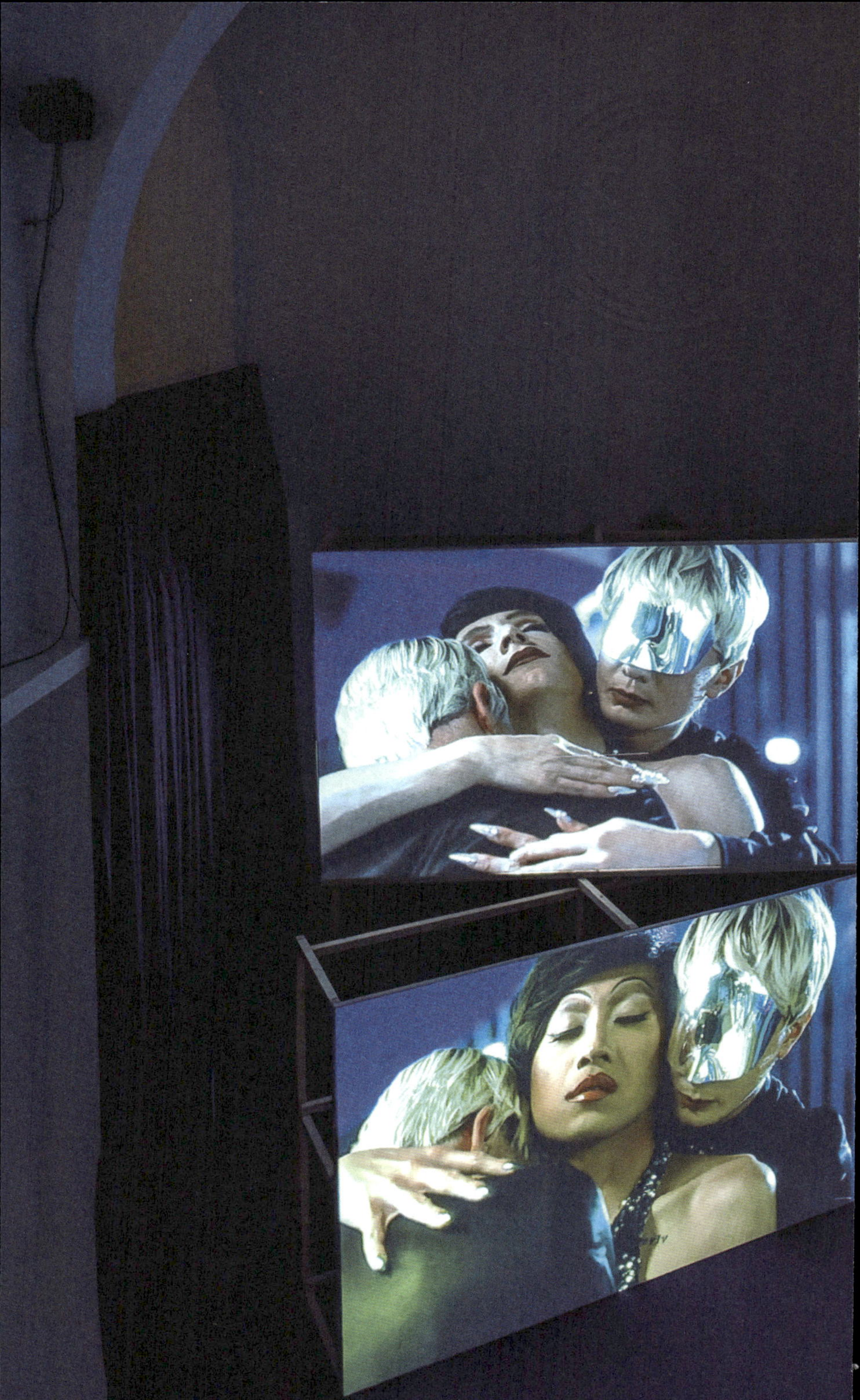

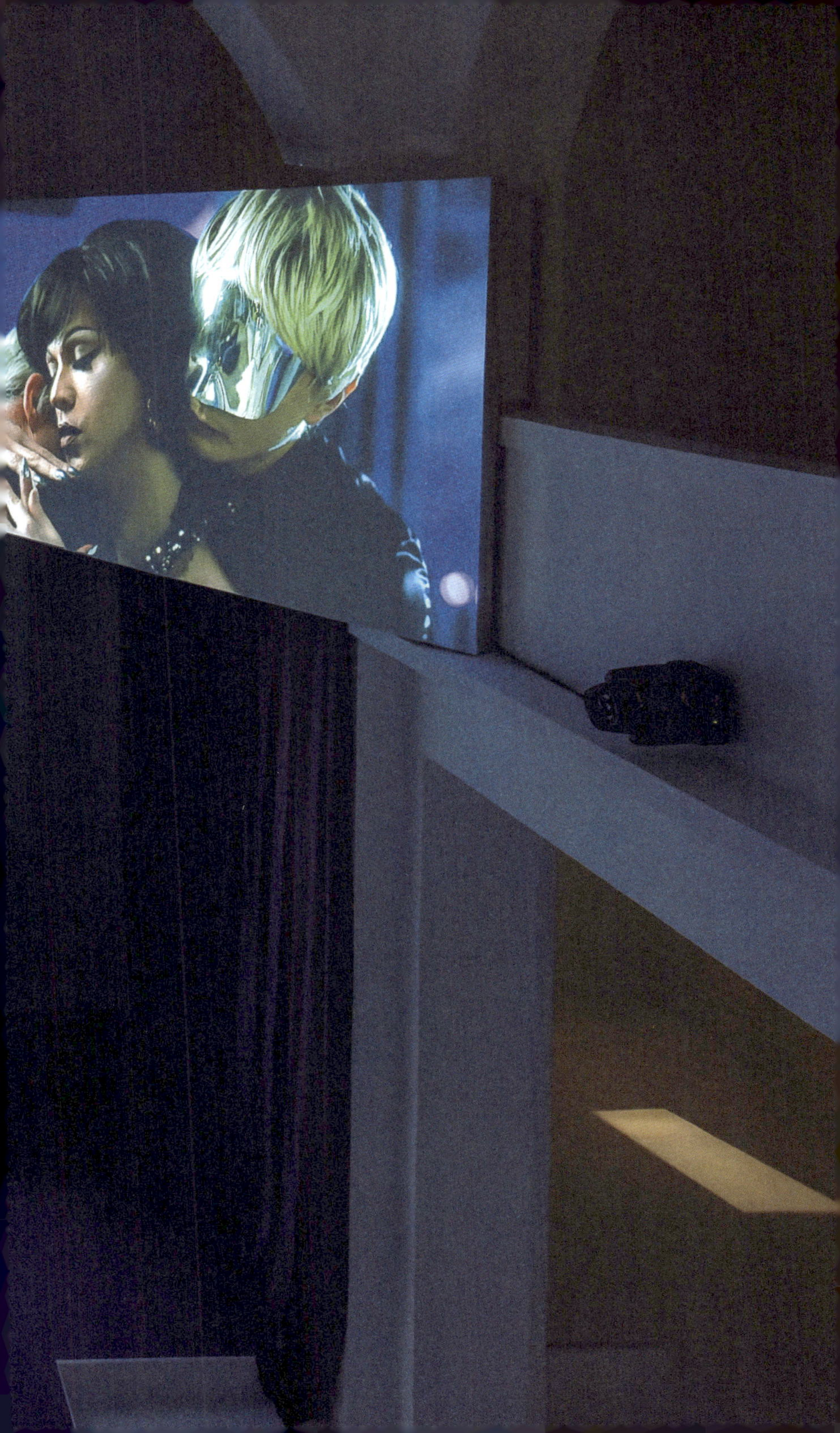

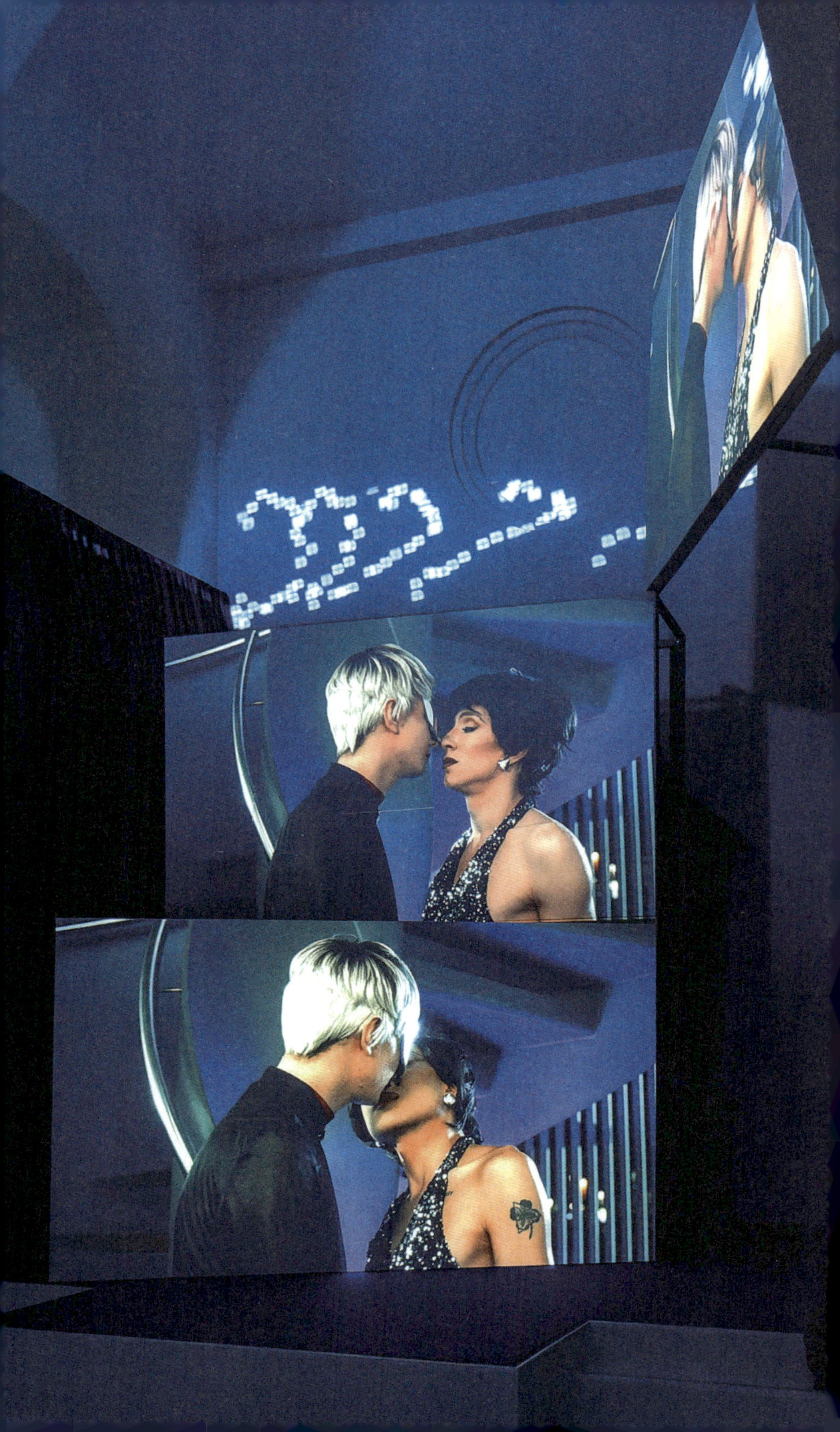

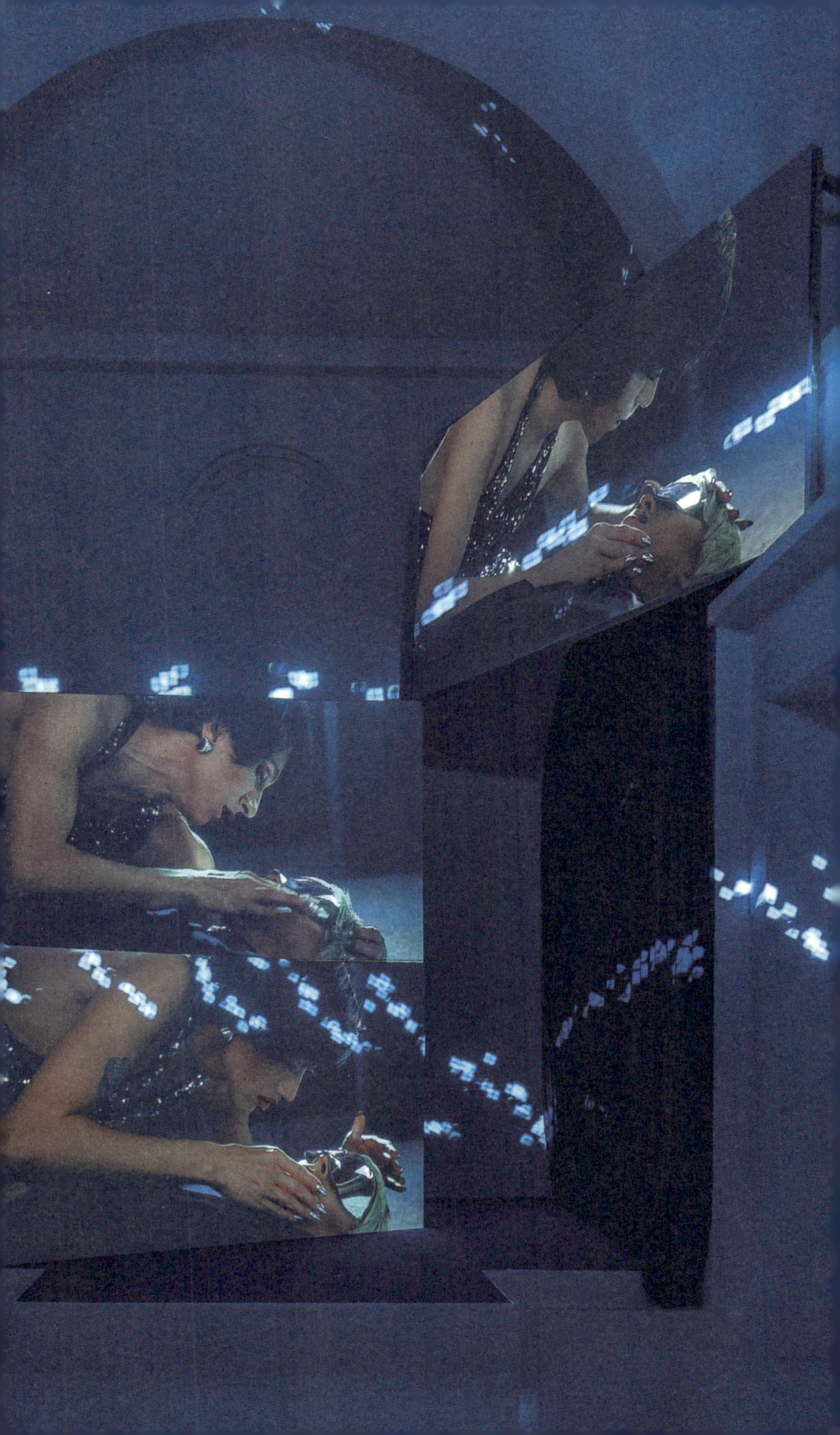

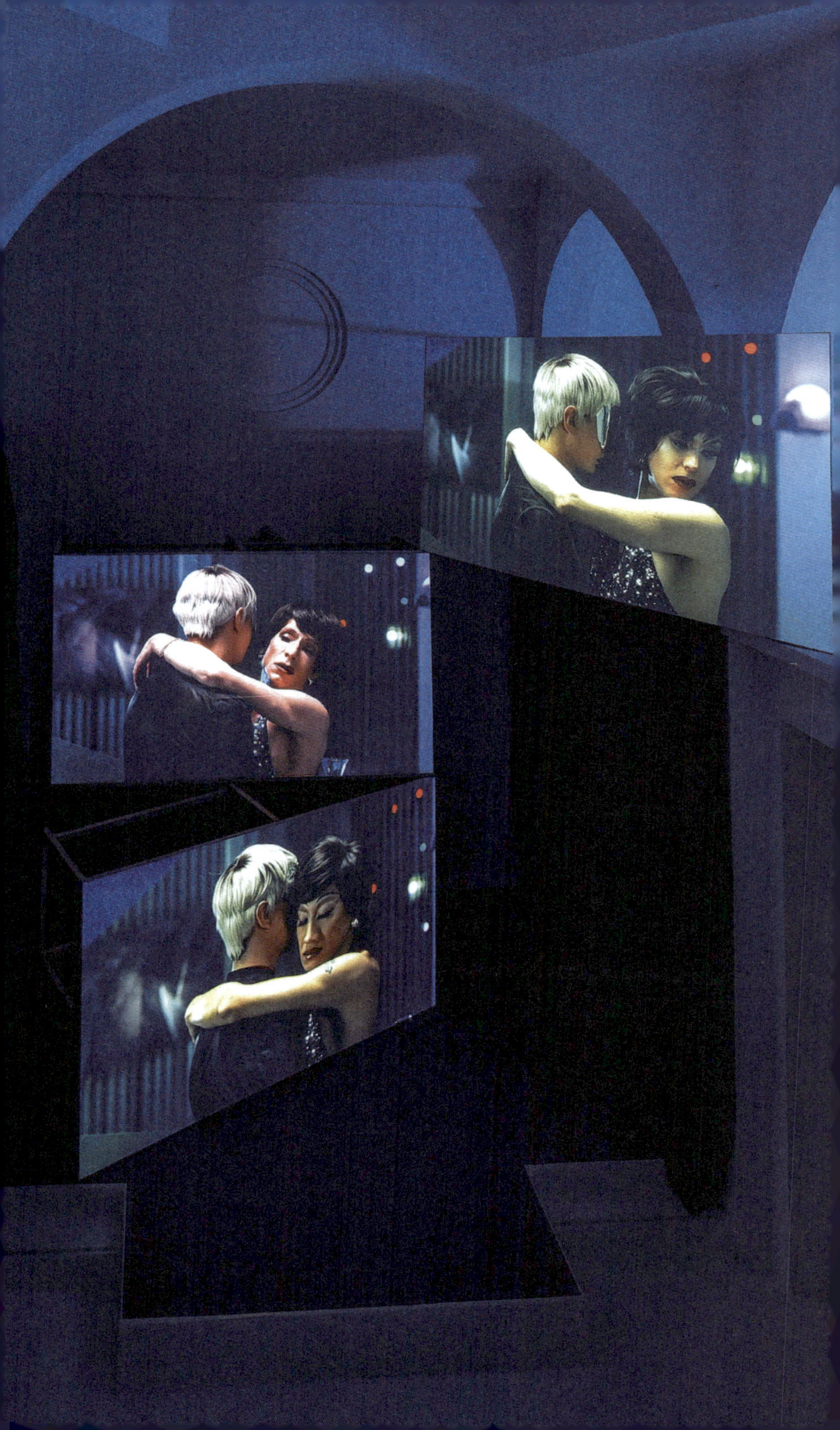

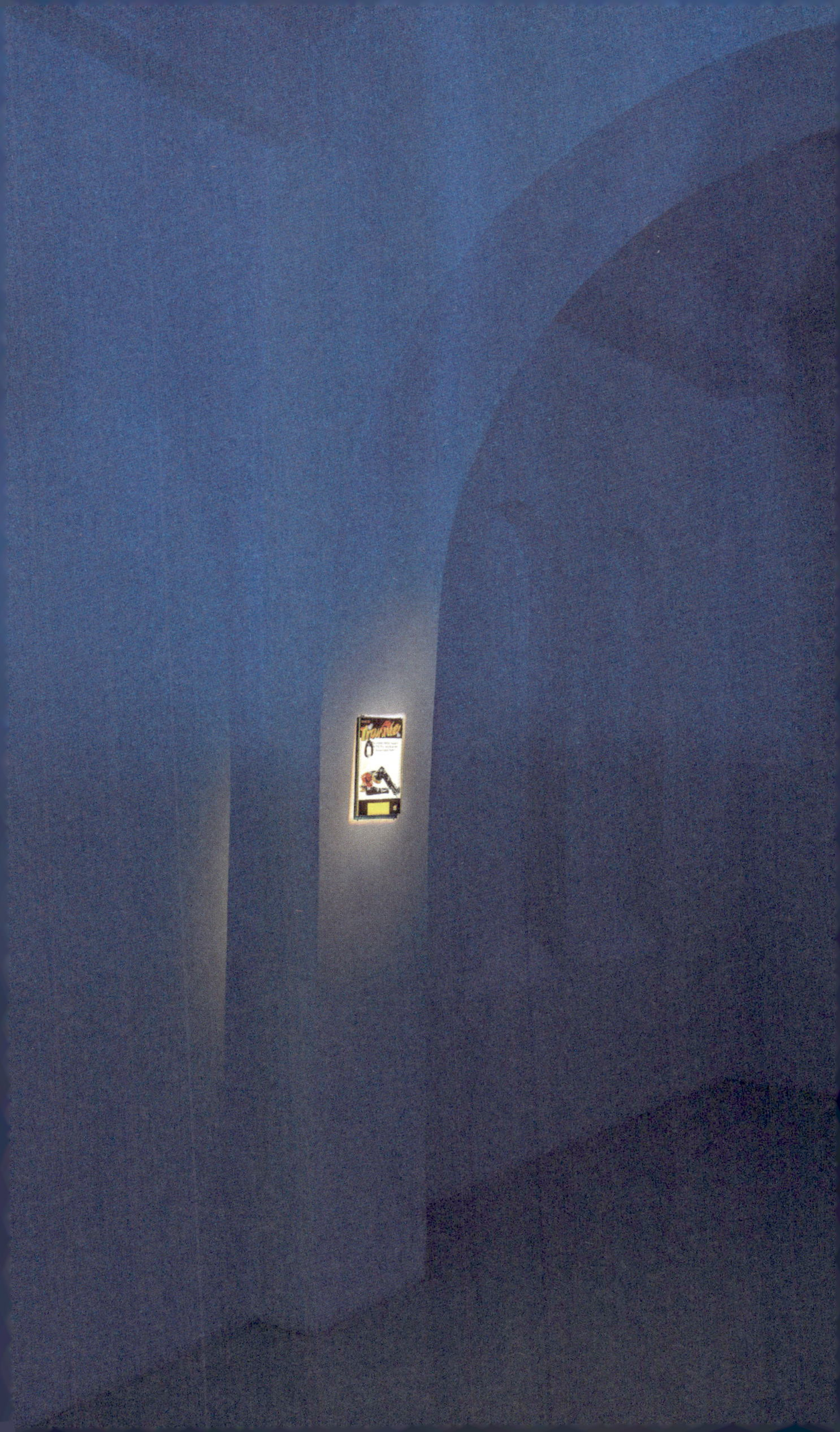

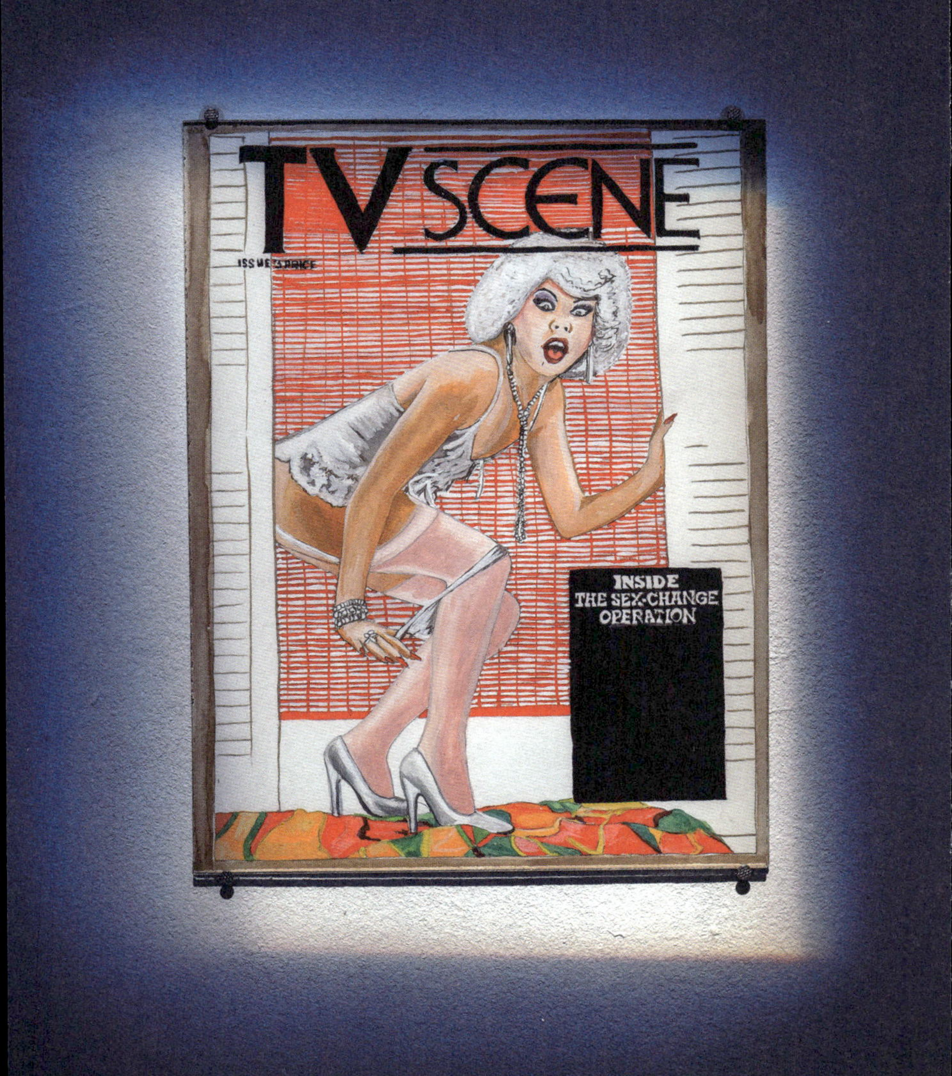
TV SCENE
INSIDE
THE SEX-CHANGE
OPERATION

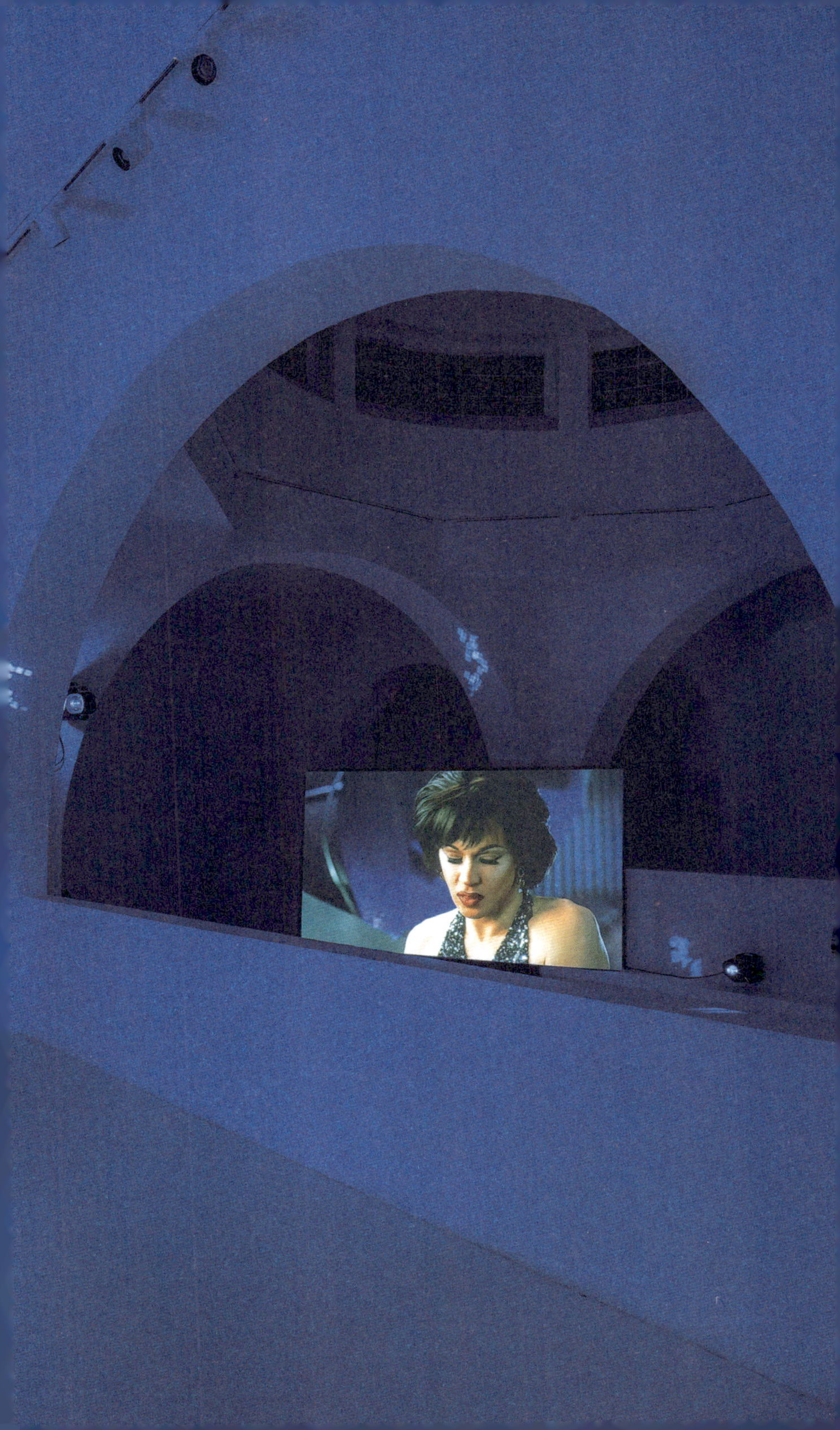

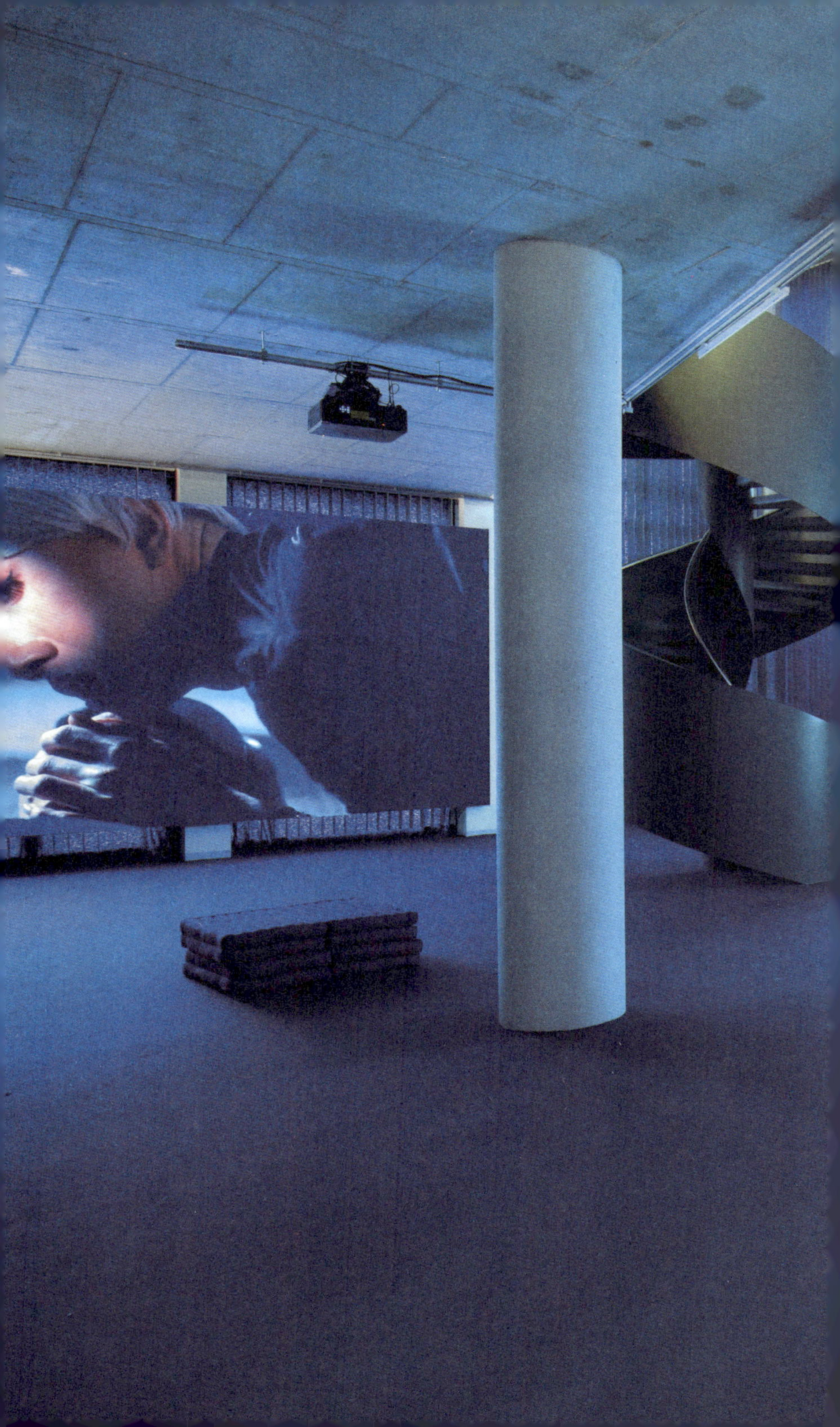

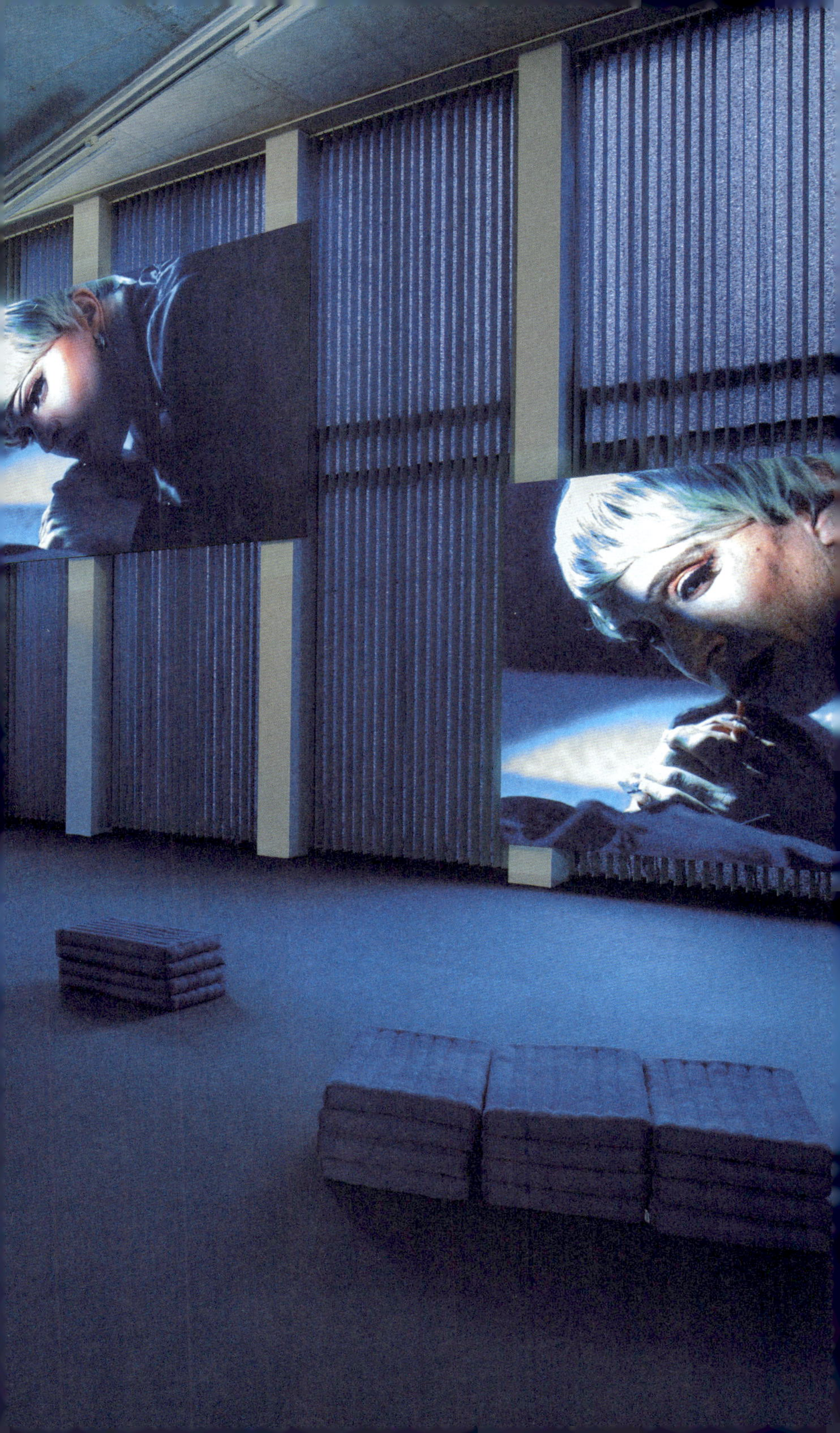

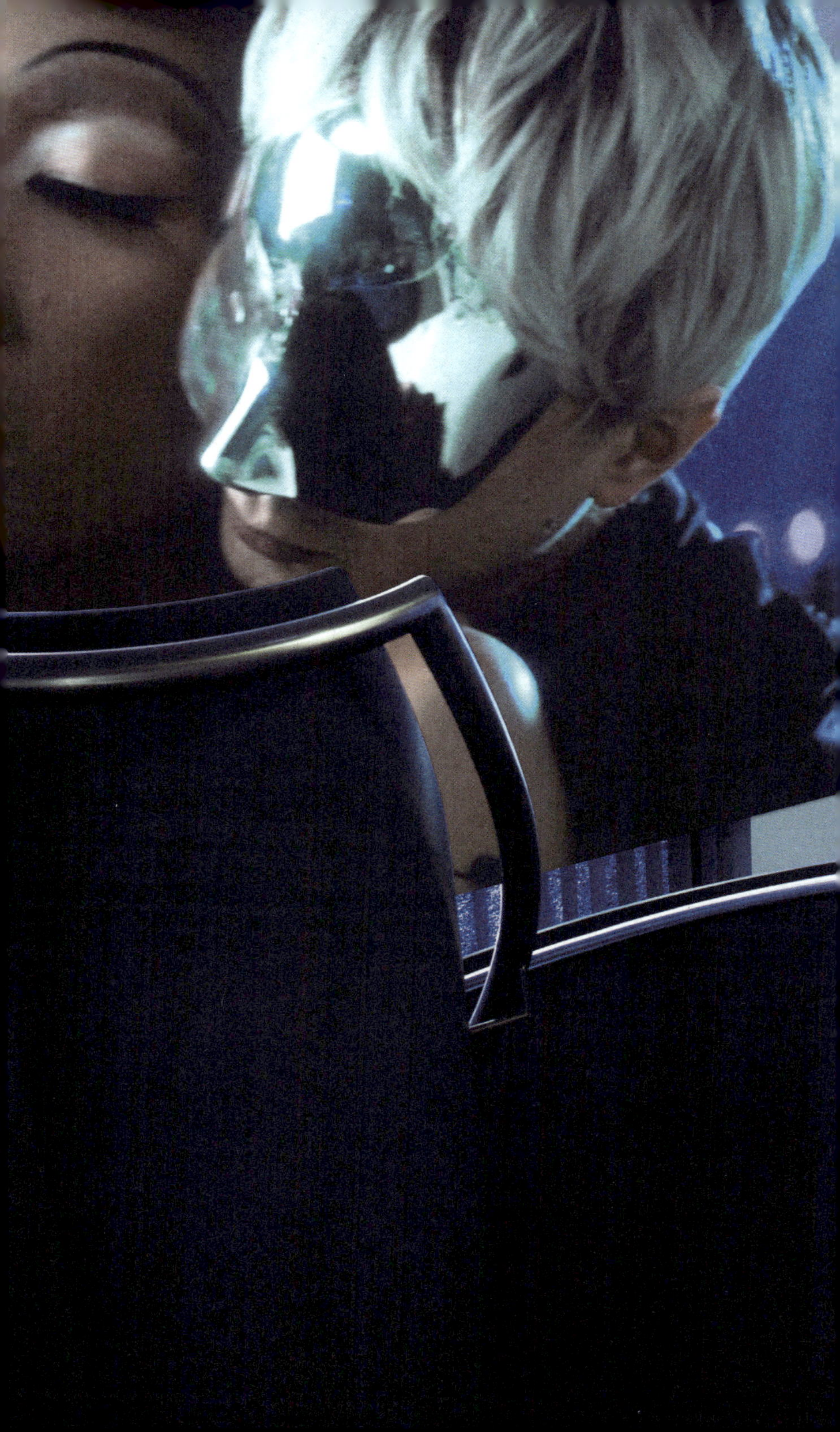

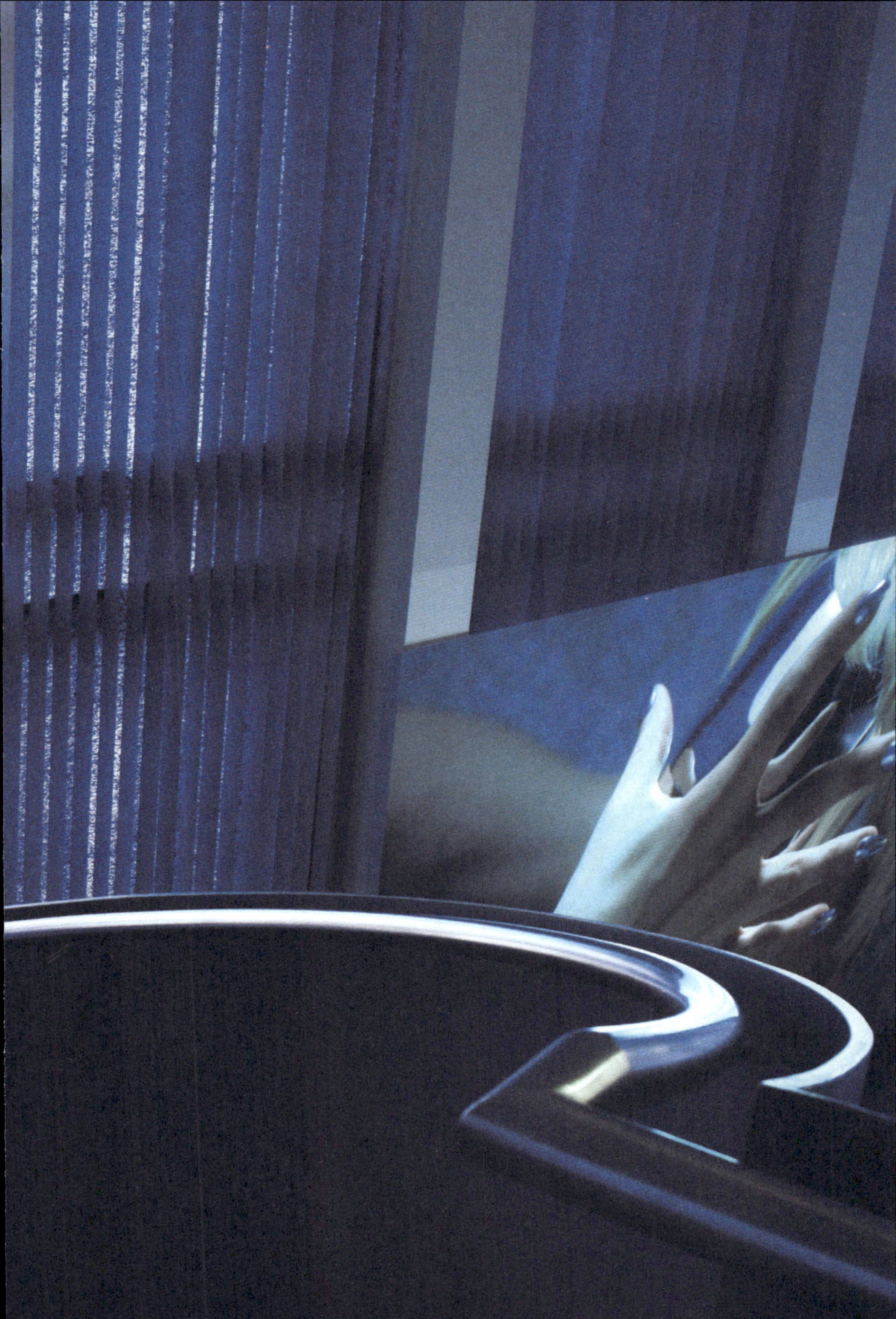

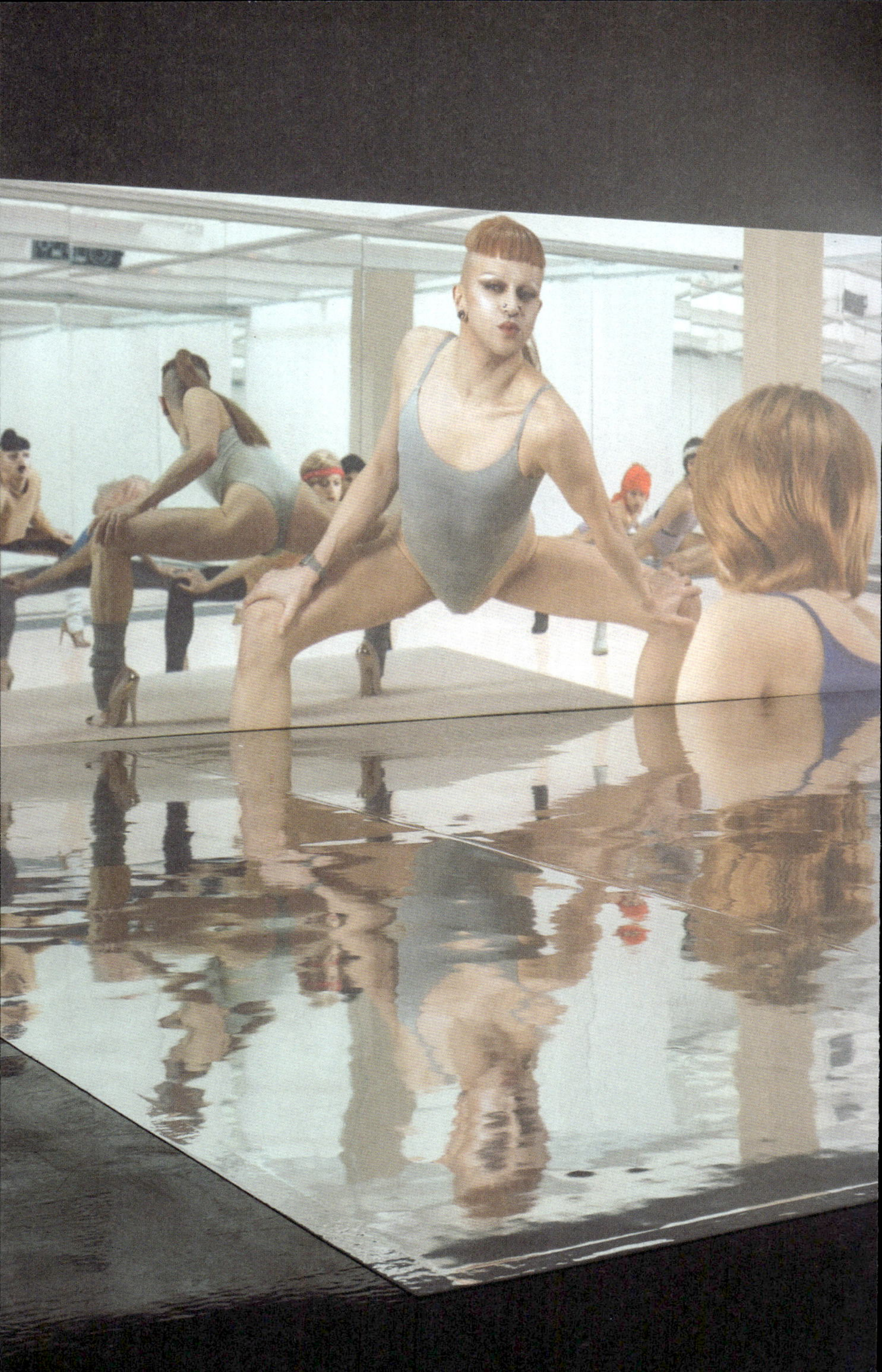

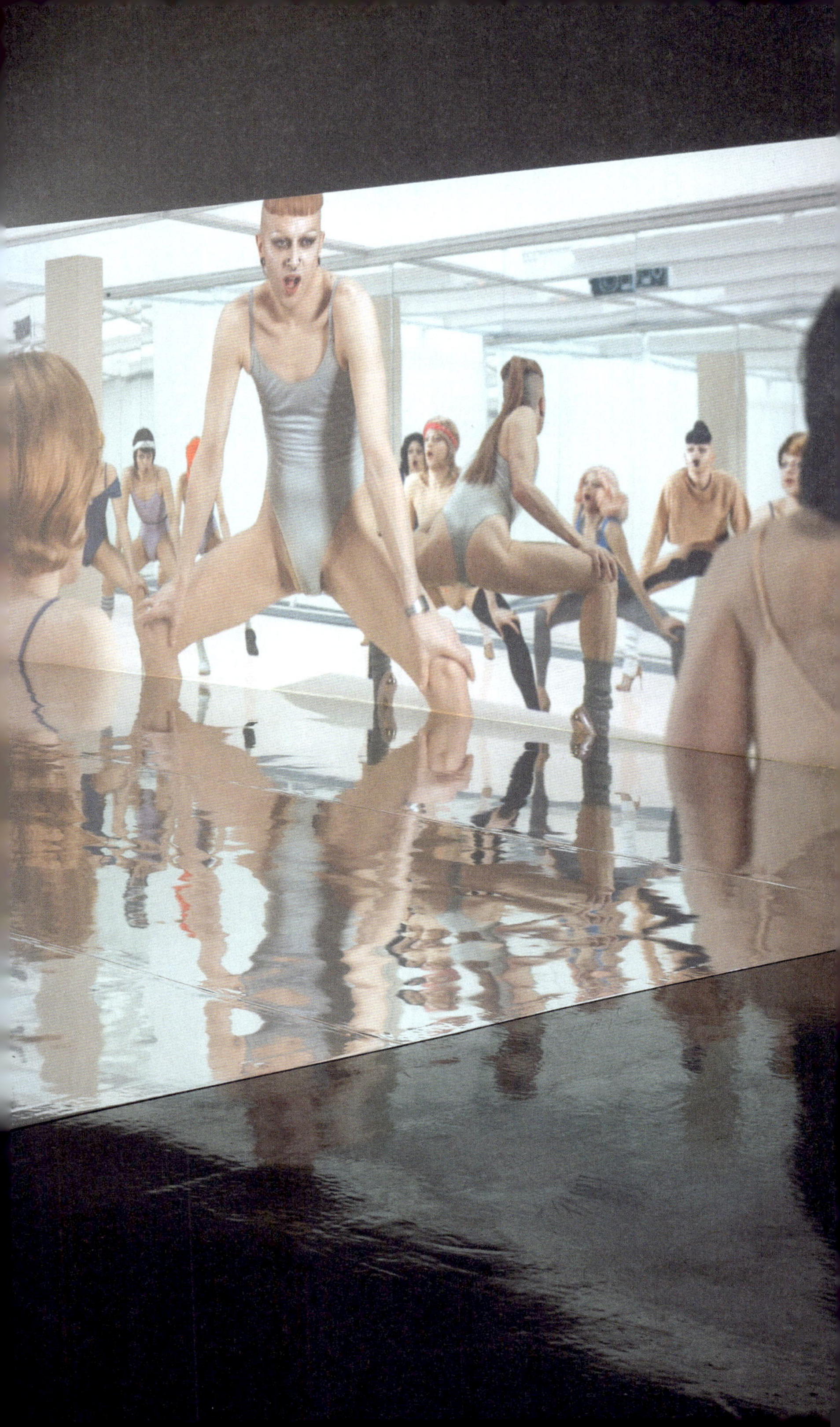

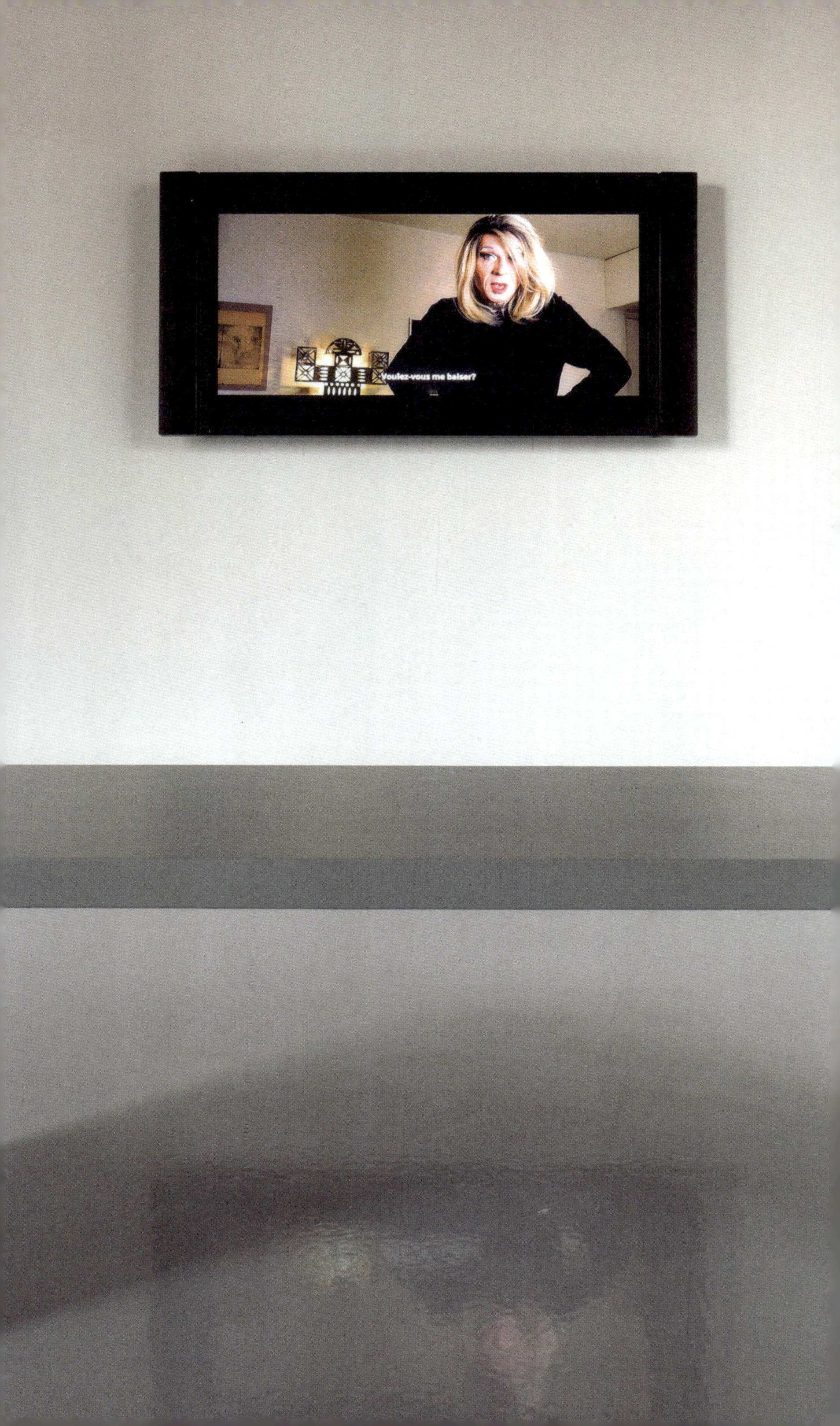
Voulez-vous me baiser?

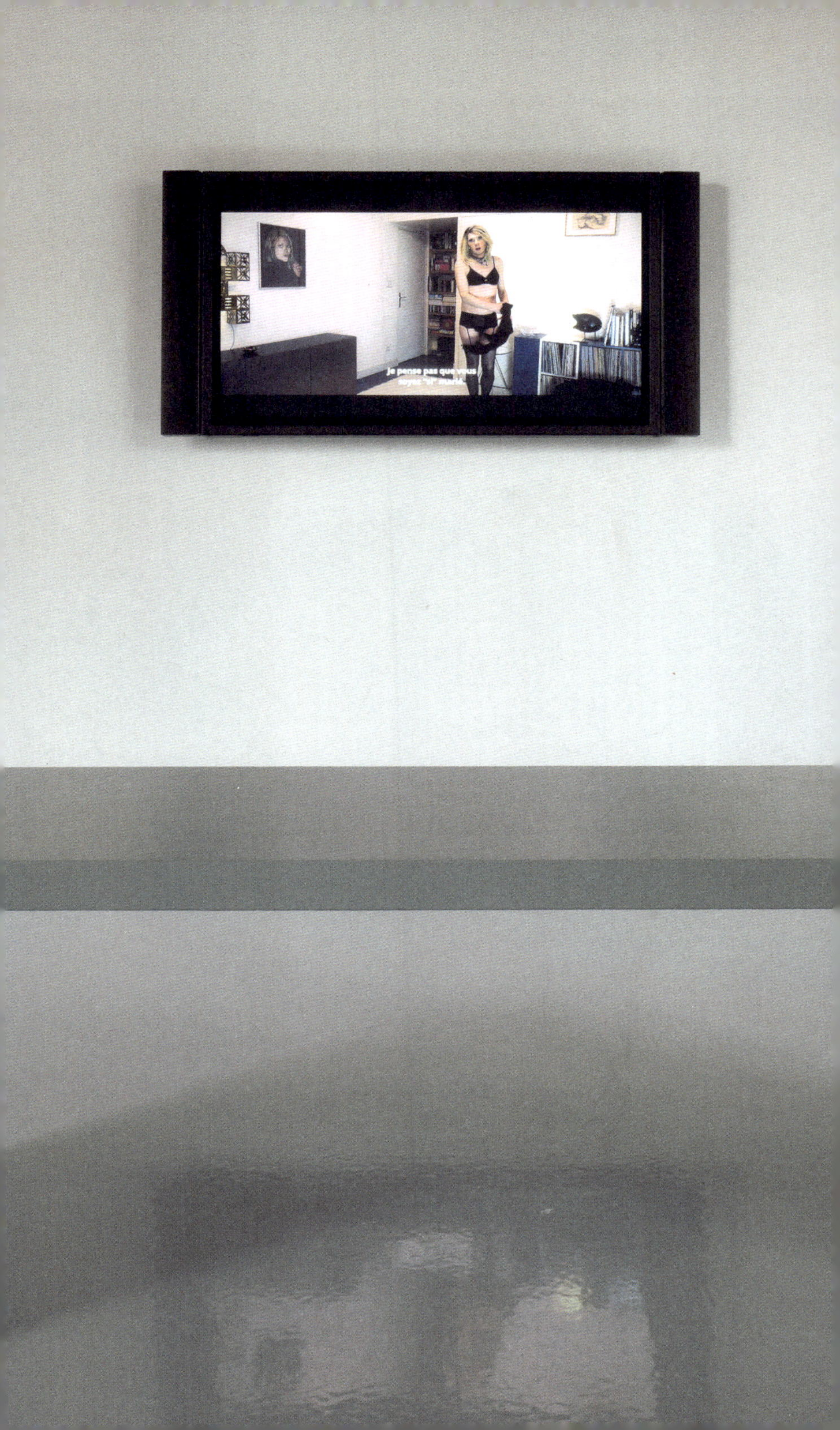
Je pense pas que vous
soyez "si" marié.

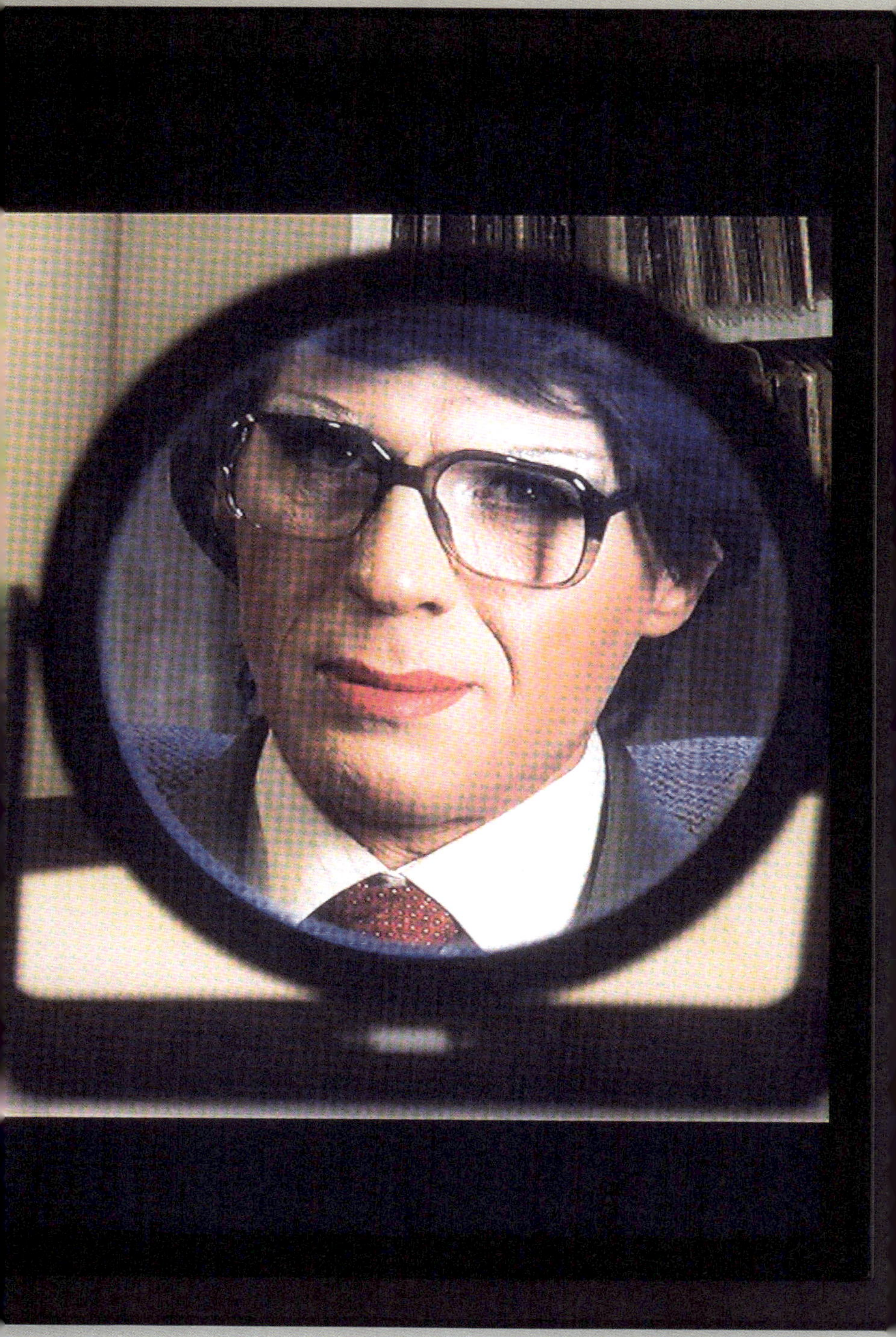

BEHIND-THE-SCENES

1, 2, 3, 6, 7, 8, 10, 11
Photo: Brice Dellsperger

4
Photo: Dana Colin

5
Photo: Gilles Martinez

9
Photo: Dorine Potel

12
Photo: Gina Folly

PHOTO CREDITS FOR EXHIBITION VIEWS:

154–166
Quitte ou Double
CAC - Passages, Troyes, France
20 Septembre – 14 December 2025
Photo: Aurélien Mole

167–175
Futurs intérieurs
CAC - la synagogue de Delme, France
5 July – 14 December 2025
Photo: OH Dancy

176–179
Jalousies
Dortmunder Kunstverein, Dortmund, Germany
26 May – 25 August 2024
Photo: Jens Franke

180–184
Solitaires
Air de Paris, Romainville, France
20 June – 30 July 2020
Photo: Marc Domage

ACKNOWLEDGEMENTS

Body Double 29
ENSA Bourges (Érik Bullot, Damien Chailloux, Arnaud Deshayes, Ingrid Luche, Gilles Martinez), Nadège Piton (Transpalette)

Body Double 32
ENSA, Bourges, France (Antoine Réguillon, Nadia Lecocq, Ingrid Luche, Chloé Nicolas, Erik Bullot, Damien Chaillou, Jean-Yves Gauthier), Marie-Claude Beaud, Célia Bernasconi, Joachim Biehler, Nicolas Müller, Jean-Luc Verna, all Kisskissbankers, François Rousselet, Jean-Michel Bertin, RVZ/Be4post

Body Double 33
Air de Paris, Jérémie Bonnefous, Dorine Potel, Clément Vidamant

Body Double 34
Jill Gasparina, Jean-Marc Guillot

Body Double 35
Simon Castets, Alison Coplan, Daniel Merritt, José Freire, Alissa Benett, Philippe-Alain Michaud, Marcella Lista, Sylvie Douala-Bell, Sylvain Wolff, Florence Bonnefous, Beau Bizarre (Nicolas Perge, David Lavialle), Thierry Durepaire (music box publishing), Clément Vidamant

Body Double 36
Air de Paris, Nicolas Perge, David Lavialle, Arnaud Olivier, Marie Canet, Arnaud Maguet, Julien Tibéri, François Tarot, Pascale Tiraboschi

Body Double 38
Marc Bembekoff, Nathanaëlle Puaud, Nina Childress

Body Double 39
Rebekka Seubert, Linda Schröer-Fabry, Michael Rother and Miki Yui, Mareike Hettler (Grönland Deutschland Gmbh), Fabrice Gomont (Panavision France), Beau Bizarre (Nicolas Perge, David Lavialle, Arnaud Olivier), Jennifer Emmel (Ordnungsamt Stadt Dortmund), Julia Wissert and Rohilat Kalmaz (Schauspiel Dortmund), Jana Rittlewski (Hotel Moxy Dortmund), Pauline Autet (Trampoline Association), Jean-Michel Bertin, Emmanuelle Laboue, Christian Phaure, Zoe Williams

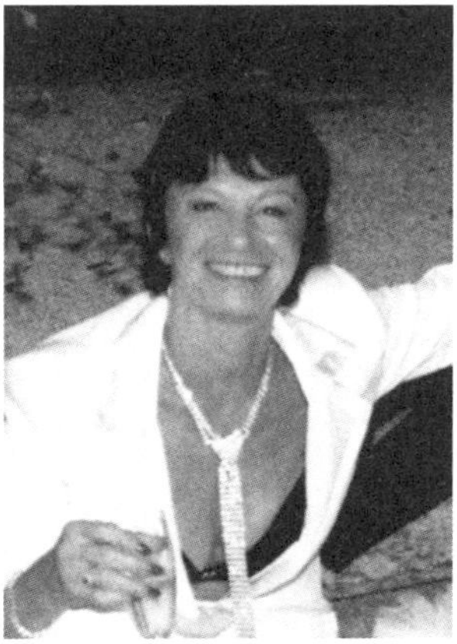

MAGGY HUE

(1950-2019)

FOR YOU, MY GIRLFRIEND
ALWAYS CLOSE TO ME

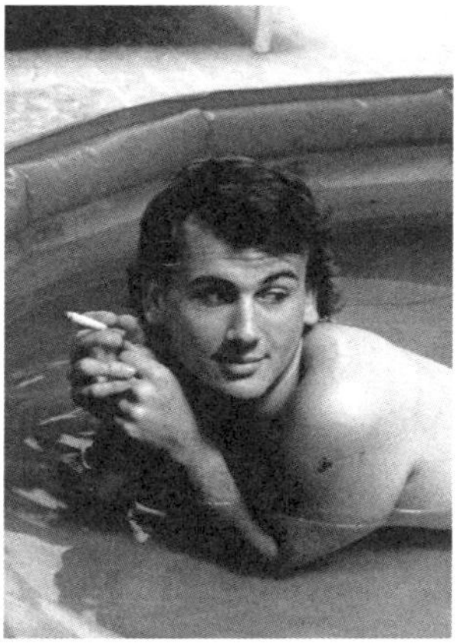

RICHARD VAN LOOT

(1975-2024)

BEAUTIFULLY HAPPY MYLÈNE-MERMAID
ALWAYS IN MY HEART

has been a wonderful r that has brought gether various public nd private institutions united by their shared love of Brice Dellsperger's films!

Twelve Body Doubles (2025) is the result of this coming together.

Published on the occasion of following Brice Dellsperger exhibitions:

Futurs Intérieurs (05.07 – 14.12.2025) at CAC - la synagogue de Delme curated by the artist and Benoît Lamy de la Chapelle;

Quitte ou Double (20.09 – 14.12.2025) at CAC -Passages curated by the artist and Maëla Bescond;

Brice Dellsperger (11.04 – 23.08.2026), Mrac Occitanie, Regional Museum of Contemporary Art Occitanie / Pyrénées-Méditerranée curated by the artist and Clément Nouet

Published and distributed by
Mousse Publishing
Contrappunto s.r.l.
Via Pier Candido
Decembrio 28,
20137, Milan–Italy

Available through
Mousse Publishing, Milan
moussemagazine.it

Publishing directors and coordination:
Ilaria Bombelli,
Florence Bonnefous,
and the artist

Graphic design:
Massimiliano Pace

Texts:
Evan Moffitt,
Rebekka Seubert

Translation:
Salomé Mercier,
Emilie Notéris

First edition
2025

Printed in Italy by
Tipografia Negri

ISBN 978-88-6749-707-2

€ 30 / $ 35

Published with the support of CAC - la synagogue de Delme and CAC - Passages.

A collaboration made possible thanks to the 'Mieux Produire Mieux Diffuser' programme implemented by the Ministry of Culture and supported by the DRAC Grand Est, the Grand Est Region and the City of Troyes.

MINISTÈRE
DE LA CULTURE
Liberté
Égalité
Fraternité

PRÉFET
DE LA RÉGION
GRAND EST
Liberté
Égalité
Fraternité

La Région Grand Est

Troyes

CAC - la synagogue
de Delme
33 rue Raymond Poincaré
57590 Delme, France
https://cac-synagoguedelme
.org

CENTRE D'ART CONTEMPORAIN
LA SYNAGOGUE DE DELME

Moselle
L'Eurodépartement

Communauté de communes du
Saulnois

CAC - Passages
9 rue Jeanne d'Arc 10000
Troyes, France
https://cac-passages.com

Published with the support of Musée régional d'art contemporain in Sérignan.

This project is supported by the Mrac Occitanie, Regional Museum of Contemporary Art, and is managed by the Région Occitanie / Pyrénées-Méditerranée. The museum receives support from the French Ministry of Culture, Prefecture for the Region Occitanie / Regional Directorate of Cultural Affairs, Occitanie.

Mrac Occitanie,
Regional Museum of
Contemporary Art
Occitanie /Pyrénées-
Méditerranée
146 avenue de la plage
34410 Sérignan, France
http://mrac.laregion.fr/

PRÉFET
DE LA RÉGION
OCCITANIE
Liberté
Égalité
Fraternité

La Région
Occitanie
Pyrénées - Méditerranée

Mrac
Occitanie

Published with the support of the fonds de dotation agnès b.

fonds de dotation
agnès b.

Published with the support of the Foundation Pernod Ricard.

Fondation
d'entreprise
Pernod
Ricard

TextWork
Plate-Forme Éditoriale Fondation Pernod Ricard

Published with the support of Air de Paris.

à

Romainville, Greater Paris

The artist would like to thank for this publication

Florence Bonnefous, Edouard Mérino, and Sebastian Quévedo Ramirez

Benoît Lamy de la Chapelle and Patricia Couvet

Maëla Bescond

Antonia Scintilla, Pauline Autet, and Vincent Duché

Agnès B., Clément Douala, and William Massey

Eric Mangion

Clément Nouet

and for the shows, everyone who participated in the memorable adventures: the team at Air de Paris, the team at CAC - Passages, the team at CAC - la synagogue de Delme, the team at Dortmunder Kunstverein

Sara Agutoli, Stéphanie Hue, Jean-Baptiste Monteil

for their beautiful energy, Rebekka Seubert and Ewan Moffitt

and for the love, Robin, Marcel, Jump, and Valmont.

♥